Pattern Languages of Program Design

Edited by

James O. Coplien

AT&T Bell Laboratories

Douglas C. Schmidt

Washington University

ADDISON-WESLEY
An Imprint of Addison Wesley Longman, Inc.

Reading, Massachusetts • Harlow, England • Menlo Park, California

Berkeley, California • Don Mills, Ontario • Sydney

Bonn • Amsterdam • Tokyo • Mexico City

Cover: Photographs by Charles Mercer, used with the permission of the Robert Allerton Park and Conference Center, University of Illinois at Urbana-Champaign.

Quotes by Witold Rybczynski in Chapter 13 are taken from *The Most Beautiful House in the World*, New York: Penguin, 1989. Reprinted with permission. Quotes by Christopher Alexander in Chapters 14 and 30 are taken from *The Timeless Way of Building*, Oxford University Press, 1979. Reprinted with permission. Figure 1 in Chapter 20 from P. Coad, "Object-Oriented Patterns," *Communications of the ACM*, V. 35 #9, September 1992, New York, New York. Figure 9. Reprinted with permission. Figures 2, 3, 4, and 5 in Chapter 20 from J. Soukup, *Taming C++: Pattern Classes and Persistence for Large Projects*, © 1994, Addison-Wesley Publishing Company, Inc., Reading, Massachusetts. Figures 2.12, 2.20, 2.21 and 2.23. Reprinted with permission. Figure 5 in Chapter 20 from Gamma/Helm/Johnson/Vlissides, *Design Patterns: Elements of Reusable Object-Oriented Software*, © 1995, Addison-Wesley Publishing Company, Inc., Reading, Massachusetts. Reprinted with permission.

The programs and applications presented in this book have been included for their instructional value. They have been tested with care, but are not guaranteed for any particular purpose. The publisher and authors do not offer any warranties or representations, nor do they accept any liabilities with respect to the programs or applications.

Acquisitions Editor: Thomas E. Stone
Associate Editor: Deborah Lafferty
Production Supervisor: Nancy H. Fenton
Cover Designer: Diana Coe
Production: Editorial Services of New England
Project Manager: Penny Stratton, Editorial Services of New England
Text Designer: Ron Kosciak, Dragonfly Design
Text Figures: George Nichols
Copy Editor: Bruce Crabtree
Senior Manfacturing Manager: Roy E. Logan

For more information about Addison-Wesley titles please visit our web site at: http://www.aw.com

Library of Congress Cataloging-in-Publication Data
Pattern languages of program design / edited by James O. Coplien,
  Douglas C. Schmidt.
      p.   cm.
    Includes bibliographical references and index.
    ISBN 0-201-60734-4
    1. Computer software—Development. 2. Object-oriented
programming. I. Coplien, James O. II. Schmidt, Douglas C.
QA76.76.D47P375   1995
005. 1—dc20   95-6731
                                                                       CIP

Copyright © 1995 by Addison Wesley Longman, Inc.

All rights reserved. No part of this publication may be reproduced, stored in a retrieval system, or transmitted in any form or by any means, electronic, mechanical, photocopying, recording, or otherwise, without prior written permission of the publisher and author.

Printed in the United States of America.

2 3 4 5 6 7 8 9 10–MA–99 98 97

Night Patterns

The coffee mug etched black inside
haunts the worn gray keys. The computer screen
amused pearlwhite lights the developer's hands
and his night still life: pencils and books, scattered
pages of code circled and crossed with notes.
Outside, along the river, white headlights flow,
red lights retreat.

Inside the agile black box it waits—the conjuring
that lifts alive vined parts,
veins flowing in forces he imagines
by circles and crosses, in dozing spells,
in whitened warmth upon noon earth,
in peach trees by the wall—
it waits to pulse the pages
toward life, the patterns of night, to bring
the quality, singing soft and hanging low.

RICHARD GABRIEL

Contents

1 Frameworks and Components

2 Systems and Distributed Processing

3 Business Objects

4 Process and Organization

5 Design Patterns and Catalogs

6 Architecture and Communication

7 Object Usage and Style

8 Events and Event Handlers

Introduction

Ralph Johnson and Ward Cunningham

PLoP was founded to create a new literature. That implies that the founders were somehow dissatisfied with the existing literature, which is true. The founders, a handful of notables in the object-oriented programming community, had come to realize that the advance of their discipline was limited by a bias in its literature. The bias, a product of the traditions of scientific publication, was to favor the new, the recent invention or discovery over the ordinary, no matter how useful. The founders' interest in the ordinary may have come from their studies of software reuse. Or it may have come from their observations that projects fail despite the latest technology for lack of ordinary solutions. What matters is that all the founders agreed to focus their attention on the dissemination of solutions. The PLoP conference is one result.

This volume is the first of a series of books dedicated to the "pattern form," our best guess at the way to share solutions. We asked authors to submit papers in the "pattern form" without actually saying what that form was. Christopher Alexander coined the term *pattern language* and explained the form well in his book *The Timeless Way of Building*. Many authors were familiar with this work, and many more were introduced to it through a series of OOPSLA workshops and Internet discussion groups. Even so, we felt authors needed considerable latitude in adapting Alexander's form to the domain of computer programs. The one thing we insisted was that each paper describe a solution, a thing that could be made to solve a problem.

You will notice as you read this volume that the authors' solutions cover an incredible range of problems. This means that you will probably not find every chapter equally interesting. We expect that as the PLoP community grows and matures that PLoP will itself splinter along traditional lines of interest. Future volumes may not demand so much versatility of their readers. For now we ask that you dig into all the chapters. Even if you do not plan to apply what you read directly, it might inspire you with new ideas of how to present patterns, and it should certainly give you a perspective on why it is so difficult to develop software.

For all this diversity in subject matter, there were some surprising agreements among PLoP authors and attendees. For one, most found that a solution, the essence of a pattern, could easily transcend the exact nature of its expression. A pattern must ultimately reside in one's own mind. So the various writing styles—from labeled sections of a standard template to running paragraphs of a more narrative style—have less to do with the success of a pattern than with some more basic elements. These include establishing a problem and its context, analyzing the forces bearing on the solution, and, most important, offering a concrete solution. Patterns that include these elements succeed.

A central feature of PLoP '94 was the writers' workshops. Instead of presenting their papers to an audience, writers listened to a small group discuss their paper and debate its strengths and weaknesses. This gave authors a chance not only to learn how they were communicating but also to discover learning alternatives to the techniques they were presenting. Writers' workshops, originated a few decades ago in the creative writing community, are an important forum where new writers learn the craft and experienced writers polish their material. We owe a great debt to Richard Gabriel for introducing us to the writers' workshop in the spring of 1994. To the best of our knowledge, this is the first time it has been used in a technical community, but it seems to work well.

So that is the vision and process that has led to this volume. We are pleased with the result and are sure you will be also. For us it is full speed ahead. Every week we see some new piece of evidence that the shift of focus that we and our authors have made will have a profound and enduring effect on the way we write programs. They will also show by example our vision of the future of software engineering.

Preface

This book is the culmination of an intensive effort to capture and refine a broad range of software development expertise in a systematic and highly accessible manner. The chapters are based on papers presented at the First Annual Conference of Pattern Languages of Programs (PLoP) held near Monticello, Illinois, in August 1994. This book is more than just a compendium of conference papers, however. It represents a broad offering from a new body of literature focusing on object-oriented design patterns. It is the first in a series of similar edited works on an ever-broadening spectrum of software patterns and pattern languages.

Design patterns capture the static and dynamic structures of solutions that occur repeatedly when producing applications in a particular context. Because they address fundamental challenges in software system development, design patterns are an important technique for improving the quality of software. Key challenges addressed by design patterns include communication of architectural knowledge among developers, accommodating a new design paradigm or architectural style, and avoiding development traps and pitfalls that are usually learned only by (painful) experience.

A large body of pattern literature already exists—not for software, but for constructing buildings. Christopher Alexander refined his architectural pattern form over 15 years ago, and isolated references to architectural patterns go back hundreds of years. Patterns have taken root in software only recently. Peter Coad noted the link between Alexandrian patterns and software architecture in a *CACM* article in 1992 (Coad 1992). It wasn't until 1993 that patterns began to enter the vernacular as the result of seminars, conference sessions, and journal publications. Drafts of Erich Gamma et al.'s *Design Patterns* (1995) were widely circulated in 1993 and 1994. This landmark work offered the first comprehensive set of software patterns between two covers and set new standards for the pattern form. Peter Coad's more recent work has culminated in *Object Models: Strategies, Patterns, and Applications* (Coad 1995). A fledgling body of diverse literature precedes the patterns collected in this volume.

As you examine the contents of this book carefully, you will observe a rich diversity of pattern forms. Some patterns draw on Alexander's style; others draw on the work of Erich Gamma and his colleagues; still others draw on the patterns of Peter Coad; and several are altogether original. We made every effort to preserve the authors' original forms. We avoided tampering with individual expression as much as possible: we made no attempt to enforce a uniform writing style. Although the book lacks the voice of a single author, we wouldn't have it any other way. We hope you join us in celebrating this diversity in the formative stage of a new body of literature.

The chapters in this book are certainly among the most intensely edited works in contemporary software literature. Editing was an ongoing, iterative effort. Before the conference, authors worked with "shepherds" from the patterns community. The goal was for each pattern to contain bare essentials: a clear problem statement, a solution addressing the problem, and a clear statement of forces that motivate the solution. Then, each chapter underwent intensive editing in writers' workshops at the PLoP '94 conference. Authors, reviewers, and other workshop participants discussed the strengths and weaknesses of each paper. Reviewers were encouraged to accentuate the positive and to suggest improvements in content, style, and presentation.

Production editing was also a team effort. Discussions with our colleagues in The Hillside Group steered early editorial decisions. While we focused on the logical organization of the material, our friends at Addison-Wesley created a unified design, swept out passive verbs and dangling prepositions, and richly supported us with logistics, copyright negotiation, and a host of details. Despite our scholarly inclinations to the contrary, page design and formatting contribute greatly to the readability of any written material. Thus, although we received manuscripts in a wide variety of formats, we have tried to integrate them in a single design while preserving the spirit of the individual formats.

We simply couldn't have done this without Deborah Lafferty, Penny Stratton, and Tom Stone, who treated this book with the same care and attention as if it were their own. We were proud and pleased—but most of all desperately grateful—to have them on our team.

Finally, we want to emphasize that this book would not have been possible without the talents, hard work, and dedication of the authors. All the copyediting in the world doesn't take the place of high-quality material. We are honored to work in the company of outstanding authors.

J.O.C.
D.C.S.

Coad, Peter (1992). "Object-Oriented Patterns." *CACM* 35, 9 (September): 152–159.

Coad, Peter, with David North and Mark Mayfield (1995). *Object Models: Strategies, Patterns, and Applications.* Englewood Cliffs, NJ: Prentice Hall.

Gamma, Erich, Richard Helm, Ralph Johnson, and John Vlissides (1995). *Design Patterns: Elements of Reusable Object-Oriented Software.* Reading, MA: Addison-Wesley.

FRAMEWORKS AND COMPONENTS

PART **1** The object paradigm has shaped how we have thought about reuse over the past decade. It's instructive to look at how our thinking has evolved since the first Smalltalk libraries appeared in the 1970s. Predominant industrial practice has evolved from general-purpose class libraries to domain-specific frameworks. Smalltalk made the transition from class libraries to frameworks in the late 1970s, and C++ followed along a decade later. The same thing has happened in other object-oriented languages, such as Eiffel and Objective C—the original classes that provided data structures and sophisticated math functions have evolved into frameworks that support graphical user interfaces (GUIs), distributed communication, and persistent objects. This evolution has culminated in widespread reuse of architectures, detailed designs, algorithms, and implementations. The chapters in Part 1 examine a number of design patterns related to object-oriented frameworks and components.

Early generations of commercial object-oriented components were generally packaged as class libraries, which cluster related operations and data to form modular programming components (for example, collections of data types such as stacks, queues, and lists). Applications typically reuse components in a class library by creating object instances and invoking methods on the objects. Objects provided a larger granularity of reuse than found in earlier C and FORTRAN subroutine libraries, but they didn't raise the level of architectural reuse significance. However, object instantiation made it possible to use a self-contained construct over and over in different architectural contexts within a single application program. Objects became the agents that could be summoned at will to serve the application architecture.

Modularity increased the scope of reuse beyond that supported by procedural libraries, and the variation in state supported by objects extended the scope even more. Inheritance provided a facility to further customize library classes through refinement and extension. Experience over the past two decades, however, indicates that it is difficult to achieve reuse and extensibility via class libraries alone. The basic problem is that the scope of a broadly reusable class is not large enough to significantly reduce the amount of application code that must be developed manually.

Effective reuse depends on understanding and capturing the pressure points of stability and variability in an application domain. These pressure points rarely correspond to the abstractions captured in class libraries. Though many library abstractions enjoy reuse in many different contexts (in the sense that windows and lists serve a limitless breadth of application domains), the abstractions don't stretch to cover the domain abstractions that are the lifeblood of an application. Even if a library captures the important abstractions of an application domain, the designer must still work hard to integrate them to support fundamental mechanisms and architectural relationships. In contrast, frameworks capture the common abstractions of an application domain—both their structure and mechanisms—while yielding control of application-specific structure and behavior to the application designer.

Extensible frameworks lead current software reuse trends. Packages such as MacApp, ET++, Interviews, Choices, MFC, OODCE (Object-Oriented Distributed Computing Environment), implementations of the OMG CORBA (the Object Management Group Common Object Request Broker Architecture) standard, and the ADAPTIVE Service eXecutive (ASX) play a larger role in contemporary architectures than the class libraries of preceding generations. A framework is a reusable design for an application or a part of an application that is represented by a set of abstract classes and the way instances of these classes collaborate (Johnson 1988). Although class libraries and frameworks share many characteristics, frameworks may be distinguished from conventional class libraries in the following ways:

1. *A framework provides an integrated set of domain-specific functionality.*
   Components in a framework typically address a particular domain (such as business data processing, telecommunications, graphical user interfaces,

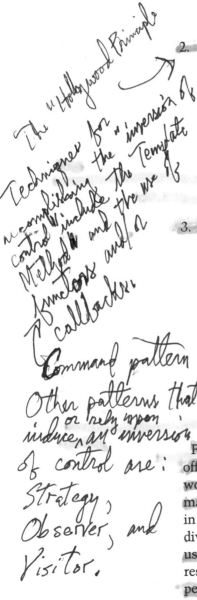

The "Hollywood Principle"

Techniques for accomplishing the "inversion of control" include the Template Method and the use of function and/or callbacks.

Command pattern

Other patterns that induce, or rely upon an inversion of control are:
Strategy, Observer, and Visitor.

databases, and distributed communication systems). In contrast, class library components are largely domain-independent (such as strings, complex numbers, dynamic arrays, and bitsets). Since a framework is more tightly integrated with a particular domain, the scope of reuse is significantly larger than with class libraries.

2. *Frameworks exhibit an "inversion of control" at run-time.* Designs based on class libraries traditionally placed the application in control. The application programmer was in charge of designing the flow of control through the application. In contrast, designs based on frameworks place the framework in control. The framework determines which methods to invoke in response to events (such as messages arriving on communication ports or user input from a mouse or keyboard). Developers write framework code that gets called by the code they are reusing, instead of writing code that calls the code they are reusing. Thus, applications reuse the flow of control that the framework provides.

3. *A framework is a "semicomplete" application.* Programmers form complete applications by inheriting and instantiating parameterized framework components (rather than simply invoking methods provided in a class library). Inheritance enables the features of framework base classes to be selectively shared by subclasses. Each base class provides default versions of (nearly) all functionality. Only those methods that need custom application-specific functionality must be overridden. Instantiation of parameterized types is a related technique that allows applications to extend framework functionality without modifying existing code. Parameterized types describe generic algorithms and container class data structures that have identical implementations, regardless of the type of their elements.

Framework developers are confronted with many challenging design trade-offs. One of the most crucial is determining which components in a framework should be variable and which should be stable. Insufficient variation makes it hard for users to customize framework components. This results in a framework that cannot accommodate the functional requirements of diverse applications. Conversely, insufficient stability makes it hard for users to comprehend and depend upon the framework's behavior. This results in a framework that is awkward to use and unable to satisfy the performance requirements of time-critical applications.

In Chapter 1, Sam Adams describes a pattern that addresses tradeoffs between functionality and performance. He notes that complex systems become increasingly inefficient as end-users insist on more features, without properly understanding their impact on performance. One unsatisfactory solution is to expose all the underlying mechanisms so that users can manually tune various system characteristics. However, this solution leads to a highly complex interface, akin to the problem of insufficient stability in a framework. Sam proposes a solution: the "Functionality Ala Carte" pattern. This pattern provides a performance tradeoff "menu" that reports the incremental and aggregate performance cost of each additional feature. Explicitly exposing this information to end users helps them understand the performance implications of their feature demands.

Historically, a major impediment to reusing nontrivial software components has been the high initial learning curve. For example, a sophisticated framework (such as ET++ or Interviews) typically has hundreds of classes and thousands of methods. In addition, tracing a thread of execution in a framework is complicated by the callback-driven flow of control. One technique for reducing the effort required to learn and reuse software components is to characterize them in terms of metaphors (such as the "desktop metaphor" that forms the basis for popular GUIs). In Chapter 2, Dirk Riehle and Heinz Züllighoven summarize their work on software for desktop applications as a pattern language. Their key idea is that most objects from an application domain should belong either to a "tool" or to a "material," hence the name of their approach: "The Tools and Materials Metaphor." Tools are the means for work that operate on materials, whereas materials are the outcome of work in a domain. For example, a compiler is a tool used by a developer to generate an executable from source code, which is a material. Other tools that work on source code are browsers or editors in a programming environment. Developers use the metaphors to discuss the application domain with users. The metaphors are supplemented by object-oriented patterns that let them create actual software designs. The use of the Tools and Materials metaphor helps bridge the gap between application requirements and the software design. In turn, this helps shorten the learning curve for application developers and end users.

As outlined above, one of the key differences between class libraries and frameworks is that components in a class library are relatively passive, whereas components in a framework are often more active. In Chapter 3, Norbert Portner describes a fundamental pattern for designing flexible command interpreters. This pattern is found in many frameworks, particularly those that parse interactive or batch input (such as an editor or an automated testing environment). Developing a flexible command interpreter requires the decoupling of the run-time command processing engine from the grammar of the command language. This decoupling enables both the processing engine and the grammar to evolve independently, as long as the core architecture of the interpreter is preserved. As with other frameworks, the key to successful decoupling is to separate the variable elements of the framework from the stable elements. Norbert achieves this decoupling by using base classes to define the stable interfaces, and at the same time delegating variation in behavior to the subclasses. This approach allows the run-time command processing engine to rely upon the stable base class interfaces, while allowing grammar changes to be reflected in the subclasses.

Many of the pioneering object-oriented frameworks (such as ET++ and Interviews) have originated in the domain of GUIs. This reflects the inherent richness of objects (such as windows and various scroll bars, buttons, sliders, and other widgets) in the GUI domain. It also reflects the fact that portability, extensibility, and elegance are often more important requirements than raw performance in a successful GUI framework. In contrast, networking is a domain that has traditionally emphasized raw performance over portability, extensibility, and elegance. However, the demand for portable, extensible, and elegant network programming frameworks is increasing as the industry migrates towards client/server systems that integrate legacy business databases with low-cost desktop computers. In Chapter 4, Kirk Wolf and Chamond Liu discuss interrelationships among a hierarchy of patterns they used in a client/server framework for integrating Smalltalk workstations with legacy database systems. They define a pattern language that helps guide client/server framework developers through the maze of potential design choices.

One key question is not discussed directly by any chapter in this section: What are the similarities and differences between design patterns and application frameworks? Clearly, both patterns and frameworks are a means to achieve large-scale reuse by capturing successful software development strategies within a particular context. The primary difference is that frameworks focus on reuse at the level of detailed design, algorithms, and implementation. In contrast, design patterns focus more on reuse of recurring architectural design themes. Often these architectural design themes are reusable even if the detailed design, algorithms, or implementations are not directly reusable.

It is important to recognize that patterns and frameworks are highly synergistic concepts, with neither subordinate to the other. Patterns have been characterized as more abstract descriptions of frameworks, which are then implemented in a particular language. Sophisticated frameworks typically embody dozens of patterns. Likewise, patterns have been used to document frameworks.

Johnson, Ralph, and Brian Foote (1988). "Designing Reusable Classes." *Journal of Object-Oriented Programming 1, 5 (June/July 1988): 22–35.*

1 Functionality Ala Carte

Sam S. Adams

Aliases   Performance Trade-off Menu

History   This pattern was discovered during the development of a large-scale, high-fidelity military logistics simulation. After continued requests for higher fidelity over several releases of the system, simulation runs became intolerably long. Furthermore, after repeated incremental improvements in system performance, a limit had been reached. There was no way a simulation run could take the same time on the same hardware with continual increases in simulation fidelity. The team decided to give users the ability to make informed decisions about the execution costs of various aspects of the simulation. The pattern's name comes from an analogy between this solution and an a la carte menu in a restaurant.

Preconditions   The system being designed requires that a user be able to enable or disable any features at will (Functionality on Demand pattern). Users complain about system performance while making unrealistic functionality demands.

Copyright © Sam S. Adams, Object Technology Practice, IBM Consulting Group. All Rights Reserved.

Problem   As a system grows in functional complexity, it often is necessary to allow users to customize system behavior by enabling or disabling some features. Very often different combinations of enabled features affect a system's overall performance differently. While having a great deal of flexibility, the user must learn by trial and error which features can be enabled simultaneously without lowering system performance below an acceptable level.

Constraints   Systems with functionality on demand often have more complex user interfaces than those without it. Adding more information to the interface runs the risk of reducing the user's overall intuitive comprehension of the system's behavior. On the other hand, leaving the user to discover the right balance of functionality and performance can lead to frustration and often the perception of a sluggish system.

Solution   Determine the incremental performance cost of each feature available on demand and present the client with the aggregate cost of the features selected. While this will not change the performance of the system, it makes the user aware of the performance consequences of his or her chosen configuration of features. If available, present a comparison of the aggregate cost with a known performance threshold such as subsecond response time. This provides the user with a benchmark for measuring the costs of the selected combination of features, thus permitting a more informed trade-off between functionality and performance. For systems such as high-fidelity simulations, showing the cost of increasing the fidelity dramatically decreased complaints about system performance, even though the performance of various features was not improved.

The price of each feature can be described to the client in the following manner: assign a "monetary value" to a length of time, as a unit of cost; then determine the average number of these units required to execute the feature. In the case of a simulation, the number of entities executing the feature will also have to be considered in the price. Depending on the application, pricing may require significant analysis and experimentation.

Setting a budget for the user requires a detailed understanding of the performance characteristics of the system as well as the price of each feature and the price points of the "performance tolerance market." If determining a performance budget beforehand is impossible or not feasible, simply presenting the total cost of the user's selections from the menu should provide enough feedback to determine a budget over time.

Sam S. Adams can be reached at IBM, P.O. Box 12195, 3039 Cornwallis Road, RTP NC 27709-2195, Attention: Department BJV/062/D300; sadams@vnet.ibm.com.

A Pattern Language for Tool Construction and Integration Based on the Tools and Materials Metaphor

Dirk Riehle and Heinz Züllighoven

1. BACKGROUND AND MOTIVATION

Why do people prefer to use certain software systems? Why do they have problems using others? What is the quality in certain software that makes people quickly feel familiar with it and lets them work efficiently? Like a lot of people who develop and use application systems in their everyday work, we found ourselves asking these questions.

We believe that this quality (in the sense of *Zen and the Art of Motorcycle Maintenance* [Pir74]) is exemplified by systems that allow people to work according to their qualifications and needs while using their skills and competence.

In order to develop software with this quality, we, a group of software engineers located at various institutions, have pulled together many of the methods and techniques that have proved useful in software engineering over the last decades and integrated them into a unified approach—the Tools and Materials Metaphor [BCS92, BZ92, BGZ95]. This approach has guided

Copyright © Dirk Riehle and Heinz Züllighoven. All Rights Reserved.

us and other developers during analysis and design and has helped us envision and finally build systems of quality. The Tools and Materials Metaphor entails a specific perspective on work:

- People have the necessary competence and skills for their work.
- There is no need to define a fixed work flow, because people know what they do and can cope adequately with changing situations.
- People should be able to decide on their own how to organize their work and their environment (including the software they use) according to their tasks.

We have found that software developed around this viewpoint makes people feel comfortable using a system, improving both the work process and its outcome. (At least, this holds true in the field we are familiar with, which is work in office environments and workshops.)

But why "tools" and "materials"? From the long tradition of craftsmanship we have learned that human work is often best defined by the tools and materials used to perform it. We have taken this basic notion as a starting point for understanding what work is, and we have attempted to extend this concept to software tools and materials, thereby bridging the gap between social requirements and a software system.

Thus the term *Tools and Materials Metaphor* characterizes our overall approach. We explain this approach and its underlying idea by using a pattern language. We start by outlining this language on its highest conceptual level, which we call its design metaphors. These design metaphors are *tools*, *materials*, *aspects*, and *environment*, representing different but related concepts. We then present the next lower level of abstraction—design patterns—for the implementation of the metaphors, and we show how to use them as a coherent language. Our notion of patterns is based on the work of Gamma et al. [GHJ+93] and Johnson [Joh92].

2. THE OVERALL APPROACH

The central elements in our approach are tools and materials. In many work situations an intuitive conceptual distinction can be made between those things that are worked upon (materials) and those things that provide the means for performing work (tools). We use these metaphors to describe the work of the application domain experts (called *users* in this paper) for whom we develop software. These metaphors provide a conceptual framework for discussion between users and software professionals (called *developers*), because most people have a sufficient understanding of what tools and materials are.

When actually developing software for a project, we follow an evolutionary and participatory approach using prototyping [Flo84, BKK+92]. Thus we organize software development as a mutual learning and design process where users and developers cooperate.

Evolutionary software development means designing software in fast feedback cycles involving all concerned parties. Thus there are various tasks to perform: We analyze the application domain by observing how users actually do their daily work, focusing on the tools and materials they use, and we discuss our findings with them. Looking at everyday work, we try to understand the professional language in use in order to build a model based on these concepts and terms. We extend this language by new concepts necessary for the envisioned system. While doing this we make heavy use of current work scenarios and models of anticipated work with the future system.

Having outlined the process model of our approach, we come to our leitmotif of humans as skilled and trained experts in their domain. To make the goals of our leitmotif concrete, we use the design metaphors of tools, materials, aspects, and environment. These metaphors are realized as objects and classes during design activities by a construction technique utilizing the design patterns of our pattern language.

As a foundation for further research, one of the authors of this paper designed and implemented an application framework for the Tools and Materials Metaphor. Its purpose was to extend and improve implementation techniques used in industrial projects. After the application framework reached a sufficient degree of maturity and had been heavily used in student projects, he reinterpreted the framework as a pattern language, which became the main part of this paper (Sections 4–6).

3. LEITMOTIF AND DESIGN METAPHORS

The context of the design metaphors described in this chapter is provided by our leitmotif of skilled experts whose work we wish to support with appropriate software. Thus the metaphors we use must conform to the given objectives of enabling skilled human work, operating without a fixed work flow, and encouraging knowledgeable interaction with software tools.

3.1 The Distinction Between Design Metaphors and Design Patterns

Before elaborating on our pattern language, we will clarify the difference between the two levels of this language—that is, between the design metaphors and the design patterns. In short, design metaphors are patterns that govern our perception of the application domain and guide us when designing the future system, while design patterns are used in the technical construction process as a kind of "micro architecture."

Our design metaphors of tools, materials, aspects, and environment express our understanding of human work (in many areas) as being composed of four different but interrelated elements. Because work frequently includes the use of computers, these design metaphors provide a guideline and a perspective on how software systems for a given application domain should be designed. They are used for understanding and analyzing the work of others. Thus they provide an approach as well as a worldview.

The well-known Model-View-Controller (MVC) paradigm is based on the metaphor of direct manipulation, as well as on a general concept of domain modeling. This concept is quite general, lacking any specific leitmotif. Our metaphors are more specifically aimed at skilled human work supported by computers.

Design patterns are based on design metaphors and are used to relate them to the technical level of designing software systems. We follow Gamma et al. [GHJ+93] in seeing design patterns as a set of related classes and objects interacting in a specific way to achieve a well-defined goal. Design patterns are described by naming the pattern components and their collaborations and responsibilities. Patterns emerge out of experience with recurring solutions in designing software systems. They describe the solution to a problem, usually making use of a problem-context-solution schema. Design patterns are used in the specific contexts for which they were invented as micro architectures—that is, they build the actual programs.

The MVC paradigm is an example of a classical design pattern, consisting of three components—Model, View, and Controller—interacting to build a software tool with an underlying domain model. In line with Gamma et al., we wish to stress that patterns are not merely technical but also capture the professional's domain-specific understanding (as guided by the underlying design metaphors).

Grown from experience, patterns as well as metaphors form the developer's language and become powerful tools for analyzing and designing software systems. We use them to communicate, document, and develop our software.

In actual projects we need a third level of our pattern language. This is the level of programming patterns—they may also be called atoms, idioms, or fundamental patterns, as on the patterns mailing list. Programming patterns provide a basic way to create a software design using a programming language and the principles of software engineering. As an example, take the distinction between objects and values and the different ways of realizing this difference in an object-oriented language [Cun95]. Pipes and filters may also be shown as basic patterns of software [Sha95]. This shows that the distinction between design patterns and programming patterns depends on experience and specific perspective.

To sum up, there are three levels in our pattern language, which we use to analyze, design, and construct software systems:

1. The design metaphors, which grow out of a leitmotif that guides our perception and our thinking

2. The design patterns that help us transform our design ideas into a concrete software design

3. The programming patterns as basic means and forms for expressing software building blocks

In the following sections we will explain the first two levels of our language, assuming that the third level is familiar to experienced software engineers.

3.2 The Tools and Materials Metaphor

The design metaphors of our approach are based on the underlying separation between tools as the means of performing work and materials as the objects of work. This tools-and-materials model leads to the metaphors of materials and tools.

The presentation of these design metaphors and patterns is illustrated by the following example: a time-planning system to keep track of dates, appointments, seminars, and so on. Figure 1 shows our first tool, a simple calendar. It consists of a list of appointments on the left and the contents of a selected appointment on the right. Looking at the calendar we encounter the tool (the calendar), its materials (the appointments), and the aspects of the material (information that can be listed and edited).

Materials: Design Metaphor

Problem   Looking at the skilled professional, we have to identify what he or she is actually working on—that is, what the relevant objects of his or her work are. In line with our leitmotif and as a basis for adequate modeling, the focus of the expert's work has to be analyzed and made explicit.

Solution   The "things" professionals work on are materials. Materials are examined, manipulated, or incorporated into other materials in order to become part of the work results. Examples of materials are forms, files, and folders.

Materials are passive entities that are taken and worked on when appropriate, like the different forms laid out systematically on a desktop. In our work we mainly concentrate on materials, and we get a feeling for directly accessing and manipulating them. Though we use tools like a typewriter or a pen to fill in a form, for example, these tools seem to disappear and we only focus on the form. We often use our hands as tools while working with tangible materials. In software systems, however, we can never access materials directly in this way, but only by using appropriate tools. Therefore, in order to maintain an understandable system model, we design "active" tools and "passive" materials. So in a software system we need a browser tool, for instance, to look at the contents of a folder.

The calendar tool in Figure 1 shows some appointment materials presented by that tool.

When designing materials we are not concerned with their graphical or textual representation or their interactive manipulation. Tools use additional graphical objects to display materials. They also provide the context for working with materials, both graphically and logically. Despite the fact that materials are always represented and manipulated by tools, they exist in their own right and should not be subordinate to a specific tool.

FIGURE 1 A Calendar (a tool) that was built from the application framework

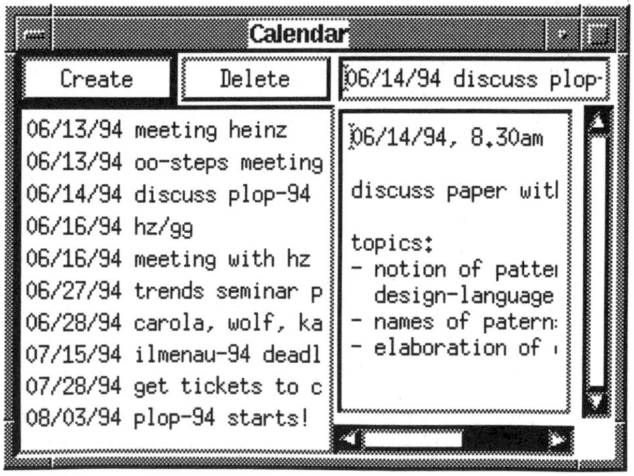

Tools: Design Metaphor

Problem   In order to accomplish a task, it is obviously not sufficient to just look at materials and wait for something to happen. Thus we need the means both to organize materials and to perform our work on them.

Solution   When manipulating materials, we use tools as a means of producing work. Computer tools are often based on a long tradition; they represent physical tools and the experience of using them to work efficiently with materials. They are manifestations of the ways and means materials can be examined and manipulated in a given application domain. Tools include calendars (as in our example), all kinds of form editors, browsers for folders, and so on.

Tools present a permanent view on materials and give users feedback about their activities. Tools have their own state, which relates to the respective work situation. For example, the calendar consists of objects that display the appointments, objects that receive user input, objects that transform this input into manipulations of an appointment, and objects that "remember" the last selected appointment.

Well-designed tools become transparent when handled by an experienced user—that is, they are nondistracting and give the user the impression of directly manipulating the materials. Despite this, tools should be marginally present and should never "disappear" in a work situation. In unclear situations or in case of errors, users need to be able to look at a tool directly.

Being a tool or a material is not an intrinsic property of thing—the distinction depends on the task at hand. A pencil, for example, is a tool when we use it to write on paper; it becomes a material when we sharpen it with a pencil sharpener. The materials for a help tool are other tools—those we wish to retrieve help about. We will see that the aspects design metaphor will establish the context that makes clear whether a particular thing is a tool or a material in a given situation.

The concept of tools and materials is compatible with that of direct manipulation, but it underpins the role of tools in human work.

Often a task can be divided into subtasks that may be performed independently. The results of these subtasks are integrated to form the overall result. We can organize tools in a similar way. The calendar allows for selecting appointments from a list and editing them. Thus we build a tool for handling a list of items (a lister) and a tool for processing the text of an appointment (an editor).

We normally use a number of different tools for working on a single material. Besides the calendar, a scheduler tool will give an overview of our weekly dates, and other tools will track appointments.

Aspects: Design Metaphor

Problem   We never work with a tool on a material in a generic way; we use our knowledge to select the right tool and to handle it in a specific way that is suitable for the combination of tool, material, and work at hand. Because the same tools and materials might be used to produce a variety of outcomes, we have to sort out the different ways of working with them and their meaning.

Context   From traditional crafts we know that not every tool is suitable for every material. We would hardly use a pencil sharpener to sharpen a ballpoint pen, for example. Furthermore, we find that in many areas the relationship between tools and materials is governed by standards—for example, the relationship between spanners and nuts. Each tool that fits a material in a specific way does so because humans designed it that way to perform a specific task. Understanding the task is relevant to understanding the relationship between the tool and the material.

Solution   We can make the relationship between a tool and a material explicit by introducing aspects. An aspect defines a single interface that provides all the necessary operations a tool needs in order to work properly with specific materials in a specific task and it will contain exactly those operations. At the same time, aspects are an abstraction of specific materials. For example, the appointments on a calendar must be listable and editable for the calendar to be able to display and edit them. The operations necessary to perform these tasks are expressed by two different aspects: listable and editable.

Aspects are just as important to a particular operation as the choice of tools and materials, because they define the necessary operations and thus the context that is needed to perform a specific task. By doing this, they formally establish the contract that binds a tool to a material [Mey91]. A tool does not know the specific materials it may be used on; neither does a material know which tools may be used on it. They only know the contract that connects them. This abstract coupling is a major aid in making our systems more flexible (see the Tool and Material Coupling pattern, below).

Aspects reflect what psychologists of work call usability. Usability refers to the usefulness of an item with respect to an intention or a purposeful task or activity. It relies on objective or subjective characteristics within a work situation that can be assessed on the background of individual needs (derived from Dzida, Wiethoff, and Arnold [DWA93]).

Environment: Design Metaphor

Problem   Tools and materials are never found in isolation. We always work in well-organized places equipped with the things we need. In a computer system there is no "natural" environment of this kind. In order to support skilled work, the notions of spatial and logical ordering and relations are of crucial importance to software systems.

Context   We perform tasks in a work environment—for example, in a workshop or on a desktop. Within this environment we physically and mentally organize and arrange our tools and materials according to our working habits and the needs of the task at hand. Tools and materials therefore have their place, their location and order. We generally do this in an implicit and intuitive way, based on our qualification and experience.

Solution   We transfer this concept of environment to the computer because it provides a means of organizing our work. For office work a familiar example is the electronic desktop, which provides a place to plan and arrange our work. It provides a space and several logical dimensions for performing work.

The notion of environment allows us to think about constraints between tools and materials. The environment must provide a means for ensuring consistency between them.

4. DESIGN PATTERNS FOR TOOL CONSTRUCTION AND INTEGRATION

Having introduced the design metaphors of our approach, we will now explain the design patterns in detail. These patterns conform to the metaphors, emphasizing certain characteristics and showing ways to efficiently implement them. Design patterns do not introduce new concepts or views distinct from those given by the metaphors, but carry over their meaning into detailed software design.

4.1 Graphical Notation

Figure 2 sketches the graphical notation used throughout Chapter 2. It is based on [RBP+91], with small deviations.

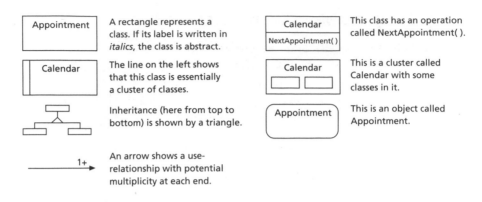

Appointment	A rectangle represents a class. If its label is written in *italics*, the class is abstract.
Calendar	The line on the left shows that this class is essentially a cluster of classes.
	Inheritance (here from top to bottom) is shown by a triangle.

An arrow shows a use-relationship with potential multiplicity at each end.

Calendar — NextAppointment( )	This class has an operation called NextAppointment( ).
Calendar	This is a cluster called Calendar with some classes in it.
Appointment	This is an object called Appointment.

Figure 2 Design notation

4.2 Road Map to the Design Patterns

This section introduces the design patterns for the construction of tools and their relation to materials, starting with patterns for integrating tools with other tools and materials in an environment. First, however, we will provide a short road map for these design patterns.

Figures 3 and 4 show an overview of the presented patterns for tool construction and tool integration, respectively. The patterns are ordered according to their range; the largest one forms the border of the aggregate layers in each figure. Some patterns break this simple ordering by range,

Figure 3 Patterns for tool construction

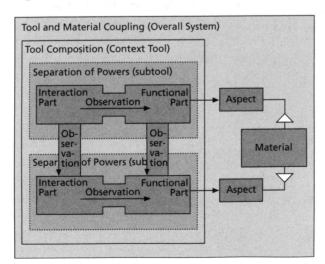

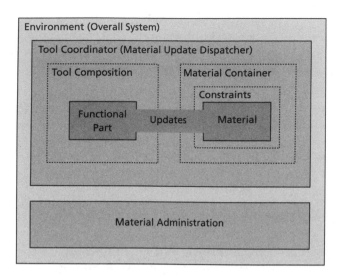

Figure 4 Patterns for tool integration

namely Separation of Powers, Event Mechanism (Observation), and Material Container, which overlap.

Each rectangle represents a design pattern, except some special classes—named Interaction Part, Functional Part, Aspect Class, and Material—whose meaning can be guessed from the metaphors and will be discussed later.

Probably the most important design pattern for tool construction is Tool and Material Coupling, which structures the overall system. Tools and materials from the metaphors become objects that are linked by aspect classes representing aspects. Tools use materials via specific aspect classes; materials are subtypes of several aspect classes. Tools are composed from simpler tools using the mechanisms of the Tool Composition pattern. Each simple tool consists of an interaction part and a functional part separating the powers of both domains. To connect the interaction and functional parts of tools, an event mechanism is used. This allows dependent components to be informed about changes, in order to react appropriately. Therefore, the interaction part of a tool depends on the state of its functional part, and it is informed by the functional part about relevant changes. This is done by announcing an event.

The design patterns for tool integration are based on the patterns for tool construction, especially on Tool Composition and Separation of Powers, which structure a compound tool. As the boundary of the overall system we use Environment, which represents the closure of a single (computer) workplace. The environment creates a Tool Coordinator to inform tools about changes to their materials that might have occurred due to side effects. These side effects are controlled by a Material Container, which groups dependent materials and provides constraints for ensuring consistency.

The functional parts of tools are made available on an abstract level to Tool Coordinator. Linked to the tool and material patterns is Material Administration, which provides an abstract way of accessing material providers (that is, databases). Material Administration and the patterns for integrating material providers constitute a pattern sublanguage of its own, which goes beyond the scope of this paper.

4.3 Design Patterns for Tool Construction

We will first look at a single tool and introduce patterns for its construction based on the tools, materials, and aspects metaphors.

Tool and Material Coupling: Design Pattern

Purpose   This pattern couples tools with materials through aspect classes that implement aspects. The pattern captures the way we work with tools on materials and represents the smallest reusable interface to materials.

Problem   Usually a tool is developed to work with a single type of material. But we wish to develop reusable tools that are not tied to specific materials. Several tools should work on the same material, and one tool should be usable for several materials.

Context   Tools and materials are represented by different objects. The interface of a material should offer all the operations a tool needs, but no more. This interface is the aspect a tool uses to work with materials. Aspects should be independent of each other. The code in Figure 5 shows the aspects Listable and Editable as C++ class interfaces.

A lister (a tool) displays items from a container used as a list to select from. An editor (also a tool) provides the means for textually editing materials. In order to work properly, both tools need to have part of the functionality of their materials expressed through the Listable or Editable aspects. As discussed under the aspect metaphor, both classes should be treated as a contract established between a tool and a material.

From a tool's point of view, aspects can be seen as properties of a material. Thus the appointment objects for the calendar should offer both the Listable and Editable aspects, because they can be listed and edited.

```
// simple interface for listable objects
class Listable {
 String GetDescription() =0;
 bool isEqual( Listable& ) =0;
 bool isLower( Listable& ) =0;
};
// simple textually editable objects
class Editable {
 String GetParagraph( int ) =0;
 void  SetParagraph( String, int ) =0;
};
```

FIGURE 5 C++ Interface of `Listable` and `Editable`. The functionality of each is independent of the other.

Solution Each aspect becomes a class interface in its own right, called an aspect class. An aspect class determines the operations necessary to make a material usable for a specific tool. The Listable and Editable aspects given above are aspect classes.

Tools are restricted to work with aspect classes. As a consequence, tools can use any material that offers the respective characteristics of the aspect class—that is, any material that fulfills the contract formalized through the aspect class interface. The appointment class implements the operations specified in Listable and Editable. The single line returned by the appointment via its Listable interface may consist of a string with the date and the name of the person to meet. Figure 6 shows the resulting class diagram for our example.

Introducing a new material into a system is done by identifying which tools should be working upon that material. Then the appropriate aspect classes are inherited and the specified operations are implemented. An aspect

Figure 6 The lister and editor tool access the same material through different aspect classes.

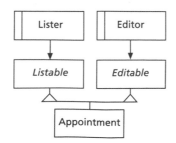

class can be seen as a partial type. Material interfaces are built out of the different aspect classes they inherit from.

An aspect class is normally an abstract class that establishes the context for interpreting a given class as a tool class and other classes as appropriate materials for this tool. A class is a tool class in context α if it uses aspect class α, and a class is a material class in context α if it inherits from aspect class α.

Aspect classes make the dependencies between materials and tools explicit. They structure a material's interface into different sections, each representing a certain way of using it. Tools working on aspect classes present this interface to users as the work context. Thus, materials cannot be active (nor "self-representing" or "self-editable"). This indirection provided by tools makes our systems more flexible.

Aspect classes provide our rationale for dealing with multiple inheritance in a constrained but efficient way. Applied properly, no diamond inheritance structures result, and thus no name or repeated inheritance conflicts emerge.

Additionally, they represent a step toward independence. From the point of view of the tools, this is achieved by the tools' ignorance of the concrete materials they work upon. They only know their respective aspects. From the point of view of the materials, no assumptions have to be made about the tools; in particular none have to be made about how materials are presented or handled at the user interface. This independence is achieved by the materials' having to implement only what is specified by their aspect classes.

Once a common understanding of an aspect class has been reached in a software design team, tools and materials can be developed by different groups or persons. Aspect classes can thus serve as a basis for cooperation and separation of work within in a design team.

Compare   Such classes of characteristics are known as Interface classes [CCH+89]. According to Wirfs-Brock and Johnson [WJ90], they also represent responsibilities.

Tool Composition: Design Pattern

Purpose   This pattern composes tools from independent subtools according to a task-subtask division, to allow for maximum reuse.

Problem   Complex tools often consist of similar parts. We frequently find elementary tasks that can be captured as basic building blocks. Examples are the lister and editor just presented. We wish to reuse these building blocks, and thus we need a guideline for building complex tools from simpler ones.

Context
We have already said that the calendar consists of simpler tools—the lister and the editor. A composition guideline for tools will have a major impact on the tools' presentation and handling; therefore it must adequately relate to the users' understanding of the tools and the working tasks.

Solution
When possible, we build a new tool using available tools. These component tools are called subtools. As each tool realizes a well-defined task, the decision about which tool to reuse and how to embed it must conform to the overall task of the tool. Thus each subtool's task must be a subtask of the embedding tool's task.

The calendar displays materials in a list and allows editing of a selected material. It embeds the lister and the editor as subtools, because each subtool realizes a subtask—listing and editing—of the calendar's overall task. In this example, the calendar's task is simply to connect both subtools to realize the way we want to work with a calendar: after an item is selected from the lister, the editor must be informed and receive the new selected material (see Figure 7).

Tools can be either simple or compound. Simple tools are self-contained; they perform their task without the help of other tools. Compound tools, in contrast, rely on other tools to perform their tasks. Listers and editors are simple tools, a calendar is a compound tool.

Every compound tool embeds some subtools that are arranged according to the so-called principle of delegation. This principle divides tasks into subtasks that can be performed with minimal information about their context. The result of a subtask is integrated into the overall task that provides the context for its interpretation. Accordingly, a compound tool is called the context tool for its subtools.

A context tool creates its subtools, delegates and coordinates subtasks, and deletes subtools on demand. It integrates the results of its subtools into its own result. Any subtool may perform its task by becoming a context tool for the subtools it creates. The resulting object structure is a tree of tools (see Figure 8).

This structure of tools and subtools should not be confused with functional decomposition of, for example, structured design. Normally each tool is

FIGURE 7 The calendar is a compound tool built from the two simple tools: Lister and Editor.

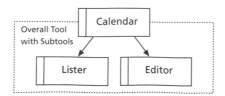

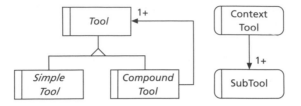

FIGURE 8 Class (left) and object diagram (right) for tool composition. Each context tool may have any number of subtools.

visible to and thus accessible by the user. No predefined control flow from the root to the leaves of the tool hierarchy is determined, but the user may interact freely with any tool.

Tools are not a collection of functions, but have a state of their own distinct from their materials' state. A tool's state captures the way a material is currently used and thus preserves vital information for the user.

Comment Though each tool can work on its own material, frequently a subtool will work on the same material as its context tool, but with fewer aspect classes. The calendar uses the aspect classes Listable and Editable to supply the lister and editor with materials. Each subtool needs its respective aspect class to work properly. The calendar, however, needs both aspect classes combined in order to be able to pass materials between the subtools. Thus, aspect classes can be composed to build complex aspect classes to satisfy complex tool requirements.

Figure 9 shows the complex aspect class Browsable as a composition of Listable and Editable. The appointment class will then inherit from Browsable. The introduction of complex aspect classes prevents complex tools from being tailored to specific materials. The reason is the same as for normal aspect classes. Tools build a tool-subtool hierarchy, and so do complex aspect classes.

Separation of Powers: Design Pattern

Purpose This pattern divides a tool into an interaction and a functional part to separate its handling and presentation from its functionality. This facilitates tools' adapting to changing requirements.

Problem Conceptually, any tool can be divided into two parts: one that deals with presentation and handling of materials and one that provides the necessary functionality for manipulating materials. We wish to use this distinction, also known as separation of interaction from function, when building tools.

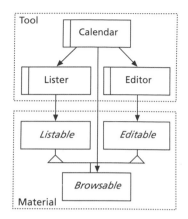

FIGURE 9 Full class diagram for the calendar, its subtools, and the simple and complex aspect classes

Context   Each tool has to provide both a user interface for presentation and handling, and the functionality reflecting the task the tool supports. Assuming a graphical user interface, it should present the various features of the tool as well as a tool- and aspect-specific view of the material. The user interface has to offer reactive behavior and as little sequencing of activities as possible. It should provide modeless interaction. The functionality of each tool should be closely related to a task or subtask within the application domain.

Solution   The general technical solution of separating functionality from presentation and handling, has been introduced by the MVC paradigm of Smalltalk (see Section 3.1). Adapting the paradigm to our approach, we compose a tool out of one or more interaction parts (IP) and exactly one functional part (FP). The interaction part manages user actions and presents materials, thereby allowing for complex interactive handling. It translates user actions either into a mere change of presentation at the interface or into calls of the functional part. The functional part interprets all actions that examine or manipulate the materials at hand. It knows the aspect classes of its materials and incorporates the application-oriented knowledge of the tool. The interaction part should be replaceable without affecting the functional part.

The lister can be divided into two objects implementing the interaction part and the functional part. The interaction part uses graphical user interface elements to present a list and to receive notification about a selection from the list. It transforms this notification into a call to a selection operation of the functional part that is parameterized with an index.

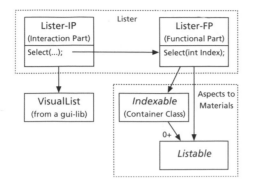

Figure 10 The lister tool, consisting of an interaction and a functional part

Compared to the MVC paradigm, the interaction part of a tool combines the responsibilities of View and Controller. The tasks of Model, on the other hand, are divided between the functional part, the aspects, and the material. So Model combines material behavior as seen from the special viewpoint of an aspect with the tool's functionality of working with materials. We believe that this extension of the model concept is one of the major achievements of the tools and materials dichotomy as compared to MVC.

Compare   See also MVC [KP88], ALV [Hil92], and CommonInteract [SP93], as well as Dodani, Hughes, and Moshell [DHM89] about the basic concepts.

Event Mechanism: Design Pattern

Purpose   This pattern provides a mechanism that automatically updates the dependencies of IPs and Context-FPs on their FP's state and also preserves the hierarchy between the components.

Figure 11 General class diagram for a tool with relation to graphical user interface objects

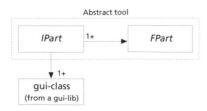

Problem   If the state of a material or the respective FP changes, the FP's IP and its Context-FP have to be informed about these changes. This has to be done anonymously in order to avoid making FPs dependent on specific IPs or Context-FPs.

Context   Any FP should make as few assumptions about its use context as possible to ensure maximum reusability. This would be easy if it were sufficient to restrict the IP and Context-FP to using the FP. But in reactive and complex interactive systems it is not feasible to permanently ask the FP (that is, the poll) about changes. Thus the FP has to take action and notify its IP and Context-FP about relevant changes.

This means that in case of relevant changes, the FP has to issue an event to notify its observers. An event is an announcement from the FP to its observers about a change and the kind of changes that have happened. Observers are the IP and Context-FP that look upon the FP. They receive an event from the FP, their observed object.

If, for example, the user selects an item from the lister's visual list, the lister's FP is informed about this through the invocation of Select(), as shown in Figure 13. It then announces an ItemSelected event, which is received by its observer, the Calendar-FP. Next, the Editor-FP will receive the new selected appointment to be edited. It will then issue the event TextHasChanged, which is received by its IP, which in turn updates its display.

It is important that the observers remain anonymous to the observed object. Otherwise, the observed object could not be used with observers other than those it has been tailored for.

Solution   In our solution, events are first-class objects that observers can register to. Each observable object—that is, each IP or FP—offers these events in its interface. Observers register by passing an anonymous reference to the event and an operation to be called.

The observed object decides when to announce an event according to changes in its state. It then calls the Announce() operation of an event, which in turn calls the operations that have been passed to it by its observers.

Figure 12   A class diagram for decoupled observer and observed objects

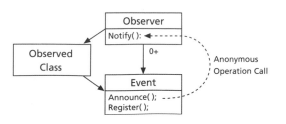

```
class ListerFP : public FPart {
 class Event {
  void Register( ... );
  void Unregister( ... );
  void Announce( FPart*, Listable* );
 } ItemSelected;

 void Select( int Index ) {
  CurrentItem = Container->Get( Index );
  ItemSelected.Announce( this, CurrentItem );
 }
};
```

FIGURE 13 The `ItemSelected` event in the lister's interface is available to clients

The parameters for Announce() differ from event to event. Usually two to three parameters suffice to inform the observers about specific changes. The first parameter is almost always a reference to the observed object itself; otherwise, the observer has to find out which of its observed objects has announced the event.

An observer should react to an event only through probing operations; it should never modify the observed object. This avoids the danger of entering into an infinite Event-Change loop.

Compare   Compare to Change-update, as in Smalltalk [GR83] or Observer/Subject [GHJ+95]; implicit invocation [NGG+93]; or callback, as in various windowing systems.

IP/FP Plug In: Design Pattern

Purpose   This pattern reconciles tool composition with tool construction by plugging in Sub-IPs into Context-IPs and Sub-FPs into Context-FPs.

Problem   Tools are structured vertically by composition out of subtools and horizontally by separating interaction from function. If we wish to dynamically create a subtool, this leads to two diverging forces that must be reconciled on the object level.

Context   Any tool consists of at least one interaction and one functional part. Creating a subtool poses the question of how to connect the subtool's IPs and FP to the IPs and FP of the context tool.

Calls and events have to be routed in a disciplined way to keep the structure and dynamics of complex tools clear and understandable. This means that a technique for dynamically plugging subtools into context tools as well as putting interaction parts on functional parts has to be provided. Creation and deletion have to be considered, too.

Solution   First we show the static structure of class relationships. For the simple case of the calendar with its lister subtool, the structure in Figure 14 results.

The calendar's IP works on the lister's IP, and the calendar's FP works on the lister's FP. Additionally, each IP works on its own FP. Each relationship in Figure 15 also indicates an observation of the used object. So the Lister-FP is observed by the Lister-IP and by the Calendar-FP.

Notifying an IP about relevant changes usually means that the display has to be updated. Notifying the FP of an embedding context tool means that something relevant to the subtool's task has happened. If a user selects an item from the list, the lister-FP will notify the calendar-FP, which in turn takes appropriate action (by handing over the newly selected appointment to the editor).

The general structure is more complicated, because a tool may have more than one interaction part. The FP of the context tool, the Context-FP, accesses the FPs of its subtools, the Sub-FPs. Every IP of the context tool

Figure 14 IP and FP coupling between calendar and lister (context and subtool)

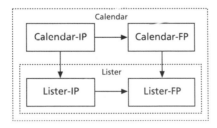

Figure 15 General object diagram between IPs and FPs of context and subtool

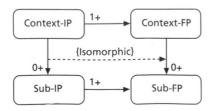

(Context-IP) may put several Sub-IPs onto each Sub-FP. The Sub-IPs work on their Sub-FP like the Context-IPs work on their Context-FP.

Again, each relationship means using as well as observing the used object. The IP is mainly interested in events that deal with presentation. The Context-FP of an FP is normally interested in logical issues related to the material or the tool's state.

We will now look at the dynamics. The decision to create a subtool is made by the Context-FP. It simply creates the Sub-FP and announces an appropriate event. Informed by this event, the IPs of the Context-FP decide which Sub-IPs are needed for the new Sub-FP and therefore have to be created. Thus, each Context-IP creates zero, one, or more Sub-IP objects for every new Sub-FP. The Context-IP introduces the new Sub-FP to its newly created Sub-IPs. The code in Figure 16 shows this interplay between the calendar's IP and FP when the Sub-FP creates the lister subtool.

Whenever a Sub-FP has to be deleted, the Context-IP deletes all Sub-IPs belonging to that Sub-FP. Then the Sub-FP is deleted by its Context-FP.

FIGURE 16 C++ code showing the interplay between events and operation calls for creating an IP for a given FP

```cpp
class CalendarFP : public CompoundFP {

 class Event {
   Announce( FPart* SubFP );
 } SubFPCreated;

 void CreateSubFPs() {
   ListerFP = new ListerFP( this );
   SubFPCreated.Announce( ListerFP );
 }
};

class CalendarIP : public CompoundIP {

  void CreateSubIP( FPart* NewSubFP ) {
   if ( NewSubFP->IsA( ListerFP ) ) {
    ListerIP = new ListerIP( NewSubFP );
   }
  }
  CalendarIP( CalendarFP* MyFP ) {
   MyFP->SubFPCreated.Register( CreateSubIP );
  }
};
```

4.4 Application of Design Patterns for a Single Tool

How do we apply the different patterns in a uniform way, like using a coherent language? Looking at Figure 17, we see a calendar tool that is composed out of the subtools lister and editor, both working on materials via the aspect classes Listable and Editable, respectively.

The Lister-FP and the Editor-FP have been plugged into the Calendar-FP as well as its IPs. Figure 17 shows that each tool is constructed of an IP and an FP, with the FP notifying its IP about relevant changes of its state. On closer examination, we have not just built a calendar but a general browser tool that works with any listable and editable material. We could enhance this design by adding another aspect class, `FormEditable`, for the structured editing of materials using fields of specific data types.

5. TOOL INTEGRATION

Next we will combine the calendar with a second tool. The additional patterns again have to conform to the metaphors of tools, materials, and environment.

FIGURE 17 Detailed class diagram for the calendar tool and the appointment with its aspect classes

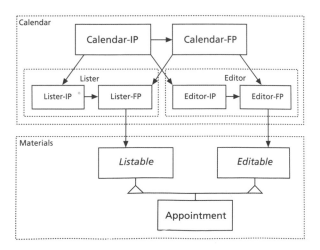

5.1 Extending the Example

Figure 18 shows a second tool, which we want to use together with the calendar. It is a scheduler for a whole week that presents all periodic dates and allows the user to directly manipulate them. While the calendar shows individual appointments, the scheduler will only show things like regular weekly meetings and seminars. The materials the scheduler uses are Time-Table objects based on WeeklyDate objects. WeeklyDate objects are distinct from Appointments in that they have no fixed date.

Figure 19 illustrates how to simplify both tool structures. Thereby we can concentrate on the problems of tool integration. The scheduler has a Time-Table containing WeeklyDate objects, and the calendar has an AppBook (appointment book) containing Appointments.

Obviously, weekly meetings can clash with individual appointments. In order to focus the discussion, a date clash will be expressed by a Boolean flag, Conflicts, on both WeeklyDate and Appointment objects. If the flag is set for a WeeklyDate object, a conflicting individual appointment exists. If the flag is set for an Appointment object, there are overlapping periodic dates. The flag is necessary for the tools to signal a date clash to the user.

FIGURE 18 A scheduler (a tool) extending our example to examine integration problems

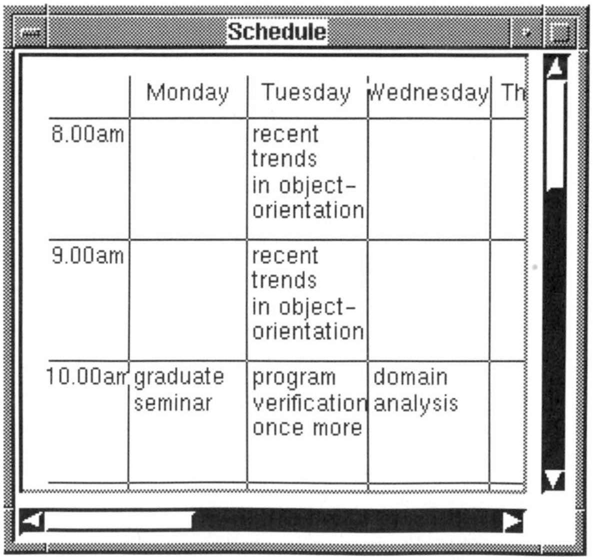

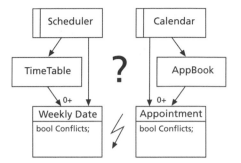

FIGURE 19 A class diagram of the two tools and their materials and an integration relationship

5.2 Design Patterns for Tool Integration

There is no need for a supertool controlling all other tools, but a fair selection of interrelated but independent tools should be at hand for the user. Dependencies may exist among materials, but not tools.

We collect dependent materials into a single material container that maintains constraints among these materials. We use tool coordinators to propagate change notifications among interrelated tools. Materials are retrieved from the Material Administration, which is a kind of object-request broker. Finally, we accomplish the workplace's closure through an Environment object.

Material Container: Design Pattern

Purpose   This pattern groups dependent materials into a single container acting as a closure so that constraints can be maintained independently from tools and in one place.

Problem   Different materials are often related and mutually dependent. Maintaining such constraints has to be independent of the tools' functionality in order to allow for easy addition of new tools.

Context   Materials like WeeklyDate and Appointment depend on each other; this fact has to be expressed and maintained as constraints of these materials. For example, adding a new appointment leads to checks and updates of the Conflicts flag on the WeeklyDate and Appointment objects.

Adding a new tool to our time-planning system which works on the same materials should not make maintenance of the materials' constraints more difficult. If the tools were responsible for maintaining material constraints, these constraints would have to be reimplemented for each new tool. Each tool then would have to know the constraints on any related materials—an undesirable situation. Thus, constraints have to be maintained independently of tools. All constraints will be localized in a single place.

The notion of constraints can be captured formally, as mathematical equations relating object attributes, for example. Our experience shows that material dependencies often produce structural implications that force rearrangements of object relationships. For the time being, we implement constraints within standard programming languages, but as constraint languages become more popular this may change.

The constraints treated here take immediate effect. They are restricted to a single workplace. We call them short-term constraints.

Solution   We enclose all materials that are mutually dependent through short-term constraints into a single container called a material container. This container provides an Update() operation that is called by a tool if a relevant change takes place (a stronger solution controls each access to the materials in a container). The container in turn triggers a constraint object, which it supplies with the changed material.

FIGURE 20   The material container hides the constraints between materials and thus localizes the dependencies.

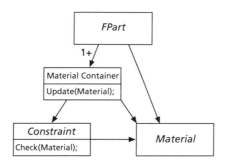

FIGURE 21   Our example has two materials (WeeklyDate and Appointment) that are constrained by a TPSConstraint object.

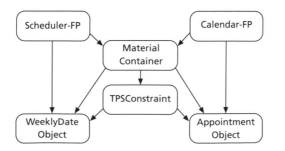

In our example, WeeklyDate and Appointment are subclasses of Material. A tailored constraint has to be written that will take care of these specific materials, called TPSConstraint (time-planning system constraint). Figure 22 shows the result.

The TimeTable and AppBook objects have been omitted for clarity. TPSConstraint will ask them for WeeklyDate and Appointment objects. A constraint object can be seen as a strategy class encapsulating an algorithm for constraint maintenance.

Introducing a new tool will cause no further changes, as constraints are taken care of in the TPSConstraint class independently of tools. If a new material is added to the time-planning system, only the integrating relationship realized through TPSConstraint class has to be updated.

Tool Coordinator: Design Pattern

Purpose   This pattern notifies tools about changes to their materials due to constraints.

Problem   If a constraint changes a material's state, the tool's state and the material's visual presentation can become inconsistent and thus need to be updated.

Context   Each tool whose material is changed by a third party needs to be informed about this change. As each container may hold several materials, usually more than one tool will be affected. Entering a new weekly date might lead to clashes with several appointments, for example. Thus all relevant—that is, the calendar and scheduler—are affected and have to be informed.

A number of possible solutions come to mind, all based on the notification mechanism. Each tool can observe its materials, the constraint, or the container that will in turn notify it about changes.

FIGURE 22 The Tool Coordinator dispatches an event received from an FP to the FPs of other tools.

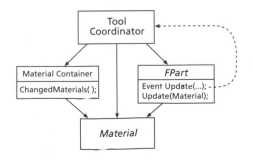

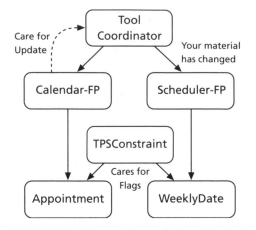

FIGURE 23 The run-time relationships between the participating objects and the resulting control flow.

We feel that using the notification mechanism this way is highly problematic. Notification should be used as sparingly as possible. Our experience shows that the system's architecture and dynamics otherwise become harder to understand.

Solution   For each material container we create a tool coordinator. This is an object that observes all functional parts working on materials in the container. If a functional part changes a material, it will issue an Update event to inform its IP or Context-FP. Additionally, this event is received by the tool coordinator.

The tool coordinator requests a list of materials that were affected by the last manipulation from the container. From this list and its internal dispatch tables, the tool coordinator derives which FPs' Update operations have to be called.

The dispatch tables can be built efficiently. The tool coordinator knows all the tools working on materials in the container. Each tool offers a list of its FPs under their abstract superclass FPart. Each FPart object offers the material it works on under the abstract superclass Material. They are held in a dictionary. The tool coordinator uses the list of affected materials it gets from the container and the dictionary in order to decide which FP has to be informed. With these superclasses, the tool coordinator can be built independently of any specific material or tool.

Compare   Compare our concept of tool coordinators and material containers with the widespread notion of mediators, as, for example, in Sullivan and Notkin [SN92] or Gamma et al. [GHJ+95].

5.3 Outlook: The System's Boundaries

We end the presentation of our pattern language by providing a brief outlook on two more design patterns. The Material Administration and Environment patterns define the system boundaries necessary for integrating the patterns into a work environment.

Material Administration

We need a Material Administration pattern for retrieving and storing materials, for controlling access to originals and copies, and for grouping materials into material containers. The Material Administration subsystem is accessible by any tool. As the result of a request, tools receive iterators on a set of materials conforming to the query.

The Material Administration pattern works with several material providers, each of them encapsulating a database service such as an OO-DBMS or a RDBMS. In addition, nonpersistent material providers may be used.

The Material Administration pattern may be seen as a combination of an object-request broker (ORB) and a portable common tool environment (PCTE) enhanced to fit our specific needs.

Environment Object

The Environment object sets up the whole system. It shows accessible tools and materials on a desktop. For each new material container, it creates the corresponding tool coordinator and takes care of technical issues during initialization (like providing screen and database services).

The Environment object is the first object to be created. After system startup it creates material providers, each of them encapsulating a database service and the Material Administration subsystem that receives the material providers. After this it opens the desktop and waits for users to launch a tool.

6. TOOLS AND MATERIALS AT WORK

We will now give a short but complete example in order to see the pattern language at work. We will describe a system for task-oriented requirements analysis (TORA) [Kei87] that is used at the University of Hamburg for teaching purposes. It consists of the graphical editor Sane for interactive manipulation of task net materials and a glossary browser for textually documenting the objects of the editor.

The tool Sane consists of a compound tool with two subtools. Each tool has an interaction and a functional part. The compound tool establishes the frame for the usual application services, like file handling, clipboard access, and so on. The Canvas subtool allows for direct manipulation of the editor's materials, which are graphical objects (GraphObjs). The TaskNet subtool works with the logical materials' TaskObj. Depending on the number of contexts it is presented in, a TaskObj has one or more graphical presentations through GraphObjs.

Access to these materials is mediated through aspect classes that establish the use context. They provide an approach for working with graphical objects that differs from what we find in most editors. The main tool works only with the aspect class Storable to store and retrieve objects from files or the clipboard. The Canvas-IP uses drag and resize wrappers to manipulate the graphical objects via its aspect classes Drawable and Sizeable. More complex functionality requires knowledge of the composite structure of TaskObj, introduced through the Composite aspect class available to the Canvas-FP through the complex Graphical aspect class.

Thinking in terms of aspects (classes) helps very much to separate different functionalities from each other and makes the evaluation of the necessary functionality easier.

Each logical TaskObj can be documented using the tool ObjectLexicon. For each TaskObj there exists a LexiconObj, which users textually edit to document the TaskObj and its GraphObj. Both materials are kept inside a material container that uses the InSane (Integrated Sane) Constraint that, for example, ensures that the label of the TaskObj is always the same as that of the LexiconObj.

FIGURE 24 The Sane tool and its materials. The materials' interface relies heavily on aspect classes separating different functionalities.

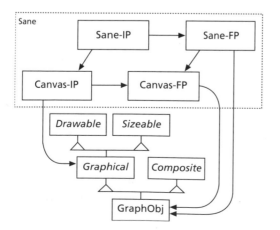

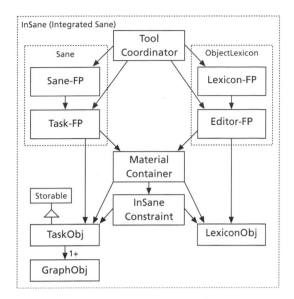

Figure 25 The integrated system shows that tools are tied together at the top (Tool Coordinator) and at the bottom (Material Container).

If a TaskObj is created or deleted or its label is changed, the tool coordinator will be notified and it in turn informs the related tool.

7. DISCUSSION OF THE TOOLS AND MATERIALS METAPHOR

The application domain of the Tools and Materials Metaphor comprises environments that fit naturally with the notion of tools and materials used by skilled human workers. It focuses on the work of people in workshops and offices. The individual craftsman, the software developer, and the office worker all fall into this category and may be supported adequately by a software system designed according to the Tools and Materials Metaphor.

To complete the Tools and Materials Metaphor, additional metaphors—like machine and the material administration for embedding databases—address other issues, which are not discussed in this paper but are needed in every major project.

When it comes to cooperative work, however, these metaphors have to be extended—a topic that is currently under discussion. For office work a possible solution seems to be obvious—namely, introducing mailboxes for incoming and outgoing materials (a concept that has been used in offices for many decades). Similar ideas are currently being discussed, with different outcomes, under the label of work-flow management.

Still more ambitious tasks remain to be solved. Close and intense cooperation on an electronic whiteboard, working on commonly shared artifacts in parallel—these are tasks that are not yet fully addressed by the Tools and Materials Metaphor. Nevertheless, we believe we have a fruitful starting point that can be further developed toward more advanced metaphors that either integrate or compete with communication and media metaphors or agents [MO92, Mae94].

8. OUTLOOK

The pattern language presented in this paper will be used to teach the Tools and Materials Metaphor to both professional software developers and students. We want to transfer the experience from the application framework to industrial projects. In the industrial settings we will carefully analyze how the metaphors and implementation techniques of our pattern language enhance comprehensibility of the overall approach, the communication among a design team, and the resulting design quality.

ACKNOWLEDGMENTS

This paper was written in close contact with Karl-Heinz Sylla at GMD St. Augustin, who proposed essential changes and amendments. We wish to thank our reviewer, Bruce Anderson, for his substantial help in making this paper readable, and Ralph Johnson for inspiring comments on early drafts. The paper profited a lot from the discussions in the writer's workshop at PLoP '94; thus we wish to thank all those who by commenting helped to improve it.

BIBLIOGRAPHY

BCS92 Reinhard Budde, Marie-Luise Christ-Neumann, and Karl-Heinz Sylla. "Tools And Materials: An Analysis and Design Metaphor." *Tools-7, Technology of Object-Oriented Languages and Systems, Europe-92.* Edited by G. Heeg, B. Magnusson, and B. Meyer. Englewood Cliffs, NJ: Prentice-Hall, 1992, 135–146.

BGZ95 Ute Bürke, Guido Gryczan, Heinz Züllighoven. "Object-Oriented System Development in a Banking Project: Methodolgy, Experience, Conclusions." *Human-Computer Interaction* 10,2 (forthcoming).

BKK+92 Reinhard Budde, Karl-Heinz Kautz, Karin Kuhlenkamp, and Heinz Züllighoven. *Prototyping.* Berlin, Heidelberg: Springer-Verlag, 1992.

BZ92 Reinhard Budde and Heinz Züllighoven. "Software Tools in a Programming Workshop." *Software Development and Reality Construction.* Edited by Christiane Floyd, Heinz Züllighoven, Reinhard Budde, and Reinhard Keil-Slawik. Berlin, Heidelberg: Springer-Verlag, 1992, 252–268.

CCH+89 Peter S. Canning, William R. Cook, Walter L. Hill, and Walter G. Olthoff. "Interfaces for Strongly-Typed Object-Oriented Programming." OOPSLA-89, ACM *SigPlan Notices* 24, 10 (October 1989): 457–467.

Cun95 Ward Cunningham. "The CHECKS Pattern Language of Information Integrity." This volume, Chapter 10.

DHM89 Mahesh H. Dodani, Charles E. Hughes, and J. Michael Moshell. "Separation of Powers." *Byte* (March 1989): 255–262.

DWA93 Wolfgang Dzida, Marion Wiethoff, and Albert G. Arnold. *ERGOguide—The Quality Assurance Guide to Ergonomic Software.* GMD, Schloss Birlinghoven, Germany, 1993.

Flo84 Christiane Floyd. "A Systematic Look at Prototyping." *Approaches to Prototyping.* Edited by Reinhard Budde, Karin Kuhlenkamp, Lars Mathiassen, and Heinz Züllighoven. Berlin, Heidelberg: Springer-Verlag, 1984.

GHJ+93 Erich Gamma, Richard Helm, Ralph Johnson, and John Vlissides. "Design Patterns: Abstraction and Reuse of Object-Oriented Design." ECOOP-93, *Lecture Notes on Computer Science No. 707* (1993): 406–431.

GHJ+95 Erich Gamma, Richard Helm, Ralph Johnson, and John Vlissides. *Design Patterns: Elements of Reusable Object-Oriented Software.* Reading, MA.: Addison-Wesley, 1995.

GR83 Adele Goldberg and David Robson. *Smalltalk-80: The Language and Its Implementation.* Reading, MA: Addison-Wesley, 1983.

Hil92 Ralph D. Hill. "The Abstraction-Link-View Paradigm: Using Constraints to Connect User Interfaces to Applications." CHI-92, *SIGCHI Conference Proceedings.* Edited by Penny Bauersfeld, John Bennet, and Gene Lynch. Reading, MA: Addison-Wesley, 1992, 335–342.

Joh92 Ralph E. Johnson. "Documenting Frameworks Using Patterns." OOPSLA-92, *ACM SigPlan Notices* 27, 10 (October 1992): 63–70.

Kei87 Reinhard Keil-Slawik. "Supporting Participative Systems Development: Task-Oriented Requirements Analysis." *System Design for Human Development and Productivity: Participation and Beyond.* Edited by Klaus Fuchs-Kittowsky and D. Gertenbach. Berlin: Akademie der Wissenschaften der DDR, 1987.

KP88 Glenn E. Krasner and Stephen T. Pope. "A Cookbook for Using the Model-View-Controller User Interface Paradigm in Smalltalk-80." *Journal of Object-Oriented Programming* 1, 3 (August/September 1988): 26–49.

Mae94 Pattie Maes. "Agents That Reduce Work and Information Overload." *Communications of the ACM* 37, 7 (July 1994): 31–41.

Mey91 Bertrand Meyer. "Design by Contract." *Advances in Object-Oriented Software Engineering.* Edited by Dino Mandrioli and Bertrand Meyer. London: Prentice-Hall, 1991, 1–50.

MO92 Susanne Maass and Horst Oberquelle. "Perspectives and Metaphors for Human-Computer Interaction." *Software Development and Reality Construction.* Edited by Christiane Floyd, Heinz Züllighoven, Reinhard Budde, and Reinhard Keil-Slawik. Berlin, Heidelberg: Springer-Verlag, 1992, 233–251.

NGG+93 David Notkin, David Garlan, William G. Griswold, and Kevin Sullivan. "Adding Implicit Invocation to Languages: Three Approaches." JSSST-93, LNCS-742, *Object Technology for Advanced Software.* Edited by Shojiro Nishio and Akinori Yonezawa. New York: Springer-Verlag, 1993, 489–510.

Pir74 Robert M. Pirsig. *Zen and the Art of Motorcycle Maintenance.* London: Corgi Books, 1974.

RBP+91 James Rumbaugh, Michael Blaha, William Premerlani, Frederick Eddy, and William Lorensen. *Object-Oriented Modeling and Design.* London: Prentice-Hall, 1991.

Sha95 Mary Shaw. "Patterns of Software Architectures." Chapter 24, this volume.

SP93 Bernhard Strassl and Franz Penz. "CommonInteract: An Object-Oriented Architecture for Portable Direct Manipulative User Interfaces." *Journal of Object-Oriented Programming* 6, 3 (June 1993): 33–39.

SN92 Kevin J. Sullivan and David Notkin. "Reconciling Environment Integration and Software Evolution." *ACM Transactions on Software Engineering and Methodology* 1, 3 (July 1992): 229–268.

WJ90 Rebecca Wirfs-Brock and Ralph E. Johnson. "Surveying Current Research in Object-Oriented Design." *Communications of the ACM* 33, 9 (September 1990): 104–124.

Dirk Riehle is a graduate student at the University of Hamburg and Heinz Züllighoven is full professor at the University of Hamburg. Both can be reached at the University of Hamburg, Department of Computer Science, Software Engineering Group, Vogt-Kölln-Str. 30, D-22527 Hamburg, Germany; {riehle, zuelligh}@informatik.uni-hamburg.de.

Flexible Command Interpreter: A Pattern for an Extensible and Language-Independent Interpreter System

Norbert Portner

Intent   This paper provides the architecture for an interpreter system that allows for flexible extension of the command language's scope and, in addition, independence from the actual grammar of the language. The interpreter should be capable of controlling real time applications.

Motivation   Many systems are controlled by some kind of command language. After the command language has been defined once, changes to the language's scope will often arise from changes in the system requirements or from extending the system's functionality.

Consider, for example, a testing system for custom PC boards. To automate the testing process, a control language is defined and interpreted by some specialized testing system. As it is not foreseeable what the testing requirements for future custom designs will be, the testing system needs to be extensible to adapt to new or changed requirements. Hard-coding the language's grammar means that the code of the interpreter will have to be changed every time new control statements need to be processed. In many cases this will lead to new code that differs only in part from the original

Copyright © 1995 Siemens AG. All Rights Reserved.

one. This process of extending conventional implementations has proved to be error-prone and costly.

Therefore, the pattern for the flexible command interpreter maps the grammar of the command language to a class structure. A program (script file) is now compiled to an instance tree instead of to some other intermediate representation. Once we have defined the class model for the grammar, extending the language's scope may often be done by subclassing existing statements. Using yacc makes it rather easy to generate a new compiler for a modified grammar, which produces the new instance tree. (The compiler is not part of the pattern and will not be discussed further.)

The following program illustrates the use of a typical command language from this domain to implement a simple test case:

```
PROGRAM test01 ;

VAR     value:          INTEGER;        // declare a variable

CHANNEL analogIn:       AI1;            // declare I/O channels
        digitalOut:     DO1;

MODULE test01m1;                        // begin a new program module

 FROM 10 TO 100: GET analogIn value;    // read analog input channel
 FROM 10 TO 100: IF value > 1024        // check channel value
          THEN
          AT +5: SET digitalOut 1   // set output channel
          ELSE
          AT +0: SET digitalOut 0;  // unset output channel
END;
```

The purpose of this small program is to read an input channel and check its value. Depending on the value of this input channel, an output channel is either set or unset (digital 1 or 0).

A special feature of this command language that is not found in general-purpose languages is the notion of time-controlled statement execution; this is a typical feature in real-time systems. In the example above, the statement FROM 10 to 100 directs the interpreter to repeatedly execute the statement following the colon within a time range of 10 ms (milliseconds) to 100 ms. If the value being read exceeds the threshold value of 1024, a digital output channel is set to 1, with a delay of 5 ms. This means that statements must not be executed at the pace of the execution vehicle, but have to follow stringent time conditions as depicted by the FROM- and AT- statements.

Figure 1 shows the pattern for a selected set of statements, together with the controlling classes (TestController, Agenda, Timer). The statement classes shown in the figure illustrate the pattern as it has been implemented in a testing system for custom PC boards. The command language is rather simple, and the testing programs mostly consist of Set and Get commands to write and read the interface pins of a board. In addition, there are control statements like If-then-else and While loops.

FIGURE 1 Class model of the interpreter system

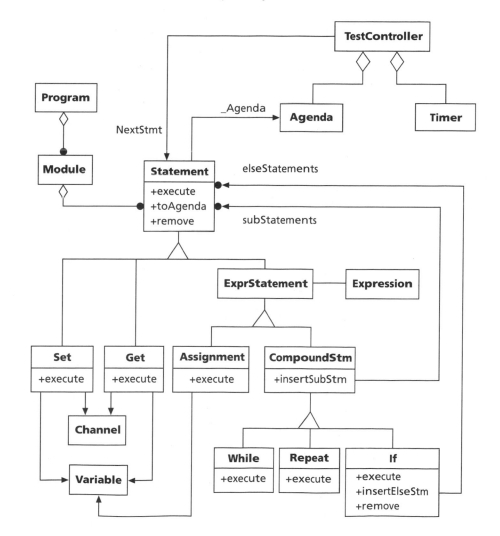

The pattern resolves three forces:

1. **Extensibility.** The class hierarchy of statement classes provides for easy extension; all statement classes provide an execute method that encapsulates the corresponding functionality.

2. **Language independence.** The flow of execution is controlled by an *Agenda*, and all statement classes provide a toAgenda method in order to activate the statement.

3. **Real-time capability.** The grammar comprises time-control statements and the TestController uses a Timer to decide upon statement execution times.

The pattern resolves force 1 by a class model in which every concrete statement is derived from the Statement superclass. Thereby every statement subclass inherits the protocol of Statement, including the execute method. Every concrete subclass needs only to overwrite the execute method to provide its specific functionality—that is, the execute method is responsible for encapsulating all necessary functionality intended by the statement. Putting this method into the superclass of all statement classes ensures that every statement can be called the same way. The interpreter no longer depends on the internals of the statement. Hence the language's scope may easily be extended by subclassing the statement class or any already-existing subclass.

Figure 2 illustrates the dynamic behavior of the interpreter when it is executing a test case; the following discussion of force 2 and force 3 refers to this behavior. In order to resolve force 2, the Statement class also defines a toAgenda method, which is responsible for putting its reference into the Agenda object of the TestController. When the TestController is started for a Module, it calls the toAgenda method of all top-level statements like Set, Get, and Compound of that Module. Within the Agenda object, all statements are sorted in a timely manner. For certain statements, like the If statement, it can only be decided later whether the then or else part needs to be executed and put on the agenda. This has to be done by the If statement's execute method, which in turn calls toAgenda for either the then or the else part.

Resolving force 3: After all top-level statements have been registered, the TestController asks for the current time from Timer and retrieves from Agenda all statements with an execution time less than or equal to the current time. For all those statement objects, TestController calls the execute method. The Statement objects return a certain value, which may be passed to the user interface (the user interface is not covered by the pattern). TestController repeats this sequence until no more Statement objects are on the Agenda.

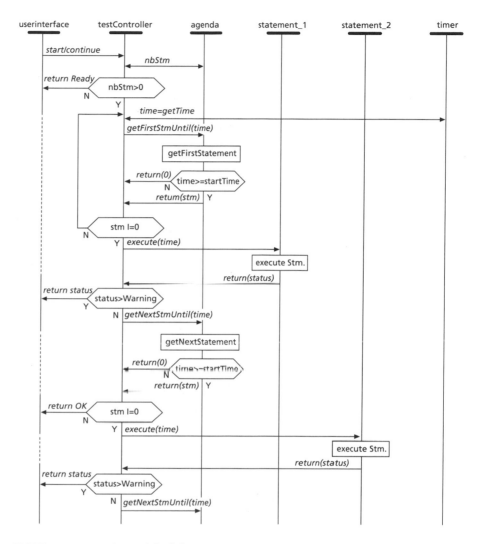

FIGURE 2 Dynamic model of the interpreter system

Modules are organized in Programs and started by the TestController in the sequence of their occurrence within the Program. For understanding and using the pattern, the concepts of Program and Module have only a minor impact.

Applicability The pattern may be used when

- Flexibility is needed for the scope of a command or program language
- The run-time portion should be unaffected by changes in the language's scope
- Time-controlled statement execution under real-time conditions is required

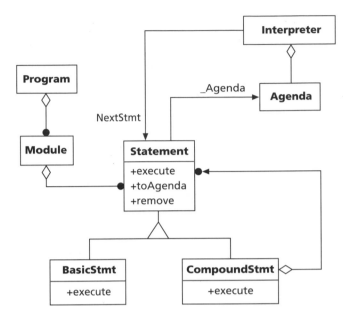

FIGURE 3 Structure of the Interpreter pattern

Structure   The Timer class is a specialty of the application in use and therefore is excluded from the general structure of the pattern. Depending on the structure of the command language, there may be a module class or not. Figure 3 shows the general structure of the Interpreter pattern.

Participants   ■ Program—an organizational unit of modules
- Module—an organizational unit of statements
- Statement—the superclass of all other statements
- BasicStmt—a basic statement not consisting of further components
- CompoundStmt—a statement consisting of further compound or basic statements; may contain control structures for deciding which basic statements to execute next
- Interpreter—a singleton object responsible for calling the execute method of statements found in the agenda
- Agenda—a singleton object holding a collection of references to statements; may be processed sequentially or, in real-time environments, controlled by timing conditions

Collaborations
- Compound statements control their enclosed basic statements.
- Interpreter is responsible for putting all top-level statements on the Agenda.
- Statements must know the Agenda (global resource, singleton) in order to put their reference there when `toAgenda` is called.
- Interpreter knows the Agenda and selects the next statements (basic and/or compound) from there and calls the execute method of the respective statements.

Consequences
- The grammar implemented using this pattern has been rather trivial so far. No experiences exist for more complex language constructs like procedures.
- Compared with conventional implementations, the price for using this pattern has to be paid in the form of reduced performance (30 percent for a C++ implementation has been observed, compared to a pure and optimized C-implementation).

Known Uses   The pattern has been used in the course of reimplementing an existing testing system. The old system was highly optimized and implemented in C. There are stringent timing conditions for the execution of statements. (Typically a statement must be executed within 100 µs; simple set/get IO statements must execute within 50 µs.) These have a certain impact on the implementation of compound statements and on their nesting levels.

After the reimplementation was done, we measured the efforts necessary to extend both systems. For the object-oriented system, efforts for modifying existing statements (for example, `IfTest` statement, trigger) and adding new statements (for example, `random` statement) could be reduced by a factor of five! The potential savings in development efforts easily compensates for the decrease in performance.

Related Patterns
- The Interpreter and the Agenda are singleton objects.
- Even though it was not done in the original implementation (due to a lack of knowledge about patterns), the behavior of existing statements could have been extended using the Strategy pattern (see Figure 4).

Figure 4 illustrates how statements may be extended by exploiting the Strategy pattern. Using the Strategy pattern could help to further stabilize the hierarchy of statement classes and thereby contributes to resolving force 1, the extensibility of the language's scope.

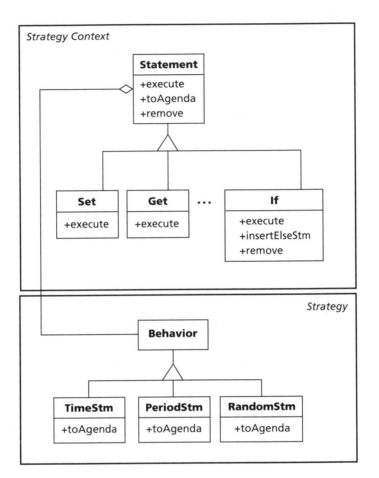

FIGURE 4 Combining Interpreter pattern with Strategy pattern

Norbert Portner can be reached at Siemens AG, Automation, P.O. Box 48. D-90327 Nuremberg, Germany; norbert@m30x.nbg.scn.de.

New Clients with Old Servers: A Pattern Language for Client/Server Frameworks

Kirk Wolf and Chamond Liu

INTRODUCTION

While developing object-oriented frameworks for Smalltalk workstations communicating with legacy host business systems, we have found that several patterns recur in mutually supportive arrangements. Many of the low-level patterns have already been described by other authors (Coad 1992; Gamma et al. 1995); our purpose is to describe how they cooperate with higher-level patterns to produce complete frameworks. Our attempt to form such a description is motivated by Christopher Alexander's pattern language (1977, 1979), with which whole metropolitan regions are designed or improved by applying successively more detailed patterns, culminating with patterns such as "half-inch trim." While Alexander's exposition proceeds top down, ours begins with low-level patterns and works up to a whole framework; this approach shows how higher-level patterns build directly on lower-level ones.

Copyright © 1994 Kirk Wolf and Chamond Liu. All Rights Reserved.

Most of the matters we discuss in this paper are of particular relevance to framework developers—the individuals who must solve infrastructure problems such as converting host data to and from client objects, coordinating persistent with nonpersistent versions of objects, utilizing communications paths economically, and windowing. Framework users, on the other hand, while having to be be conversant with the framework's externals—available services, abstract classes from which to inherit, and methods that must be overridden—must concentrate largely on business-specific matters. For example, in an order-processing application, they must focus on the data and behavior of an order: its information content, its changing states, and the behavior that supports the business rules of the legacy system. As a rough indication of scale, the project we are now working on has about eighty framework classes and four hundred domain classes. We distinguish framework developers (who program the former) from users (who program the latter), and have aimed this paper mostly at developers. Nevertheless, we believe framework developers can only succeed if they have experience as framework users, too.

Conventional descriptions of frameworks emphasize classes and their collaborations; they connote a single, fixed architecture, providing no guidance on how one might construct alternative frameworks to solve the same problem. Raising the emphasis from detailed descriptions of classes to descriptions of *patterns* suggests a more flexible approach to framework construction. Recent work by Eggenschwiler and Gamma (1992) and Johnson (1992) describes specific frameworks with the help of patterns, the latter paper with the express purpose of assisting the framework's users. We use patterns as a family of principles for framework developers; their interrelationships form an overall scheme—or pattern language—for building client/server frameworks to support business applications with traditional mainframe systems.

Although we focus here on interrelationships between patterns, we cannot overlook the classes that participate within each pattern. Unlike the elements of Alexander's architecture patterns (nouns), the elements of object-oriented design patterns (classes) are generally not part of the vernacular. Thus, software pattern descriptions must usually elaborate on participating classes. Omitting this elaboration would be like trying to describe Alexander's "light on two sides of a room" to someone who has never heard of a room.

A schematic summarizing our results appears in the concluding section of this paper. We invite readers who prefer a top-down exposition to begin there and work backward.

A NOTE ON REIFICATION

Reification is a pervasive and beneficial theme of object-oriented design. It is the act of forming objects from entities that seem very unlike objects. Reification, then, "objectifies" that which may not at first appear to be object. (This is analogous, in linguistics, to turning parts of speech that are not nouns into nouns.) The classic example of reification is the *command* pattern: designers reify user interface commands into objects in their own right so that they may be stored, retrieved, executed, and—most significantly—unexecuted or undone (Schmucker 1986; Meyer 1988; Gamma et al. 1995). Other candidates for reification are services (like *searching*; see below), constraints, *exceptions* (see below), strategies (Gamma et al. 1995), and many-to-many relationships between objects.

Reification is not so much a pattern as a broad class of patterns; specific patterns like command, search, and so on may be thought of as instances of reification. Despite this lack of specificity, reification is a useful approach to any problem that manifests unanticipated complications—reification often clarifies a design.

EXCEPTION

Problem Abnormal or unusual conditions often occur far from the point in the execution stack where a program should most naturally respond to the condition. The customary solution is to return information needed to handle the condition back through the calling chain to the handling site. Alternatively, global variables are sometimes used to exchange such information. The first solution results in considerable code clutter, especially when the information is complex, and the second exposes too much information to unconcerned portions of the system.

Solution Defining these conditions as specializations of class Exception classifies them into hierarchies of conditions. Furthermore, the *exception* pattern decouples detection of conditions from their handling and widens the bandwidth from lower-level services to their upper-level clients, without the clutter that the conventional call-return protocol causes. This pattern is built into C++ and some Smalltalk implementations, and it is well documented elsewhere. (See Hinkle and Johnson [1992, 1993] and Dony [1990].)

SOLITAIRE

Problem   Some objects occur once in an application. This phenomenon should appear explicitly in a framework, for the sake of both developers and users.

Solution   A class for which one instance, may occur is called *Solitaire* or *Singleton* (Gamma et al. 1995). Two roles for solitaires are prominent here: as *identifiers*, which are responsible for recognizing whether two objects actually have the same identity; and as *keepers*, which are responsible for maintaining a cache of valuable resources. Identifiers mediate integrity, and keepers improve performance.

OBJECTS FROM RECORDS

Problem   Exchanging data between object-oriented clients and legacy host database systems is complicated by the impedance mismatch between rich, deeply nested objects and flat relational rows. Records (strings of bytes) are inherent in legacy host systems, and therefore must participate in any architecture for exchange. The client must transform these records to and from full-fledged Business objects—the objects at the core of the problem domain, such as Order in an order processing system. The record's distinct fields must be transformed to and from the Business Object's instance data.

Solution   *Objects from Records* provides for flexible, efficient exchange of data between a client and host server. This pattern moves the data access responsibility from the Business Object to a Record object. The class Record is responsible for getting, setting, and committing field objects to and from a string of bytes. Each instance of a concrete subclass (like Order) of Business Object has a corresponding instance of record. We like to think of each Business Object as wrapping behavior around a Record, which represents the object's instance data.

Records collaborate with RecordMaps; a RecordMap defines the layout for all Records of the same kind. This layout is in turn specified by FieldMaps; a FieldMap defines the structure of a type of record field and is responsible for converting objects to and from a string of bytes. Thus a RecordMap consists of an array of FieldMaps and an array of corresponding positions within the record structure. Concrete subclasses of FieldMaps handle conversions for dates, time stamps, numeric types (often built with the Pas de deux pattern [Liu 1993]), character strings (by code-page), or more domain-specific objects such as PhoneNumber, Address, and so on. FieldMaps raise *exceptions* when encountering conversion errors.

Since all Records for a single kind of Business Object share a single RecordMap, the storage overhead for Records themselves is small. Just as all records are instances of a single Record class, so all record maps are instances of a single RecordMap class. RecordMap instances may be generated directly from Cobol record definitions or host data dictionaries and are kept in a RecordMapRegistry (a *solitaire*).

For high-performance access to field objects, Records cache the first access to a field, so that subsequent accesses bypass conversion. Changes to RecordFields only change the cache, until the changes are committed.

REQUEST

Problem   Client/server frameworks use different communications interfaces—APPC, TCP/IP sockets, Remote Procedure Calls, and so on—to exchange information with host applications. The API models and requirements for maintaining connection states vary between these interfaces. These variations should be invisible to client applications.

Solution   The *request* pattern removes dependencies on the particular communications interface. A client instantiates a Request object, which atomically exchanges a collection of input records for a set of output records. A Request object thus encapsulates a unit of work, or transaction, which is executed by the host/server. Requests mediate access to the protocol of a particular communications service, maintain connections to the communications layer, mediate user authentication with the host, and raise exceptions to their clients.

Note: Because our units of work are limited to the duration of a Request, we use an optimistic transaction strategy to detect and recover from integrity errors from concurrent updates to data. Thus each updatable record contains a time stamp, and the host rejects update requests unless this time stamp matches the time stamp in the corresponding database row.

MATERIALIZATION

Problem   A fundamental property of an object-oriented client/server framework is that it renders objects at the client from the server, whether the server supports objects or not (as is the case with the conventional transaction-based host systems considered here). Moreover, application code on the client should be unaware of how or when this rendering occurs.

Solution   The *Materialization* pattern uses the *request* and *objects from records* patterns to transform host data to and from objects. To make this transformation invisible to application code requires a *proxy* (Gamma et al. 1995) or *ghost* pattern. A proxy is an object inserted between an object and its clients; to the clients, the proxy appears to be the underlying object. The proxy establishes an indirection that can mask the extent to which the underlying object has been materialized. A ghost manifests none of the behavior of the underlying object. Messages intended for the underlying object are not understood by the ghost; rather, the ghost intercepts the first such message, whereupon it materializes the object and then "becomes" it, finally redispatching the message. In other words, a ghost metamorphoses into the materialized object upon first use. By contrast, a proxy embeds the materialized object within itself upon first use and survives as the only external interface to the object. Ghosts are impractical to implement in C++.

Both these forms are "on-demand" or "lazy"—they defer materialization until absolutely needed. Proxies may, alternatively, be "eager," which means that they embed the materialized object prior to first use. When materializing complex networks of business objects, proxies may mix eager and lazy materialization to balance fast initial materialization against fast subsequent use, while remaining transparent to the rest of the system. Proxies also go by the name "handle-body" (Coplien 1992). The "handle" is the proxy itself, and the "body" is the underlying object.

In situations where communications bandwidth must be conserved, especially when retrieving lists of objects instead of single objects, a framework may partially materialize an object, producing a *skinny object* with a subset of the complete object's protocol. Should a skinny object receive a message intended for the complete object, the skinny object behaves as a ghost, transparently morphing into its full form.

FINALIZATION

Problem   Applications often need an opportunity to take some explicit action at the moment of an object's demise—that is, at the moment that the last reference to an object is removed. The classical example occurs when the last reference to a handle of an operating system resource is removed; the application needs an opportunity to free the resource at that time. As we will see in the next pattern, there are other occasions when the application or framework must be informed when an object is no longer used by any other objects.

Solution   The *finalization* pattern provides a facility for taking action at an object's demise. Smalltalk-80 provides direct support for finalization through class WeakArray: a WeakArray references its elements just as an ordinary Array would, except that it doesn't impede their garbage collection. When the last reference to an element disappears—that is, when the element is garbage collected—the WeakArray is informed, giving it an opportunity to act. In other Smalltalk implementations or C++, finalization may be implemented by using techniques that resemble reference counting. (Our own implementation uses "dependency"—finalization of an object occurs when it loses its last "dependent." The full treatment of dependency appears later, in its more customary user interface context.)

IDENTITY MANAGEMENT

Problem   Because objects *materialize* from identity-less records, the application is prone to materializing multiple copies of the same object. It is therefore conceivable for multiple order objects to represent the same order with the same order number. Such multiplicity needlessly clutters the workplace, distracts the user, and introduces the risk of inconsistent versions of the object.

Solution   To prevent multiplicity of business objects, we use the *identity management* pattern. The responsibility resides in an abstract class we call File. File is an *identifier solitaire* that manages the identity of business objects to ensure that if, for instance, two lookups produce the same business object, the second lookup references the existing object instead of producing another copy of it. We use a separate File for each kind of business object. Each File maintains a set or dictionary of the objects whose identity it manages. Business objects register themselves with their File when they materialize; when they are no longer referenced, they must be unregistered. In other words, File relies on *finalization* to know when to unregister one of its objects.

Files also provide users with a conceptual representation of a repository for business objects; users imagine that orders are housed in an order file, or order repository. The fact that File also implements identity management for its business objects is transparent to users.

MEGA-SCROLLING

Problem   A request may return a collection of objects that is too large to materialize practically on the client.

Solution   *Mega-scrolling* (which we also call *Virtual lists*) limits the size of the returned collection. This limited subcollection may satisfy the user, but if not, *mega-scrolling* issues another request to retrieve an adjoining subcollection. In practice the business objects materialized by mega-scrolling are often skinny objects that contain only enough state to render summary views of the objects.

Mega-scrolling may be designed so that the user explicitly requests the next subcollection or so that the user interface anticipates the need for the next subcollection on behalf of the user. Either way, each mega-scroll requires the client and host to exchange context information that defines the next subcollection. Our current implementation provides sufficient information to drive a brand-new host transaction for each succeeding mega-scroll; alternatively, succeeding mega-scrolls could refer to a persistent host resource such as an SQL cursor.

SEARCHING FOR BUSINESS OBJECTS

Problem   The act of locating an object of interest is an elemental activity, so mundane that it risks being taken for granted. Screening a repository by certain criteria or merely extracting from it a single element identified by a unique key are both examples of this act. Note that searching is something that may need to be retried, only somewhat differently, because the original results aren't what the user hoped for or because she would like to filter or reorder the results.

Solution   *Searching for business objects* can be reified by defining an abstract class called Search. Search objects define the criteria that govern a search or lookup. Since they can persist after a search operation has finished, they are available for modification and reuse and they are a basis for subsequent filtration, reordering, or *mega-scrolling*. The *search* pattern unifies lookup and searching. All searches for business objects, no matter how trivial, begin by constructing a Search object defining criteria for the search. A File receives a message to search, with the Search object as a parameter. The result is a List (or a single object if the intent of the search is really just a lookup). Note that the result may be null if the search fails to locate anything. Searching relies on *identity management* to avoid rematerializing an object that is already present at the client.

DEPENDENCY (MODEL-VIEW, BROADCAST, OBSERVER, MVC)

Problem   Coupling business objects to the views that render and control them is bad engineering and is ultimately bad for users as well. Such coupling complicates code and design maintenance and also inevitably clouds the underlying conceptual model: the behavior of the model gets inextricably tangled with the behavior of the user interface, both for developers and for users.

Solution   The loose coupling between model objects and their views, pioneered in the late 1970s at Xerox PARC as the Model-View-Controller (MVC) has been one of the most durable patterns in the history of object-oriented programming. Nowadays the original MVC triad more often coalesces into an MV dyad. Nevertheless, the essential benefit remains: the model objects are oblivious to the specific expectations of their views, thereby uncoupling the task of developing model objects from the task of developing the user interface. A full exposition of MVC appears in Collins (1995). The pattern goes by various names: *observer* [Gamma et al. 1995], which implies the obliviousness of the "observed" model object, and *broadcast* [Coad 1992], which refers to the mechanism by which models inform views that changes have occurred. Because we also apply this pattern to non-UI situations (see the next section), we often refer to it as *dependency*. (Views "depend" on models, but not vice-versa.) As suggested earlier, dependency can also be exploited for reference-counting purposes.

CREATING AND UPDATING BUSINESS OBJECTS

Problem   Business objects must come into existence and change over time. These actions usually initiate at a client and must eventually be reflected in the host. These actions become more complicated when objects depend on other objects. For example, an order is likely to depend on its customer, so that changes to the latter must affect the former.

Solution   A File uses materialization (more precisely, "dematerialization") to apply changes to its business objects. Updates must propagate to dependent objects so that the dependents have an opportunity to update as well. We propagate updates with the *Dependency* pattern; the objects in question are not views, but they behave exactly as views do. That is, they are dependents of another object, just as views are, and they receive broadcasts of updates, just as views do. Dependency is the inverse of the *composite* pattern (Gamma et al. 1995); either pattern solves the problem of cascading updates to other objects. However, we prefer dependency because it supports two-way communication between the objects: the dependent can gather whatever information it chooses to from the broadcaster.

Broadly interpreted, updating includes practically any public behavior of a business object. An order, for example, may experience several state transitions (enter, bill, suspend, validate, cancel, and so on) during its life cycle. The transitions and states are specific to the particular business and may entail extensive analysis and design that is well beyond the concerns of a framework's mechanisms. (The pattern *objects from states* [Beck 1994] can help organize state transition problems like this.)

FACTORY METHOD

Problem   When creating a view object for a model, it is better for client code to assume as little as possible. The client generally shouldn't even know the class of the view.

Solution   A *factory method* (Gamma et al. 1995) creates an object to be associated with an existing object, like a window or view object to be associated with a model object. Different classes of objects implement the factory method polymorphically, so that, for instance, each different class of model object may create a different kind of associated view. A factory method frees its client of the need to know the kind of object to be associated with its receiver.

WINDOW-KEEPING

Problem   Building complex windows from scratch in a graphical user interface can be expensive. For example, moderately complex windows can take many seconds to appear, even on high-performance desktop systems. Users do not tolerate such performance characteristics. Another usability problem occurs if, when an application identifies a business object for which a window already exists, the application opens a new, redundant view on the object instead of resurfacing the existing view.

Solution   Class WindowKeeper is a *solitaire* that keeps track of the application's windows. When the user dismisses a window, the window-keeper simulates closing it, then caches it. Should an object subsequently require a window of this class, the window-keeper disinters the cached window and opens it on the object. This all but eliminates the penalty for building a window for the object. Moreover, since the window-keeper tracks all of the application's windows, it knows when to resurface an existing window to avoid redundant windows on the same object.

VIEWING

Problem   Besides finding and creating or updating business objects, the only remaining function of an application is to provide visibility to them. Most projects use the machinery of a platform specific user interface framework or toolkit to build this function. Regardless of the quality of the framework or toolkit, however, we frequently see several design shortcomings of applications built around them: client code burdened with knowledge of the view(s) that apply to a particular kind of model object, design complicated by intertwining models and views (ultimately clouding the user's conceptual model of the application), slow window creation, and proliferation of redundant windows on the desktop.

Solution   Viewing generally uses the rich variety of functions provided by some user interface toolkit. Beyond this function, *viewing* also requires the *factory method, dependency,* and *window-keeping* patterns to overcome the problems outlined above. These patterns together help maintain clear separation in user interface design and provide practical desktop management.

A CLIENT/SERVER FRAMEWORK

Problem   An object-oriented client/server framework for communicating with a legacy host system, reduced to its most elemental terms, must let its user locate objects of interest, examine them, and change (or create) them.

Solution   The client/server framework pattern, then, is an aggregation of *searching,* *viewing,* and *updating/creating* patterns. A successful framework depends on the quality with which these three patterns are implemented, which in turn depends recursively on the quality with which their constituent patterns are implemented.

CONCLUSION

In the spirit of Christopher Alexander's pattern language for designing a human community, we have outlined the patterns and their interrelationships for designing a coherent client/server framework. The figure here summarizes the key relationships. An arrow indicates that a higher-level pattern relies on a lower-level pattern.

This schematic amounts to an informal pattern language that anchors our thinking about framework designs and limits the space of potential framework development paths to a subspace of possibilities that can reasonably be grappled with. We hope that this subspace—or language—proves helpful

FIGURE 4 Key client/server framework relationships

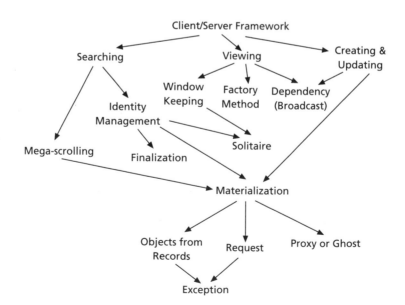

to other developers, and we would also like to know what other framework languages for client/server computing might look like.

ACKNOWLEDGMENTS

We are grateful to the referees and workshop participants of PLoP '94 for their many constructive suggestions to earlier iterations of this paper.

REFERENCES

[Alexander 1977] Christopher Alexander, Sara Ishikawa, and Murray Silverstein, with Max Jacobson, Ingrid Fiksdahl-King, and Shlomo Angel. *A Pattern Language*. New York: Oxford University Press, 1977.

[Alexander 1979] Christopher Alexander. *The Timeless Way of Building*. New York: Oxford University Press, 1979.

[Beck 1994] Kent Beck. "Death to Case Statements (Part 2)." *The Smalltalk Report* 3, 4 (January 1994). 8–9.

[Coad 1992] Peter Coad. "Object-Oriented Patterns," *Communications of the ACM* 35, 9 (September 1992): 152–159.

[Collins 1995] Dave Collins. *Designing Object-Oriented User Interfaces*. Redwood City, CA: Benjamin/Cummings, 1995.

[Coplien 1992] James O. Coplien. *Advanced C++ Programming Styles and Idioms*. Reading, MA: Addison-Wesley, 1992.

[Dony 1990] Christophe Dony. "Exception Handling and Object-Oriented Programming: Towards a Synthesis." *ACM SIGPLAN Notices* (OOPSLA ECOOP '90 Proceedings) 25, 10 (October 1990): 322–330.

[Eggenschwiler and Gamma 1992] Thomas Eggenschwiler and Erich Gamma. "ET++ Swaps Manager: Using Object Technology in the financial Engineering Domain. "*ACM SIGPLAN Notices* (OOPLSA '92 Proceedings) 27, 10 (October 1992): 166–177.

[Gamma et. al. 1995] Erich Gamma, Richard Helm, Ralph Johnson, and John Vlissides. *Design Patterns: Elements of Reusable Object-Oriented Software*. Reading, MA: Addison-Wesley, 1995.

[Hinkle and Johnson 1992] Bob Hinkle and Ralph E. Johnson . "Taking Exception to Smalltalk, Part 1," *The Smalltalk Report* 2, 3 (November/December 1992).

[Hinkle and Johnson 1993] Bob Hinkle and Ralph E. Johnson . "Taking Exception to Smalltalk, Part 2," *The Smalltalk Report* 2, 4 (January 1993).

[Johnson 1992] Ralph E. Johnson. "Documenting Frameworks Using Patterns," *ACM SIGPLAN Notices* (OOPSLA'92 Conference Proceedings) 27, 10 (October 1992): 63–76.

[Liu 1993] Chamond Liu. *Duets, pas de deux, and double dispatch.* Position paper, 1993 OOPSLA Patterns Workshop.

[Meyer 1988] Bertrand Meyer. *Object-Oriented Software Construction.* Hertfordshire, England: Prentice Hall International, 1988.

[Schmucker 1986] Kurt J. Schmucker. *Object-Oriented Programming for the Macintosh.* Hasbrouck Heights, NJ: Hayden, 1986.

Kirk Wolf can be reached at Wolf Associates, Inc., 305 Willowpointe Drive, St. Charles, MO 63304; wolf@mo.net. Chamond Liu can be reached at 2 Clarity Computing, 4 Eldorado Drive, Poughkeepsie, NY 12603; chamond@acm.org.

SYSTEMS AND DISTRIBUTED PROCESSING

PART 2

The demand for extensible, robust, and efficient distributed systems is increasing. This increased demand is driven by technological, economic, and sociological factors. In the past decade, advances in VLSI technology and fiber optics have increased host processing power by two to three orders of magnitude and network channel speeds by five to six orders of magnitude. During this time, the price for network and computer hardware has fallen dramatically. Together, these technological and economic factors have unleashed a seemingly insatiable demand for global connectivity among researchers, developers, and end users. The explosive growth of the Internet and its associated interworking tools (such as email, Netnews, the World Wide Web, Mosaic, and the Multicast Backbone [MBone]) are changing the ways we live, work, and play. As evidence of the scope of these changes, it is now cliché to mention that the authors, editors, and publishers of this book collaborated almost exclusively via email and ftp.

Now that much of the communication and computing infrastructure is available, the challenge for software developers is to realize the potential of distributed computing. Realizing this potential requires a blend of strategic and tactical skills. Strategic skills require mastery of analysis, architecture, and design techniques for developing and reasoning about distributed systems. Tactical skills require mastery of tools such as object-oriented programming languages and reusable frameworks, such as implementations of the OMG Common Object Request Broker Architecture (CORBA) standard and the OSF Distributed Computing Environment (DCE). The design patterns contained in Part 2 help systematically capture, associate, and express the recurring strategic and tactical themes that pervade distributed software systems.

Software systems that effectively utilize distribution are capable of delivering increased system throughput, reliability, scalability, and cost effectiveness. Designing and implementing distributed systems (such as global personal communication systems, telecommunication switch management platforms, video-on-demand servers, and real-time market data monitoring systems) is a challenging task, however. These complex systems exhibit reliability, functionality, efficiency, and portability requirements that are hard to satisfy simultaneously.

Distributed computing and its complexity brings its own set of challenges. One type of complexity arises from limitations with tools and techniques used to develop distributed software. For example, many programming environments lack type-safe, reentrant, portable, and extensible libraries for distributed applications. Fortunately, this type of "accidental" complexity is diminishing as vendors and developers adopt standard tools such as CORBA, DCE, or OLE COM.

A more insidious type of complexity stems from the inherent challenges of developing distributed systems. For example, minimizing the impact of communication latency between hosts, detecting and recovering from partial network and host failures, and efficiently partitioning services among hosts to balance the system workload are inherently complicated tasks. Efficient, robust, and widely available solutions to these problems (such as the Isis reliable distributed computing toolkit) are only beginning to emerge from research labs.

Chapter 5, by Dennis DeBruler, presents a pattern language that addresses complexity inherent in building distributed systems. His pattern language focuses on strategies for decomposing complex software systems across processing nodes. It is difficult to determine how to partition system data and functionality into separate components, and where to distribute these components throughout nodes in a network since workloads and behavior may vary over time. One of the patterns Dennis describes for addressing this problem is to omit functionality at lower levels (such as retransmission of a lost message at the link layer or network layer) in a distributed system that will be provided by higher levels (such as the transport layer). Interestingly, this pattern expresses the philosophical underpinnings of the entire Internet protocol architecture, where it has been named "the end-to-end argument in system design" [Saltze et al. 1984].

Large-scale distributed systems are inherently concurrent since each host is an autonomous computer capable of acting independently. Likewise, large-scale distributed systems also tend to be designed and implemented as a series of layers to reduce unnecessary complexity and enhance extensibility. Chapter 6—by Amund Aarsten, Gabriele Elia, and Giuseppe Menga—and Chapter 7 by Barry Rubel, present a set of patterns that form the basis for developing layered concurrent and distributed systems. Their application domains are computer-integrated manufacturing and real-time systems, respectively. However, the patterns they discuss address issues (such as layering, asynchronous event handling, mutual exclusion, synchronization, and service demultiplexing) that arise in all complex distributed systems. Many of the patterns in these two chapters also recur in Part 6. A particularly important pattern that emerges in these two chapters concerns the assignment of threads of control to tasks in a system. A distributed system consists of both active objects (which execute tasks autonomously in their own threads of control), as well as passive objects (which must borrow the thread of control from their caller to perform a task). Chapter 6 describes the performance and design tradeoffs inherent in the active versus passive object pattern.

Chapters 5–7 focus extensively on patterns for decomposing objects on a host into layers and assigning tasks to each layer. Gerard Meszaros' chapter, "Half Object+Protocol," focuses on an orthogonal pattern that guides the decomposition of an object across multiple address spaces that span hosts. The challenge is to determine an appropriate partitioning of tasks across a distributed system. Gerard describes a pattern whereby an object is divided into two interdependent "half objects" (one in each address space on a different host). His pattern strives to hide an object's remoteness, so that clients are shielded from explicitly handling distribution. Moreover, the pattern strives to make all interactions with the object synchronous, rather than forcing clients to deal with potential asynchronicity if the object implementation is remote. Since events may now arrive at a half object from multiple sources (i.e., the network or local clients), some type of concurrent demultiplexer (such as the Reactor described in Chapter 29) may be used to process incoming events without blocking indefinitely.

Distributed systems often require substantial effort to achieve levels of fault tolerance equivalent to those expected from nondistributed applications. Detecting and recovering from failures is often extremely complicated since volatile state information may be lost when hosts fail independently.

One technique for improving fault tolerance is to replicate services in a distributed system. A common technique for replicating services within a distributed system is described by Frank Buschmann in his "Master-Slave" pattern (Chapter 9). This pattern enhances fault tolerance and robustness by performing computation redundantly on multiple slave hosts. The master host initiates and controls the slaves. As long as at least one slave completes its tasks and returns its results to the master without crashing, the computation will succeed. In addition to being used as a means to increase reliability, the Master-Slave pattern is frequently used to increase performance by performing different computations on the slave hosts in parallel. Whichever slave finishes first reports back to the master, thereby reducing the execution time of a distributed algorithm.

The richness of the distributed software domain is evident by the fact that nearly half the chapters in this book (Chapters 4, 5, 6, 7, 8, 9, 17, 21, 22, 23, 24, 28, 29, and 30) present patterns related to distributed systems. A thorough reading of these chapters reveals that certain key themes recur, each from different perspectives and orientations. Interestingly, a number of other key distributed processing patterns (such as distributed two-phase commit and patterns for group communication) are not addressed in the PLoP proceedings. We expect that the distributed systems domain will prove to be fertile ground at future PLoP conferences.

Saltzer, J. H., D. P. Reed, and D. D. Clark (1984). "End-to-End Arguments in System Design." *ACM Transactions on Computer Systems 2* (November).

A Generative Pattern Language for Distributed Processing

5

Dennis L DeBruler

This paper consists of three sections. The first section is a "meta" section containing some thoughts about patterns and their use. The second section fulfills the charter of these proceedings with an edited version of the conference patterns. I learned a lot at the conference, and thus the editing was actually a rewrite. Unfortunately, I have been unable to change all of the patterns, and the third section records the conference patterns I have not been able to revisit. In short, this paper is like the patterns movement in general—it is only a beginning.

SOME THOUGHTS ON PATTERNS AND THEIR USAGE

Our experience at the conference indicated that even a very cryptic description is sufficient among experienced practitioners. In this form, patterns can be used as a tool to identify and solidify experience. However, we also learned

Copyright © 1995 AT&T. All Rights Reserved.

that a much better description and some examples are needed to use patterns as a teaching tool.

I have become comfortable with formally labeled sections of a pattern—such as name, context, forces, problem, solution, resulting context, and design rationale, and so on—as long as the solution section immediately follows the problem section. The reason the problem and solution sections should be adjacent is that I have tried to follow the advice that the problem section should build up a tension for which the solution section provides a catharsis.

The "forces" section is currently rather weak because the many missing patterns of this "distributed computing" pattern language need to be identified before one can properly begin to identify and sort out the forces. Working with patterns has given me additional insight as to why I have such a difficult time with the waterfall "*myth*odology." I generate programs by tackling different levels of abstraction in parallel. For example, at the beginning of a development I'll discuss both high-level structural issues such as the boundary between the application and the platform, low-level issues such as what kind of protocol to use over a fiber link, and a myriad of miscellaneous issues such as source code control strategy and tools. However, there are other topics, such as measurement collection, that I don't even want to start designing until after most of the code has been implemented. I can envision a methodology based on generative pattern languages that allows the design of some aspects of the system to precede by a considerable interval the design of other parts of the system. For several years I have thought of the software-development cycle as a pail of water freezing into ice. It doesn't freeze top-down or bottom-up, it starts crystallizing throughout the pail around loci of impurities. In the case of software design, I prefer to think of loci of understanding or insight rather than loci of impurities.

One lesson I learned at the writers' workshop was the conflict between the initial reading of the patterns as expository material and reading them later as reference material. In the expository mode many examples should be included. But in the reference mode, many examples make it more difficult to find the nuggets of information. Ultimately we may be able to use hypertext to resolve this conflict. While we are constrained to the printed page, I'm experimenting with using a smaller font for the examples so that they may be easily skipped during subsequent references to the pattern.

My experience with these patterns ranges from having used a pattern systematically since the early 1970s to having just learned about one. As Alexander contends, each pattern's utility will eventually have to be graded. However, I have yet to undertake a project in which all of these patterns are systematically utilized. One reason is that until this documentation effort many of these patterns were the result of intuition rather than knowledge. Another reason is that some of my colleagues think object-based programming means coding in C++, rather than my meaning, "understand your data." Culture clash is a force I haven't even begun to consider how to resolve. Another reason I haven't systematically practiced this pattern language is that there are many patterns still missing.

TOWARD A PATTERN LANGUAGE FOR DISTRIBUTED COMPUTING

To provide continuity one would like all of the examples in the paper to be drawn from the same application. However, to explore the scope of a pattern language it is useful to draw examples from several different applications. I compromise here by choosing several rather distinct applications—the data processing–oriented application of cable television advertising and the hardware intensive, real time–flavored problem domain of a video server.[1] I also draw examples from telephony, because that is the application I am most familiar with. Each example will begin with a header that indicates which of these applications the example draws from. The examples also assume that the paper is being read sequentially and that the previous examples will have been read.

NAME: DEFINE THE DATA STRUCTURE

Context   The beginning of a software design project has a seed team consisting of at least two areas of expertise: marketing and software. Some projects also have a hardware subteam. The marketing subteam provides a "vision," but they are a long way from providing specific requirements. Performance and availability[2] requirements are not yet well understood.

---

[1] The video server is a "box" that has many disk-drive interfaces (SCSI standard) and many fiber interfaces (ATM SONET standard). The job of the video server is to play out movies stored in a digital format on the disks onto the appropriate fiber interface. In a typical application, the fiber interface carries 155 million bits per second (Mbps) and each movie plays out at a rate of 3 Mbps on a Virtual Channel.

[2] I design for applications where unavailability is specified in terms of a few (1–3) minutes a year.

Forces   Forces are to be determined, as mentioned in metacomments in the first section.

Problem   For a large, distributed programming problem, how do you begin the architecture/design?

Solution   Ignoring anything that is known about the distributed nature of the hardware architecture, do a data structure analysis.

Resulting After the data structure analysis, the state data and the relationships that
Context   model the "real world" of interest will be well understood. Note that I have avoided the word *done.* If an application is successful, this activity continues for years, if not decades. However, for any one release cycle, it will settle down. Several of the lower-level patterns have the property of reducing the risk of getting the data model "just right," which helps reduce the time to market.

In addition to the patterns discussed here concerning the data structure, other patterns, concerning aspects of architecture and design such as identifying application programming interfaces [Rubel94], are also needed.

Design   A data analysis exercise is complex enough without the problems of distrib-
Rationale uted computing, so do a first phase of the analysis while ignoring processor boundaries.

NAME: IDENTIFY THE NOUNS

Context   This is the beginning of the Describe the Data Structure phase.

Forces   Everybody is frozen by the immensity of the job that lies ahead [Cunningham94].

Problem   For a large programming problem, how do you begin the architecture/design? Note, it is not a large *distributed* programming problem.

Solution   Brainstorm the values, attributes, and roles of the system, and give them precise names.

It continues to amaze me how simply naming things helps the brain go from the "vision" stage to the "reality" stage. Don't worry at this point whether a noun is an attribute or a role. It should be easy to identify values and their associated enumerated types, however. These should be recorded directly in the project's programming language. That is, it is OK to produce some code during the architecture and design phases concerning details. Furthermore, producing some code early in the waterfall helps force the project to address topics such as source code control before they become critical path issues.

Some enumerated types are easy to identify, but the identification of the values for those types will continue throughout the development of the code—including, unfortunately, system testing. Nonetheless, whenever a new value is identified, it should be recorded directly in the programming language. Any other medium, such as a design document, is simply a waste of keyboarding effort. (One can always include selected code files into a design document, if such detail is desired.)

> ***Telephony Example*** *The attribute Cause Value [Bellcore92] is defined as the result code in a call disconnect report. It contains values such as normal clearing, destination out of service, invalid call reference, and message unimplemented. It has been interesting to watch this list of values grow over the years.*

Resulting Context The resulting context includes enumerated value definitions under source code control and the beginnings of a glossary of roles and their attributes.

Design Rationale This is essentially the first stage of any data analysis or object-oriented analysis, except that we introduce an intermediate notion between attributes and objects/entities, called roles. The notion of role will be defined later as we describe additional patterns.

NAME: FACTOR OUT COMMON ATTRIBUTES

Context A first cut at a list of things and their attributes has been developed by the **Identify the Nouns** pattern.

Forces Reuse of software must be maximized.

Problem During the coding phase of a project there is sometimes a need to copy code and edit it because basically the same operation needs to be done but there are small differences that preclude the use of procedures. Copying code is great for getting your Non-Commentary Source Line (NCSL) count up; but it creates a maintenance nightmare, because whenever a change is needed it must be made in all of the copies.

Cable TV Advertising Business Example   *There are a remarkable number of companies involved in getting a local advertisement to appear on a cable TV show. We define a record for each of these companies. The name of the record is indicated in parentheses.*

- *The cable networks (Network), which schedule programming and identify periods of time that are available for the insertion of advertisements by affiliates.*
- *The cable system advertising business units (CSABU), which are responsible for selling the advertising slots for all of the channels for all of the neighborhoods they serve.*
- *The advertising agencies (Agent), which buy advertising slots for their client companies.*
- *The advertising sales representatives (ASR), who function as brokers between the CSABUs and the advertising agencies.*
- *The video preparation facilities (Preparer), which produce and prepare the spot for each of the CSABUs that will run the ad.*
- *The ad insertion locations (Inserter), which accept, store, retrieve, and insert the spots at the appropriate times into the appropriate channels.*
- *The verification locations (Verifier), which independently verify that a video spot has run.*

All of these companies have an Address attribute. Three years after the software is deployed, all seven records have to be changed because the existing address becomes the Mailing Address and an optional Shipping Address must be added.

Video Server Hardware Example   *Let us assume that four board designs are used—Clock, Disk, Fiber3, and Fiber12. The Clock board derives a clock from one of the fiber terminations or from a local oscillator and distributes that clock to the other boards. The Disk design implements two Small Computer System Interfaces (SCSI). The Fiber3 design implements four OC3 (155 Mbps SONET) interfaces, and the Fiber12 design implements one OC12 (620 Mbps SONET) interface. The design of the Disk and Fiber boards includes a powerful RISC processor with several million bytes of memory. These "smart" boards share methods to diagnose the processor and the memory. Later in the design cycle, an Ethernet chip is added to the processor core to facilitate program development.*

Thus an additional method must be added to each of the smart board types to diagnose the Ethernet chip.

Each of the board types also contains attributes that record the hardware's Current and Goal states. The Current state indicates if the hardware is currently in service (ACTIVE), out of service because it is being tested (OOS-TEST), out of service because the hardware has failed (OOS), out of service because the board has yet to be connected to equipment and turned up for service (INACTIVE), or out of service because a user has removed it from service (OOS-RMV). The Goal state indicates which current state is desired; its legal values are a subset of the current state's values. For example, being OOS because of a failure would never be a goal. Later, while implementing diagnostics,[3] one discovers that when the test is completed it is unknown if the goal should be changed from OOS-TEST to ACTIVE or from OOS-TEST to INACTIVE. Thus each board type definition must be modified to add a Policy state attribute that records the long-term goal of ACTIVE versus INACTIVE.

Solution   Identify the attribute inheritance structure. The reader will recognize this pattern as one of the basic tenets of object-oriented design. However, we use the term *role* instead of *object* because object programming not only implies attribute inheritance, it also implies a specific way of animating data. As we will see later, there are other ways to animate data, but the notion of attribute inheritance makes sense for these other techniques as well. Factoring out shared attributes will introduce new roles of a more general nature that are inherited by the more specialized roles. An object-oriented programming language supports this structure directly. A more traditional language must resort to unions or a field that points to another structure containing the specialized attributes.

> *Cable TV Advertising Business Example*   *We note that all of the different types of companies listed in the previous example are specializations of a more fundamental entity type: Company. Thus a Company role should be defined that has the Mailing Address and optional Shipping Address attributes. The more specialized roles should inherit the Company role and define their own attributes, such as Media Format[4] for the Inserter role. Even if a role currently does not have any additional attributes, it*

---

[3]   We use the term *diagnostics* for hardware tests that affect service. That is, the equipment must be taken OOS while they run.

[4]   We assume that this attribute indicates the transmittal format used by its video equipment, such as Betamax analog tape, Betamax digital tape, MPEG 28mm digital tape, and MPEG-2 delivered over an ATM SONET interface.

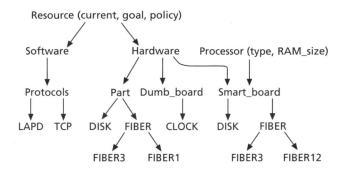

FIGURE 1 Part of the role inheritance structure of the video server

should still have a distinct name because it may acquire additional attributes later in the program's life cycle.

Video Server Hardware Example *To avoid having to edit multiple board definitions whenever another attribute or method is identified that applies to several board types, we introduce the more general role of Board. Furthermore, the processor-related attributes such as Type—for example, 80960 versus 68360, RAM size, and diagnostic methods—are factored out into a Processor mix-in. Note that the maintenance states of Current, Goal, and Policy also apply to each of the interfaces on the Disk and Fiber interfaces. Thus we introduce the role Port to model the common aspects of these hardware interfaces. Noticing that both boards and ports share the maintenance states, we introduce an even more general role of Hardware. Further investigation discovers that some Software roles, such as protocols, also have the notion of a maintenance state. For example, it makes sense to talk about a TCP connection being ACTIVE or OOS. Thus we introduce the role Resource as a generalization across Software and Hardware roles. Figure 1 summarizes this inheritance structure.*

Resulting   The resulting context is a graph recording the inheritance structure among
Context   the roles.

   To facilitate software reuse, we try very hard during the design phase to make our inheritance tree rather deep. That is, we strive for more and more generalization. I like to use the term *entity* for the most fundamental base objects discovered by this generalization process and use the term *role* for the "typical" objects of the problem domain used in the data-structure diagrams.

Design Rationale   The utility of inheritance is discussed extensively in the existing literature.

NAME: NORMALIZE THE ROLES

Context   A diagram of the program's inheritance structure exists.

Forces   Programming languages provide good support for aggregating attributes into records, but they do not provide good support for recording relationships between records.

Problem   Attributes are defined for one large role that instead should be defined for multiple related roles.

> ***Cable TV Advertising Business Example*** *In addition to the company roles of Agent and ASR defined previously, the* **Identify the Nouns** *exercise defined a role, Sale, to record the sale of ad time from an ASR to an Agent. The attributes of the Sale role are contract number, ASR, broker, commission, agent, account manager, date of sale, ad ID, start date, end date, slot ID. The broker is an employee of the ASR, and the account manager is an employee of the agent. The ad ID keys another role that records such things as the name of the ad, the client company for which it was made, and the media formats that are available. The slot ID keys a role that records the play time and channel number of the time being sold. Assume that an ASR employee, Jane, has several active contracts. If we assume that her commission has changed, we have the update problem of consistently changing the Commission attribute of all the role instances associated with her contracts. This is an example of the "update anomaly" [Date81]. Now assume that while she is on vacation all of her contracts expire. We can no longer determine her commission. This is an example of the "deletion anomaly."*
>
> *By including the address attributes in the company role, we can't accommodate companies that have multiple locations without the risk of repeating information that is unique for a company, such as its legal and common names.*

Solution   Apply the normalization techniques developed for relational database models. Descriptions of these normalization techniques can be found in Tsichritzis and Lochovsky [TL77] and Ullman [Ullman82]. Notice that there is a one-to-many relationship between a role with a key of $<k_1, \ldots, k_{n-1}>$ and a role

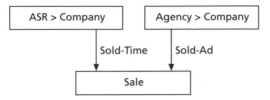

FIGURE 2 Initial data structure diagram of ad sales

with a key of $<k_1, \ldots, k_{n-1}>$. These one-to-many key-subset relationships should be diagrammed using Bachman's data structure diagram [Bachman69]; however, we use the diagrams in the spirit of his later thinking, when he introduced the notion of roles. Specifically, we don't interpret a node in a data structure graph as a record; instead we interpret it simply as a set of attributes with a strong logical cohesion. How to map roles to storage concepts such as records or objects comes later, when we consider how to animate the data.

To summarize the conventions of a data structure diagram, the role with the key $<k_1, \ldots, k_{n-1}>$ is said to be the owner and the role with the key i$<k_1, \ldots, k_n>$ is said to be the member. Boxes are drawn to represent each of the roles, and the name of the role is placed in the box. An arrow is drawn from the owner to the member role, and the name of the relationship is placed near the arrow.

Alternatively, one can view each arrow of a data structure diagram as a functional mapping. Specifically, the role at the arrow's tail is the range and the role at the arrow's head is the domain. The arrow's name becomes the name of the functional mapping.

> ***Cable TV Advertising Business Example*** *The original roles are diagrammed in Figure 2. The ">" symbol is used to indicate the inheritance ancestry of a role. We convert the roles ASR, Agent, and Sale to third-normal form by introducing roles for each of the employees. We also notice that several different time slots may be sold at the same time between the same two people. Thus we add another role that records the time slot–specific data. To accommodate multiple locations, we introduce a Location role between an employee and a company. The normalized roles are diagrammed in Figure 3.*

Resulting Context As a result of using this pattern, additional roles have been introduced and several one-to-many relationships have been identified. But there remain additional relationships to identify using the pattern: Identify Problem Domain Relationships.

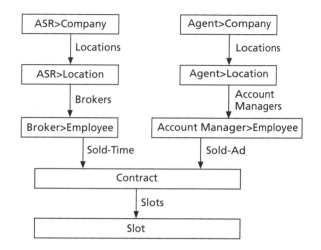

FIGURE 3 Normalized data structure diagram of ad sales

Design Rationale The relational-model objectives of normalization [TL77] that apply to programming are (1) the removal of undesirable insertion, update, and deletion dependencies, and (2) the reduction of the need to restructure relations as additional information is added to the model. Documenting a relational model using a data structure diagram helps me formulate the equijoins that are needed to access attributes during implementation.

NAME: IDENTIFY PROBLEM DOMAIN RELATIONSHIPS

Context The inheritance structure has been diagrammed by **Factor out Command Attributes**, and the one-to-many mappings that result from mechanically decomposing compound keys have been diagrammed by **Normalize the Roles**.

Forces The application has relationships that have not yet been diagrammed.

Problem Many relationships, such as Sale, are implicitly identified as compound roles during the Identify the Nouns brainstorming. But "pure" relationships may need additional effort to capture.

> *Video Server Hardware Example While developing the maintenance-state model of resources, it quickly becomes evident that there are dependencies between resources. In fact, there are two types of*

dependencies: Supporting/Supported and Composite [Bellcore93]. The Supporting/Supported relationship is many-to-many, and it records the fact that some resources cannot be ACTIVE if a resource it depends upon is not ACTIVE. For example, if a Fiber3 port fails, then all of the TCP/IP and video stream connections that it was carrying become OOS. Furthermore, the TCP/IP connections not only need the port, they also need the Fiber3's RISC processor to be ACTIVE. The Composite relationship is one-to-many, and it records physical containment (for example, the four OC3 ports contained by a Fiber3 printed circuit board). Other examples of the Composite relationship are the 24 DS0 (64000 bps) circuits that are carried on a single DS1 (1.544 Mbps) facility and the 2048 DS0 circuits that are carried by an OC3 fiber facility.

Solution   Convert many-to-many relationships to two functional mappings and a new role.

*Video Server Hardware Example The Supporting/Supported relationship is very general and thus is associated with the most general role— resource. As the Bellcore name implies, this relationship consists of two functional mappings: those resources that this resource supports (*Supporting *in their terminology and* Sponsers *in our terminology) and those resources needed by this resource (*Supported *and* Dependent*). The new role is* Dependency.

The Composite relationship can be modeled with an arrow labeled Contains *that has the Resource role for both its range and domain roles. However, other roles, such as* Connections*, can also have this relationship. So we define a new role,* Node*, that can be inherited by both resources and connections. The Contains arrow now points from and to the Node role instead of the Resource role. Figure 4 summarizes the pattern. We use overlapping rectangles to model the inheritance of the same mix-in by different roles.*

Resulting Context   The result is the end of the **Define the Data Structure** effort.

Design Rationale   There are several reasons why I convert many-to-many relationships to two functional mappings and a new role. One is that the new role is needed by both relational- and network-implemented database-management systems. In the case of the network implementation, the two functional mappings are required. In the case of the relational implementation, the two functional mappings will appear on the data structure diagram because of the pattern **Normalize the Roles**. Another reason is that it is not uncommon for

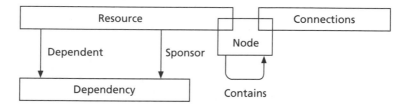

FIGURE 4 Data structure diagram of resource relationships

additional attributes to be associated with the relationship. If a double arrow is used for many-to-many relationships, then how does one depict a many-to-many-to-many relationship? In the case of functional mappings, it just requires adding another arrow with a third range role. Finally, a double-ended arrow tends to get lost in the diagram. I find it very easy to spot the boxes that have more than one arrow pointing to them. Since much of the complexity and dynamics of a system is associated with these low-level roles that model many-to-many mappings, I like them to be very visible in the diagrams.

NAME: INTRODUCE VIRTUAL ATTRIBUTES

Context   The context is that every functional mapping has been identified.

Forces   Forces are to be determined, as mentioned in a metacomment in the first section.

Problem   A network implementation of the data model introduces the need for tedious navigation code, which breaks easily if the model must be changed. The relational model also has this problem for non-key attributes.

> *Cable TV Advertising Business Example   Consider the Broker role in the example for the pattern* **Normalize the Roles***. To obtain the attribute Company Name, one must traverse two functional mappings. Worse yet, if the Location role was not identified during the original design, all code that obtained the Company Name of a Broker (and an Account Manager) must be changed.*

Solution   Access all attributes with accessor functions, and post-process a data-definition language to automatically generate accessor functions to attributes defined by range roles. Apply the range role analysis recursively. That is, as long as there is a unique path to an ancestor node, all of the attributes of all of the roles in the path are propagated down as virtual attributes of the role under consideration. In practice it is sufficient to provide virtual access functions for reading an attribute but not for creating or updating an attribute. One reason for this is that there are typically few places in the code that create or change an attribute, compared to the many places that use an attribute. Another reason is that code that changes data should "know what it is doing." In general, I feel that subschemas should be read-only.

Cable TV Advertising Business Example *All of the attributes of the Company and the Location roles can be accessed from a Broker instance using the same mechanism that accesses the "native" attributes such as broker name.*

Resulting Context   For code that uses, as opposed to changes, a role, the role appears to have many attributes.

Design Rationale   Virtual attributes minimize the impact on existing code of adding additional roles to the data structure. This reduces the need to get the data model "just right" early in the program-development process.

NAME: ANIMATE THE DATA

Context   The Define the Data Structure phase of the software-development cycle has reached the point of diminishing returns.

Forces   Forces are to be determined, as mentioned in the metacomments.

Problem   Any application uses a data model to model the relevant aspects of the real world. Thus the essence of the application's actions becomes updating data based on events and transactions from the real world, making decisions based on those events and transactions, sending controls and transactions back to the real world, and generating various views of what is happening in the real world by interrogating the data and/or generating reports. Also, the data itself becomes an issue, because the accuracy of the data must be maintained in spite of challenges such as computer failures.

Solution   See the following patterns, which decompose this pattern.

Resulting Context   Each role has been mapped onto an actor, and each actor has been mapped onto a processor. The paradigm of communicating finite-state machines has been chosen instead of the paradigm of remote function calls.

Design Rationale   Roles provide a layer of indirection between determining *what* must be done and *how* it is done [Lea94]. For example, the mapping of actors to processors can be changed from a design decision to a run-time decision and can be used to help solve problems such as load balancing and processor fault recovery.

NAME: TIME THREAD ANALYSIS

Context   The beginning of the **Animate the Data** phase.

Forces   Forces are to be determined as mentioned in a metacomment in the first section.

Problem   How are the data created and changed?

Solution   Use time-thread analysis [BC93]. First, list the problem domain events and transactions that the real world generates. Then, for each event, trace the causality flow through the roles of the data structure and note the actions performed by each role.

> *Cable TV Advertising Business Example*   *The following are examples of external events that need to be traced:*
>
> - *Joe Ford's advertising executive calls his account manager to request that his current advertisement be played during each of the local high school football games aired this fall on the local cable channel.*
> - *A sports event has a commercial opportunity, such as a time-out call or a change of innings.*
> - *Programming determines that a particular movie is going to be aired during a 7:00 p.m. time slot; a promotional spot for that movie needs to be scheduled for earlier that day and for sometime during the previous day.*
> - *A commercial features a star who has just committed an unsavory act; all showings of that commercial must be yanked.*
> - *A tornado has been spotted, and the graphics overlay feature of the commercial-insertion equipment is used to display a warning on all cable channels.*

- *A display of unsold time for the next week is requested.*
- *An invoice is prepared by an advertising sales representative for an advertising agent.*

Resulting Context   The result is that the actions needed by roles to animate the data have been identified.

Design Rationale   As Buhr and Cassleman note [BC93], this type of analysis has typically been done already informally. We might as well capture the insights it provides.

NAME: DETERMINE THE ACTORS

Context   The actions that each role needs to perform in response to outside events have been identified.

Forces   The forces are to be determined, as mentioned in a metacomment at the beginning of this chapter.

Problem   How to determine what lines of code get executed when an event happens.

Solution   Use objects, callbacks, and Finite-State Machines (FSM). One technique is to view each role as an object and add methods to its definitions, along with the attributes that have already been identified. This works fine for role-specific actions that are not state-dependent. For example, it is quite appropriate to define an Alert method for a specific phone type to cause a phone of that type to ring. At this phase of the design process, assume that each role has a dedicated actor that runs on its own computer. That is, each role is implemented as an object within its own computer.

However, for actions that are not role-specific, such as removing a piece of equipment from service, the object-oriented paradigm requires that the bulk of the code be implemented as before and/or after methods. For these generic types of actions I prefer the callback paradigm exemplified by the X Window System.[5]

Video Server Hardware Example   To remove a resource requires changing the Goal attribute to OOS-RMV and recording the identity of the user entering the remove *request as the cause code. The program must also recursively change the Goal of all the resources the removed resource*

---

[5] This is a trademark of the Massachusetts Institute of Technology.

sponsors. Furthermore, the program recursively changes the state of all the resources the removed resource contains. When the current state of all the sponsored and contained resources have transitioned to OOS-RMV, the "down" handler of the requested resource is called to transition it to OOS-RMV. If a sponsored resource does not transition to OOS-RMV within a generous time-out value, such as a minute, an error is logged and the resource is removed anyhow. To implement a new hardware role, only a few (typically simple) handlers need to be defined. The typical handlers are Init, Up, and Down. With these handlers defined for each resource type, several rather complex actions such as Remove, Restore, Diagnose, Error Detection, and Fault Recovery can be handled by centralized, generic code.

Resulting Context   The result is a massively distributed design because each object is assumed to be running on its own computer.

Design Rationale   A reason to assume during this phase that each actor runs on its own computer is that "with each object residing on its own computer, you cannot afford to ignore interference problems that are at the heart of most distributed system design errors" [Lea93].

RAW CONFERENCE PATTERNS

This section contains some "rules of thumb" as they appeared in the conference draft. They should become patterns in the more detailed part of a distributed pattern language.

Process Considered Harmful   "Real-time operating system" is an oxymoron: use finite-state machines instead of processes.

Processes were invented to implement time sharing systems to give each user a virtual machine. Nowadays, if an application calls for the emulation of a machine, just give it a real machine. For other types of applications, three problems with processes are context switching overhead, wasted stack space, and unnecessary message buffering.

Consider the structure of a typical process in a distributed system:

```
main()
{
  while (1) {
    select(...);
    recvfrom(...);
```

```
    switch (message_opcode) {
    case SETUP: /* setup code */
    case FLASH: /* call feature code */
    case HANGUP: /* call teardown code */
    etc.
    }
  }
}
```

There may be many processes of this nature—each roadblocked until an event happens. While each is roadblocked, its nearly empty stack represents wasted memory. Memory is cheap, but it is not free. For embedded system coding, I prefer an infrastructure that understands the event structure of "the box" under development and that dispatches the event handlers directly, rather than using classical operating system models.

In many event handlers there will be calls to the operating system's "send message" primitive. Unfortunately, in every operating system I am aware of (UNIX plus about five so-called real-time operating systems), the message is queued, even if the target process is resident in the same processor. If the program counter were to follow the message rather than fall through to the statement following the "send message" statement, I would have less concern with a process structure. This would allow the system to finish current work before beginning new work, and it would remove the headache of trying to engineer message buffer utilization. (The engineering headache in this case is not so much memory consumption as it is additional processing delay.)

Time Granularities   There is no such thing as immediate. First, determine the order of magnitudes of the event processing times. The granularities I have experience with are microseconds, a few milliseconds, tenths of a second, and fractions of an hour. Fortunately I haven't had all of these granularities in one system! For the tight granularities (a few milliseconds or less), determine if the short processing time is required because of latency/delay requirements or because of total throughput requirements. If you have requirements of a few microseconds due to throughput (such as for ATM cell processing), dedicate a microprocessor to the problem and support the other granularities with another microprocessor. Otherwise, these granularities can be handled using interrupts.

Queues should be used only when an event handler discovers work that should be handled at a slower granularity of time. For example, if an Ethernet interrupt handler discovers that an incoming UDP packet contains an SNMP command rather than a call-processing command, it will put that packet on the tenths-of-a-second queue. The SNMP handler may discover that the command requests a diagnostic that will take several minutes to run. The SNMP handler will add the diagnostic request to the fractions-of-an-hour queue.

Run to Completion

Minimize the use of interrupts. If the smallest granularity of time is around a hundredth to a tenth of a second, interrupts can be avoided altogether.

We do not use time-slice interrupts to force an event handler to give up control for another event handler. Instead, we require that each event handler periodically call a special scheduling primitive that allows handlers with a finer granularity to run. That is, a handler is allowed to run to completion or until it voluntarily gives up control. (We do have a sanity timer interrupt, but it is considered a very serious error if it fires.) For embedded software, giving up control is usually a simple matter of placing the scheduler call at the end of each loop in the code. Avoiding preemptive scheduling greatly simplifies critical region programming.

We avoid error handler interrupts by designing hardware with error counters that can be periodically polled.

Alarm Triage

The importance of an alarm is relative. A lesson from Three Mile Island is that there should be no more than seven red lights on a display. Normally, if a line to a customer fails it is a major alarm. However, if an OC12 fiber link (which can carry 8064 connections) fails, a failed customer line is no longer major compared to the OC12 break. The alarms for lines whose calls were being carried by the failed fiber are of especially low priority. Unfortunately, we have yet to develop a system architecture that successfully implements relative alarm priority.

Invent System-wide "Pressure Gauges"

Put some of the "computing" into the message transport subsystem. If the job of a software module is to sum the contents of many messages together, then whatever processor that module is assigned to will become the focal point of a large set of messages. Instead, if we design the message transport nodes to recognize whenever there is more than one message in its buffer that is destined to the same "summing" module to replace the messages with one message that contains an intermediate sum, then only one message is delivered to the systemwide summing module, and the total message traffic in the network is significantly reduced.

One of the big differences between a real-time system and a time-sharing system is shedding load. If a system has the capacity to do n jobs satisfactorily but $n + m$ jobs are submitted to the system, a time-sharing system will do $n + m$ jobs poorly, whereas a real-time system will kill (or ignore) m jobs so that it can continue to do n jobs satisfactorily.

It is rather easy for distributed elements to shed work if they can detect that the system is overloaded. The real problem is determining a systemwide load factor. To do this we define a centralized software module to compute the needed systemwide load parameters and "broadcast" the computed parameters back to each element. (Broadcast is in quotes because in a WAN, broadcasting usually has to be implemented using many point-to-point connections or a spanning tree.) These centralized software modules are also useful for driving interfaces that allow humans to see the "big picture." The "intelligent message nodes" technique can be used so that these centralized modules don't become a bottleneck as the size of the system is scaled up.

The same technique can be used to help implement alarm triage. In this case the "pressure gauge" is measuring system alarm severity rather than traffic load, and the intelligent nodes are computing a maximum rather than a sum. Also, if a new alarm is of less severity than the current severity level of the system, it would not be reported in the first place. This helps to lower message traffic when the system is in trouble.

Strategy Versus Tactics Use the messaging capability of the distributed system to centralize strategy. Traditionally, algorithms have been either centralized or distributed. In many cases a hybrid approach would be beneficial. Pressure gauges are a simple example of a hybrid approach. The load- or alarm-shedding logic is distributed, but the determination of the current state of the system is centralized. Another example of a hybrid algorithm is in the realm of network routing. The network design algorithm that I use takes about ten hours to run on a Sun 3 for a 100-node network. On a Sparc 10, this algorithm takes ten minutes. Telephony networks gather and log traffic measurement data every fifteen minutes. Thus processing power has become cheap enough that one can now redesign the entire network during each traffic collection period. The tables that are distributed to each network element can be simplified, because they don't have to cover as many contingencies. This, in turn, simplifies the routing algorithms in the network elements that use these tables.

Don't Retransmit at the Link Level You can add increased reliability at the application layer, but you can't decrease delays. Most Layer 2 protocols are a legacy from the 1970s, when modems struggled to deliver 300 baud. Nowadays, especially with fiber optics, messages are lost due to internal congestion rather than bit errors. Thus link level retransmission is not going to compensate for most lost message problems. Thus you have to accommodate for lost messages at the application level anyhow. Furthermore, for some applications, such as process control, it is easier to send "fresh" data than it is to store and retransmit stale data. In fact, a retransmitting frame delaying a frame with newer information simply adds even more delay. The upper layers of the protocol stack can always add more reliability; however, no layer can reduce a delay after it has been introduced. So it is important that the lower layers be "lean and mean."

Dennis L DeBruler can be reached at AT&T Bell Laboratories, P.O. Box 3033, 2000 North Naperville Road, Naperville, IL 60566-7033; d.l.debruler@att.com.

REFERENCES

Bachman69: Bachman, C.W. "Data Structure Diagrams." *Data Base* 1,2 (1969): 4–10.

BC93: Buhr, J.A., and Casselman, R.S. *Designing with Timethreads.* SCE-93-05. Ottawa: Carleton University.

Bellcore 92: Bellcore Technical Reference: TR-NWT-000303, Issue 2, December 1992, pp. 12-34 to 12-35.

Bellcore93: Bellcore Technical Reference: TR-NWT-001093, Issue 1 (*Generic State Requirements for Network Elements*), September, pp. 2-7 to 2-8.

Cunningham94: Personal conversation with Ward Cunningham, PLoP Conference, August 4, 1994.

Date81: Date, C. *An Introduction to Database Systems.* Reading, MA: Addison-Wesley, 1981.

Lea93: Email from Doug Lea dated September 12, 1993.

Lea94: Personal conversation with Doug Lea, PLoP Conference, August 5, 1994.

Rubel94: Rubel, Barry. "A Pattern for Generating a Layered Archictecture." Chapter 7, this volume.

TL77: Tsichritzis, D.C., and Lochovsky, F.H. *Data Base Management Systems*, Section 2.5. New York: Academic Press, 1977.

Ullman82: Ullman, J.D. *Principles of Database Systems.* Rockville, MD: Computer Science Press, 1982, Chapter 7.

G++: A Pattern Language for Computer-Integrated Manufacturing

6

Amund Aarsten, Gabriele Elia, and Giuseppe Menga

ABSTRACT

A design of any sort is defined by patterns found in the relationships between the design's elements; each of these patterns is also in itself a rule that directs a design choice for a certain number of design problems. Together these patterns form a language—a "pattern language"—which can be used to approach a certain class of problems.

These ideas, introduced by Christopher Alexander, an architect [1], have been transferred to the field of object-oriented (OO) design. Objects are the (system) design elements that form patterns; the patterns are discernible in clusters of cooperating objects, linked by certain relationships, that are repeatedly found in the solutions to a particular class of problems. This has led to the definition of a pattern language (and a supporting framework of reusable classes) for the design of concurrent and possibly distributed information systems, with applications in computer-integrated manufacturing (CIM).

The objective of this paper is to raise reusability in OO design from the component to the architectural level and to offer a conceptual model for concurrent and distributed architectures.

Copright © Amund Aarsten, Gabriele Elia, and Giuseppe Menga. All Rights Reserved.

1. INTRODUCTION

The OO paradigm claims to promote reuse. Originally, reusability was intended for the system-component level, and component reuse was achieved through establishing libraries of reusable classes organized in hierarchies of inheritance (what are now called frameworks of classes). However, attention has now shifted from component reuse to architecture reuse, attaching more importance to the fundamental role that the patterns of the relationships between system elements have in any design. It is generally accepted, in fact, that designers have always been driven by personal patterns when making choices. Christopher Alexander formalized these ideas into the concepts of "pattern" and "pattern language" [1,2].

Alexander suggests that each design pattern consists of a three-part rule that expresses a relationship between a certain context, a design problem, and its solution. Moreover, all these rules—or patterns—are part of a larger system, that is, a "pattern language" that contains the experience of generations of designers in solving a certain class of problems. However, if such a pattern language is to be shared and to become a part of the collective knowledge in addressing a "certain" problem, it must be structured; the structure of the language is created by a network of connections between individual patterns.

Alexander's definition of a pattern fits perfectly into OO software design, where each pattern incorporates one aspect of the problem analysis into the design (elucidating, at the same time, the use of the framework of classes that are the elements of the architecture). However, the whole set of patterns, together with their structuring principles, becomes a high-level language and a design method that is used throughout the software's development, from analysis to final implementation.

This paper extends previous work and presents, within the OO context, an attempt to bring the concept of a pattern language closer to Alexander's idea of a whole design method for a specific application domain.

1.1 The Application Domain

The application domain targeted here is that of large client-server control architectures. A pattern language, as defined by Alexander, is the best answer that can be offered to the question of establishing a standard architecture in such a domain.

The CIM domain, by its very nature as an aggregation of heterogeneous elements, is a challenging environment in which to define architectural patterns and frameworks of classes, and it will be used as a case study. The examples described in Section 2 are, in fact, taken from the design of a flexible manufacturing system (FMS), that is, a factory shop, made up of production cells composed of machine tools, stores, and automatic transportation systems, that manufactures lots of different types of pieces concurrently. (A lot is an administrative entity representing a group of identical pieces manufactured together.)

However, as the questions raised here relating to managing the complexity of systems and their concurrent and distributed nature are very similar to those raised for other application domains. Therefore, these ideas can be readily transferred into other fields, such as business administration or telecommunications.

The approach leads naturally to a CASE environment, which has actually been implemented, merging a framework of C++ classes and the tools that automate the development. Examples of its application can be found in Menga et al. [19].

1.2 Paper Organization

This paper is organized as follows: Section 2 describes the proposed patterns and their structure through the presentation of examples, and Section 3 compares the interpretation of patterns presented in this paper with other related results.

2. THE PATTERN LANGUAGE

The problem addressed by the pattern language presented here involves the design of large software systems that contain layers of concurrent control modules on a distributed computer architecture. The chosen development process is evolutionary; it is obtained by exploiting transformations that first map the analysis into a logical design to be locally prototyped and then map the logical design into a physical design.

Patterns in this language are structured, following Alexander, as in the tree shown in Figure 1; each oval denotes a pattern, with branches representing the relationship between larger and smaller patterns. Each pattern depends both on the smaller patterns it contains and on the larger pattern within which it is contained; it is the network of these connections between patterns that creates the language.

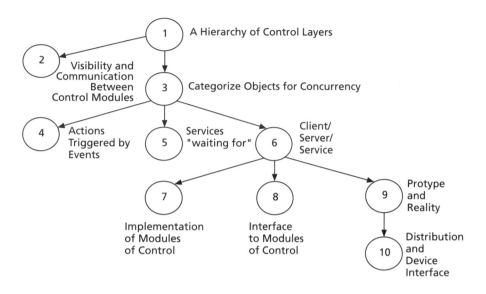

FIGURE 1 The pattern language for designing distributed applications

The template used to describe an OO pattern is inspired by proposals in the literature [5, 10, 11, 16], by the "pattern mailing list," [21] and by the works of Alexander himself.

It has the following fields:

the pattern name

the context in which we discuss the pattern

the problems the pattern addresses, related to the context

the solution offered by the pattern in terms of the framework of classes (including a graphical representation of the solution in which we tried to show the "balance of forces" in the pattern)

an example of the pattern in the case study (for example, CIM)

the definition and design rules of the pattern, trying to define rules for an operative use of the pattern

references to lower-level patterns of the language

As patterns are mostly aggregates of classes, they can be described by means of entity relationship diagrams, where a rectangle with rounded vertices represents a class (upper identifiers) or an instance (lower identifier); a character on the left side of the label indicates whether the object is active, sequential, blocking, and so on. Pure data attributes, methods, and names of events issued are represented as a comment on the side of the icon. Relationships are represented using the OMT notation, to which have been added the links of USE (in the logical design space) and COM (indicating interconnection through a communication network involving a stub and a remote context) in the physical design space. The links implying use relationship may also show the method names of the messages flowing through them. The OMT generalization/specialization relationship of the analysis, applied to the design, indicates implementation inheritance. If it is necessary to specify interface inheritance (that is, to include subtyping), an ISA label is added to the link.

PATTERN 1: A HIERARCHY OF CONTROL LAYERS

Any complex system organizes its functions within an architecture of hierarchical layers of control modules.

Context   Large, distributed engineering systems, characterized by multiple concurrent activities, are difficult to design and manage; moreover, it is important to be able to reuse some parts in different systems.

Solution   In order to cope with complexity, it is worthwhile to organize system functions in hierarchical, decentralized control architectures. Each layer of the hierarchy encompasses modules of control that contain similar classes of functions. A module of control is an entity characterized by the presence of

- autonomous decision-making capabilities
- a series of available services that are offered to the outside (for example, in manufacturing: planning products, executing piece production, executing a machine operation, storing or moving pieces)
- a pool of controlled resources

Modules of control are objects, and they should be organized using two basic structuring principles: inclusion (encapsulation) and use.

Any organization defines its own control modules; they are shaped according to the organization's internal principles and can be functional, logical, or simply dictated by tradition. In the manufacturing field they are traditionally indicated either as business or technical processes, arranged as in Figure 2 (according to McLean, Mitchell, and Barkmeyer [18]). Modules should encompass functions in such a way that they can be reused for different

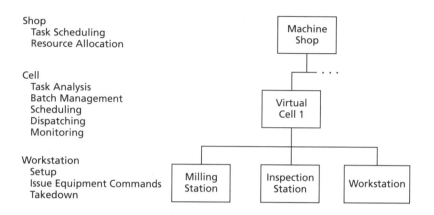

FIGURE 2 The USA-NBS reference model for manufacturing

projects. A pattern language for the definition of modules of control will be highly application-specific and is not discussed here.

Example: The FMS

Figure 3 describes the analysis of a typical FMS for producing mechanical components. This is a production shop composed of two cells—one for machining and the second for assembling. Each cell is made up of a set of numerically controlled machines, an automatic inventory system for raw and finished pieces, and an automatic guided vehicle (AGV) system for moving pieces. Integration is achieved through a network encompassing shop and cell computers, along with computerized numerical controls (CNC) for the machines and programmable logic controllers (PLC) for the inventory and AGV systems. Production is characterized, at any period of time, by the presence in the cells of several concurrent small lots of different types of pieces. Each of these lots undergoes a sequence of operations, each one on a different machine according to the piece type. The cell, with a real-time dispatcher, assigns pieces to the machines as soon as they become idle, and issues mission requests to the AGV system, monitoring the shop-floor lot production. A database is present containing technological data (operation, piece type, machine type) and management data (order, piece, lot), together with their relationships, which allows the shop and the cells to control production.

> *To organize a system in modules of controls, there must be objects with a certain degree of autonomy that are capable of offering well-defined services managing a set of resources. There must be a hierarchical structure to these modules—a structure that applies the principles of inclusion or external use.*

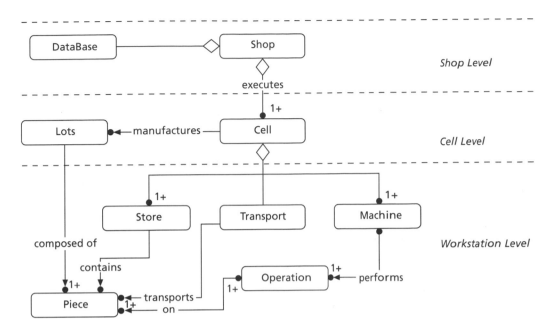

FIGURE 3 Analysis of an FMS

PATTERN 2: VISIBILITY AND COMMUNICATION BETWEEN CONTROL MODULES

Each module in the hierarchy performs services, requests services from other modules, or signals events so as to inform other modules of its state.

Context Complex systems are developed over a relatively long period of time. There are two possibilities: the first is to build modules that will be plugged into preexisting designs; the second is to build "frameworks" that have to integrate preexisting control modules. In the former case, the designer has "visibility" of the environment in which they will operate; in the latter case this does not happen.

In CIM systems the evolution is bottom-up. A higher-layer control module (for example, a shop controller or a cell controller) acting as a client integrates lower-level controllers, which act as servers (for example, machines, transports, and buffers).

Modules communicate, however, and the way their communications are established depends on their visibility to each other. Control-module communications can be imperative, as in a command issued by one module to the other, or they can be reactive, as in event monitoring. The two situations have a direct relationship with the two basic mechanisms of communication between objects, here called caller/provider (C/P) and broadcaster/listeners (B/L), described in Figure 4.

- The C/P mechanism is involved when an object invokes another object's method and is deeply rooted in OO programming, so it will not be discussed further.

- The B/L mechanism (used in Smalltalk dependencies and X-Window callbacks) is achieved by giving all the objects in a framework the ability to broadcast and listen to events. The term *event* is used here to indicate a broadcasted message issued at a certain instant of time by an object; and event is identified by a symbolic name and has some data associated with it.

Solution   Reusability in a hierarchy of layers of control will improve by avoiding visibility loops and by not allowing two controls at the same layer to communicate directly. Follow these rules instead (see Figure 4):

1. Two modules at the same layer should not be entitled to communicate directly.

2. When a client addresses a message (command) to a server, it should be done explicitly in C/P fashion.

3. When a server answers (by sending monitoring information, for example), this should be done by signaling events through a B/L mechanism.

FIGURE 4   The communication mechanisms

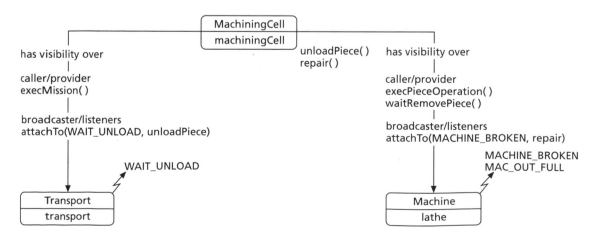

Gamma et al. [11] call this pattern *Observer*. It has the same logic of reusability as the `changed: update:` mechanism of the Model-View-Controller (MVC) paradigm, which has already been documented in the Smalltalk browser [17].

Example: Communication in the FMS

The cell for machining, detailed in Figure 4, asks for services directly from the machines (`execPieceOperation()`, `waitRemovePiece()`, and so on) and from the transport (`execMission()`) (it should be noted here, in fact, that inclusion also implies use); but the evolution of the cell production has to be driven by the events broadcasted by its components, for example, MAC OUT FULL when a piece enters the output buffer of a machine.

All modules of a control system are entities that communicate with each other through C/P or B/L mechanisms. Communication between controls takes place using a C/P mechanism that operates from the layer containing newer (or more volatile) modules to the layer containing older (or more stable) ones, and a B/L mechanism that operates in the reverse.

PATTERN 3: CATEGORIZE OBJECTS FOR CONCURRENCY

Control modules in the system perform services concurrently, and concurrency assumes different scales of granularity.

Context

The first problem is that there are concurrent activities occurring in a complex system and that concurrency assumes different scales of granularity. Small-grain concurrent activities are made up of simple actions with a weak cohesion, as in a multiwindow graphical interface. Larger-grain concurrency may be represented by operations composed of an ordered sequence of actions and having a stronger cohesion, for example, the production processes of different (logically concurrent) lots of pieces managed by a cell controller. Even larger concurrency is represented by control modules operating in parallel, such as distinct machine controllers executing independent operations.

A second problem is that modules of complex concurrent systems interact in various ways:

- through entities where services can store data
- through entities where services enter into conflict over the sharing of limited resources, such as buffers of parts or pools of carts for transportation
- through entities that perform (sub)services developed over time

Solution   Use concurrent processes to express concurrency in its larger forms. In G++ concurrent processes are encapsulated in proper, active objects; in this case processes represent the services offered by an object in response to a request for an operation.

The distinction between passive (sequential or blocking) objects and active objects is now widely accepted:

- Passive objects do not possess threads of control; they depend on client threads for the execution of their functions. They can be further subdivided into sequential or blocking objects. The semantics of sequential objects is guaranteed only in the presence of a single thread of control; such classes have an S in their label. Blocking objects, which are designed to maintain their semantics when more than one thread accesses them, offer the *wait* primitive, the indispensable element needed to block client threads and allow them to interact; such classes have a B in their label.

- Active objects differ from passive objects in that they possess, create, and internally manage one or more independent threads of control that govern the execution of their services. A class `ThreadOfControl` is used for representing a concurrent service. Active objects are the natural candidates to represent modules of controls; they have an A in their label.

Example:
Active Objects
in the FMS

In the FMS example, the following control modules (that is, active objects) are identified in Figure 5:

- the shop—`shop`
- the cells—`machiningCell` for machining and `assemblingCell` for assembly of lots
- the machines—a collection of machines is indicated with the label `machines`
- the transport system—`transport`

Instead, stores for semiworked and finished pieces (named `storeIn` and `storeOut`) are modeled as blocking objects, since they act as shared resources between different lot production services.

Model the concurrent activities of a complex control architecture (according to their level of granularity) by actions triggered by events, by sequential processes (services) interacting through shared resources, or by concurrent modules exchanging requests for services. Moreover, in order to support concurrent services, identify sequential, blocking, and active objects and represent modules of control as active objects.

Related
Patterns

The role of each of these three basic elements—sequential, blocking, and active objects—is detailed in a specific pattern (see Patterns 4 to 6).

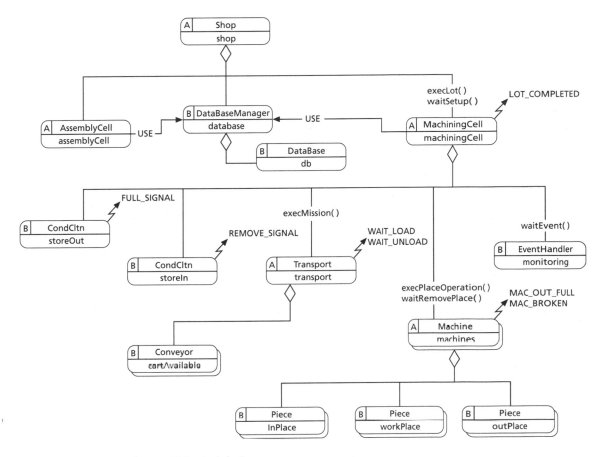

FIGURE 5 The complete FMS logical design

PATTERN 4: ACTIONS TRIGGERED BY EVENTS

Communication through events can be either intraservice, generating a small-grain concurrency, or interservice, resulting in a larger-grain concurrency.

Context In developing an application it is possible to find intraservice concurrency requirements (as in the case of activating rules in a rule-based decision-making system for scheduling production) or interservice ones, when two objects in two distinct concurrent processes and modules of control want to communicate by exchanging events (for example, in the FMS the piece-machining service of a workstation raises a failure event that is listened for by the cell's lot-production service).

Solution   The B/L mechanism to raise and listen to events, which is introduced with control modules for communication between the older and newer ones that encapsulate them, is implemented just once in the Object class and is inherited by all classes of the framework.

Use the B/L mechanism to model fine-grained concurrent actions (by the interaction between sequential objects bound to a service offered by an active object). Use this same mechanism for communication between lower layers of control modules and higher ones.

Related Patterns   The interaction between services through events is discussed further in Pattern 5.

PATTERN 5: SERVICES "WAITING FOR"

Services offered by a control module have to wait for a condition to occur or for data to be transferred from or to a shared resource before they can perform an action in concurrency with others.

Context   In a manufacturing system, for example, the lot production service in the cell must wait for the event MAC OUT FULL from a machine, while the transport service provided by the conveyor system is blocked while it waits for the first available cart from a pool of free carts. In both situations, an entity is needed to manage the interaction between services.

Solution   Blocking objects are useful entities for solving this problem. In fact, in an OO world the only way a service can enter into a particular state is to suspend itself by sending a message (or asking for a service, which implies waiting for a condition) to a blocking object. The flow will be resumed with a transition from this waiting state whenever the appropriate condition on the blocking object occurs.

Condition is the abstract class used by the framework to define any blocking object; from it specific implementations such as timers, semaphores, event handlers, and shared queues (bounded buffers, that is, CondCollection) can be derived by inheritance or encapsulation (see Figure 6). Conditions as a way of synchronizing threads are discussed in Andrews and Schneider [3].

Example: Blocking Objects in the FMS Cell   In the FMS example, there are different blocking objects (see Figure 5):

- The storeIn and storeOut buffers are CondCollection, belonging to the MachiningCell class. They act as a bounded buffer: the cell service

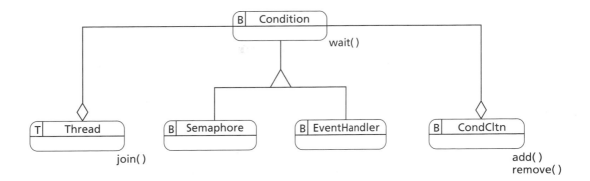

FIGURE 6 Blocking objects

automatically stops if it tries to remove a piece when the `storeIn` is empty or add a new piece when the `storeOut` is full.

- `inPlace`, `workPlace`, and `outPlace` are, similarly, `CondCltn` and act as blocking objects of the `Machine` services.
- The database is modeled as a blocking object, as it is a shared resource between the cells.
- The `MachiningCell` has an `EventHandler`, which is used to block its services while waiting for the events from transport, machines, and stores. Here the cell controller uses an `EventHandler` to monitor its resources (for example, `MAC OUT FULL` or `WAIT NOT FULL`) and to take the appropriate actions.

Use blocking objects to model the shared resources of the control module every time interaction between its concurrent services is needed.

Related Patterns The synchronous request made to an active object for a service, as will be seen in Pattern 6, is one example that shows the presence of a `Condition` inside a `ThreadOfControl`.

PATTERN 6: THE CLIENT/SERVER/SERVICE MODEL: IMPLEMENTING MODULES OF CONTROL

Modules of control are active objects that offer multiple concurrent services. They are present at different levels in the hierarchical architecture of the system.

Context In the design of control modules, a first requirement is that there be more than a single service available, at every moment, to their clients: for example, a cell may manage more than a single lot of pieces. Another requirement is for a common representation of the control modules at the different levels of the hierarchy, for standardization purposes and to enforce reusability and facilitate the task of distributing the application. That is, it is necessary to represent a system as a structure of hierarchically layered virtual machines.

Finally, modules of control should have the capability to encapsulate the resources and services that manipulate them.

Solution   These requirements are satisfied by the Client/Server/Service model proposed in this pattern, which was derived from the programming paradigm of SR (Synchronizing Resources) [4]. Two classes are needed to support it: the Service and the Server (see Figure 7):

- The Service extends the ThreadOfControl so that it becomes an extended finite-state machine, embedding the dynamics of the application and having the following characteristics: it always belongs to a unique Server owner, it has internal data (sequential objects), it maintains a symbolic state value, and it broadcasts events with the incoming state name every time a state transition occurs. It rarely needs to be redefined, as it delegates the execution of its dynamics to a private behavior method of the server owner.

- The Server is an abstract class that defines the common implementation of active objects; it must be redefined in order to build concrete servers. It contains a Collection of Service objects: each service executes the

FIGURE 7 Client/Server/Service

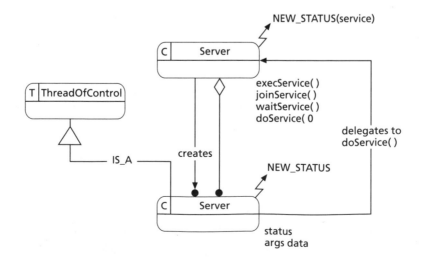

server operations in concurrency while sharing the same set of resources. A server's `Service` can, in turn, use another (sub)server, and in this case it acts as a client for that server. To be accessed, the `Server` offers three public methods—`execService()`, `waitService()`, and `joinService()`—which represent asynchronous, synchronous, and deferred-synchronous service requests, respectively. They accept, as arguments, sequential objects only by value; blocking and passive objects are accepted by reference, too. Whenever each one of these three public methods is called, a new `Service` is forked and added to the list of ready services. By default it is executed in the private method `doService()` of its `Server`. The method `doService()` must be redefined in the derived concrete classes. Moreover, the `Server` relays its service events externally so that its state can be monitored by other objects.

The Client/Server/Service pattern is fundamental to our pattern language; it contains the essential structuring solution for concurrent programs. Much in the same way that a Smalltalk programmer structures virtually all userinterface code after the Model-View-Controller pattern, we use Client/Server/Service for concurrent programming at all levels. Moreover, since the control modules in the CIM reference model of Figure 2 are active objects, the pattern applies throughout a CIM control system.

> *Inherit form `Server` and redefine `Server::doService()` to have a simple active object with multiple concurrent threads of control that share the `Server` components, such as common resources, between them.*

Related Patterns   Modules of control are implemented using this pattern and specializing in the `Server` class, as described in Patterns 7 and 8. The prototype objects mentioned in Patern 9 are often interfaces to `Server` objects.

PATTERN 7: IMPLEMENTATION OF "MULTIPLE KINDS OF SERVICES" CONTROL MODULES

Control modules manage different pools of shared resources and can offer different kinds of services. They may in fact need to offer multiple kinds of services and not simply multiple concurrent services of the same type.

Context   The `Server` class offers an active object with a standard interface, represented by the `execService()`, `waitService()`, and `joinService()` methods, and executes multiple instances of the same service.

Solution   "Multiple Kinds of Services" control modules can be obtained by inheriting from a `Server` (see Figure 8) and using the following guidelines:

- Identify the resources the control module needs. The resources shared by the services of an active object can only be blocking objects (`Condition` or `CondCltn`) or other active objects (`Server`). There are no sequential objects inside the `Server`, as they are suitably encapsulated into blocking objects or bound to the services.

- Identify the different types of services offered (for example, for the class `MachiningCell`, the `LotProduction` and `MachineSetup` services). Specify their behaviors in terms of finite state machines, extended by the necessary sequential objects bounded to the service and implemented by private behavior methods (for example, `doLotProduction()` and `doMachineSetup()`).

- Use a graphical notation to specify `Service` behaviors. This will add expressiveness to the formalism—and because it is possible to animate it, debugging will be easier. Specify a `Service` behavior with an OO exten-

FIGURE 8 Implementation of control modules

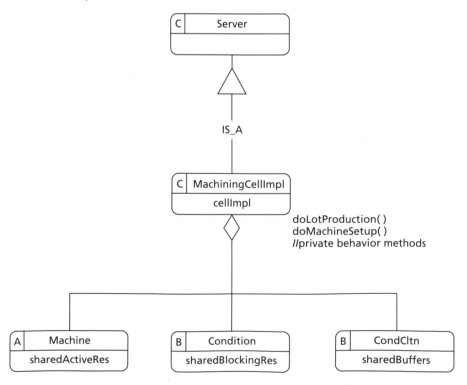

sion of SDL (the Specification and Description Language standardized by CCITT). This leads to the automatic generation of the behavior method by the CASE environment.

- Redefine the `Server::doService()` method. This will allow it to become a switch case (which is controlled by a name parameter) and access the different types of service. The CASE environment supporting the framework does this automatically when the class is generated.

The practical reason for this behavior is that in the G++ library it is easier for the `exec-join-wait`Service triad to always fork the `doService()` method execution.

The representation of all service behaviors in the framework with the unique `doService()` method of the `Server` is an alternative design choice to the `Command` pattern described by Gamma et al. [11]. `Command` "objectifies" services, by modeling them as different "behavior objects."

Instead, Client/Server/Service uses a pattern that we would call *Delegated Environment*, in which service behaviors are methods of the object that offers them (and not of "objectifying" objects), but they can be executed concurrently thanks to the context delegated from instances of the `Service` class. This solution has the double advantage of offering a protected execution environment for each service instance, while at the same time allowing all services inside a server to share the server resources without visibility problems.

**Example: The class
`MachiningCellImpl`**

At this point it is possible to consider the design of the FMS machining cell, defined by the class `MachiningCellImpl`. It inherits from `Server`, and its member data (see Figure 5) are the AGV system transport (an instance of class `Transport`), the collection of machines `machines`, and stores of semiworked and finished pieces (`storeIn` and `storeOut`, of class `CondCltn`).

The service of routing pieces between machines and stores is expressed by the method `doLotProduction()`; more than one service can be active at a certain moment. Other services handle machine setup and maintenance.

> *Control modules are implemented by inheriting from the `Server`, by encapsulating or referring to shared resources (which must be blocking objects or other active objects), and by specifying the behavior methods of its services in terms of extended finite-state machines.*

Related Patterns   The companion `Interface` class is discussed in Pattern 8.

PATTERN 8: THE INTERFACE TO CONTROL MODULES

Control modules offer different kinds of operations to their clients.

Context   The classes derived by inheritance from the `Server` in Pattern 8 are "heavyweighted" classes, which carry the property of being active objects but also the resources encapsulated by the control module they represent. In C++ it is not convenient to inherit directly from them if they need to be substituted by proxy objects, such as for distributed implementation. Anyway, we don't want to change the client code because of this substitution.

Solution   Use an `Interface` object to access each server (see Figures 9 and 10). The `Interface` offers the server's operations to clients.

When a new active object is conceived and the services it offers one identified (for example, the `MachiningCell` can perform `LotProduction`, `MachineSetup`, and `Maintenance`), a new class `Interface` is generated, assigning to itself the following features for each type of service:

- a link to the implementation object
- an interface operation, which delegates one-to-one, according to the three synchronization semantics of the specification and its functions, to the standard three Server methods. (For example, `execLotProduction()` is asynchronous and calls `execService()`, `waitMachineSetup()` is synchronous and calls `waitService()`, `joinMaintenance()` is deferred-synchronous and calls `joinService()`.)

Figures 9 and 10 present two alternative architectural solutions for this pattern, where interface and implementation are linked by inheritance and use relationships, respectively; Gamma et al. [11] consider both these solutions in the `Adapter` pattern.

In both cases the `Interface` object can be generated automatically by a CASE environment from the specification of the active object. For active objects, even those that will not be distributed as described in Patterns 9 and 10, this separation often favors reusability.

Client control modules have to refer to their server control modules by `Interface` *objects linked to their* `Implementation` *through an inheritance or use relationship.*

Related Patterns   This pattern follows the trend among C++ designers to separate an object definition into two distinct interface and implementation classes. The interface class is called a handle by Stroustrup [25] and a proxy by Decouchant [9]. It also corresponds to the `Proxy` described by Gamma et al. [10].

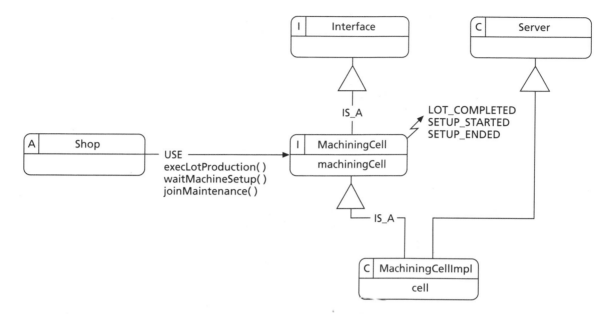

FIGURE 9 Interface and implementation linked by inheritance

FIGURE 10 Interface and implementation linked by use

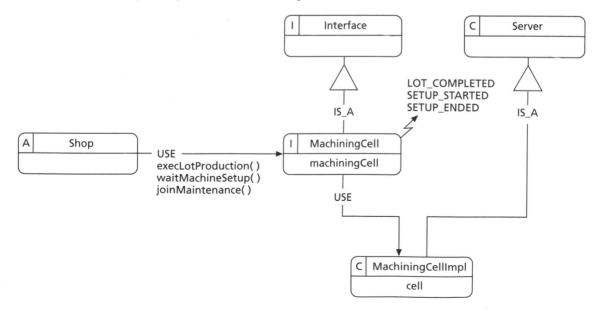

The switch from prototype to reality, as described in Pattern 9, is usually enabled by the use of this pattern.

PATTERN 9: PROTOTYPE AND REALITY

Any complex application requires prototyping and simulation of the different elements that have to be integrated, before an implementation is derived.

Context There is a particular need for prototyping and simulation in CIM control systems, as well as in other types of applications that interface to hardware controllers or are by nature distributed. For instance, one cannot test and debug a factory-control application using the actual controllers and machines at the factory.

The evolution from a simulation to a real system should be as seamless as possible. The nonsimulated components (that is, the rest of the system) should remain unaffected by this evolution.

Solution The following patterns consider the transition from logical to physical design that is obtained by replacing the prototypes in the program with their physical counterparts.

For any object that needs to be simulated, maintain two coexisting versions:

- the "simulated-time prototype" or "emulated-time prototype," which simulates or emulates the object's behavior
- the "reality object," which embeds the physical object

The "reality object" could be a hardware device driver, an encapsulation of an external function (like a relational database), or a surrogate for an external object (stub), as described in Pattern 10.

When going from simulation to reality, replace the simulation object with the object (such as a device driver) that interfaces to reality. Consistency in this transition is guaranteed either by inheriting the two implementations from a common base class that defines their interface, or by application of Pattern 8, substituting the desired implementation object in the interface object's use relationship.

Maintaining two distinct implementations of a certain conceptual entity and switching from one to the other is an application of the Bridge pattern described in Gamma et al. A reality object that encapsulates an external functionality is an example of their Adapter pattern. Installation can be speeded up by switching from prototype to physical implementation in the same program, which is achieved by using a suitable design pattern such as their Abstract Factory [16], which allows the user to decide at run time the specific class he needs.

Evolution from logical to physical design and from prototype to implementation is achieved by maintaining two representations of the same entities (the prototype and the reality object), transforming the prototype into the reality by exploiting polymorphism or use relationships.

Related Patterns   Going from prototype to reality when reality is a remote (distributed) object is described in Pattern 10.

PATTERN 10: DISTRIBUTION OF CONTROL MODULES

Control modules usually reside on remote computers or peripheral devices and are interconnected through a common communication network. These modules define the physical architecture that must be realized by the final, distributed system.

Context   Complex distributed systems share a need for simulation, as discussed in the previous pattern. When going from a nondistributed simulation to the distributed reality, the objects that are moved to remote nodes are no longer part of the original program; they must become independent programs in their own right.

As in the previous pattern, the rest of the system should not be affected by moving some objects to a remote node. In addition, moving objects to remote nodes should be kept relatively easy, in order to avoid preventing the system from changing with the physical architecture; that is, we want to exploit an evolutionary approach.

Solution   Create large-grain objects (called remote contexts in G++), one for each node that will contain remote objects. Remote contexts contain one or more (typically active) objects, along with the services these objects need in order to function as an installable program.

The remote context supports (1) listening for requests coming over the communication network from other nodes, (2) unpacking these requests, and (3) forwarding them to the correct object. These functions correspond to those of the "server skeleton" and the "object adapter" of the OMG CORBA reference model. If objects in a remote context will be making requests to objects residing on other nodes, the installable program must also contain the necessary Stub objects, as explained below. See also Figure 11.

In the original system, replace objects that have been moved to other nodes with Stub objects that encapsulate the distribution and communication interface. These stubs have the same interface as the object they replace, and they forward each request over the network or communication link to the remote object they represent. As in the previous pattern, consistency is ensured either by inheritance polymorphism (as in Figure 12) or by delegation (as in Figure 13). The functionality of the Stub object corresponds to that of the CORBA stub.

Each Stub and each RemoteContext encapsulates an instance of the class Network. While the former two classes are rarely modified, Network might need to be adapted to the particular communication platform. Note that a sufficiently intelligent CASE tool could automate the transition to a distributed system by generating the necessary stubs and remote contexts and replacing the original simulation objects with the stubs. For certain platforms this transition could be as simple as generating CORBA IDL interface descriptions.

FIGURE 11 Prototyping and distribution

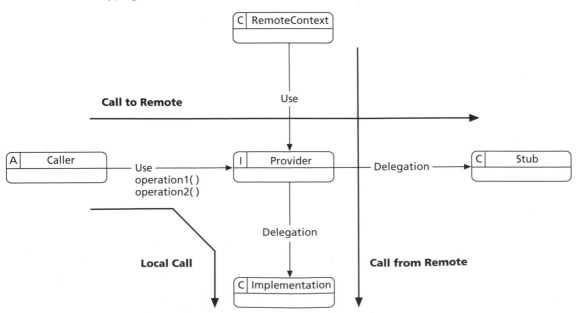

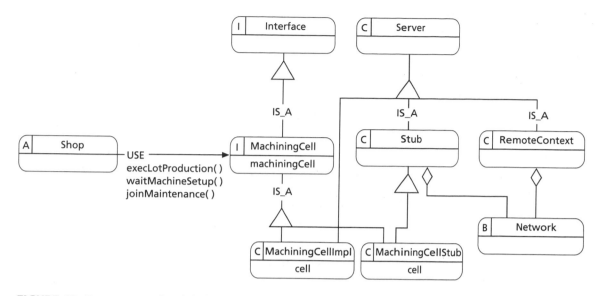

FIGURE 12 Prototype and stub linked by inheritance

FIGURE 13 Prototype and stub linked by use

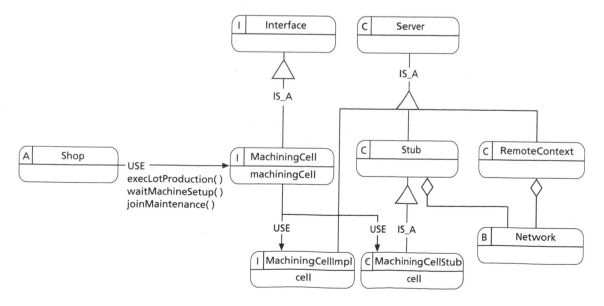

`Stub` and `RemoteContext` are the natural interface between the large grain of concurrency (represented by separate modules) and the smaller one (represented by services inside modules) supported by the G++ model.

`Stub` is an application of the `Proxy` pattern described by Gamma et al. Switching between a simulation object and the corresponding `Stub` is an application of their `Bridge` pattern [11].

Example:
Distribution
of a Shop
and a Cell

We assume that the `Shop` and `MachiningCell` control modules are installed on different computers connected through a factory-wide backbone network and that cell peripherals, in particular the collection of machines, are connected to the cell computer through shop-floor LANs.

Focusing on the cell distribution, Figure 14 shows how the `Machining-CellStub` substitutes for the `MachiningCellImpl` (the prototype of the cell control module) in the shop controller. `MachiningCellStub` communicates with the corresponding `RemoteContext`, which encapsulates `Machining-Cell`. In turn, the `MachiningCellImpl` contains a collection of `Machine` objects, whose implementations have also been replaced by their respective stubs.

To develop a prototype into a distributed application, use `Stubs` *to create alternative implementations of remote control modules, and substitute them for the prototype modules in the model. Use* `Remote-Context`s *that encapsulate these remote control modules and provide a context for them. These two classes are a matched pair offered by the framework. They are rarely modified, as they delegate the implementation of low-level protocols to a* `Network` *object, which wraps the communication drivers (ORB, for example). It should be provided for in each different implementation.*

3. COMPARISON WITH THE "DESIGN PATTERN CATALOG"

In order to compare the patterns presented here with those described in the literature, patterns may be classified as elemental, basic-design, and domain-dependent. Elemental patterns determine the language (the elements of the architecture) in which the whole application has to be written; they include *A Hierarchy of Control Layers, Concurrency, Actions Triggered by Events, Services "Waiting For,"* and *Prototype and Reality*. Basic design patterns, similar to those discussed in Gamma et al. [11] and with the

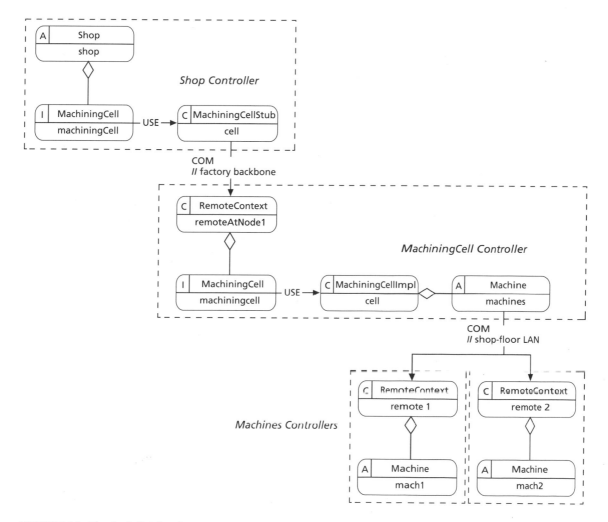

FIGURE 14 Physical distribution

same level of abstraction, propose OO design solutions as intermediary building blocks, such as Client/Server/Service, which by their very nature are fairly application-independent. The others—*Visibility and Communication Between Control Modules, Implementation of Control Modules, The Interface to Control Modules,* and *Distribution of Control Modules*—are domain-dependent and are very similar to Johnson's concepts [16]: they provide guidelines for using the framework's classes to solve specific problems. They obviously exploit basic OO design patterns, in turn, for their implementation.

4. CONCLUSION

A set of patterns for designing concurrent distributed systems has been defined and has been illustrated using CIM applications. These patterns are the documentation that makes it possible to understand and use the many event handling, concurrency, and distribution functions offered by a framework of basic reusable classes.

Each pattern proposes a design choice for a particular aspect of the problem. In addition, taken together the patterns form a language, that is, an organized set of rules that guide the designer from analysis to physical implementation, with the objective of raising reusability from the component to the architectural level and of easing the designer's task of making choices in the sophisticated environment of OO programming. This is possible due to unambiguous rules that reduce the semantics gap between the problem and the software architecture. In fact, patterns, as a media in which analysis evolves into design, are an answer to the problems of the seamless transition from analysis to design raised by Høydalsvik and Sindre at the 1993 OOPSLA conference [15].

Finally, one contribution this paper makes is to allow dynamic behavior to be seen as a property of the whole architecture rather than an attribute of each single object in isolation; this has been achieved by embedding the design into a well-defined framework that resulted from the application of the pattern language.

ACKNOWLEDGMENTS

We wish to thank our "shepherd" at the PLoP conference, Jim Coplien, for his help and advice, and Professor Ralph Johnson of the University of Illinois at Urbana-Champaign, together with John Brand, Brian Foote, and Don Roberts, for their rich suggestions and their careful review of the paper.

This work has been supported by Consiglio Nationale delle Ricerche under grant no. 92.01602.PF69 *Progretto Finalizatto Sistemi Informatici e Calcolo Parallelo*, grant no. 92.01940.PF67 *Progretto Finalizzato Robotica*, and by the Changer of Commerce of Turin—Standards in CIM.

REFERENCES

[1] C. Alexander, S. Ishikawa, and M. Silverstein. *A Pattern Language: Towns, Buildings, Construction.* New York: Oxford University Press, 1977.

[2] C. Alexander. *The Timeless Way of Building*. New York: Oxford University Press, 1979.

[3] G. R. Andrews and F. B. Schneider. "Concepts and Notations for Concurrent Programming." *ACM Computer Surveys* 15, 1 (March 1983): 3–43.

[4] G. R. Andrews. "An Overview of the SR Language and Implementation." *ACM Transactions on Programming Languages and Systems* 10, 1 (1988): 51–86.

[5] K. Beck and R. Johnson. "Patterns Generate Architecture." In *ECOOP'94 Conference Proceedings*, Bologna, Italy, July 1994.

[6] B. W. Boehm. "A Spiral Model of Software Development and Enhancement." *IEEE Computer* (May 1988).

[7] G. Booch. *Object-Oriented Design with Applications*. Redwood City, CA: Benjamin/Cummings, 1991.

[8] R. S. Chin and S. T. Chanson. "Distributed Object-Based Programming System." *ACM Computing Surveys* 23 (March 1991): 91–124.

[9] D. Decouchant. "Design of a Distributed Object Manager for the Smallltalk–80 System." *OOPSLA'86 Proceedings*, pp. 444–451.

[10] E. Gamma, R. Helm, R. Johnson, and J. Vlissdes. "Design Patterns: Abstraction and Reuse of Object Oriented Design. " In *ECOOP '93 Conference Proceedings*, Kaiserlautern, Germany, April 1993.

[11] F. Gamma, R. Helm, R. Johnson, and J. Vlissides. *Design Patterns: Elements of Reusable Object-Oriented Software*. Reading, MA: Addison-Wesley, 1995.

[12] P. B. Gibbson. A Stub Generator for Multilanguage RPC in Heterogeneous Environments. *IEEE Transactions on Software Engineering*, 13(1):77–87, January 1987.

[13] A. Goldberg and D. Robson. *Smalltalk80: The Language and its Implementation*. Reading, MA: Addison-Wesley, 1983.

[14] R. Halstead, *Multislip: A Language for concurrent symbolic computation*. ACM Transactions on Programming Languages and Systems 4, 4 (October 1985).

[15] G. M. Høydalsvik and G. Sindre. *On the purpose of Object-Oriented Analysis*. OOPSLA'92 Washington, DC, September 1993.

[16] R. E. Johnson. *Documenting Frameworks using Patterns*. OOPSLA'92 Proceedings, Vancouver, BC, Canada, October 1992.

[17] G. E. Krasner and S. T. Pope. "A Cookbook for Using the Model–View–Controller User Interface Paradigm in Smalltalk–80. "*Journal of Object-Oriented Programming* (August/September 1988).

[18] C. McLean, M. Mitchell, and E. Barkmeyer. "A Computer Architecture for Small-Batch Manufacturing." *IEEE Spectrum* 20,5 (1983): 59–64.

[19] G. Menga, G. Elia, and M. Mancia. "G++: An Environment for Object Oriented Design and Prototyping of Manufacturing Systems. In W. Gruver and G. Boudreaux, eds., *Intelligent Manufacturing: Programming Environments for CIM*. New York: Springer–Verlag, 1993.

[20] D. L. Parnas, P. C. Clements, and D. M. Weiss. "The Modular Structure of Complex Systems." *IEEE Transactions on Software Engineering* 11,3 (March 1985): 259–266.

[21] Pattern Mailing List. Send email to `patterns-request@cs.uiuc.edu` to subscribe.

[22] A. Rockstroem and R. Saracco. "SDL-CCITT Specification and Description Language." *IEEE Transactions on Communications*, COM-30, June 1982.

[23] J. Rumbaugh, M. Blaha, W. Premerlani, F. Eddy, and W. Lorensen. *Object-Oriented Modeling and Design.* Englewood Cliffs, NJ: Prentice Hall, 1991.

[24] R. M. Soley. *Object Management Archictecture Guide.* OMG, Inc. 492 Old Connecticut Path, Framingham, MA 01701. November 1990.

[25] B. Stroustrup. *The C++ Programming Language,* 2nd ed. Reading, MA: Addison-Wesley, 1991.

[26] R. Wirfs-Brock and R. Johnson. "Surveying Current Research Issues on Object Oriented Design. Communication of the ACM 33, (September 1990): 105–124.

[27] D. A. Young. *The X Window System Programming and Application with Xt.* Englewood Cliffs, NJ: Prentice-Hall, 1989.

The authors can be reached at the Department of Automatica e Informatica, Politecnico di Torino, Corso Duca degli Abruzzi n. 24, 10129 Torino, Italy; {amund, gelia, menga}@polito.it.

7
Patterns for Generating a Layered Architecture

Barry Rubel

ABSTRACT

Although many system developers recognize that layered architectures are beneficial, the problem lies in how to create one. This paper presents patterns that lead practitioners to a natural decomposition of system requirements into a layered architecture. The discussion uses mechanical control systems as an example, to illustrate the concepts of the general pattern.

BACKGROUND

Real-time systems respond to external asynchronous events, which typically originate from several sources, such as an operator or equipment. Figure 1 shows the operator interfaces to Command, Monitor, and Alarm (CMA) software, which in turn relies upon a hardware interface to supply connectivity to the equipment. Commands originate at the operator and travel

Copyright © 1994 Harris Corporation. All Rights Reserved.

through each of the domains, affecting the equipment. Some commands involve closed-loop control that utilizes feedback from the equipment to calculate a control signal. Status travels up from the equipment, through the domains, to the operator. Once the equipment status reaches some predefined state, a CMA system may deliver an alarm to the operator. The system also typically delivers an alarm when a fault occurs. For example, if the oil pressure in an engine drops below a predefined threshold value, a warning light is illuminated on the console.

Grady Booch states that "a complex system that works is invariably found to have evolved from a simple system that worked" [9]. Typically, a mechanical engineer develops a mechanical process with a hands-on approach, and then the process is automated by inserting the following patterns between the engineer and the equipment.

PATTERNS

Pedestal

Problem   Although many system developers recognize that layered architectures are beneficial, the problem lies in how to create one.

Context   You are developing a mechanical-process control system. The control system involves many engineering domains: mechanical engineering, controls, systems engineering, operator interface, electrical engineering, software engineering, operating systems, and so on.

Forces   Developers have a need for organization. Organization facilitates the development of simple solutions to complex problems. For example, early parser developers found that Chompski's hierarchy, with its context-free grammar, simplified parser implementation. This reduced the complexity of parser development so much that it became the popular choice of compiler developers. Parser implementation is possible without this method of organization, but it is more difficult. In a similar manner, a good architecture will simplify the implementation of a system.

The need for organization is amplified because object-oriented methods, although growing in popularity, cannot be layered as easily as structured methods' data flow diagrams (DFDs). In DFDs a process can be expanded into a lower-level DFD. The data-flows to and from a process are consistent at each level and are therefore subject to rigorous consistency checking. Although

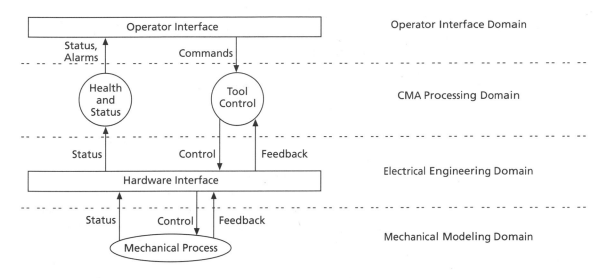

FIGURE 1 A typical CMA system   **FIGURE 2** Domains and support products

Rumbaugh's method has the subsystem and Booch's method has categories of classes, these do not support a leveling organization as well as DFDs.

Creating a layered architecture supplies organization for a system; but the question of *how* to create one still remains.

Solution   Generate a layered architecture, such as the one in Figure 3, in the following manner:

1. Select and order a set of domains. The software domain must be in the selection.

2. Reflect the real-world domains into the software domain to form a model of the real world. The real-world domains form architectural layers.

3. Add a layer, on top of the software model, that contains objects that organize the behavior of the model.

4. Add another layer that connects the previous layers to a client. This is usually an operator interface layer, but in the case of an embedded system it could be a communication layer.

Select and order domains based on the domains' purpose in the system. The purpose of the final system is to automate a mechanical process—thus the mechanical domain is a terminal domain of the order, and so we would place it at the bottom of the hierarchy in Figure 2. The purpose of the electrical domain is to supply connectivity between the mechanical entities and the software domain. The purpose of the software world is to model the real world and to organize this model into system behavior. The purpose of the operator interface is to supply connectivity between the operator and the software domain. Thus the ordering consists of the mechanical domain followed by the electrical domain followed by the software domain followed by the operator-interface domain, as shown in Figure 2.

Practitioners may observe symmetry in the lowest portion of the pattern. The axis of symmetry, shown in Figure 3 and Figure 4, provides a boundary interface between the real world and the software world. The real world consists of the mechanical and electrical domains. Figure 3 shows the lower boundary of symmetry; the axis of symmetry sets the scope of the real world. The symmetry exists between real-world entities and those that the analyst reflects as image objects into the software model of the real world. The upper boundary of symmetry is a reflection of the lower boundary. Consequently, the upper boundary of symmetry and the axis of symmetry define the scope

FIGURE 3 A CMA architecture

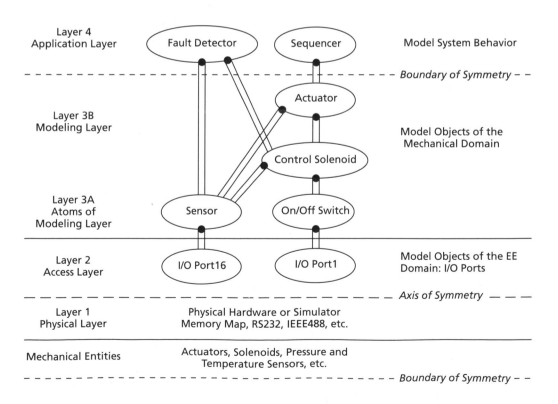

```
Operator Interface
─────────────────────────
Management of Model
───────────────────────── Upper Boundary of Symmetery
Model of Real World
─ ─ ─ ─ ─ ─ ─ ─ ─ The Axis of Symmetery
         Real World
───────────────────────── Lower Boundary of Symmetery
```

FIGURE 4 The pedestal form

of the software model reflecting the real world. The real-world domains are reflected into the software world as architectural layers.

We organize the software model of the real world with software objects that are more abstract than the real-world objects the model reflects. These software objects are more abstract in that they do not have any real-world counterpart. They exist solely to organize the behavior of the software model of the real world. Consequently these objects are more procedural in behavior, and they may be defined with state machines. Some examples of these objects include sequencers and fault detectors.

Resulting Context

See Figure 4.

Design Rationale

Selecting a minimal set of essential architectural domains enhances understandability. The software domain is always essential. The operator-interface domain is nearly always essential. In this context—mechanical process control—the mechanical engineering and electrical engineering domains are also essential. All other domains are left out of the pattern intentionally. This is a form of information hiding. Including nonessential domains would increase complexity and therefore decrease understandability. The Non-Architectural Domains pattern (to be written) describes relationships between architectural domains and excluded domains.

The pedestal form is very understandable. The practitioner may use the pedestal form to communicate decisions to professionals of various fields involved in the system, such as mechanical and electrical engineers, technical managers, customers, and so on.

Related Patterns

(Backward) Layered Architecture

(Forward) Bridge

(To be written) Non-Architectural Domains (NAD)

(Forward) Symmetrical Reuse

(To be written) Application Layer and Polymorphism (ALP)

Bridge

Problem   Given the context resulting from the Pedestal pattern, what do you do with the joystick? Although it is part of the real world, it is in a different domain than a motor.

Context   The context results from the Pedestal pattern.

Forces   Forces include the real worlds and the corresponding models to communicate with it. Some of the most abstract objects in the system are located between the operator interface software and the electromechanical software.

Resulting Context   Figure 5 shows the bridge, consisting of two vertical columns topped with a lintel. The low region of the bridge contains two separate bases, one for each real-world domain: the operator interface domain and the mechanical domain. The intermediate region consists of corresponding models of each real world, capping each base. The upper region contains the lintel, providing a communication channel between the two bases and ultimately between the real-world domains.

Aqueduct-style bridges can be formed in applications that have three or more columns based on varying real worlds.

Design Rationale   Creating separate real words for different terminal domains yields a more cohesive structure (the column). Information transfer between the terminal domains is achieved above the upper boundary of symmetry. Communication between objects of different terminal domains anywhere below the upper boundary of symmetry would reduce the column's cohesion.

Related Patterns   (To be written) Vertical Symmetry between Pedestals

FIGURE 5 The bridge form of the pattern

Management of and Communication between Models		Upper Boundary of Symmetry
Model of OI World	Model of Mechanical World	The Axis of Symmetry
Operator Interface Real World	Mechanical Real World	Lower Boundary of Symmetry

Symmetrical Reuse

Problem   Given the context resulting from the Pedestal pattern, developers need to understand the opportunities for reuse and the factors supporting reuse.

Context   In an automated assembly line there are many stations. Each station has a mechanical component, an electrical component, and a software component, all working together to perform a mechanical process unique to a particular kind of workstation.

Different kinds of stations support mechanical assemblies tailored for specific purposes. Although the stations' assemblies are different, they are constructed from a common set of mechanical building blocks, such as motors, actuators, heating elements, temperature sensors, pressure sensors, and so on.

Different kinds of stations consist of various commercial VME cards, such as analog input cards, digital output cards, intelligent motor controller cards, and so on. Although the VME cards vary in quantity and type between kinds of stations, it is common for the same type of card to appear in different kinds of stations. For example, the PMAC motor controller card may control up to eight motors. One kind of station may have four motors, requiring one PMAC card, while another class of station may have forty motors, requiring live PMAC cards.

Forces   ■ The common use of mechanical building blocks and VME cards among the stations is related to the particular software component in use at each station.

■ A stable architecture increases opportunities for reuse.

■ In real-time systems there are various methods for multitasking and asynchronous interobject communications.

Solution   Apply the Pedestal pattern to each kind of station. Use the axis of symmetry as a reference for reuse. If a practitioner reuses a card in a chassis, he or she can likely reuse the layer-2 objects supporting the card. Applying this to Figure 6, if we reuse the PMAC card we can likely reuse the corresponding PMAC object in the software domain. Other object-image pairs in this figure are the analog-to-digital card and the sensor object, as well as the digital-output card and the switch object. These items, previously mentioned, are all immediately adjacent to the axis of symmetry. Extending farther from the axis of symmetry, if mechanical engineers reuse an item in their domain, then we are likely to reuse the comparable layer-3 object. For example, if mechanical engineers reuse a motor, then we are likely to reuse its layer-3 motor object.

Use the same architectural support software among the workstations. Architectural objects will have stable relationships for implementation details, that is, multitasking and asynchronous interobject communications.

Resulting Context   See Figure 6.

Design Rationale   The architecture provides a vertical stability. Each layer in the architecture has a stable relationship with adjacent layers. Reuse of the architecture among the various stations facilitates reuse of the architectural objects through the vertical stability.

   The architecture provides the opportunity for another degree of stability—horizontal stability. Each architectural object in the software world has a relationship with its supporting implementation domain. Providing this horizontal stability among stations increases the reusability of their architectural objects.

FIGURE 6 Reuse of object about the axis of symmetry

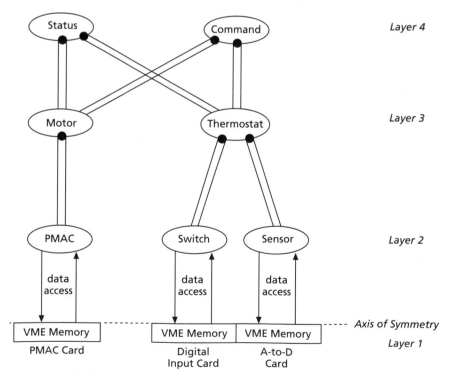

The architecture reflects the fact that there are two degrees of stability: vertical and horizontal. The architectural stability provides a supporting context for an object. This stability minimizes the differences between instances of the same kind of object. The differences between object instances may be parameterized as data. For example, an instance of a motor at the modeling layer (layer 3) may hold a reference to a PMAC motor controller at the access layer (layer 2). When the same motor class is instantiated on different stations, the different references to each PMAC card may appear as a parameter to the constructor of each motor object.

The layers of the architecture tend to support reuse by leading the practitioner to develop objects that are similar to virtual devices. Encapsulation hides the details of how the layer-3 motor object uses layer 2 and layer 1 (the access and physical layers) to communicate through the hardware interface. This helps when moving to a different implementation of layer 1 and layer 2 while using the same mechanical motor and its layer-3 motor object. For example, say that after development requirements changed. The use of a PMAC card in the system was not acceptable, but the motor was to remain, as well as all of the motor's client software. New hardware could replace the PMAC card. Developers could develop new layer-2 software components to support the new hardware. It would be less of an impact on the client software if the new layer-2 software provided the same interface to its layer-3 client, the motor object. This organization of software should minimize the software impact for this type of change. This provides a ripe environment for producing an application-specific framework, by providing interchangeable run-time components as well as interchangeable development-time support tools.

Related Patterns   (To be written) SCT at Each Layer Elevate References to Enhance Reuse (ER2)

Elevate References to Enhance Reuse (ER2)

Problem   How should designers model a relationship between two objects?

Context   You are modeling two actuators: A and B. A constrains B, in that B may not be moved unless A is at a position of 0 inches.

Forces   Developers decrease an object's reusability by having it directly reference other objects at the same level in the architecture. In this context, developers decrease the reusability of actuator B by having it directly reference actuator A.

Solution   Implement the relation in an additional adjacent object that is higher in the architecture. This object is more abstract, and thus its relationships tend to have a vertical factor. Knowledge of the reference is directed from the top down. Avoid horizontal references and references that are constructed from the bottom up.

Resulting Context

The sequencer that has existing references to both actuators, A and B, implements the constraint. When a command to activate actuator B arrives, the sequencer verifies the constraint (actuator A is at 0 inches) before passing the command to actuator B.

Design Rationale

The modeling of the actuator is cohesive. Actuator B does not have an intrinsic physical relationship to actuator A. This relationship is a rule developed by an expert, usually a systems engineer. Representing this rule in the actuator reduces the cohesion of the actuator. It amounts to taking an entity in the engineer's mind and putting it into an object modeling the physical world. The physical object should only model relevant physical characteristics. Cohesion of the object is also reduced if it references another object that is higher in the architecture.

REFERENCES

Booch, Grady. *Object-Oriented Design with Applications,* 2nd ed. Redwood City, CA: Benjamin/Cummings, 1994.

Rumbaugh, James. *Object-Oriented Modality and Design.* Englewood Cliffs, NJ: Prentice Hall, 1991.

Barry Rubel can be reached at 348 Sheridan Avenue, Satellite Beach, FL 32937; (407) 777-9561.

Pattern: Half-object + Protocol (HOPP)

8

Gerard Meszaros

Applicability Once you decide upon your objects and their associations, it is time to determine how your objects will be mapped into the address spaces in which they will execute. This pattern helps determine where the objects are placed and their positions relative to the address space boundaries.

Problem Sometimes objects must appear in more than one computing context (that is, address space.) How can we make the difference between one and multiple address spaces (for example, single versus distributed processing) transparent?

Forces The forces affecting the placement of objects into address spaces include complexity, distribution, information availability, cost, and performance.

Many computer systems are forced to be implemented across multiple address spaces for reasons of cost, size, physical distribution, disparity of programming environments, regulatory reasons, and so on. Sometimes these systems can be easily decomposed into objects that each live in exactly one address space. Some objects are constrained to exist in certain address spaces

Copright © 1994 Bell Northern Research, Ltd. All Rights Reserved.

by coupling to hardware (such as sensors, disk drives, and so on), and others can easily be placed based on such couplings. Sometimes, however, a concept exists in both spaces, so you can't easily decompose it; or an object may have to interact with other objects in more than one address space, because it requires information from more than one address space to carry out its behavior. Similarly, unsolicited requests arriving from objects in either address space may need to be handled. See Figure 1.

In the figure, the single-headed arrows represent particular "use-cases" that require the participation of the object needing to be represented in both address spaces. In this case, neither address space can carry out the task in isolation. Therefore, at least one object may have to exist in more than one address space. The object or objects in question may have to be split into one or more object per address space. Splitting an object across the address spaces introduces additional complexity, since a single object is simpler than two half-objects with a protocol between them. (We use the term "half-object" to refer to each distinct part of the object even though each part may implement significantly more than 50 percent of the object's functionality.) One half-object can implement all the behavior, interacting with the other object whenever it needs information retrieved or actions carried out.

If these interactions are frequent, the cost (in terms of execution time, or delay) of building message objects and sending them to an object in another address space may be unacceptable.

Splitting an object into two equal parts allows each part to respond to many local requests without consulting the other address space, but it may result in duplicated functionality and a need to keep the two objects synchronized.

FIGURE 1 Where should the distribution boundary be?

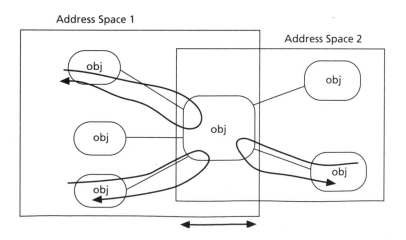

Address Space 1

Address Space 2

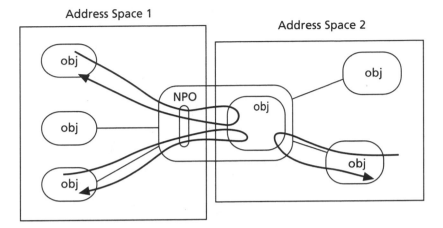

FIGURE 2 The network proxy object (NPO) passes all requests back to the real object.

It does isolate the object's interface from the protocol used between the half-objects.

Solution Divide the object into two interdependent half objects, one in each address space, with a protocol between them. In each address space, implement whatever functionality is required to interact efficiently with the other objects in that address space. (This may result in duplicated functionality,

FIGURE 3 Synchronization Protocol. Half-objects respond to local requests; they synchronize their activities through the Synchronization Protocol.

Address Space 1

Address Space 2

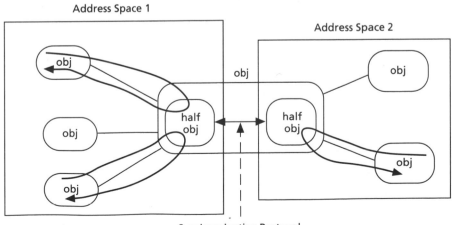

Synchronization Protocol

that is, functions implemented in both address spaces.) Define the protocol between the two half-objects such that it coordinates the activities of the two half-objects and carries the essential information that needs to be passed between the address spaces.

Related Patterns   Once the functions of each half-object are determined, the protocol between them may be defined. This leads to the use of patterns in designing the protocol (Message as Object, Message Parameter as Object) and the mechanisms to handle the creation (information collection, formatting) and reception (parsing, handling) of the message.

Examples   *Physical distribution:* Non-native debuggers, telephone services distributed across the national telephone network, systems accessing hardware devices (such as sensors), user interfaces remote from information (such as central databases), distributed (replicated) databases.

Size: Systems where functions must be carried out in slave microprocessors due to real-time costs of the function.

Disparity of programming Environments: A user interface for a C++ debugger implemented in Smalltalk.

Regulatory Reasons: Service control points (SCPs) in the telephone network contain software created by the telephone company to modify calls carried through switches in the telephone network. This software may not be allowed to run in a switch. (This is also an example of disparate programming environments, since switches have proprietary environments while SCPs typically have UNIX-based environments.)

Gerard Meszaros can be reached at Bell Northern Research, Canada, P.O. Box 3511, Station C, Ottawa, ONT K1Y 4H7, Canada; gerard@bnr.ca.

9 The Master-Slave Pattern

Frank Buschmann

ABSTRACT

The pattern presented in this paper, the Master-Slave pattern, handles the computation of replicated services within a software system to achieve fault tolerance and robustness. It separates independent components that all provide the same service (the slaves) from a component (the master) that is responsible for invoking them and for selecting a particular result for further use from the results they return. Clients of the service communicate only with the master component. The principles behind the Master-Slave design pattern are separation of concerns and organizing the computation of services.

1. INTRODUCTION

The Master-Slave pattern was developed as part of a comprehensive system of patterns for software architecture [Buschmann+94]. This system of patterns

Copyright © Siemens AG. All Rights Reserved.

includes patterns of various scale ranges, beginning with patterns for defining the basic structure of an application and ending with patterns describing how to implement a particular design issue in a concrete programming language. All the patterns in this system are described in a uniform way, according to a template consisting of the following slots:

1. **Name:** The pattern's essence is succinctly conveyed.
2. **Rationale:** The motivation for developing the pattern is presented.
3. **Applicability:** A rule is presented stating when to use the pattern.
4. **Classification:** The pattern is classified according to its general properties (see below).
5. **Description:** The participants and collaborators in the pattern are described, as well as their responsibilities and relationships to each other.
6. **Diagram:** A graphical representation of the pattern's structure is given.
7. **Dynamic behavior:** The dynamic behavior of a pattern is illustrated.
8. **Methodology:** The methodology (steps) for constructing the pattern is listed.
9. **Implementation:** Guidelines for implementing the pattern are presented.
10. **Variants:** Possible variants of the pattern are listed and described.
11. **Examples:** Examples for the pattern's use are presented.
12. **Discussion:** The constraints of applying the pattern are discussed.
13. **See also:** References to related patterns are given.

To guide the selection of a pattern for a given design situation, the system of patterns includes a classification scheme by which all patterns are classified. This classification scheme consists of three categories of criteria or design issues that play a significant role in software development:

1. **Granularity:** Developing a software system requires dealing with various levels of abstraction, beginning with the basic structure of an application and ending with issues regarding the concrete realization of particular design structures. Thus granularity is an important category for classifying patterns.

   Three levels of granularity can be specified:

   - *Architectural frameworks* represent fundamental principles for structuring software systems into subsystems and the relationships between them.

- *Design patterns* describe basic schemes for structuring subsystems and components of software architecture, as well as their relationships.

- *Idioms* describe how to implement particular components (parts) of subsystem and component functionality, or their relationships to other components within a given design.

2. **Functionality:** The second category by which patterns can be classified is functionality. Each pattern serves as a template for implementing a particular functionality. However, the various classes of functionality are of a general nature rather than specific to a certain application domain.

   The following functionality categories can be distinguished:

   - *Creation of objects:* Patterns may specify how to create particular instances of complex recursive or aggregate object structures.

   - *Guiding communication between objects:* Patterns may describe how to organize the communication between a set of collaborating objects that may also be independently developed or that run in a remote context.

   - *Access to objects:* Patterns may describe how to access the services and state of shared or remote objects in a safe way, without violating their encapsulation of state and behavior.

   - *Organizing the computation of complex functions:* Patterns may specify how to distribute responsibilities among cooperating objects to solve a more complex function or task.

3. **Structural principles:** To realize their functionality, patterns rely on certain architectural principles:

   - *Abstraction:* A pattern provides an abstract or generalized view of a particular (often complex) entity or task in a software system.

   - *Encapsulation:* A pattern encapsulates details of a particular object, component, or service to remove dependency on the pattern from its clients or to protect these details from access.

   - *Separation of concerns:* A pattern factors out specific responsibilities into separate objects or components to solve a particular task or provide a certain service.

   - *Coupling and cohesion:* A pattern removes or relaxes the structural and communication relationships and dependencies between otherwise strongly coupled objects.

The Master-Slave pattern presented in this paper is described and classified according to the overall frame set by the system of patterns.

2. THE PATTERN

Rationale

Fault tolerance is a critical factor in many industrial software systems. Such systems must ensure that services are executed correctly and that service computations and access to service suppliers do not fail. Replication of services and the delegation of the same task to several independent suppliers is a common strategy to handle such cases.

Applicability

The Master-Slave design pattern can be used whenever it is necessary to replicate a particular service, to organize its multiple and simultaneous computation, and to select the result that is to be returned to the clients of the service out of the results produced by various suppliers. The Master-Slave pattern is suitable for all programming paradigms supporting abstraction facilities like abstract data types or modules.

  The Master-Slave design pattern can be applied whenever it is necessary to handle the computation of replicated services within a software system.

Classification

The structural and functional principles behind the Master-Slave design pattern are separation of concerns and organizing the computation of services. The design pattern separates independent components providing the same service from the component invoking them and selecting a particular result for further use from the results the components return.

Description

The Master-Slave design pattern consists of two kinds of components, the master component and at least two slave components. The master component is responsible for providing a service for which fault tolerance, safety, or correctness is critical. However, the master component does not provide this service directly; it delegates it to several suppliers, the slave components. All slave components solve the same task or provide the

Class	Collaborators
Slave • implements a service	—
Master • organizes the invocation of replicated services • decides which of the results returned by its slaves is to be passed to its clients	Slave(s)
Client • requires a certain service in order to solve its own task	Master

FIGURE 1 Participants and collaborators of the Master-Slave design pattern

same service. Each slave is also completely independent of other slaves participating in the pattern. The slave components may also use different strategies for providing the service they are responsible for.

The master component delegates the requested service to its slaves and selects which of their returned results to use for further computation of the application. It may select the first result returned, the one returned by most of the slaves, the average result of all slaves, the one returned by a slave that did not fail, or sometimes none of them, (for example, if all slaves return a different result). Clients of the service provided by the Master-Slave design pattern communicate only with the master component rather than with the various slaves. Although all participants of the pattern are generally responsible for the same service, their interface may not necessarily be the same; for example, different strategies used by the slaves may require different interfaces. In parallel or distributed software systems the various slave components are often placed on different environment nodes and executed concurrently.

Dynamic Behavior

The behavior of a Master-Slave pattern is usually simple (see Figure 3). A client invokes the service offered by the master. The master invokes its associated slaves. All slaves start computing the requested service, usually concurrently. The results the slaves return are collected by the master.

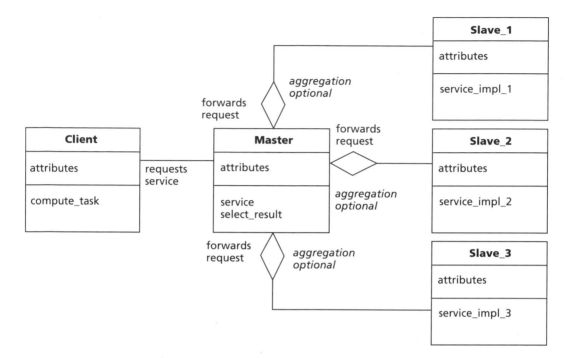

FIGURE 2 The Master-Slave design pattern

The master also decides what concrete result is to be used for further computation of the software. The master returns this result to its client.

Methodology

1. A master component is introduced for every service that should be replicated and organized with the help of the Master-Slave design pattern. This component must offer the requested service in its public interface and it must be associated with its clients.

2. The required number of slave components is specified, each of them implementing the service provided by the master. The slave components must be completely independent of each other. If possible (and desired), they may also use different solution strategies for implementing the service.

3. The master component is associated with the slaves specified in the previous step.

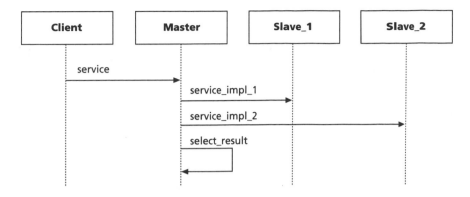

FIGURE 3

4. A strategy is specified for the master to use in selecting a result from those returned by its slaves. The master returns this result to its clients.

Implementation

Every participant in the Master-Slave design pattern is implemented as a separate component or class. If all the slaves in the pattern offer the same or a similar interface, and if the programming language used for implementation supports inheritance, it may be appropriate to implement the slaves in a hierarchy with an abstract base.

   If, in addition, both the master and the slave classes offer the same or a similar interface, this hierarchy may be extended with a further abstract base, from which the master class as well as the abstract base for the slaves are derived. (Note that neither case is illustrated in the above diagram of the design pattern.) If the slaves are only used by a single master instance and they do not live in a distributed environment, the slave classes may be implemented as explicit parts of the master, with the help of the Composite-Part pattern.[1] Otherwise the slaves should only be referenced by the master.

---

[1] The Composite-Part pattern is briefly introduced in the paper "A System of Patterns" (Buschmann+94) and is fully described in a later paper (Buschmann+95).

Examples

- Many safety-critical software systems use structures equal or similar to the Master-Slave pattern to handle replication of services. In a material flow–control system for flexible manufacturing (automation domain; see Meyer+88), the pattern is used to organize the generation of transport instructions for work pieces. The algorithm for generating transport instructions can be based on various strategies, such as on an optimal machine tool or transport system occupation. The distinct algorithms are based on information from different sources. However, when the system is calculating a transport instruction, this information might not be accessible (for example, because machine tools cannot respond to a request for information about their state immediately or in an appropriate time). Since it is necessary to continuously organize the material flow, various components for calculating transport instructions—all based on different algorithms—are introduced and organized with the Master-Slave pattern.

- Other application domains in which the Master-Slave design pattern is applied are aircraft control systems and telecommunications systems (ATM93).

- The concept of gaggles (Black93) is similar to the Master-Slave pattern. Gaggles provide a mechanism for accessing distributed replicated services in an object-oriented software system.

Discussion

The Master-Slave design pattern introduces redundancy, fault tolerance, safety, and correctness into a software system. A Master-Slave structure does not rely on a single supplier to provide the service it is responsible for; rather, it implements the service at least twice. Thus, if any slave fails—for example, if a slave cannot finish its computation in the required time, if the master is not able to open a connection to it, or if the existing connection or the slave itself throws an exception—there is still a good chance of accomplishing a valid and usable solution for the requested service. As long as at least one slave provides a result, the failure of all the other slaves has no effect on the application's computation—the master component is still able to serve its clients. In addition, the pattern compares the results returned by the various implementations of the service and selects one of them to return to its clients (for example, the most accurate one).

The main advantage of the Master-Slave pattern is that it factors out all responsibilities related to the handling of replicated services into a separate component, the master. Clients of the master do not know that they communicate with a replicated service. Thus the Master-Slave pattern supports changeability and helps to handle system complexity.

Another possible use of the Master-Slave pattern is for when the algorithm on which the computation of a particular service is based varies dynamically; for example, when it depends on the current state of the overall computation within the software system. Other patterns, such as the Envelope-Letter pattern, also address this problem; but it might be more appropriate to have all possible implementations of the service directly available and to let a master component decide which one to invoke, rather than to load the appropriate implementation on demand.

A Master-Slave structure is based on the Actor-Agent-Supplier variant of the Actor-Supplier design pattern. The client can be compared with an actor, the master with the agent, and the slaves with the suppliers. The Master-Slave design pattern can be implemented most efficiently within parallel and distributed software systems. In such systems all slaves can be executed in parallel, either in different processes or on different machines, which increases the power and efficiency of the structure introduced by the pattern. However, this does not mean that the pattern cannot be used in nondistributed software systems effectively. For example, when it is necessary to select among results computed according to different algorithms, it may be sufficient to calculate these results sequentially.

A problem may arise if the various slaves rely on slave-specific types in their public interfaces. To achieve a flexible configurability of the master with different slaves, such slave components have to be encapsulated by wrappers or provided with an adapter. This may cause several problems, however. First, the structure becomes more complex and inefficient, because additional components need to be introduced. Second, wrappers and adapters have a tendency to spread [Hölzle93]. A better solution to this problem is to use only built-in types of the selected programming language within the slaves' public interfaces, or make the interfaces configurable with generic or template types that can be defined by the master. However, this solution does not solve the problem completely.

See Also   Actor-Supplier pattern, Composite-Part pattern, Envelope-Letter pattern. (See Buschmann+94.)

REFERENCES

[ATM93] Siemens AG, Komplexspezifikation ATM-Switch, internal document, Siemens AG, 1993.

[Black93] Andrew P. Black and Mark P. Immel. "Encapsulating Plurality." *ECOOP 7 Proceedings.* Berlin: Springer-Verlag, 1992, pp. 57–79.

[Buschmann+94] F. Buschmann and R. Meunier. "A System of Patterns." Chapter 17, this volume.

[Buschmann+95] F. Buschmann, C. Jäkel, R. Meunier, H. Rohnert, and M. Stal. "Principles and Foundations for Object-Oriented Software Architecture." In preparation.

[Hölzle93] Urs Hölzle. "Integrating Independently Developed Components in Object-Oriented Languages." *ECOOP 7 Proceedings*. Berlin: Springer-Verlag, 1993, pp. 36–56.

[Meyer+88] Walter Meyer and Siegfried Paul. "Objektorientierung in der Automatisierungstechnik. "Laboratory report, Siemens AG, ZFE IS SOF 3, 1988.

Frank Buschmann can be reached at Siemens AG, Corporate Research and Development Department: ZFE BT SE 2, Otto Hahn Ring 6, 81730 Munich, Germany; frank.buschmann@zfe.siemens.de.

BUSINESS OBJECTS

PART 3 The chapters in Part 3 focus on problems for a particular application area, namely business software. We have organized most of the other chapters around solution constructs; here, we group the patterns for the community they address.

Ward Cunningham's CHECKS pattern language (Chapter 10) provides a pragmatic strategy for separating valid input from invalid input. The CHECKS language does not try to solve the entire problem domain (e.g., writing error handlers). Instead, it focuses on dealing with the wide range of values that a real "industrial-strength" program must face. The form and style of the CHECKS language set a good example for small pattern languages: the patterns are small but powerful, and the pattern language makes clear the relationship between them. Though the pattern adopts an object-oriented vocabulary, parts of it are equally applicable to a more general level of design. Hardware engineers (and scientific and engineering programmers as well) will recognize relationships between parts of this pattern and the IEEE floating point standard. In a slightly more abstract form, this pattern extends well beyond the business domain to address the much broader question of tolerance for software error values.

William Wake's Account Number (Chapter 11) is a single pattern that develops the rationale for using account numbers in enterprise data designs. It is reminiscent of an old saw that claims many interesting problems in computer science reduce to what's in a name, and can be solved by one more level of indirection (a pattern seen in Dennis DeBruler's Chapter 5). At first glance, account numbers seem like a simple concept. However, the pattern explains account number structuring, using an example that shows how a 10-digit phone number doesn't scale to handle communities of 10 million people who share an area code. This pattern helps explain why the account number on a water bill has 12 digits and four letters in a service area of 75,000 people. It also examines reasonable alternatives to brute-force numbering schemes.

Steve Peterson's Stars pattern language (Chapter 12) provides patterns that support ad hoc queries of data bases that weren't originally designed with ad hoc access in mind. Stars is a rich pattern that touches on enterprise modeling (i.e., making a model of business entities and activities), data base design, objects, and other facets of a broad and mature business perspective. It uses the metaphor of people, places, and things, which is a recurring world model in recent computing literature. Note the similarity between this language's Whole Business Entities pattern, and the Whole Value pattern from CHECKS. In addition, Stars is one of many patterns that deal with data duplication; compare Chapters 5 and 8 with the Stars patterns.

These three business patterns capture a tiny fraction of one of the largest and richest computing domains today. As the pattern form matures, and as business computing, distributed processing, and telecommunications become more tightly integrated, we are likely to see greater coupling between business object patterns and patterns with other legacies.

The CHECKS Pattern Language of Information Integrity

10

Ward Cunningham

Any program that accepts user input needs to separate good input from bad and make sure that little of the latter gets recorded. The CHECKS pattern language tells how to make such checks without complicating programs and compromising future flexibility.

The language has eleven patterns, presented here in three sections. The first section describes values as they should be captured by the user interface and used within the domain model. The second and third sections discuss detecting and correcting mistakes, first during data entry and then after posting or publication. The patterns draw from the author's experience developing financial software in Smalltalk. They are written as if they are part of a larger language, and therefore they may seem sketchy or incomplete. This paper is as much an experiment in the selection and linking of patterns as an attempt to communicate practical knowledge.

Copyright © Ward Cunningham. All Rights Reserved.

SECTION 1. First, consider quantities used by the domain model. Your domain code must express the "logic" of the business in its richest (often illogical) detail. Every clause of every statement should be motivated by some business fact of life. Other concerns will be pushed into the specialized values described in this section or pulled out into objects described later. This section discusses these patterns:

1.   Whole Value
2.   Exceptional Value
3.   Meaningless Behavior

---

1. WHOLE VALUE

Besides using the handful of literal values offered by the language (numbers, strings, true and false) and an even smaller complement of objects normally used as values (date, time, point), you will make and use new objects with this pattern that represent the meaningful quantities of your business. These values (like currency, calendar periods, or telephone numbers) will carry whole, useful chunks of information from the user interface to the domain model.

When parameterizing or otherwise quantifying a business (domain) model, there remains an overwhelming desire to express these parameters in the most fundamental units of computation. Not only is this no longer necessary (it was standard practice in languages with weak or no abstraction), it actually interferes with smooth and proper communication between the parts of your program and between the program and its users. Because bits, strings, and numbers can be used to represent almost anything, any one in isolation means almost nothing.

Therefore: Construct specialized values to quantify your domain model and use these values as the arguments of their messages and as the units of input and output. Make sure these objects capture the whole quantity, with all its implications beyond merely magnitude; but keep them independent of any particular domain. (The word *value* here implies that these objects do not have an identity of importance.) Include format converters in your user interface (or better yet, in your field and cell widgets) that can correctly and reliably construct these objects on input and print them on output. Do not expect your domain model to handle string or numeric representations of the same information. Consider these messages and answers:

the message: `contractDurationInDays`

answers: 21

the message: `contractDurationInDaysAsString`

answers: `'21'`

Both of these messages use a wordy protocol and return answers in quantities devoid of meaning. The following, simpler message returns a whole value with an obvious, isolated meaning:

the message: `contractDuration`

answers: `Weeks(3)`

You will find that these objects will capture some of the irregularity and (possibly) ambiguity of the domain model. Expect particular classes to grow into hierarchies over time, but do not extend whole values to include nonapplicable or exceptional quantities better represented by an Exceptional Value (2). Also, avoid undue reasoning regarding inappropriate combinations of values, so long as Meaningless Behavior (3) will eventually result.

2. EXCEPTIONAL VALUE

A business model will normally be composed of a basic case or abstraction that is specialized and/or refined to capture the diversity present in the business. However, there will often be circumstances where the inclusion of all business possibilities in the class hierarchy would be confusing, difficult, or otherwise inappropriate. You will therefore at times need to extend the range of an attribute beyond that offered by a Whole Value (1). Consider a pollster who collects answers like "agree," "strongly agree," and so on. Answers that defy quantification, like "illegible" or "refused," are better represented outside the range of values, no matter how fuzzy they may be. However, the structure of a domain model should leave a place for this sort of missing data, for it may appear later. In fact, missing values are impossible to avoid during the creation (data entry) of all but the most trivial domain models.

Therefore: Use one or more distinguished values to represent exceptional circumstances. Exceptional values should either accept all messages, answering most of them with another exceptional value, or reject all messages (with `does not understand`), with the possible exception of identifying protocols like `isNil` or `printOn:`. Interface widgets should produce `nil` on blank input and produce blank, given `nil`, on output. Domain models should accept `nil` or other exceptional values as legal input, at least temporarily. In Smalltalk it is possible to make refinements of `UndefinedObject` that can carry an explanation. If you do, note that `aValue == nil` no longer means the same thing as `aValue isNil`.

```
purchaseDate
        ^(buys := self trades select: [:each | each isPurchase])
        size <<= 1
                ifTrue: [buys first settleDate]
                ifFalse: [ExceptionalValue reporting: 'various']
```

Exceptional values simplify the domain model hierarchy and method structure. It should not be necessary to explicitly test for exceptional values in methods, because they will either absorb messages or produce Meaningless Behavior (3). The little exceptional-value handling that is required can be concentrated extremely close to the user interface. For example, the report writer needs to detect exceptional values to correctly compute a weighted average. Properly objectified, the WeightedAverageColumn object can perform this computation on behalf of any domain object and thereby separate concerns. Deferred Validation (6) is responsible for testing completeness, recognizing that Hypothetical Publication (8) may not require completeness.

3. MEANINGLESS BEHAVIOR

Given that the Whole Values (1) used to quantify your business logic will exhibit subtle variations in behavior and that Exceptional Values (2) may appear throughout the computations, it is possible that the methods you write will stumble in circumstances you cannot foresee. Keep in mind that the rules of business apply only selectively, and that the evolution of your business practices can wiggle around even those rules that "must" apply. In your domain models you are chartered to express business logic with no more complexity than its original conception or current expression.

Therefore: Write methods without concern for possible failure. Expect the input/output widgets that initiate computation to recover from failure and continue processing. Output will remain blank, because any other output would be an attempt to attach meaning to meaningless behavior. Users will interpret unexpected blanks to mean that inputs do not apply and/or outputs are unavailable.

Trying to be meaningful:

```
weightedAverageCost
        |total weight|
        total := self weightedTotalCost.
        total isCurrency ifFalse:
                [^ExceptionalValue reporting: 'N/A'].
        weight := self totalWeight.
        (weight isNumber and: [weight isZero not]) ifFalse:
                [^ExceptionalValue reporting: 'Empty'].
        ^total / weight
```

Accepting possible meaninglessness:

```
weightedAverageCost
        ^self weightedTotalCost / self totalWeight
```

Note: Some readers have assumed that this pattern is about writing error handlers. It is not. It is about writing domain methods in the presence of diversity. It does assume that a near trivial error handler is in place in the input/output system, which is not always the case. You can view meaningless behavior as an alternate implementation of Exceptional Value (2), and in many cases the two are indistinguishable to the user. Choose meaningless behavior unless a condition can be anticipated that has domain meaning (as opposed to merely operational meaning, such as *not-yet-filled-out*). At times there may be something very wrong inside the program, so it is important that some clues surface. Echo Back (4) exposes failure by echoing blank. Serious trouble will cause input screens that report Visible Implications (5) to blank too. Deferred Validation (6) should demand meaningful behavior where corruption of records is the alternative.

SECTION 2. A person must reach through a program's interface in order to manipulate the domain model. Although the interface is itself a program (an interface model and graphical machinery), its purpose is to enable the direct manipulation of the domain model as transparently as possible. The user interface is programmed to create the illusion of control in the mind of the user. To this end it must provide sufficient clues of the model's state so that sensible operation is the norm. These patterns offer the required feedback:

4. Echo Back
5. Visible Implication
6. Deferred Validation
7. Instant Projection
8. Hypothetical Publication

---

4. ECHO BACK

Field and cell widgets will be able to construct and deliver Whole Values (1) to the domain model. As is normal in object-oriented programming, the domain model is free to extract, interpret, or reject any information presented to it. The Echo Back pattern considers the domain model's modest obligation to explain such selection.

You can expect users to enter values in small batches and follow up with a quick review to look for typing errors. This cycle is repeated, but not always with the same batch boundaries. Since you will have no way of knowing exactly when a review takes place (it can be just a quick glance), you must inform users of their success in entering values as each field or cell is processed. Furthermore, when problems occur you must provide this information without disrupting the cycle.

Therefore: Provide for the read-back of any information written into a domain model. Expect field and cell values to be retrieved and echoed back immediately after each entry. Answer reconstructed values using a protocol trivially derived from the original. *Note:* The usual getters & setters convention (that is, `attribute` and `attribute:`) meets this requirement, though the requirement applies to more than just attributes. The full turnaround echo of entered values allows the user to observe any selection or interpretation of entered values.

Do not expect the domain model to explain its interpretation of marginal or incorrect values through notifiers. Such initiative on the part of the model would be misplaced, because it would break the small-batch entry behavior. For example, consider the entry of a pay date:

user types:	5/8/94	
echo back:	05/08/94	(the whole value May 8th, 1994, standard format)

user types:	5/5/94	
echo back:	05/08/94	(the model has chosen the nearest payday, always a Friday)

The leading zeros appear for the simple reason that the original six characters entered are discarded and replaced with the standard print representation of the date echoed back by the model. In the second case the actual numbers are different because the model has chosen to handle bad input by choosing to store the closest legal input in its place. The echo back makes this choice visible. Equally justifiable alternatives would be for the model to ignore the bad value or accept it unconditionally (possibly as an exceptional value). The point here is not that one choice is better than another, but that once a choice is made it must be visible to the user without disruption. Following this point of view further, meaningless setters would be ignored, and meaningless getters would print as blank.

This pattern counters the common practice of ringing bells and flashing lights at the first sign of trouble. You will have plenty of opportunity to protest bad values in Deferred Validation (6).

5. VISIBLE IMPLICATION

By combining the mechanisms of Echo Back (4) with methods that compute attributes, we simplify some entries and improve the effectiveness of the visual review for others.

People find many ways to quantify things. Their measurements often duplicate each other, with only a portion of a measurement actually required to completely characterize a thing. Often there is a sense that some attribute values are more fundamental than other, derived quantities. Other times, the duplicate measurements are simply another way of looking at the thing.

Therefore: Compute derived or redundant quantities implied by those already entered. Display the computed values in fields or cells alongside those that are changed. Where possible, allow a derived quantity to be entered, and work backward to compute the more fundamental measurements. Where the choice of fundamental measure is ambiguous, choose the unspecified over the specified or the more variable over the less variable.

given quantity: 12

and unit price: 6 . 50

compute total: 78 . 00

given quantity: 12

and total: 72

compute unit price: 6 . 00

given unit price: 7 . 00

and total: 77 . 00

compute quantity: 11

Perform this logic in the accessing methods of the domain model. Write getters that try to compute missing values from other inputs:

```
unitPrice
  ^unitPrice notNil
    ifTrue: [unitPrice]
    ifFalse: [total / quantity]
```

Or write setters that transform redundant quantities into the chosen fundamental measurements:

```
total: a Value
  unitPrice isNil
    ifTrue: [unitPrice := total / quantity]
    ifFalse: [quantity := total / unitPrice]
```

Keep the domain model's implication logic simple. Also, do not try to encode field dependencies into the user interface. Instead, simply refresh all fields when any one field changes.

You can expect Meaningless Behavior (3) whenever a thing is incompletely specified. Expect these to show as blanks, which will reinforce the incompleteness in the user's mind. Be sure that all implications can be computed in a small fraction of a second. Longer calculations, or those unsafe to perform on partial specifications, are best left to Instant Projection (7).

6. DEFERRED VALIDATION

The Whole Values (1) that quantify a domain model have been checked to ensure that they are recognizable values. They may also have been further edited for suitability by the domain model and Echoed Back (4) to the user. All of these checks are immediate on entry. There is, however, a class of checking that should be deferred until the last possible moment.

As the user completes a series of entries, there will come a point when he or she wants more extensive action by the computer. This may be a simple query ("How am I doing?"), a pause in activity ("I'll finish this tomorrow"), or a change in responsibility ("You take it from here"). The exact integrity needs will not be known until the computer's action is called for.

Therefore: Delay detailed validation of a domain model until an action is requested. Also, tailor the extent of the validation to the specific action. Saving incomplete work in a private location will not require as much validation as posting finished work in a public place. Validation checks may (but don't always) form a structure in which more complex actions require all the checks of simpler activities—and then some. Write methods for your domain model that encode its anticipated use. Have these methods delegate to simpler validations before making their own checks. Checks should be made in passes, so the most specific problems are reported first. Check to make sure that required quantities are present before checking that they are consistent with others, as we do in this example:

```
validateForPublication: notificationHandler
    self validateForSave: notificationHandler.
    self validateForComputation: notificationHandler.
    self validateVariablesForPublication: notificationHandler.
    self validateRelationsForPublication: notificationHandler
```

Expect the individual validation methods to be complex and subject to regular modification. As such, they may invoke systems designed specifically to validate business rules and restrictions.

Deferred validations are hurdles domain objects must clear on their way into the more public portions of a system. The system demands validation so problems can be brought to the user's attention before publication. The user, on the other hand, may be aware of potential problems beyond those detectable by any strict validation. Instant Projection (7) and Hypothetical Publication (8) offer the user two related strategies for further assessment of information entered into the system.

7. INSTANT PROJECTION

As you collect information for future use, you display the Visible Implications (5) of the entries in the hope that inconsistency will be noticed. Now, as the user's attention shifts from entry to publication, you will want to further carry your prediction of that publication's impact.

We collect information so we can use it later on. *How* it gets used will depend on future events we cannot predict. Even so, we have a notion of a likely chain of events and expectations of how things will probably work out.

Therefore: Offer to project the consequences of any publication before that publication is actually made. You may require the entry of additional assumptions, or you may offer alternative forecasting techniques. Expect the interpretation of a projection to take some effort. Consider opening a "projection window," with various tabulations and summaries. Obsolete tabulations will be useful for observing parameter sensitivities.

A projection anticipates a question that will likely be asked of a soon-to-be-published domain model. Asking the question has no impact on the system other than reporting the answer. In a situation where questions concern multiple publications, Hypothetical Publication (8) offers a versatile, though more cumbersome, alternative to projection.

8. HYPOTHETICAL PUBLICATION

A complicated domain model might pass all Deferred Validations (6) required for publication but still be in doubt if the risks of publication are high. The risks may come more from taking an action described by the model than from incorrectly describing an action already taken. This is all the more reason to consider an elaborate mechanism for detecting mistakes.

When one publishes information (or posts it, or otherwise completes entry of it), that information is expected to travel to many destinations. It may be difficult to assess the full impact of any piece of information out of context and independently of other, also questionable, data.

Therefore: Allow your user to make any number of hypothetical publications that can be released into the system in a controlled way. Limit their distribution to subsystems on the user's own workstation, or clearly mark them for other users as tentative. Provide mechanisms to retract hypotheticals individually or en masse.

Hypothetical Publication can substitute for Instant Projection (7) when forecasting tools are available for published models. Hypotheticals are also useful when large quantities of historical information must be entered and checked.

SECTION 3. Now consider mechanisms that address the long-term integrity of information. Both patterns address one form or another of questionable information. They recognize that many quantities in business are ambiguously specified or otherwise open to interpretation. These patterns lead up to the treatment of accounting integrity (which, unfortunately, has been omitted from this language). These patterns are described in this section:

9. Forecast Confirmation
10. Diagnostic Query

---

9. FORECAST CONFIRMATION

Real-world events often run ahead of their computer model counterparts. When real-world events can be anticipated, it makes sense to mechanically generate appropriate computer models and publish them for public use. However, when the computer system does catch up with reality, it is important that reality be accurately modeled.

Therefore: Provide a mechanism for adjusting and confirming values associated with mechanically published events. Consider this sequence:

Thursday: We predict an automatic deposit of $187,655.47 for Friday.
Friday: We mechanically post $187,655.47 to the cash account.
Monday: Bank records show that $187,655.50 was deposited on Friday. We adjust accordingly.
Later: Records for the month are closed showing no unusual activity.

What is important here is that the best information was available at every moment, even though no one was technically accountable for the posting until after the fact. Forecast confirmations look like original entries from the point of view of accounting integrity. Forecast confirmations apply only to mechanically generated models. Once confirmed, the model's values become subject to accounting integrity.

10. DIAGNOSTIC QUERY

Whole Values (1) and Exceptional Values (2) accumulate useful information that may not always be visible in the user interface due to rounding or other simplification. That information (and more) must be retrievable from the point where values are displayed.

As various business activity records are cross-checked, disagreements are sure to arise; much published information will be in doubt until the nature of any errors is determined. Tracking down a recording error is substantially different from observing the operation of normal business. However, if we turn to completely new observation mechanisms we lose track of the familiar, making for tedious work.

Therefore: Incorporate mechanisms for the diagnostic tracing of every value in the system. Make every display that rounds or summarizes offer the unprocessed values for inspection:

```
Normal display:      67%
Diagnostic display:  66.6454329
Normal display:      652 MM USD EQV
Diagnostic display:  622,456,325.07 USD + 3,624,878,450 JPY +
                     23,549.54 FRF
```

Likewise, where rules and formulas have been applied, make them retrievable from the system itself and format them with variable names and the values bound in the particular calculation. Since the trace will ultimately lead to a value entry, make sure you can report the date, time, and identity of the source:

```
Normal display:      22%
Diagnostic display:  ROR = 22% = internal rate of return
                     ( P0, P1, CFi)
                     P0 = 32,454.55 = market value (1/1/93)
                     P1 = 36,537,39 = market value (12/31/93)
                     CF1 = 354.00 = cash flow
                     (3/15/93, #1000324)
                     CF2 = -400.00 = cash flow
                     (7/31/93, #1000378)
                     CF3 = -100.00 = cash flow
                     (8/30/93, #1000412)
```

Correction of input errors offers another source for diagnostic information. Prior values and the time and identity of all sources should be available for diagnosis.

Ward Cunningham can be reached at Cunningham & Cunningham, Inc., 7830 S.W. 40th Avenue, Portland, OR 97219; ward@c2.com.

11

Account Number:
A Pattern

William C. Wake

PATTERN

If:

- Information (an account) is associated with a person.
- Two different persons might have the same name.
- Traversal is commonly from name to account.

Then:

Assign each person a unique account number.

Problem A single name may correspond to many people. Also, each person may use a number of different names, depending on the situation. We want to examine or update account information for a particular person. Given that person's name, how do we find the corresponding account object?

Copyright © 1994 William C. Wake. All Rights Reserved.

Forces   **Account search** We often want to go from a person's name to the corresponding account. For example, when you go to a doctor's office, they'll ask for your name so they can locate your medical records.

Shared names Any particular name may be shared by many people. Almost any American phone book will list more than one John Smith, for example.

Multiple names A person may have many valid names, including a formal name used on legal documents, an everyday name, a maiden name, a nickname, a pen name, a stage name, and many others. Depending on the situation, a person may use any of these.

Many-to-many relationship Thus, names and people are in a many-to-many relationship, as illustrated in Figure 1.

No unique attributes Not only are names insufficient to identify people, no other combination of attributes of a Person object is guaranteed unique. For example, two people named John Smith might have the same birthday, live at the same address, and share a telephone. And even where attributes sufficient for identification do exist, it may be socially infeasible or too expensive to use them: people are not willing to have their DNA sampled just to obtain a library card.

Solution   Rather than depending on a person's name or other attributes, we introduce an artificial name: an account number (see Figure 2).

Assign exactly one account number to each person, and assign each account number at most once.

Name: the object encapsulating a name.

FIGURE 1 Names and people: a many-to-many relationship

FIGURE 2 An account number is an artificial name.

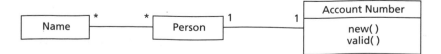

Person: the object representing a person. In addition to being related to a set of Names, the Person object is in one-to-one correspondence to an AccountNumber object.

AccountNumber: the generated account number. The AccountNumber class must be able to issue new numbers and validate whether a supposed AccountNumber is in fact valid.

Collaborations

- Given a name, we can identify a set of "matching" people. If there is more than one person in that set, we can use the account number (and possibly other attributes) to select among them.

- Alternatively, given a valid account number, there is exactly one corresponding person, and we can verify the name through the Person object.

Implementation

Numbers or not? It's not necessary for account numbers to be strictly numeric.

Fixed or variable length? Account numbers are often of a fixed length. This is convenient for the software (and hardware) that must work with these numbers. However, it limits expansion, and it makes the choice of how many digits an important up-front decision. Some numbering schemes don't have this restriction. For example, the ISO object identifier numbering scheme [Rose] uses a hierarchical numbering scheme of essentially unlimited depth.

Unstructured or structured numbers? One way to issue account numbers is to have a central issuer maintain a counter, starting at 1 (or some other convenient number), and issue successive numbers. This is an unstructured system: there is no relationship between the number and the account holder or issuer.

An alternative is to develop structured numbers. One or more digits are reserved for particular issuers or specific attributes of the account holder. Each issuer is responsible for a certain range of numbers. For example, credit card numbers are sixteen digits long; the first digit indicates the type of credit card (such as MasterCard or Visa). This method lets each issuer choose its numbers independently. A disadvantage is that the account numbers tend to be larger, to enable easy encoding of fields.

How many digits? If an account number has a fixed length, it should accommodate the maximum potential number of accounts. Particularly with fixed-length, structured numbers, you should try to ensure that one group won't run out while another has numbers to spare.

Consider the case of telephone numbers in the United States [Townson]. (The following is an example of assigning numbers, but not of the Account Number pattern.) U.S. telephone numbers are structured as a three-digit area code and a seven-digit local number. In principle this allows for ten billion numbers. This would seem sufficient: enough to give every person in the world two phone numbers. However, because of the way numbers are assigned, only about a billion numbers are actually available. (Plans are in place to expand this to about six billion numbers.)

Unfortunately, there are only ten million numbers within each area code. Large metropolitan areas approach having this many occupants. These areas run out of numbers, while smaller areas may have numbers to spare. Because area codes are limited to specific geographic regions, a region with extra numbers can't share them with a region that needs them.

Making things even worse, many people need more than one phone number (perhaps one for home and one for work). The phone system was originally designed for people, but fax machines and computers need telephone numbers as well. In addition, companies need phone numbers that are not tied to any particular person.

Thus, the demand for telephone numbers has outstripped the supply. Ten billion numbers seems like a lot, until you start restricting them, structuring them, and providing multiple numbers for individual persons. Changing the numbering scheme has been expensive and time-consuming.

Variations

One name per person. We're often not interested in recording all the names for a person; a single, "formal" name may be sufficient. This will make `Name:Person` a one-to-many relationship. While this reduces storage and management requirements, it doesn't affect the fundamental problem of shared names.

When restricting people to one name each, we may let someone change their name, but we will not normally issue a new account number.

Attributes of name relationships. The `Name:Person` relationship can be very complicated: the relation may have attributes indicating when the name is valid, the type of name, and so on.

Relationships between names. The Account Number pattern can describe a situation in which various names are related to a person but not to other names. Thus while we might recognize *Jack* as a possible nickname for *John*, not every person named John will use that nickname. However, in some situations we are interested solely in the names themselves. If we were developing a database of possibly related names, for example, *John* and *Jack* might be linked together independent of any particular person.

Examples   **Accounting systems for businesses.** Most business accounting systems (for utility companies, credit card companies, and so on) issue account numbers for people rather than trying to locate records by names.

Keys in databases. In a database, each record is identified by a key that is unique to that particular record. The key consists of a combination of one or more attributes of the record. The non-key attributes correspond to Name, the record itself to Person, and the key to AccountNumber.

Social Security numbers. In the United States, most citizens have a Social Security number, issued by the government. No one may legally have more than one number. However, this identification number is susceptible to errors and misuse—either by intentional fraud or by unintentional transposition or copying errors. There is no check digit in the coding of these numbers, so almost any nine-digit number is potentially valid [Hibbert].

International Standard Book Number (ISBN). Many publishers use ISBNs to identify their books, as titles aren't unique. This is a ten-digit number, the last digit of which is a check digit [Hamming, pp. 33–34]. (The check digit allows one to detect transpositions of adjacent digits, single substitutions, and several other errors.) In this example, the title of the book corresponds to Name, the book to Person, and the ISBN to AccountNumber.

REFERENCES

[Hamming] Hamming, Richard W. *Coding and Information Theory.* Englewood Cliffs, NJ: Prentice-Hall, 1980.

[Hibbert] Hibbert, Chris. "Social Security Number FAQ." Posted to Usenet newsgroup news.answers, May 3, 1994.

[Rose] Rose, Marshall T. *The Open Book.* Englewood Cliffs, NJ: Prentice-Hall, 1990.

[Townson] Townson, Pat, et al. "How Numbers Are Assigned." In `ftp://lcs.mit.edu/ telecom-archives/areacodes/how.numbers.are.assigned`, March 28, 1990.

ACKNOWLEDGMENTS

This work took place while I was partially supported by National Science Foundation Grant #IRI-9116991.

I'd like to acknowledge discussions with and comments from my advisor, Dr. Ed Fox (Virginia Tech); my brothers, Steve Wake (MSL, Blacksburg, Virginia) and Doug Wake (University of Hawaii); and the conference reviewers and participants.

William C. Wake can be reached at the Department of Computer Science, Virginia Polytechnic Institute, Blacksburg, VA 24060; wakew@cs.vt.edu.

12 Stars: A Pattern Language for Query-Optimized Schemas

Stephen Peterson

For years organizations have deployed and used large on-line transaction processing (OLTP) systems to automate and record their business activity. The challenge now is to allow business analysts—chartered to support decision makers by producing reports—to access this data in an ad hoc manner. While OLTP schemas are optimized for data entry, they seldom provide an acceptable solution for data analysis.

The star-schema concept presented here is the product of many discussions over the years between the author and consultants specializing in decision-support systems (DSS). The star schema has also been called a star-join schema, data cube, data list, grid file, and multidimensional schema by practitioners in the field. The name star schema comes from the pattern formed by entities and relationships on an entity-relationship diagram (ERD): typically there is a business activity in the center of the star, surrounded by the people, places, and things that come together to perform it (forming the star's points).

The star-schema pattern language presented here attempts to provide a method for developing a schema that is easy to query. Seven patterns are presented; all are part of a larger pattern language that supports the field of DSS, a branch of business data processing systems. The seven patterns are discussed in two sections: the first section addresses finding and organizing

Copyright © Sequent Computer Systems, Inc. All Rights Reserved.

relevant factors in the business needing analysis; the second section deals with implementing these factors into a star schema for a query system.

SECTION 1. Analysis. To begin, make a list of those things that are meaningful to your situation. Try to isolate the relevant entities for the part of the business you are responsible for. Your model should contain the name of everything that is readily recognized by anyone working in your area. As the model is refined, it should reflect those activities (and the parties involved in them) that are directly relevant to trends your business influences and is influenced by. The following patterns are discussed in this section:

1. Query-Optimized Database
2. Whole Business Entities
3. Key Business Activities and Influences

---

1. QUERY-OPTIMIZED DATABASE

Whatever your business area, be it sales, marketing, manufacturing, engineering, or whatever, a need will arise to analyze its ongoing operations in order to solve a problem (such as correcting poor performance) or address a need (such as seeking new opportunities). Solutions and opportunities are usually found by analyzing data captured as part of the ongoing activities of the business. This data is usually found in a company's OLTP databases.

OLTP database schema are usually optimized for recording business transactions. The normalization process for OLTP schema design takes descriptions of entities from the business domain and breaks them into a number of small tables; these small tables can then be handled by the database management system (DBMS) in an efficient manner. Breaking up entities into small tables also reduces the amount of redundant data stored in the database, since each table can be joined with other tables to form more than one business entity. Reducing data redundancy means that a single piece of data is stored only once. This avoids the problem of updating multiple copies when data changes.

Two problems arise when you want to query an OLTP schema. First, the fields that describe a particular business entity are distributed among a number of tables, and these need to be joined together in order to form the things you want for your analysis. These joins can require a significant amount of processing by the database system. Second, since these small OLTP tables must be rejoined to form the original entity, there will usually be multiple combinations from which to choose. These multiple ways of joining tables can lead to varying answers when the tables are used in a query. Even if different combinations happen to yield the same answer, the joining process can produce errors in the hands of a person who is not knowledgeable about the details of the schema.

Therefore: Develop a new database that is optimized for the purpose of easy querying rather than for entering and updating data. The new database will most likely have to be implemented on a separate machine from the one that hosts the OLTP database, since long queries could adversely affect data entry if the two databases are run on the same machine. Besides performance, another reason to separate the two types of databases is that the DSS database will need to have stable data in order to perform meaningful analyses. If the DSS is implemented as views on an OLTP database, the data within the views will be constantly changing as the data entry process captures new data and updates old data. The problem with trying to analyze constantly changing data is that you cannot hold some variables constant while selectively changing one or two others in order to see the effects of these variations on the result. This is called the "twinkling data problem."

The new database you develop and the machine it runs on will incur additional costs for ongoing administration and maintenance. The issue of transferring data between the OLTP and DSS databases will also need to be addressed, as the DSS database will need to be refreshed with new data on a periodic basis. Having data from the OLTP system appear on reports generated by the DSS will bring to light errors that occur during the data capture process. These errors will need to be corrected in the OLTP database, either by scanning and cleaning up the data before each transfer to the DSS or, better yet, refining the data capture process to catch and reduce errors at data entry.

The rest of this pattern language is concerned with finding the entities you need to model an easy-to-use schema. Create whole business entities (see Pattern 2) from your OLTP database that are relevant to your domain. Grouping together all of the relevant data for a given entity will reduce the number of joins in a query. In essence, you will denormalize the OLTP schema to a degree that will allow for faster queries. This shouldn't present a problem in the DSS database, since it should only be updated on a periodic basis (usually in a batch mode). Updates to the DSS database can be controlled using batch processing since they are only coming from one source. This is much more manageable than updating an OLTP database, where updates come from multiple sources in an ad hoc fashion.

Once you have a list of reconstituted entities to model your business area, use Key Business Activities and Influences (Pattern 3) to focus on those events, and the factors that influence them, that are critical to your area of responsibility. It is important to make the relationships between these activities and the influences on them simple and clear so that forming queries will be easy and accurate. There should be only one possible join between any two tables, and the meaning of that join should be clear to the person performing the query.

The schema will be developed by defining and implementing two kinds of tables. The first kind of table, called a fact table, will be a transaction history (see Pattern 4) of the key business activity being modeled (see Figure 1). The second kind of table, called a dimension table, will record the people, places, and things (see Pattern 5) that are involved in each kind of transaction. Another dimension table, Time (Pattern 6), is considered separately since it appears frequently in business analysis and deserves special attention. Dimension Roll-up (Pattern 7) is another kind of dimension table; it helps the person querying the database to specify groups of dimension records.

Relationships between patterns can be seen in Figure 2. These relationships show how problems and solutions in one pattern are explained further in subsequent patterns.

2. WHOLE BUSINESS ENTITIES

In order to understand a schema developed for your business, you will need to use easily recognized names for the objects in your query-optimized

FIGURE 1 Generic star schema layout

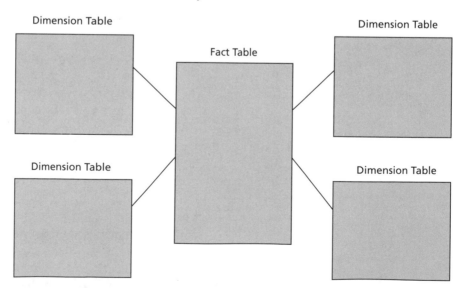

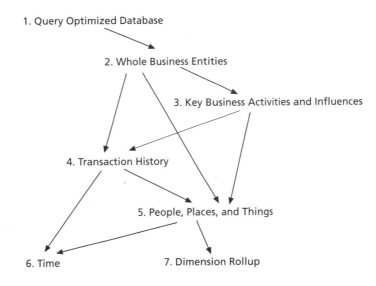

FIGURE 2 Interactions in the Stars pattern language

database (see Pattern 1). Names for the objects in your schema should reflect those things in your environment that you deal with in your day-to-day endeavors. Each object should be whole, in the sense that all of the things that uniquely describe it should be found in one place.

The business entities on your business activity reports are usually scattered into a number of small tables in the OLTP database, because of the need for normalization. The names for these small tables are usually concatenations of abbreviations for the business functions they participate in. Your job in this case, whenever you want to form a query, is like solving a jigsaw puzzle. Unfortunately, the same piece can be used in more than one place, but you only get one copy of each piece. You'll usually need to ask for help from someone intimately familiar with the details of the OLTP schema. This can produce a formidable bottleneck.

Therefore: Find the entities in your domain that are directly relevant to your problem by examining the reports you use to monitor your business. The report titles and column headings are the best places to focus on. As you find these entities, make a list of them. Put a short definition next to each entry. Another place to look is on entity relationship (ER) diagrams of the original analysis done for the OLTP database before it was normalized. The database administrator (DBA) for your OLTP database may have these diagrams available.

Example: **List of entities in a sales model**

Customer	the people and companies we sell to
Product	the things we sell
Sales	a transaction between our company and a customer
Sales planning	setting sales goals and procedures for the coming period
Sales plan	a statement of goals for sales and the steps to achieve those goals
Date of sale	the date of a sales transaction
Distribution channel	the means by which the product was sold to the customer
Salesperson	the person who sold the product to the customer
Competitors	other companies that offer competing products
Sales office	a location where a group of salespeople are managed

The entities you find here will need to be made whole again from the pieces found in the OLTP database. The fact tables and dimension tables will be where you group together the information for each entity. At this point, though, not all of the entries in your list will become tables. You will need to home in on the things that are important to you by finding the key business activities and influences (see Pattern 3) you need to analyze. Don't worry about including too many entities at this point; it is more important to brainstorm and find as many as you can. Entities that seem superfluous at first may lead you to other, useful ones.

3. KEY BUSINESS ACTIVITIES AND INFLUENCES

The activities and their participants you find in your business all have a role in the processes that produce your product. Finding the role of each thing is as important as finding the thing itself. Starting with whole business entities (see Pattern 2), you will characterize these objects according to how they are related to one another. By defining these relationships, you are also defining the role of each thing. The two categories of things that you will be concerned with will be the activities your department is responsible for and the various factors that influence them.

Tables in an OLTP database can have circular references. This usually occurs because normalized tables participate in a number of relationships, since the data in the table is reused. This reuse occurs to reduce data redundancy. What this means is that I can start specifying, in more than one way, the joins between a number of tables that refer to one another in a circular fashion. This can lead to problems, because the order in which I join tables in one query can yield an answer that is different from that of a query using the same tables joined in another order. Depending on the question I'm trying to answer, each pattern of joins may result in an answer that might be right or wrong. Without knowing the meaning of each join beforehand, I can't reliably form a query that will give me the answer I expect. Unfortunately, neither the database nor the query language can help me validate the joins against my intentions, since the meaning of the relationships between tables isn't stored anywhere.

Therefore: Determine the key business activities in your domain and find the people, places, and things (dimensions) that play some part in one or more of those activities. The people, places, and things will be found in the transactions recorded for your key business activities. Each transaction will usually describe who, what, when, and where in relation to the event. These are the simple relationships you need to define between each dimension and its activity. Be careful that the dimensions you choose are related to each other only through the key business activity and not directly. There should be no direct relationships between dimensions except in the case of a Dimension Roll-up (Pattern 7).

In all cases, there should be no circular relationships between the dimensions or the facts, or between any combination of tables. It is important to make the relationship between each dimension table and fact table clear so you can see the effect any one of these dimensions has on your business activity. Your job as an analyst will be to see how a change in the value of one of these dimensions influences your key business activities. Starting from the opposite end, once you spot a trend in a business activity you'll want to identify the changes in value of your dimensions to find correlations between the activity and the dimensions.

Choose the key business activities for your area of responsibility from Whole Business Entities (Pattern 2). The short business entity definitions you entered earlier will help you spot these. Although these activities should already be on your list, you may need to look deeper into your business environment to come up with all the activities you'll need to consider. Limit the key activities you choose to those that are directly related to your department's mission. Some of the activities on your list may be supporting processes for main activities; focus on the main activities, since these will be critical to your business's survival and growth. Each key business activity will become a fact table to hold a transaction history (see Pattern 4) in the query-optimized database you will build.

For each of the main activities you identify, make a list of the people, places, and things related to it. Again, you will probably find these in Whole Business Entities (Pattern 2), but some may not be present there and will only be found through further analysis. Also, be sure to look at your short definition for each item, as it will usually include descriptive words that will give you important clues for finding the people, places, and things you are looking for. Each of these will become a dimension table in the query-optimized database. The following example assumes that sales is the key business activity you should focus on from the example list in Whole Business Entities (Pattern 2).

Example: **List of people, places, and things involved in sales**

Customer

Distribution channel

Product

Salesperson

SECTION 2. Implementation. In order to start analyzing your business model, each relevant business entity needs to be represented in your query system. Each entity should take the form of a table or the field of a table (whichever is appropriate for your particular query system). Each table should be complete insofar as when a report is created all the fields that need to appear on the report, or are needed to specify the report, are available. The tables will be used in the following patterns:

4. Transaction History
5. People, Places, and Things
6. Time
7. Dimension Roll-up

---

4. TRANSACTION HISTORY

Some activities are critical to the life of your business. These activities, along with the factors that influence them, are your key business activities and influences (see Pattern 3). For any specific activity, it is convenient to have one place where you can refer to all of its dimensions (see Figure 3). You need to build a fact table to contain these references—this will be the center of your star. In addition, the transactions that are recorded for each activity should capture the units of work that are the basis for measuring your business's output. These are the "facts" about the transaction.

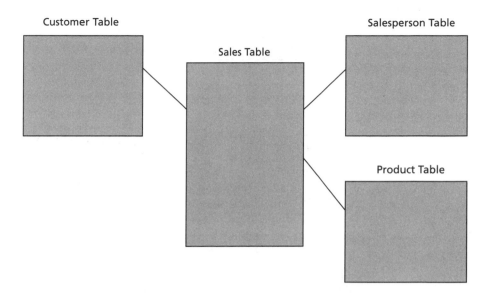

Customer Table   Salesperson Table

Sales Table

Product Table

FIGURE 3 An outline of a star schema for sales

In an OLTP schema, the facts representing your key business activities and their dimensions may be scattered throughout the database because of the normalization process. Chains of tables may have to be joined together in order to find all the relevant facts and dimensions. This chain may include tables that are irrelevant to your business question; they may be needed, however, simply because they contain references to other tables in your query. This can be wasteful in terms of performing expensive joining processing when producing your whole business entities (see Pattern 2). In addition, the joining process itself can be error prone, as discussed in Key Business Activities and Influences (Pattern 3).

Therefore: Construct a fact table for each business activity that is relevant to your analysis. Each fact table will contain the transaction history for the activity being modeled. Put the numeric data, or facts, that are unique to the transaction in the fact table. The fact table is the agent that binds together all the pertinent facts and dimensions for a transaction (see Figure 4). It describes the who, what, when, and where by pointing to the dimension tables, and it also contains the amounts of the things that changed hands between the parties of the transaction. Note that it is important at this point to confirm with a person knowledgeable about the details of the OLTP schema, typically the DBA, that the data needed to build the fact and dimension tables exists in corporate databases.

Facts are usually numeric quantities that describe how much of a product has been sold and how much money has been received for the product. This

Sales Table

Customer
Salesperson
Date of Sale
Product
Quantity Sold
Total Amount($)
Discount

FIGURE 4 Example of the sales table layout

numeric data can be summed when a group of fact records are selected. This sum represents the total activity for a particular set of criteria specified in the query. Data that is descriptive in nature, like textual names and enumerated type codes, should be placed in the appropriate dimension table. Sometimes there will be descriptive data that isn't related to any of the dimensions but is nevertheless associated with the transaction. Such hard-to-place data will usually be put in the fact table when there are not enough fields to form another dimension table. In some instances facts will not be numeric values but instead will consist only of coded fields that capture one of a predefined set of values. In programming terms this is called a field containing an enumerated type. For instance, a fact table storing the results of an opinion poll would contain mostly enumerated types.

The fact table should have an ID field for each dimension representing a person, place, or thing (see Pattern 5) related to the transaction. The IDs can be used in two ways. An ID in the fact table can be used to retrieve descriptive information from the dimension table. This is useful when you want to specify on a report the who, what, where, or when of a transaction. Another use of an ID field is to find out what has taken place for a combination of people, places, or things. This is accomplished by taking the ID values from each dimension table and matching their combinations against those stored in the records of the fact table.

The relationship of the records in a dimension table to the records in the fact table is one-to-many: one record from a dimension table can be related to many records in the fact table. The opposite will usually not be true, since most of the time you will only want to identify a single person, place, or thing involved in a transaction, to simplify your analysis. In the case of the dimension of time, for example, a transaction will usually only occur at one particular time.

When transferring data from an OLTP database to a query-optimized database (that is, the DSS), you will need to keep in mind that you will probably be aggregating data from the OLTP database. The OLTP database will have data that is captured at the time each transaction occurs. If the transactions occur daily, then the OLTP data will be stored daily, as they occur. If the time frame (see Pattern 6) for storing data in the query-optimized database covers a longer period, then you will need to aggregate the OLTP data while you make your periodic batch transfers.

Here's an example of the need for aggregation. Suppose you are storing monthly sales transaction records in your DSS. You have determined that the dimensions for sales are customer, salesperson, and product. Therefore you will need to aggregate the daily OLTP records into a monthly record for each combination of customer, salesperson, and product that produced a transaction. You would calculate the total number of records that could possibly be created for this fact table by multiplying the total number of records for each of the time unit (month), customer, salesperson, and product dimensions together: 12 months × 10 customers × 20 salespeople × 5 products = 12,000 possible records. Since, typically, not all of these possible combinations will occur every month, there will only be a fraction of that number of records created for each month.

5. PEOPLE, PLACES, AND THINGS

An important part of analyzing your business will be to detect trends in key business activities and influences (see Pattern 3). In order to understand the cause of a trend, you will have to look at the different dimensions of the activity and discover correlations between the data values in the dimension tables and the fact table. Here is where you will create those dimension tables that describe the people, places, and things that each record in the fact table will reference. The dimension tables are the points of the star.

In an OLTP schema, the information describing a dimension is usually scattered throughout a number of tables. This can make generating reports a challenge, as the information needed for a report must be constructed by joining together tables that contain the needed fields. Besides the complexity of properly determining the joins, the joining process itself is computationally expensive. Without the capability to easily query your business data in an ad hoc manner with a reasonable response time, the process of analyzing your data may be prohibitive.

Therefore: Develop a table for each person, place, or thing that has a part in the transactions you are examining. These dimension tables should model a person, place, or thing completely, insofar as they will contain all the fields you need for your queries. The fields will hold quantitative and qualitative values that will be used to display information on reports and to filter records for calculations. (See the sales star schema for examples of dimension tables.)

Since each record in a dimension table represents a real thing in your business, you should have an ID field for each record that contains a value that uniquely identifies it. The ID field will be used in the fact table as well, so that records between the two tables can be joined. Therefore, querying a database with a star schema entails starting from the points of the star (the dimension tables) and specifying criteria for each point so as to select a particular set of records from the center of the star (the fact table). The following example uses the sales star schema illustrated in Figure 5.

```
SELECT      c.Customer_ID, Customer_Name,
            Address, sum(Quantity_Sold)
FROM        Sales s, Time t, Product p, Customer c
WHERE       Month = 3
AND         Year = 1993
AND         UPC_Code = 12678754390     -- Gum Balls
AND         s.Time_ID = t.Time_ID
AND         s.Customer_ID = c.Customer_ID
AND         s.Product_ID = p.Product_ID
GROUP BY    c.Customer_ID
ORDER BY    c.Customer_ID;
```

In this example the name and address of each customer who bought gum balls is found, along with the total quantity purchased in the month of March 1993, using SQL syntax. Implicit in the example is the fact that all of the dimensions are related to each other only through the sales fact table. Thus, forming queries using this type of schema consists of having a set of simple one-way joins, from each dimension to the fact table. Since no circular joins between tables are possible, at least (if you design your schema correctly) there is no ambiguity about where to start querying. Only in cases where there is a dimension roll-up (see Pattern 7) will there be a need to directly relate the dimension tables to one another without first relating both dimension tables to the fact table.

In general, when analyzing a trend in one of your fact tables, start your query by specifying values for some of your dimension tables (constrain them, in other words), and look for correlations in the data values between the unconstrained dimensions and the fact table. For example, if you wanted to find out why a particular product wasn't selling well in a given sales office, you could start by holding the product and time constant and listing the types of distribution channels available for all sales offices. It could turn out that the distribution channel mix in the poorly performing sales office is significantly different from that of the other sales offices, giving you a starting point for further investigation. This process of investigation is called "drilling down" into the data.

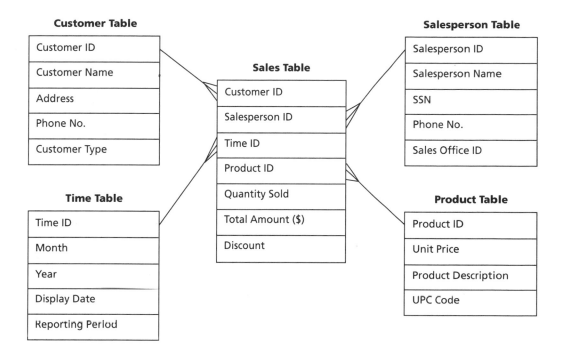

FIGURE 5 Example of a sales star schema

6. TIME

In order to measure changes in business activity, data from a range of specified times must be analyzed. Changes in activity may reveal a trend over a series of subsequent time periods. Such trends will mark places to look for causal relationships between activities and their dimensions.

Transactions in an OLTP database usually are not grouped by inherent time periods, since all that is needed is a running activity log from which to track a continuous process. On the other hand, when analyzing a particular business activity, it is best to deal with groups of transactions in order to get a feel for what's going on without getting bogged down in details. Another problem in analyzing OLTP data is that time can vary between transactions, since they are entered in an ad hoc manner. Nevertheless, the units of time you chose to group transactions should be uniform so that direct comparisons can be made between time periods. These uniform units of time should not be chosen arbitrarily, but should be meaningful to your analysis.

Therefore: Build a dimension table containing units of time that correspond to some significant event in your business. These will usually be the reporting periods management expects in summaries of the business's activity. The unit of time chosen will determine the level at which your transaction data will be aggregated in your transaction history (see Pattern 4). For example, if you choose months (since reports are made to upper management monthly), then daily transactions from the OLTP database will need to be aggregated into monthly transactions. For efficiency, when the data is loaded into your fact table it should be ordered by month so that it doesn't have to be sorted for each query.

7. DIMENSION ROLL-UP

There will be times when you'll want to "roll up," or aggregate, the level of activity in your business so that you can see the "big picture" for some group of records found in one of your dimension tables. This higher level of aggregation is a convenient technique used in querying. The convenience comes from only having to specify one record in the roll-up table to represent many records in the associated dimension table.

The transaction history (see Pattern 4) will already have been modeled, with some level of aggregation assumed. These aggregation assumptions are based on intuition about how the data will normally be used. For instance, if you are mainly concerned with tracking the performance of individual sales-people, your fact table will be defined for transactions that reflect the sales of individual salespeople. If the requirement arises to analyze sales perform-ance by geographic area, like sales offices, then all the sales for the sales-people in each office will need to be analyzed together. Specifying each salesperson in every sales office can be laborious. On the other hand, designating a field in the salesperson table for a coded value signifying a particular sales office may be inadequate, since there may be other informa-tion about the sales office that will need to appear on a report.

Therefore: Design a table for the new entity representing the larger organi-zation that will encompass your existing business dimension. As with People, Places, and Things (Pattern 5), this new table should include all the information related to the thing to be included on a report or used as a filtering criterion in a query. You may find that these kinds of things are already listed in your whole business entities (see Pattern 2).

Like all the dimension tables found in People, Places, and Things (Pattern 5), the table should have an ID field that will uniquely identify each record. This ID field will also be found in the dimension table for which it aggregates records (see Figure 6). By having the two tables related by a common ID field, you will be able to easily specify a group of records in the lower-level dimension table by specifying the appropriate value for the ID field in the dimension roll-up

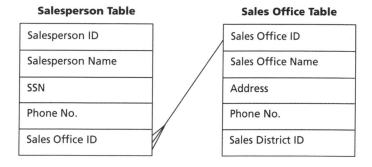

FIGURE 6 Example of a sales office table

table. Each of these lower-level dimension records will in turn be related to their associated records in the fact table, since these too are related by a common ID field. The fact records can then be summed to yield a quantity that relates back to the roll-up dimension. Note that roll-up dimensions can be nested to an arbitrary depth to reflect your business's structure.

The following example uses the sales office table to find out the total dollar amount of gum balls the Portland sales office sold in the month of March 1993, using SQL syntax:

```
SELECT      Sales_Office_Name, Product_Description,
            sum(Total_Amount)
FROM        Sales s, Time t, Product p,
            Salesperson sp, Sales_Office so
WHERE       Month = 3
AND         Year = 1993
AND         UPC_Code = 12678754390    - - Gum Balls
AND         Sales_Office_Name = 'Portland'
AND         s.Time_ID = t.Time_ID
AND         s.Salesperson_ID = sp.Salesperson_ID
AND         sp.Sales_Office_ID = so.Sales_Office_ID
AND         s.Product_ID = p.Product_ID
GROUP BY    Sales_Office_Name;
```

Stephen Peterson can be reached at Sequent Computer Systems, 15450 S.W. Koll Parkway, Beaverton, OR 97006; stevep@sequent.com.

PROCESS AND ORGANIZATION

PART 4 When we named this book, we wanted the title to encompass software-related activities that transcend programming. The chapters in Part 4 go beyond software design per se to present pattern languages of software development processes and organizational pragmatics. These pattern languages apply to people building and using software, the relationships between these people, and the relationships between people and software.

The process and organization patterns in this section abstract away from detailed design and implementation concerns to capture successful management practices that support iterative software development. These patterns address general development problems that all software organizations must face. In contrast, most of the other sections of this book focus on patterns that capture more concrete design artifacts. Owing to the scope of the subject matter, the patterns in this section have notable differences from other sections. For example, the section contains no patterns in isolation, only pattern languages. This breadth does not detract from the directness or pragmatism of these patterns. In general, the ability to capture recurring themes at multiple levels of abstraction is an important contribution to design patterns.

The title of this part is "Process and Organization," but it might as well have been "Patterns Supporting Design." Design is a process whose products include architectures and implementations. A design process is an inherently creative activity that often engages many players. It is during the design process that software developers use the patterns presented elsewhere in this book.

Each of the pattern languages in Part 4 addresses iterative software development. Iterative development is not a new concept, but it has found newfound credibility and insights in the context of design patterns. In particular, the movement away from a "waterfall" development model (characterized by linear process tasks) to an iterative development model provides a fertile field for patterns as a tool to capture, evaluate, and prescribe successful software development processes. The pattern languages of this section provide an interesting foundation for further work in this area.

Chapter 13, by James Coplien, is based in part on well-known patterns of successful software development organizations. Part of his paper is based on a two-year research program to discover recurring patterns in highly productive and successful organizations. Cope's pattern language suggests the overall structures of a healthy work group of individuals building software. The languages take cues not only from software development but from the socio-urban planning models of Christopher Alexander, and from social network analysis techniques used in the social sciences. The language generates a sociological structure—a culture—but stops short of the day-to-day details that generate a method.

Chapter 14, by Brian Foote and William Opdyke, fits well in Part 4 because it focuses on the object-oriented life cycle. It proposes a long-term iterative development process that starts with foresighted analysis, incorporates prototyping, expands the prototype into an implementation, and then consolidates the implementation. (Compare these steps to ones in Kent Beck's patterns: "Make it run; make it right; make it fast; make it small"). The chapter also contains a tantalizing list of design rules and refactoring patterns that are expanded in the references. Like RAPPeL (see below), this language marries a broad view of software development with practical design rules that shape classes and their relationships.

Bruce Whitenack's RAPPeL language (Chapter 15) captures a specific development culture at Knowledge Systems Corporation. His language addresses notations and detailed practices (e.g., Moore and Harrell machine models) as well as broad business concerns. RAPPeL is a design method that encompasses organizational and process concerns, as well as object-oriented design rules. It can be used both by those shaping an organization and by those who belong to the organization and do its work. RAPPeL's pattern form puts both kinds of users in the driver's seat, where they can use their contextual insight and experience to apply the language tastefully. In contrast, traditional design methods often overconstrain users by prescribing a single solution process without considering the context in which the solution is applied. The pattern languages described by Cope and Bruce have broad overlap: e.g., compare Bruce's Use Case Descriptions, Prototypes, and CRC Cards map to Cope's Scenarios Define Problem, Prototype, and Group Validation, respectively.

Norm Kerth's Caterpillar's Fate (Chapter 16) conjures the image of a magical transformation from caterpillar (analysis) to butterfly (completed design). This pattern language tells how to keep from contaminating analysis with premature design structuring. This process-savvy perspective earns this chapter a spot in this part of the book. Like RAPPeL, Caterpillar's Fate also provides software engineering guidelines and design rules that transform analysis abstractions into objects. Many of Norm's patterns are reminiscent of the system and distributed processing patterns in Part 2 and foreshadow the tone of the architecture and communication patterns in Part 6. His patterns go beyond a general method to generate a discipline for building software systems. The discipline is broad (from analysis all the way to some sticky engineering concerns) yet specific (it tells what modeling techniques apply to which circumstances; it tells when to use critical regions). Norm ends by asking if the Caterpillar's Fate technique, which has proved itself under the guiding hand of a software consultant, can be internalized and applied by others. He looks to us for the answer.

The study of process and organization is a mature domain that has been waiting for broad acceptance of the pattern form to find new expression. Organizational analysis is a much more mature discipline than software. For instance, *The Art of War* by Sun Tzu is a centuries-old collection of patterns about military organizations that continue to apply to business organizations today. More recent organizational sciences such as cultural anthropology have well-developed organizational models based on patterns. The volume of the pattern languages in this section suggests that the process and organization domain is especially ripe for patterns.

A Generative Development-Process Pattern Language

13

James O. Coplien

1. INTRODUCTION

This paper introduces a family of patterns that can be used to shape a new organization and its development processes. Patterns support emerging techniques in the software design community, where they are finding a new home as a way of understanding and creating computer programs. There is an increasing awareness that new program-structuring techniques must be supported by suitable management techniques and appropriate organization structures; organizational patterns are one powerful way to capture these.

Patterns are particularly suitable for organizational construction and evolution. Patterns form the basis of much modern cultural anthropology, which defines a culture in terms of its patterns of relationships. Also, while the works of Christopher Alexander discuss how patterns in town planning and architecture support human enterprises and interactions (Alexander 1979), it can be said that organization is the analogue to architecture in contemporary professional organizations. Organizational patterns have a first-order effect on the ability of people to carry out their work. We believe

Copyright © 1995 AT&T. All Rights Reserved.

that the physical architecture of office and industrial buildings is the dual of the organizational patterns; these two worlds cross in the work of Thomas Allen at MIT (Allen 1977).

There is nothing new in taking a pattern perspective on organizational analysis. What is novel about the work presented here is its attempt to use patterns in a generative way. All architecture is fundamentally concerned with control (Carlin 1994). Here we use organizational architecture to supplant business processes as an (indirect) means of controlling people in an organization.

Patterns not only help us understand existing organizations, they also help us build new ones. A good set of organizational patterns helps (indirectly) to generate the right process; this indirectness is at the core of Alexander's generative patterns. In fact, organizational patterns might provide the most promising generative approach for software architecture as well. Alexander notes that architectures "can't be made, but only generated, indirectly, by the ordinary actions of the people, just as a flower cannot be made, but only generated from the seed" (Alexander 1979, p. xi). A set of simple patterns can cause complex emergent behavior. As with many of the principles in *Timeless Way*, this is curiously reminiscent of the Way of Nonaction *(Yin)* of the Tao-te-ching; it is also reflected in the triple-loop thinking of Swieringa and Wierdsma's organizational learning model (Swieringa and Wierdsma, 1992).

As of this writing such work is speculative: only limited use has been made of these patterns in formulating new organizations. The "goodness" or "badness" of such patterns is difficult to test by experimentation. First, any metric of organizational goodness is necessarily multidimensional and complex. Second, it is difficult to design large-scale social experiments that could validate patterns, without creating an explosion in the number of control variables. Third, such an experiment would require a long-term commitment (months or years), which is more than most software organizations are willing to make, in light of fragile and evolving markets.

For these reasons we must fall back on case studies and common sense. I look at recurring patterns of interactions in organizations, note recurring matches between those patterns and some measure of "goodness," and then do an analysis to explain the correlation. The patterns presented here all combine empirical observations with a rationale that explains them. My claim that the language as a whole captures the essential characteristics of high-productivity organizations has been validated by the CEOs of many small, highly productive organizations who have read these patterns.

The patterns also follow informal conventions that have been established in patterns practice. Each pattern is stated as a problem or an opportunity. Each pattern is analyzed for the forces at play within it. Each pattern instructs us to do something explicit. This form follows the pattern work of Alexander, whose books on architecture serve as a model for the modern software patterns movement. Some of these organizational patterns hark back to Alexander; where appropriate, a distinctive reference appears in the text (§*pattern number*) to refer the reader to a pattern in Alexander's *A Pattern Language* (1977).

Though there are organizations that exhibit these patterns, combining patterns to build a new organization from scratch is a daunting task. The ideal organization envisioned by these patterns differs greatly from the state of the art in software development. These patterns are drawn from singular organizations with unusually high productivity. The patterns describe practices that are much different from those found in most project management texts.

1.1 Language Context

This paper presents generative patterns that can be used to build an organization and guide its software development process. By "organization" I mean not so much an institutional organization as a community of mutual interest, of the sort that forms naturally in any culture. These communities are sometimes called *instrumental organizations* (Swieringa and Wierdsma, 1992, p.10). An organization is usually responsible for some deliverable. The endeavor of building that product within that organization is called a *project*. The patterns of activity within an organization (and hence within its project) are called a *process*. Organization, project, and process can be viewed as partial facets of each other. We might also look at hierarchies or networks of organizations; the patterns described here apply especially to the innermost ones, and in lesser degrees to the more encompassing organizational structures (see Pattern 32, Divide and Conquer).

I am not so much interested in small (that is, simple) projects as in ambitious, complex commercial endeavors that may comprise hundreds of thousands or millions of lines of code. Such projects are common in telecommunications development, and their processes and organization are a challenge to designers. The organizations undertaking the type of projects considered here range in size from a handful of people to a few dozen. Larger organizations (containing hundreds or thousands of people) are beyond the scope of most of the patterns in this language. If large organizations can be broken into smaller, *decoupled* organizations, the patterns apply to each of the parts.

This pattern language probably applies more to young, emerging organizations than to older organizations. Established organizations, particularly in the public service and utilities sectors, are almost always bureaucracies (Swieringa and Wierdsma, 1992, p.8). Young organizations proceed through several stable stages of growth, starting with a visionary and a tightly knit group. Roles emerge and become more refined as these organizations grow. The organization may grow to the point where it exhibits an internal structure of suborganizations, each potentially a subject for the patterns presented here. The organization atrophies as it goes into maintenance mode, taking on a stable structure. The patterns in this language aim at changing, growing organizations, which don't often lend themselves to traditional corporate structures.

All development organizations serve a purpose. This paper does not explore patterns for chartering a development organization, but presumes that an organization is formed within the industry or within a company to meet a particular business need. Questions of business practicality are beyond what can be dealt with in depth here. One might look at Web of Shopping (§19) and Household Mix (§35) in Alexander (1977) as analogies to how such groups should be formed. Even grosser patterns, such as Site Repair (§104), provide analogies to corporate contexts that are suitable for high-productivity organizations.

There are "common sense" considerations that don't appear in the contexts or solutions of these patterns. Cultural taboos and standards will leave many of these patterns outside the reach of some organizations. For example, Domain Expertise in Roles (Pattern 6) presumes that experts are available in the job market. If the domain is breaking brand new ground, experts may not yet be available. Even in familiar territory experts are scarce, and the culture may not allow the extravagant measures necessary to procure them. As another example, the pattern language makes every attempt to avoid setting project benchmarks by working back from an end date (see Pattern 4, Size the Schedule). Customers often want to see intermediate benchmarks at agreed intervals, and intermediate benchmarks drive some cultures too deeply for an individual development group to fix. These problems do not invalidate the language, but they may require that some patterns be skipped for a given organization. It is likely that some of these patterns are foundation patterns, which have a larger impact than others if skipped: Domain Expertise in Roles (Pattern 6), Organization Follows Location (Pattern 9), Architect Also Implements (Pattern 15), and others are likely foundation patterns.

The success of this pattern language is almost certainly sensitive to contexts that demand future research and exploration. How well defined is the product at the outset? How much external tool support is available? How short should the edit-compile-go turnaround cycle be? How sensitive is the organization to the fault density or fault tolerance of the product system? We also need to study in more depth the degree to which these are or are not drivers for successful organizations.

1.2 Forces Driving the Language

While the language encodes well-known, reasonable folklore and practice about organizations, it also draws on unconventional insights gained through empirical studies of outstanding organizations. This pattern language builds on three years of research in development processes and organizational analyses carried out by AT&T Bell Laboratories. The data comes both from within AT&T and from other companies in computer-related fields. During this research we used a largely visual representation of the organizations we studied, and we built a catalog of "Gamma patterns" of organizations, their structures, and their processes (Gamma, 1992). These Gamma pattern visualizations are the source of many of the recurring generative patterns encoded here. For example, the pattern Engage QA appears as a tight coupling between the QA role and the process as a whole in many highly productive organizations we studied. The original visualizations for these organizations are shown along with Developer Controls Process (Pattern 11) and Engage QA (Pattern 19).

This language builds a system that is part of a larger system: a development culture in a corporate environment. Executing this language perfectly is no guarantee of success. While the language attempts to deal with interfaces to marketing and to the corporate control structure (for example, through Pattern 24, Fire Walls), the remainder of the organization must be competent, and other patterns are needed to shape it. We find hints of appropriate patterns for this in the pattern languages of Kerth (1994) and Whitenack (1994).

This language certainly works best when the raw materials are available to build an enthusiastic organization. While the patterns work better when building an organization from scratch, they may be applied to an anemic organization to restore the ability to excel that people may once have had before the culture drained it away. Some "Site Repair" (§104) would likely be necessary before these patterns could be applied to such an organization. Some patterns are in fact best suited to the problems of mature organizations experiencing difficulties (Pattern 29, Work Flows Inward; Pattern 32, Divide and Conquer; Pattern 34, Hub-Spoke-and-Rim; Pattern 30, 3 to 7 Helpers per Role).

1.3 The Quality Without a Name in Organizations

Some organizations have the "quality without a name": they are true to their purpose because they profit their stockholders, serve their customers well, and provide a sustaining, fulfilling, and supporting workplace for their employees. Organizations that reach this level of maturity are likely to excel in all other measures. Do the patterns presented here make it possible to construct such an organization? While these patterns define a culture that helps sustain morale and business success, they don't address quality of work life and morale directly. These patterns touch only lightly on key factors such as the mutual trust between worker and peer, employee and employer, and company and customer. Other factors, such as cultural diversity, the corporation's community involvement, and extracurricular activities at work, are beyond the scope of this language. I don't omit these factors here because I feel they are unimportant, but defer these issues to experts in organizational psychology and sociology (for example, see Katz and Kahn 1978). Though many of the patterns presented here have sociological overtones and will likely have a generative effect on morale and other social indicators, other pattern languages must be woven in with this one to round out the sociological picture. This perspective leads to the obvious conclusion that these patterns alone do not guarantee success—but it also provides a guiding light for further research.

1.4 Language Rationale

This language takes inspiration as much from Alexander's architectural language as from his pattern language principles. The opening phrases of the language evoke the same sizing and context perspectives as we find in Alexander. Many of the organization patterns are refinements of Alexander's Circulation patterns (§98). The philosophy of establishing stable communication paths across the industry has strong analogies with the Alexandrian patterns establishing transportation webs in a city (§16). Here we are concerned with transportation of information between individuals and development groups. We capture the communication between roles, which represents a higher-order abstraction than individual actors.

1.5 Notations

This work draws on data gathered as part of the Pasteur process research program at AT&T Bell Laboratories (see Cain and Coplien 1993). In the

Pasteur program we studied software development organizations in many companies worldwide, covering a wide spectrum of development cultures. The Pasteur analysis techniques are based in part on organizational visualization. Many of the patterns in this pattern language have visual analogues in the Pasteur analyses. I sometimes use visualizations to illustrate a pattern.

There are two kinds of pictures used in the Pasteur studies. The first is a social network diagram, also called an adjacency diagram. Each diagram is a network of roles and the communication paths between them. The roles are placed according to their coupling relationships: closely coupled roles are close together, and decoupled roles are far apart. Roles at the center of these pictures tend to be the most active in these organizations, while those nearer the edges have a more distant relationship with the organization as a whole.

The second kind of picture is an interaction grid. The axes of the interaction grid span the roles in the organization, ordered according to their coupling to the organization as a whole. If a role at ordinate position p initiates an interaction with a role at coordinate position q, we put a point at the position (p,q). The point is shaded according to the strength of the interaction.

The pattern texts, and particularly the design rationales, often make reference to documents or projects that typify the pattern. "QPW" refers to Borland's QuattroPro for Windows development and to process research conducted there by AT&T Bell Labs in 1993. The research is further discussed in the proceedings of BIC/94 (Coplien 1994a), in a column by Richard Gabriel (1994), and in an article in *Dr. Dobb's Journal* (Coplien 1994b).

The notation "ATT1" refers to a high-productivity project inside AT&T, characterized by concurrent engineering in a small-team environment. Findings from research on that project have not yet been published.

The analyses occasionally make reference to the work of Thomas Allen, whose relevant perspectives can be found in his book on technology information flow (1977).

I often draw from a whimsical book on architecture called *The Most Beautiful House in the World*, by Witold Rybczynski (1989).

1.6 Acknowledgments

Brendan Cain supported much of the early process research underlying these patterns. The research of Peter Bürgi, who spent time as a cultural anthropologist in our research department, has strongly influenced the pattern language. The language took shape and had its first applications in the formative months of the Global Configurator Project at Indian Hill, whose many members I thank for the opportunity to work with them. Joint work with Neil Harrison of AT&T's Global Business Communications Systems helped refine, validate, and prove many of the patterns. Many thanks to Richard Gabriel, Ward Cunningham, Desmond DeSouza, Richard Helm, and Ralph Johnson for participating in a structured review of these patterns; Gabriel also facilitated the review at PLoP. Many thanks to the many people at PLoP who also reviewed these patterns, and especially to Larry Podmolik, Mary Shaw, Dennis DeBruler, Norm Kerth, Bill Opdyke, Brian Foote, Bruce Whitenack, Steve Berczuk, Frank Buschmann, and Robert Martin. Kent Beck was the PLoP shepherd for this document. Mary Zajac and Joe Maranzano in AT&T provided much useful feedback from a management perspective. Mary proposed the patterns Phasing It In and Apprentice. Many comments and pattern ideas—the most noteworthy of which is Mercenary Analyst— came from Paul Chisholm at AT&T.

2. THE PATTERN LANGUAGE

Pattern 1: Size the Organization

Problem   How big should the organization be?

Context   You are building a software development organization to meet competitive cost and schedule benchmarks. The first release of the end product will probably have more than twenty-five thousand lines of code. The development organization is part of a larger organization, usually a sponsoring enterprise or company (see Design Rationale). This applies specifically to organizations that create software, and may not apply as directly to organizations whose job is to integrate existing software, for example.

Forces   If the development organization is too large, you reach a point of greatly diminishing returns. Large organizations are ships that are hard to steer. On the other hand, if it's too small, you don't have critical mass. Overly small organizations have inadequate inertia and can become unstable.

Size affects the deliverable in a nonlinear manner. Communication overhead increases as the square of the size, while the "horsepower" of the organization goes up only linearly.

New people interact much more strongly with others in the organization— and more broadly across the organization—than do mature members of the society, who have assimilated its context.

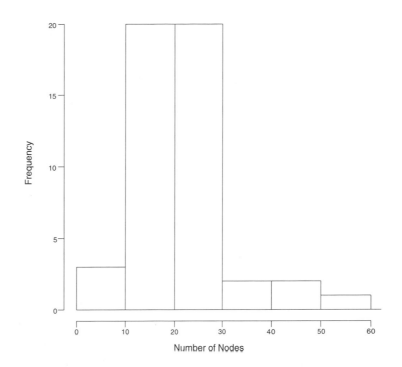

FIGURE 1 Pattern 1: Size the Organization. Most organizations we have studied have a remarkably similar number of roles. This graph is a histogram of the distribution of roles (nodes) per process. While this is not the same as the staff level (which is the number of actors, not the number of roles), it provides guidance in sizing an organization.

Solution
By default, choose ten people; experience has shown that a suitably selected and nurtured small team can develop a 1,500 KSLOC project in thirty-one months, a 200 KSLOC project in fifteen months, or a 60KSLOC project in eight months. Do not add people late in development or try to meet deadlines set by working backward from a completion date.

Resulting Context
This pattern produces an organization where nearly everyone can have "global knowledge." We have found empirically that most roles in a project can handle interactions with about six or seven other roles; with ten people, you can almost manage total global communications (and a fully connected network may not be necessary). On the other hand, ten people is a suitable "critical mass."

This pattern is closely coupled to the patterns below that support organizational growth (Pattern 7, Phasing It In; Pattern 8, Apprentice). This pattern also interacts with Pattern 37, Prototype.

Rationale   Keeping an organization small makes it possible for everybody to know how the project works. Projects that do well have processes that adapt, and processes adapt well only if there is widespread buy-in and benefit. The dialogue necessary to bring about this buy-in and benefit flourishes only in small organizations. Tom DeMarco (1993a) has noted that everybody who is to benefit from the process should be involved in process work and process decision making. Having ten people at the start is probably overkill, but it avoids the expense and overhead of adding more people later.

This pattern is for large projects. Projects larger than 25KSLOC can rarely be done by an individual (see Pattern 3, Solo Virtuoso).

Different management styles (leadership-based, manager-based) lead to the success or failure of different organizational types (democracy, republic, oligarchy). Leadership-based management styles help these organizations work; the need for democracy is less compelling, because project members feel they are well represented under an appropriate management style.

A single team is better than a collection of subteams. The faster a team breaks up into subteams worrying about their own responsibilities rather than those of the larger team, the less effective the overall enterprise will be.

Many software development cultures support technical manager groups up to this size. Adding more people would force a group to split, which can cause a large decrease in productivity, all other things being equal.

Further study might evaluate the relationship between this pattern and Alexander's Distribution of Towns (§2) and related patterns. Here we stipulate that the social organization must be small; it reflects a subculture boundary (§13) and an identifiable neighborhood (§14). Alexander emphasizes the grander architectural context that balances support for nature's ecology with the economies of scale large towns can provide, while supporting the xenophobic tendencies of human nature. Small organizations like the one being built here rarely exist in isolation, but in the context of a broader supporting organization. This relationship to the larger organization invokes Pattern 12, Patron.

As to adding people late in development, staff-month myths abound. One manager writes: "On [one] project, I grew from ten to twenty people to meet a customer contract. With [the] new people, [I] wound up three months late because of 'absorption' of new folks into the organization."

Pattern 2: Self-Selecting Team

Problem   There are no perfect criteria for screening team members.

Context   You are building a software development organization to meet competitive cost and schedule benchmarks. You are staffing up to meet a schedule in a given market.

Forces   Empowerment depends on competency and the distribution of knowledge and power. The worst team dynamics can be found in appointed teams. The best team dynamics can be found in self-selecting teams.

Broad interests (music and poetry, for example) seem to indicate successful team players.

Solution   Build self-selecting teams, doing limited screening on the basis of track records and broad interests.

Resulting Context   An empowered, enthusiastic team willing to take extraordinary measures to meet project goals.

Pattern 3: Solo Virtuoso

Problem   How big should the organization be?

Context   You are building a software development organization to meet competitive cost and schedule benchmarks. The first release of the end product will probably be less than 25KSLOC. Rapid growth is not anticipated after the first release.

Forces   Some select individuals are able to build entire projects by themselves.

Organization size affects the deliverable in a nonlinear manner. Communication overhead increases as the square of the size, which means that the organization becomes less cohesive as this overhead increases quadratically while the "horsepower" of the organization goes up only linearly.

Solution   Do the entire design and implementation with one or two people.

Resulting Context   The result is an organization limited to small developments. Though there is a singleton development role, other roles may be necessary to support marketing, toolsmithing, and other functions. The productivity of a suitably chosen singleton developer is enough to handle sizable projects; here we establish 25KSLOC as a limit, but see Design Rationale, below, for further parameters.

This pattern is not "License to Hack." Don't give up technical review, validation, and verification at appropriate times in the development (see Pattern 16, Review the Architecture; Pattern 20, Engage Customers).

This approach is rarely applicable, as it doesn't resolve some of the forces (many of them applicable) mentioned in Pattern 1, Size the Organization. Where those forces don't apply, this pattern is a big win.

Rationale   There are numerous examples of successful single-person developments. The dynamics of these developments are different from those of a small team. The productivity of a single individual can be higher than that of a collection of productive individuals. We have seen single-person developments generate 25KSLOC of deliverable code in four months (a craft interface for a telecommunications system) and two-person developments do 135 KSLOC in thirty months. These projects usually adhered faithfully to all stipulated reviews and verification steps.

Success, of course, depends on choosing the right person. Boehm notes a twentyfold spread between the least and most effective developers. A telecommunications developer recently told me that "having the right expertise means the difference between being able to solve a problem in a half hour and never being able to solve the problem at all." This pattern reduces the "truck number" of the organization (the number of people whose absence would threaten the organization were any of them hit by a truck).

Pattern 4: Size the Schedule

Problem   How long should the project take?

Context   The product is understood and the project size has been estimated.

Forces   If you make the schedule too generous, developers become complacent and you miss market windows. If the schedule is too ambitious, developers become burned out and you miss market windows. In addition, product quality suffers; compromised architectural principles establish a poor foundation for future maintenance.

Projects without a schedule to motivate the developers tend to go on forever, spending too much time polishing details that are either irrelevant or don't serve customer needs.

Solution   Reward developers for meeting the schedule. Use financial bonuses, at-risk compensation (see Pattern 42, Compensate Success), or extra time off. Keep two sets of schedules: one for the market and one for the developers. The external schedule is negotiated with the customer, the internal schedule with development staff. The internal schedule should be shorter than the external schedule by two or three weeks for a moderate project. If the two schedules can't be reconciled, customer needs or the organization's resource commitments—or the schedule itself—must be re-negotiated.

Resulting Context The result is a project with flexible intermediate benchmarks. Dates are always difficult to estimate; DeMarco notes that one of the most serious signs of a project in trouble is a schedule that is set by working backward from a targeted end date (DeMarco 1993b).

Keep the schedule current with Pattern 38, Take No Small Slips; also see Pattern 40, Interrupts Unjam Blocking. Other mechanisms are necessary as well, to ensure that a hurried development doesn't compromise quality.

Rationale The pattern can be found in QPW. One manager suggested that the skew between internal and external schedules should be closer to two months than two weeks, because if you slip it usually reflects a major oversight that costs two or three months.

Pattern 5: Form Follows Function

Alias Aggregate Activities into Roles

Problem A project lacks well-defined roles.

Context You know the key atomic process activities.

Forces Activities are too small, and their relationships too dynamic, to be useful process building blocks. Activities often cluster together by related artifacts or other domain relationships.

Solution Group closely related activities (that is, those that are mutually coupled in their implementation, manipulate the same artifacts, or are semantically related to the same domain). Name the abstractions resulting from the grouped activities, making them into roles. The associated activities become the responsibilities (job description) of the roles.

Resulting Context The result is a partial definition of roles for a project. (Some roles—mercenary analyst, developer—are canonical rather than derived from this pattern.)

Rationale   The quality of this pattern needs to be reviewed. The idea came from the approach taken in a large reengineering project I worked on in March 1994.

Louis Sullivan is the architect credited with the primordial architectural pattern of this name (Rybczynski 1989, p. 162).

This pattern interacts with other structural patterns, such as Pattern 9, Organization Follows Location; Pattern 10, Organization Follows Market; and Pattern 15, Architect Also Implements. See in particular Pattern 20, Engage Customers.

One manager notes: "In my experience from Project Management Audits . . . projects both leave out roles (e.g., no named architect) and define several people with the same role. The second [situation] is most problematic, since it causes staff confusion. But the missing role also occurs because projects have inexperienced managers. This is a big problem . . . around System Engineering roles, or [the] lack thereof."

Pattern 6: Domain Expertise in Roles

Problem   How do you match staff (actors, people) to roles?

Context   You know the key atomic process roles, including a characterization of the Developer role.

Forces   All roles must be staffed (with qualified individuals). Spreading expertise across roles complicates communication patterns. Successful projects tend to be staffed with people who have already worked on successful projects.

Solution   Hire domain experts with proven track records. Any given actor may fill several roles. In many cases, multiple actors can fill a given role. Domain training is more important than process training. Local gurus are good, in all areas from application expertise to expertise in methods and languages.

Resulting Context   This pattern is a tool that helps assure that roles can be successfully carried out. It also helps make roles autonomous.

Other roles (Architect, Mercenary Analyst, and others) are prescribed by subsequent patterns.

Rationale   Highly productive projects (such as QPW) hire deeply specialized experts.

Alexander's Old People Everywhere (§40) talks about the need for the young to interact with the old. The same deep rationale and many of the same forces of Alexander's pattern also apply here.

Pattern 8, Apprentice, helps maintain this pattern over the long term.

A seasoned manager writes: "The most poorly staffed roles are System Engineering and System Test. We hire rookies and make them System Engineers. (In Japan, only the most experienced person interacts with customers.) We staff System Test with 'leftovers' after we have staffed the important jobs of architecture, design, and developer."

Pattern 7: Phasing It In[1]

Problem   You need to hire long-term staff beyond the initial experts.

Context   Key project players have been hired and cover the necessary expertise, but the project needs more staff.

Forces   You need enough people to achieve the right critical mass. Staff members are not plug compatible and interchangeable.

   The right initial set of people sets the tone for the project, and it's important to hire the key people first. However, too many people too early creates a burden on the core team.

Solution   Phase the hiring program. Start by hiring experts, and gradually bring on new people as the project grows.

Resulting Context   The organization can "staff up" to meet development loads. This pattern is closely coupled to Pattern 8, Apprentice.

Rationale   This is a well-known management technique that allows a project to establish an identity early on and to grow graciously.

Pattern 8: Apprentice[2]

Problem   You can't always hire the experts you need.

Context   The project is staffing up incrementally after the first round of experts have been brought on board.

---

[1] Proposed as a pattern by Mary Zajac at AT&T.

[2] Proposed as a pattern by Mary Zajac at AT&T.

Forces You need enough people to achieve the right critical mass. Staff members are not plug-compatible and interchangeable.

Solution Turn new hires into experts through an apprenticeship program (see Pattern 6, Domain Expertise in Roles). Every new employee should work as an apprentice to an established expert. (The expert must function as more than just a mentor.) Most apprenticeship programs will last six months to a year—the amount of time it takes to make a paradigm shift.

Resulting Context It will be possible to maintain expertise in the organization. This pattern also increases the organization's "truck number" (the number of people whose absence would threaten the organization were any of them hit by a truck) by spreading knowledge around. Also, the "masters" feel valued, and the apprentices are provided with a good environment in which to learn.

Rationale It is better to apprentice people than to put them through a "trial by fire" that may damage the project. This approach makes it possible to form domain-specific teams.

Pattern 9: Organization Follows Location

Problem You must assign tasks and roles across a geographically distributed workforce.

Context A product must be developed in several different hallways, on different floors of a building, in different buildings, or at different locations.

Forces Communication patterns between project members follow their geographic distribution. Coupling between pieces of software must be sustained by analogous coupling between the people maintaining that software. People avoid communicating with people who work in other buildings, other towns, or overseas (see Rationale). People in an organization usually work on related tasks, which suggests that they communicate frequently with each other.

Solution The architectural partitioning should reflect the geographic partitioning, and vice versa. Architectural responsibilities should be assigned so decisions can be made locally (that is, in terms of geography).

Resulting Context The result is suborganizations that can be further split or organized by markets or other criteria (see Pattern 10, Organization Follows Market; Pattern 29, Work Flows Inward; and others). You still need someone to break logjams when a consensus can't be reached, perhaps using Pattern 15, Architect Also Implements; or Pattern 12, Patron.

If the organization is modularized along geographic boundaries but the architecture is not, then it will be impossible to apply Pattern 15, Architect Also Implements.

Rationale Thomas Allen has found that social distance goes up rapidly with physical separation (see also Alexander's §37, House Cluster). Our empirical experience with codevelopment projects overseas reveals that failure to follow this pattern can lead to complete project failure. This is a crucial pattern that is often overlooked or dismissed out of consideration for political alliances. Peter Bürgi's studies of geographically distributed organizations in AT&T underscore the importance of this pattern.

We have seen few geographically distributed organizations that exhibit positive team dynamics. There are exceptions, and there are rare occasions when this pattern does not apply. Steve Berczuk at MIT notes: "Communications need not be poor between remote sites if the following items are true: (1) The number of developers on a project, including all sites, is small. (2) Most of the communication is done via something like email (wide distribution and asynchronous communication—in [one case] . . . more people were in the loop than if the primary means of communication had been hallway chats). (3) The people involved have been together for SOME time, so that they feel like they know each other. (4) Folks aren't so burned out by 'unnecessary' travel that they are willing and happy to travel when it is needed. In some situations [this pattern] is not possible because of the nature of the project, so we need a way to address the issue of remoteness" (Berczuk 1994).

There are times when the market demands geographic distribution; see Pattern 10, Organization Follows Market.

Pattern 10: Organization Follows Market

Alias Framework Team

Problem There is no clear role or organizational accountability to individual market segments.

Context The market comprises several customers with similar but conflicting needs. The project has adopted sound architectural principles, and can organize its software according to market needs.

Forces   The development organization should track and meet the needs of each customer. Customer needs are similar, and much of what they all need can be done in common. Different customers expect results on different schedules.

Solution   In an organization designed to serve several distinct markets, it is important to reflect the market structure in the development organization. One frequently overlooked opportunity for a powerful pattern is the conscious design of a "core" organization, which supports only what is common across all market segments. Ralph Johnson calls this a framework team. It is important to put this organization in place up front.

Resulting Context   The result is an organization that can support a good architecture. The success of this pattern is necessary to the success of Pattern 15, Architect Also Implements. Pattern 15 should be seen as an audit, refinement, or fine-tuning of this pattern.

Rationale   Most of the rationale is in the forces. Two of the major forces relate to individual customer schedules and to positioning the organization to respond quickly to customer requests. Two important aspects of domain analysis are (1) broadening the architecture (for example, by working at the base class level) and (2) ensuring that architectural evolution tracks the vendor's understanding of customer needs. A single organization can't faithfully track multiple customer needs, and this organization allows different arms of the organization to track different markets independently.

The developer is central to all activities of this end-to-end software development process (see Pattern 11).

Pattern 11: Developer Controls Process

Problem   What role should be the focal point of project communication?

Context   There is an imperfectly understood design domain, where iteration is key to development.

Forces   Totalitarian control is viewed by most development teams as a draconian measure.

The right information must flow through the right roles. You need to support information flow across analysis, design, and implementation.

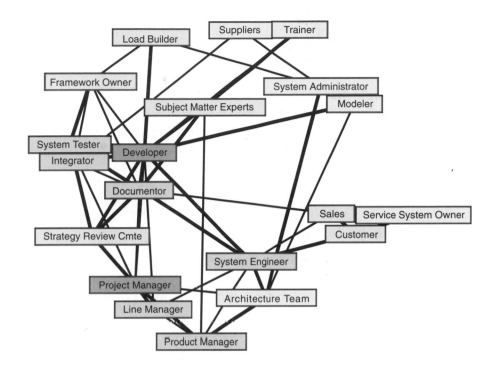

FIGURE 2 A developer-centric design and implementation process (Pattern 11)

Managers have some accountability. Developers should have ultimate accountability, as well as authority and control over the product; these are often process issues.

Solution   Place the Developer role at a hub of the process for a given feature. A feature is a unit of system functionality, implemented largely in software, that can be separately marketed and for which customers are willing to pay. The Developer is the process information clearinghouse. Responsibilities of Developers include understanding requirements, reviewing the solution structure and algorithm with peers, building the implementation, and unit testing.

Note that other hubs may exist as well.

Resulting   The result is an organization that supports its prime information consumer.
Context   The Developer can be moved toward the center of the process using Pattern 29, Work Flows Inward; and Pattern 27, Move Responsibilities.

Though Developer should be a key role, care must be taken not to overburden it. This pattern should be balanced with Pattern 23, Mercenary Analyst; Pattern 24, Fire Walls; and more general load-balancing patterns like Pattern 28, Buffalo Mountain.

Rationale   There is no role called Designer, because design is really the whole task. Managers fill a supporting role; they are rarely empirically seen to control a process, except during crises. While the Developer controls the process, the Architect controls the product. (In Figure 2, the Architect role is split across Framework Owner and Architecture Team.) This communication is particularly important in domains that are not well understood, so that iteration can take place to explore the domain with the customer.

Pattern 12: Patron

Problem   How do you give a project continuity?

Context   You are working with a development organization where roles are being defined. Patron works only if Pattern 11, Developer Controls Process, is in place.

Forces   Centralized control can be a drag; anarchy can be a worse drag. Most societies need a king/parent figure. An organization needs a single, ultimate decision maker. The time needed to make a decision should be less than the time it takes to implement it.

Solution   Give the project access to a visible, high-level manager who champions the project cause. The patron can be the final arbiter for project decisions; this provides a driving force for the organization to make decisions quickly. The patron is accountable for removing project-level barriers that hinder progress, and is responsible for the organization's morale (sense of well-being).

Resulting Context   Having a patron gives the organization a sense of well-being and a focus for later process and organizational changes. Other roles can be defined in terms of the patron's role.

The Manager role is not meant to maintain totally centralized control, but rather to act as a champion. That is, the scope of the manager's influence is largely outside those developing the product itself, but it includes those whose cooperation is necessary for the success of the product (support organizations, funders, test organizations, and so on). This role also serves as a patron or sponsor; the person is often a corporate visionary.

Rationale   We have observed this pattern at work in QPW, in managers for C++ efforts at AT&T, for a manager in a high-productivity Network Systems project; and in another multilocation AT&T project.

This pattern relates to Pattern 24, Fire Walls, which in turn relates to Pattern 25, Gatekeeper.

Block (1983) talks about the importance of influencing forces over which the project has no direct control.

Putting the developer in charge of the process implies that management titles become associated with support roles (see Pattern 24, Fire Walls). This works only in a culture where the manager decides to be the servant of the developer (an insight from Norm Kerth).

Pattern 13: Architect Controls Product

Alias   Planning and Architecture[3]

Problem   A product designed by many individuals lacks elegance and cohesiveness.

Context   A development organization that needs strategic technical direction.

Forces   Totalitarian control is viewed by most development teams as a draconian measure—the right information must flow through the right roles.

Solution   Create an Architect role. The Architect role should advise and control the Developer roles and communicate closely with the developers. The Architect should also be in close touch with the customer.

Resulting Context   This pattern does for the architecture what the Patron pattern does for the organization: it provides technical focus and a rallying point for technical as well as market-related work.

There is a rich relationship between this pattern and Pattern 12, Patron, that should be explored.

Resentment can build against a totalitarian Architect; use patterns like Pattern 16, Review the Architecture, to temper this one.

Rationale   There is no role called Designer, because design is really the whole task. Managers fill a supporting role; they are rarely empirically seen to control a

---

[3]   Joe Maranzano at AT&T envisions both functions together in one role.

process, except during crises. While the Developer controls the process, the Architect controls the product. The Architect is a "chief developer" (see Pattern 15, Architect Also Implements [αρχι τεκτον]). Their responsibilities include understanding requirements, framing the major system structure, and controlling the long-term evolution of that structure.

The Architect controls the product in the visualization accompanying Pattern 19, Engage QA.

> *Les oeuvres d'un seul architect sont plus belles . . . que ceux d'ont plusieurs ont taché de faire. [The works of a lone architect are more elegant than those attempted by several together.]*
>
> Pascal, *Pensées*

Pattern 14: Conway's Law

Alias   Organization Follows Architecture, or Architecture Follows Organization

Problem   How do you align the organization and its architecture?

Context   An architect and development team are in place. The architecture is fairly well established.

Forces   Architecture shapes the communication paths in an organization. The de facto organizational structure shapes the formal organizational structure, and the formal organizational structure shapes the architecture. Early architectural formulations are only approximations and are unstable.

Solution   Make sure the organization is compatible with the product architecture. At this point in the language, it is more likely that the architecture should drive the organization than vice versa.

Resulting Context   The organization and product architecture will be aligned.

Rationale   The design rationale is historical. Gerard Meszaros (Bell Northern Research) (1994) notes that you want to bind the organization to the architecture only after the architecture has stabilized. If you bind the organization to the architecture too early, architectural drift will lead to interference between individuals' domains of control.

Pattern 15: Architect Also Implements (αρχι τεκτον)

Problem How do you preserve the architectural vision through to implementation?

Context The development organization needs strategic technical direction.

Forces Totalitarian control is viewed by most development teams as a draconian measure—the right information must flow through the right roles.

Solution Beyond advising and communicating with Developers, Architects should also participate in implementation.

Resulting Context The result is a development organization that perceives "buy-in" from the guiding architects and can directly avail itself of architectural expertise.

Rationale The importance of making this pattern explicit was underscored for me in a recent project. The architecture team was being assembled across wide geographic boundaries with narrow communication bandwidths between them. Though general architectural responsibilities were identified and the roles were staffed, one group expected that the architects would implement code, while the other group did not.

One manager suggests that on some projects architects should focus only on the implementation of a common infrastructure, and that the implementation of noncore code should be left solely to the Developer role.

Rybczinski notes:

> *It would be convenient if architecture could be defined as any building designed by an architect. But who is an architect? Although the Académie Royale d'Architecture in Paris was founded in 1671, formal architectural schooling did not appear until the nineteenth century. The famous Ecole des Beaux-Arts was founded in 1816; the first English-language school, in London, in 1847; and the first North American university program, at MIT, was established in 1868. Despite the existence of professional schools, for a long time the relationship between schooling and practice remained ambiguous. It is still possible to become an architect without a university degree, and in some countries, such as Switzerland, trained architects have no legal monopoly over construction. This is hardly surprising. For centuries, the difference between master masons, journeymen builders, joiners, dilettantes, gifted amateurs, and architects has been ill defined. The great Renaissance buildings, for example, were designed by a variety of non-architects: Brunelleschi was trained as a*

goldsmith, Michelango as a sculptor, Leonardo da Vinci as a painter, and Alberti as a lawyer; only Bramante, who was also a painter, had formally studied building. These men are termed architects because, among other things, they created architecture—a tautology that explains nothing (Rybczynski 1989, pp. 9–10).

In *The Ten Books on Architecture*, Vitruvius notes:

Architects who have aimed at acquiring manual skill without scholarship have never been able to reach a position of authority to correspond to their pains, while those who relied only upon theories and scholarship were obviously hunting the shadow, not the substance. But those who have a thorough knowledge of both, like men armed at all points, have the sooner attained their object and carried authority with them (Vitruvius 1960).

Pattern 16: Review the Architecture

Problem   There are blind spots in the architecture and design.

Context   A software artifact's quality is to be assessed and improved.

Forces   Architectural decisions affect many people over a long time. Nevertheless, individual Architects and Designers can develop "tunnel vision." A shared architectural vision is important.

Even low-level design and implementation decisions matter.

All things are deeply "interwingled" (Ed Yourdon).

Solution   All architectural decisions should be reviewed by all Architects. Architects should review each other's code. The reviews should be frequent—even daily—early in the project. Reviews should be informal, with a minimum of paperwork.

Resulting Context   This pattern sets the context for Pattern 23, Mercenary Analyst. It will also solve potential problems with Pattern 17, Code Ownership.

The intent of this pattern is to increase coupling between those who have a stake in the architecture and implementation, which solves the stated problem indirectly.

Rationale   The pattern is based on QPW, and on a successful object-oriented project at AT&T.

Pattern 17: Code Ownership

Problem   A Developer cannot keep up with a constantly changing base of implementation code.

Context   You have a system with mechanisms to document and enforce the software architecture, and you are working with an organization that has developers to write the code.

Forces   Something that's everybody's responsibility is no one's responsibility.

You want parallelism between developers, so multiple people can be coding concurrently.

Most design knowledge lives in the code; navigating unfamiliar code to explore design issues takes time. Furthermore, provisional changes never work.

Not everyone can know everything all the time.

Solution   Each code module in the system is owned by a single Developer. Except in unusual, explicit circumstances, code may be modified only by its owner.

Resulting Context   The architecture and organization will better reflect each other. Related patterns include Pattern 15, Architect Also Implements; Pattern 10, Organization Follows Market; and Pattern 40, Interrupts Unjam Blocking.

Pattern 16, Review the Architecture, helps keep Designers and Architects from developing tunnel vision from strict application of this pattern.

Rationale   Lack of code ownership is a major contributor to discovery efforts in large-scale software development today. Note that this goes hand in hand with architecture: to have ownership, there must be interfaces. This is a smaller-scale form of Conway's Law (see Pattern 15, Architect Also Implements; and Pattern 14, Conway's Law).

There have been many arguments against code ownership, but empirical trends uphold its value. Typical concerns include the tendency toward tunnel vision, the implied risk of having only a single individual with an in-depth understanding of a given piece of code, and breakdown of global knowledge. Other patterns temper these problems (see Pattern 16, Review the Architecture; and Pattern 20, Engage Customers).

Tim Born argues that there is a relationship between code ownership and encapsulation, in the sense that C++ protection keeps one person from accessing the implementation of another's abstraction. Rousseau ascribes social order to ownership and property (Rousseau, 1972, p. 63).

It has been argued that code ownership should be applied only to reusable code. Such a constraint would be worthy of consideration if someone were to come up with a workable distinction between usable code and reusable code.

Pattern 18: Application Design Is Bounded by Test Design

Problem   When do you design and implement test plans and scripts?

Context   You have a system with mechanisms to document and enforce the software architecture, and you are working with an organization that has developers to write the code. A testing role is being defined.

Forces   Test development takes time, and it cannot just be started as soon as the system is done (that is, when you "know what you have to test").

Scenarios are known when requirements are known, and many of these are known early.

Test implementation requires detailed knowledge of the details of message formats, interfaces, and other architectural properties (to support test scripts and test jigs). Implementation changes daily; there should be no need for test designs to track ephemeral changes in software implementation.

Solution   Scenario-driven test design starts when scenario requirements are first agreed to by the customer. Test design evolves along with software design, but only in response to customer scenario changes: the source software is inaccessible to the tester. When development decides that architectural interfaces have stabilized, low-level test design and implementation can proceed.

Resulting Context   This provides a context for Pattern 19, Engage QA; and Pattern 22, Scenarios Define Problem.

Rationale   Making the software accessible to the testers causes them to see the developer's view rather than the customer's view. This leads to the chance that the tester may test the wrong things or concentrate on the wrong level of detail. Furthermore, the software will continue to evolve from requirements until the architecture gels; there is no sense in causing test design to fishtail while interfaces settle down. In short, test design kicks off at the end of the first major influx of requirements and touches base with design again when the architecture is stable.

This is related to the as-yet unspecified pattern "Testing First-In, Last-Out"; to Pattern 19, Engage QA; and to Pattern 22, Scenarios Define Problem.

Pattern 19: Engage QA

Problem   How do you guarantee product quality?

Context   You need some sort of filter between the roles in your development organization and your customer, in order to ensure product quality.

Forces   Developers feel they get everything right, but it's hard to create perfect software.

Quality is too often deferred, even though success depends on high quality. Early feedback on fundamental quality problems is important.

Solution   Make QA a central role. Couple it tightly to Development as soon as Development has something to test. Development's testing plan can proceed in parallel with coding, but developers must first declare the system ready for testing.

FIGURE 3   The development organization for Borland's Quattro Pro for Windows. Quality Assurance (QA) was central to the development of Quattro Pro (see Pattern 19).

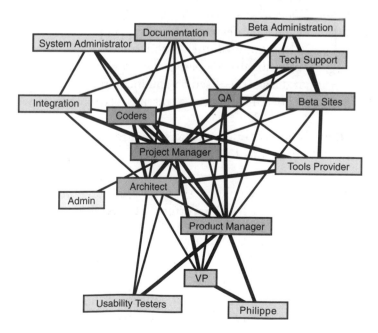

The QA organization should be outside the context of the project: QA should not have to give the development organization an account of its test plans.

Resulting Context   Having engaged QA, the project will be ready for preliminary customer input. With QA and the customer engaged, the quality assurance process can be put in place (use cases gathered, and so on).

Rationale   There are at least two reasons for making QA a separate organization from the one holding the Developers' allegiance: First, test development shouldn't be blindsided by the Developers' perspective. If both the Developers and QA perform their own tests, testing becomes a double-blind experiment. Second, QA should be outside the development organization's realm of influence, in the interest of objectivity.

This is an obvious pattern in QPW. See also Pattern 18, Application Design Is Bounded by Test Design.

Pattern 20: Engage Customers

Problem   How do you best maintain customer satisfaction?

Context   You need to devise a way to provide input to QA.

Forces   Developers used to be called "loose cannons on deck." Requirements change even after design reviews are complete and coding has begun.

Missing customer requirements cause serious problems. Customers are traditionally not part of the mainstream development process, which makes it difficult to discover and incorporate their insights.

There needs to be a trusting relationship between managers and coders.

Solution   Closely couple the Customer role to the Developer and Architect roles, not just to the QA role.

Resulting Context   The new context supports requirements discovery from the customer, as required by the Pattern 22, Scenarios Define Problem; and Pattern 37, Prototype. Pattern 24, Fire Walls, also builds on this pattern.

Rationale   QPW. Also, see Floyd et al., *Software Development and Reality Construction* (1992), and especially the works of Reisin and Floyd therein.

Some processes and methods are founded on customer engagement, such as IBM's Joint Application Development. Other methods are conducive to customer engagement, such as Beck's CRC design technique (Beck 1991). Other methods, particularly many CASE-based methods, are indifferent or harmful to customer engagement.

This pattern is called "Engage Customers," in the plural, to support a domain view and to avoid being blindsided by a single customer.

The project must be careful to temper interactions between Customers and Developers, using the patterns mentioned under Resulting Context. Note that maintaining product quality is not the problem addressed here—product quality is only one component of customer satisfaction. Studies have shown that customers leave one company for another when they feel that they are being ignored (20 percent of the time) or that the attention they receive is rude or unhelpful (50 percent of the time). Only 9 percent of customers that experience a problem that costs over one hundred dollars to fix would buy from the company again if the company does not fix the problem. Eighty-two percent would do business with the company again if the problem was quickly resolved after they issued a complaint (Zuckerman and Hatala 1992, pp. 81–83).

Maranzano notes that this pattern probably should come earlier in the language. However, it is important for project roles to be defined first—particularly those that interact with the customer and those that are driven by customer input (such as QA). Said in another way, the organization exists to serve the customer, so the organization should be in place before the customer is fully engaged.

Pattern 21: Group Validation

Problem   How do you ensure product quality?

Context   The quality of analysis, design, or implementation is to be assessed.

Forces   QA's job is to assess quality. It usually assesses the quality of the end product, doing only black-box validation and verification.

A group setting brings many insights on product problems and opportunities. Individuals may not have the insight necessary to discover a bug plaguing the system (this may be an issue of objectivity).

Solution   Even before engaging QA, the development team (with customer input) can validate the design. Techniques such as CRC cards and group debugging help to socialize the design issues and solve any problems. Members of a validation team can also work with QA to fix root causes attributable to common classes of software faults.[4]

Resulting Context   The result is a process in which the quality of the system is constantly brought into focus before the whole team. Problems will therefore be resolved sooner. The cost of this pattern is the time expended in group design and code debugging sessions.

Rationale   The CRC design technique has been found to be a great team builder and an ideal way to socialize designs. Studies of projects in AT&T have found group debugging sessions to be unusually productive.

Bringing the customer into these sessions can be particularly helpful. The project must be careful to temper interactions between Customers and Developers.

There is an empirical research foundation for this pattern. An article in *CACM* ("An implementation of structured walk-throughs in teaching CO-BOL programming"; 1979) found that team debugging contributes to team learning and effectiveness. A contrary position can be found in G. J. Meyers (1978), though this study was limited to fault detection rates and did not specifically evaluate the advantages of team learning.

Compare this pattern with Pattern 39, Developing in Pairs.

Pattern 22: Scenarios Define Problem

Problem   Design documents are often ineffective vehicles for communicating the customer's vision of how the system should work.

Context   You want to engage the customer, and you need a mechanism to support other organizational alliances between the Customer and Developers.

Forces   There is a natural distance and mistrust between Customers and Developers. However, communication between developers and customers is crucial to the success of a system.

Solution   Capture system functional requirements as use cases, a la Jacobson (1992).

Resulting Context   The problem is now defined, and the architecture can proceed in earnest. See also Pattern 23, Mercenary Analyst, which captures scenarios and uses them for project documentation (both internal and external).

---

[4] Suggested by Joe Maranzano.

Rationale   Jacobson; also Curtis (1988). Also Rubin and Goldberg, who take scenarios all the way to the front of the process, preceding even design. Also see Hsia et al. (1994).

Pattern 23: Mercenary Analyst

Problem   Supporting a design notation, and the related project documentation, is too tedious a job for people directly contributing to product artifacts.

Context   You are assembling the roles for the organization. The organization exists in a context where external reviewers, customers, and internal developers expect to use project documentation to understand the system architecture and its internal workings. (User documentation is considered separately).

Forces   If developers do their own documentation, it hampers their doing "real" work.
  Documentation is often write-only.
  Engineers often don't have good communication skills.
  Architects can become victims of the elegance of their own drawings (see Rationale).

Solution   Hire a technical writer who is proficient in the necessary domains but does not have a stake in the design itself. This person will capture the design using a suitable notation and will format and publish the design for reviews and consumption by the organization itself.
    The documentation itself should be maintained on-line if possible. It must be kept up-to-date (therefore Mercenary Analyst is a full-time job) and should relate to customer scenarios (see Pattern 22, Scenarios Define Problem).

Resulting Context   The success of this pattern depends on finding a suitably skilled individual to fill the role of Mercenary Analyst. If the pattern succeeds, the new context is a project whose progress can be reviewed (see Pattern 16, Review the Architecture) and monitored by community experts outside the project.

Rationale   Design rationale includes QPW and many AT&T projects (a joint venture based in New Jersey, a formative organization in switching support, and others). It is difficult to find people with the skills to fill this role. Contemporary software architectures would be wise to take cues from classic architecture:

> *Here is another liability: beautiful drawings can become ends in themselves. Often, if the drawing deceives, it is not only the viewer*

who is enchanted but also the maker, who is the victim of his own artifice. Alberti understood this danger and pointed out that architects should not try to imitate painters and produce lifelike drawings. The purpose of architectural drawings, according to him, was merely to illustrate the relationship of the various parts. . . . Alberti understood, as many architects of today do not, that the rules of drawing and the rules of building are not one and the same, and mastery of the former does not ensure success in the latter (Rybczynski 1989, p. 121).

Pattern 24: Fire Walls

Alias Manager

Problem Project implementors are often distracted by outsiders who feel a need to offer input and criticism.

Context An organization of developers has formed in a corporate or social context scrutinized by peers, funders, customers, and other "outsiders."

Forces Isolationism doesn't work: information flow is important.

Communication overhead goes up nonlinearly with the number of external collaborators. Many interruptions are noise.

Maturity and progress are more highly correlated with being in control than being controlled.

Solution Create a Manager role to shield Development personnel from interaction with external actors. The manager's responsibility is to "keep the pests away."

Resulting Context The new organization isolates developers from extraneous external interruptions. To avoid isolationism, this pattern must be tempered with others, such as Pattern 20, Engage Customers; and Pattern 25, Gatekeeper.

Gatekeeper and Fire Wall alone are insufficient to protect developers in an organization whose culture allows marketing to drive development schedules.

Rationale The design rationale is QPW and ATT1. See also Pattern 20, Engage Customers, which complements this pattern. Pattern 25, Gatekeeper, facilitates the effective flow of useful information; Fire Walls restricts the flow of detracting information.

Sun Tzu, a Chinese general of 25 centuries ago, notes: "He will win who has military capacity and is not interfered with by the sovereign (Tzu 1983)."

Pattern 25: Gatekeeper

Problem   How do you foster communication with typically introverted engineering personalities?

Context   An organization of developers has formed in a corporate or social context scrutinized by peers, funders, customers, and other "outsiders."

Forces   Isolationism doesn't work: information flow is important.

Communication overhead goes up nonlinearly with the number of external collaborators. Many interruptions are noise.

Maturity and progress are more highly correlated with being in control than being controlled.

Solution   One project member, a Type E personality, rises to the role of Gatekeeper. This person disseminates leading-edge and fringe information from outside the project to project members, "translating" it into terms relevant to the project. The gatekeeper may also leak project information to relevant outsiders. This role can also manage the development interface to marketing and to the corporate control structure.

Resulting Context   This pattern provides balance for Pattern 24, Fire Walls, and complements Pattern 20, Engage Customers (to the extent that customers are still viewed as outsiders). Gatekeeper and Fire Walls alone, however, are insufficient to protect developers in an organization whose culture allows marketing to drive development schedules.

Rationale   Gatekeeper facilitates the effective flow of useful information; Fire Walls restricts the flow of detracting information. The value of Gatekeeper has been verified in practice. In the discussion of this pattern at PLoP/94, many of the reviewers noted that creating a Gatekeeper role had served them well.

Engineers are lousy communicators as a lot, so it's important to take advantage of an effective communicator when one is found.

Alexander notes that while it is important to build subcultures in a society (as we are building a subculture here in the framework of a company, or of the software industry as a whole), such a subculture should not be closed (see Alexander's Mosaic of Subcultures, §8; and Main Gateways, §53). One might muse that the Gatekeeper takes an outsider through any rites of passage necessary for more intimate access to the development team, by analogy to Alexander's Entrance Transition (§112).

Gatekeeper can serve the role of "pedagogue," as in Alexander's pattern Network of Learning (§18).

Maranzano notes that the same person often must fill both the Manager and Gatekeeper roles, because of the relationships to external people who need the info.

Pattern 26: Shaping Circulation Realms

Problem Patterns of interaction in an organization are not as they should be, as prescribed by other patterns.

Context This pattern is a building block for other patterns in the language, including Pattern 10, Organization Follows Market; Pattern 11, Developer Controls Process; Pattern 15, Architect Also Implements; Pattern 19, Engage QA; Pattern 20, Engage Customers; Pattern 28, Buffalo Mountain; and others. This pattern may also apply to circulation realms outside the project, such as Pattern 24, Fire Walls; and many others.

Forces Proper communication structures between roles are key to organizational success. Communication can't be controlled from a single role; at least two roles must be involved. Communication patterns can't be dictated; some second-order force must be present to encourage them. Communication follows semantic coupling between responsibilities.

Solution Give people titles that create a hierarchy or pecking order with a structure that reflects the desired taxonomy. Give people job responsibilities that suggest the appropriate interactions between roles (also see Pattern 27, Move Responsibilities).

Physically collocate people whom you wish to have close communication coupling (this is the dual of Pattern 9, Organization Follows Location).

Tell people what to do and with whom they should interact; people will usually try to respect your wishes if you ask them to do something reasonable that is within their purview and power.

Resulting Context The goal is to produce an organization with higher overall cohesion, with subparts that are as internally cohesive and externally decoupled as possible.

Rationale   This pattern follows Alexander's pattern of the same name (§98) and has strong analogies to the rationales of House Cluster (§37). The same rationale can also be found in Thomas Allen. Note that Pattern 27, Move Responsibilities, is closely related. See related notes in the Design Rationale for Pattern 25, Gatekeeper.

Pattern 27: Move Responsibilities

Aliases   Load Balancing; Chief Programmer Team

Problem   Unscrutinized relationships between roles can lead to undesirable coupling at the organizational level.

Context   This pattern applies in any organization or process.

Forces   You want cohesive roles and cohesive organizations. Decoupled organizations are more important than cohesive roles, however. There may be fundamental trade-offs between coupling and cohesion.

   Moving an entire role from one process or organization to another doesn't reduce the overall coupling, but only moves the source.

Solution   Move responsibilities from the role that creates the most undesirable coupling to the roles coupled to it from other processes. Simply said, this is load balancing. The responsibilities should not be shifted arbitrarily; a chief programmer team is one good way to implement this pattern (within the context of the Developer role's responsibilities).

Resulting Context   The new process may exhibit more highly decoupled groups. It is important to balance group cohesion with decoupling, so this pattern must be applied with care. For example, the Developer role is often the locus for a large fraction of project responsibilities, so the role appears overloaded. Arbitrarily shifting Developer responsibilities to other roles can introduce communication overhead. A chief programmer team can help balance these forces.

   Pattern 28, Buffalo Mountain, is an alternative load-balancing pattern.

Rationale   Most of the design rationale follows from the forces themselves. This is isomorphic to Mackenzie's model, in which task interdependencies, together with the interdependencies of task resources and their characteristics, define project roles (Mackenzie 1986).

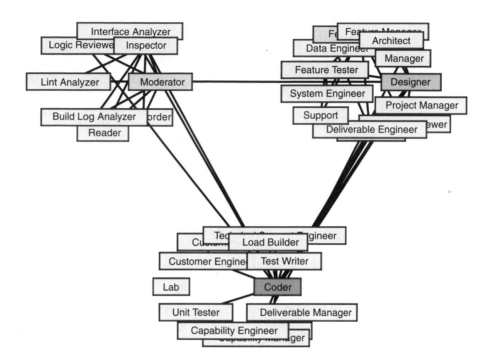

FIGURE 4   Sociogram showing clusters for activities design, coding, and review. Coupling in this partitioned design/coding process can be reduced by rearranging the Coder's responsibilities (see Pattern 27).

Pattern 28: Buffalo Mountain[5]

Problem   You want to optimize communications in a large software development organization whose members are working together on a common product.

Context   The development organization straddles several domains; effective interdepartmental communication is key to project success. A nominal "hub" may already have been established for the organization.

Forces   Communication overhead goes up nonlinearly as staff size increases. Information starvation and role isolation can cause people to develop unsuitable subproducts.

---

[5] The pattern's name comes from the similarity between the visual graph and the characteristic shape of a mountain in Colorado, and from the analogies that can be made about the forces contributing to each.

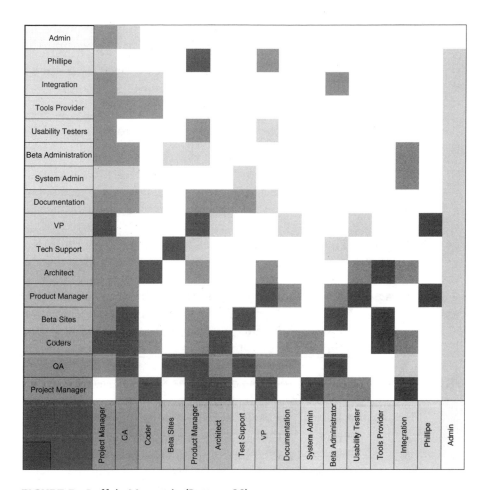

FIGURE 5   Buffalo Mountain (Pattern 28)

Being a communication bottleneck leaves no time to do work. Furthermore, such bottlenecks cause queues in organizational work flows that keep other people from doing work.

Fully distributed control tends to lead to control breakdown.

Solution   *Subpattern 1:* For any significant project interaction, the distance of two collaborating roles from the "center" of the organization should together be less than the shortest distance spanning the entire organization.

Subpattern 2: Avoid coupling with neighbors (anyone who is the same distance from the center of the process as yourself—that is, anyone who is equally coupled to the process as a whole) if you are in the outlying 50 percent of the organization.

Subpattern 3: The intensity of any collaboration should be inversely proportional to the sum of the interacting roles' distance from the center of the process.

Means A: Shuffle responsibilities between roles in a way that moves the associated collaborations to assume the above patterns (see Pattern 27, Move Responsibilities).[6]

Means B: Physically relocate people to enhance their opportunity to communicate (see Pattern 29, Work Flows Inward).

Means C: Increase the span of control of a role in the project (akin to merging multiple roles into one). It is probably best to Merge Roles with Similar Responsibilities—or better, Merge Roles with Similar Collaborations (other patterns!).

Resulting Context

The new organization has more balanced communication across its roles.

Rationale

Most of these patterns are empirical rather than derived from first principles. I think it is important to recognize this path to patterns as a positive and potentially fruitful one. If it works, go with it.

Subpattern 1 is empirical. It is the dominant subpattern. It infuses a level of "distributed control with central tendency" that lends overall direction and cohesion to an organization. Another way of stating subpattern 1 is that most points on the interaction grid tend to live near the axes.

Subpattern 2 avoids cliquish splinter groups. It also helps avoid linear event ordering in the distant (support) parts of a process. Linear event ordering (or pipelining) causes points on the interaction grid to line up right below the diagonal. A pattern that avoids points on the diagonal is likely to encourage more parallelism and independence.

Subpattern 3 tempers subpattern 1, allowing points further from the diagonal but not too far from the origin. This allows for a tight "core" at the middle of the process. It also helps to even the distribution of load across roles in the process. Many organizations are bimodal: they interact tightly in the core, but virtually not at all in the outlying roles. Subpattern 3 evens the load across all roles.

The overall (and difficult to explain) nature of these subpatterns is that they improve product quality and reduce the time to market. They tend to correlate with high spans of control. That in turn reduces the number of people necessary to complete a project, further reducing communication overhead, improving cohesion, and causing the pattern to recursively feed on itself. It's wondrous to watch this happen in an organization.

---

[6] This is Robert Lai's idea; it's simple, but profoundly effective.

Pattern 29: Work Flows Inward

Problem Work that adds value directly to the product should be done by authoritarian roles.

Context You are working with an existing organization where the flow of information can be analyzed. The organization exhibits a management pecking order.

Forces Some centralized control and direction are necessary.

During software production, the work bottleneck should be at the system's center (in the adjacency diagram sense; see Section 1.5, Notations). If the center of the organization's communication center generates more work than it does, then organization performance can become unpredictable and sporadic.

The developer is already sensitized to market needs through Pattern 24, Fire Walls; and Pattern 25, Gatekeeper (a centralized role need not fill this function).

Solution Work should be generated by customers, filter through supporting roles, and be carried out by implementation experts at the center. You should not put managers at the center of the communication grid: they will become overloaded and make decisions that are less well considered and that do not take day-to-day dynamics into account.

Resulting Context The result of this pattern is an organization whose communication grid has more points below the diagonal than above it (see Figure 6).

Rationale Katz and Kahn's analysis of organizations (1978, p. 314) shows that the exercise of control is not a zero-sum game (Katz and Kahn 1978, p. 314). The work should focus at the center of the process; the center of the process should focus on value-added activities (see Pattern 11, Developer Controls Process).

Organizations run by professional managers tend to have repeatable business processes, but they don't seem to reach the same productivity plateaus as organizations run by engineers. In programmer-centered organizations the value-added roles are at the center of the process (see Pattern 11, Developer Controls Process; and Pattern 15, Architect Also Implements). The manager should facilitate and support these roles and their work (see Pattern 12, Patron; and Pattern 24, Fire Walls).

Mackenzie characterizes this pattern using M-curves that model the percentage of task processes per task process law level (planning, directing, and execution) (Mackenzie 1986).

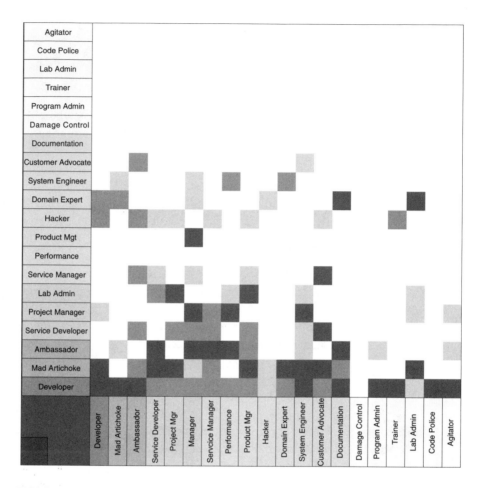

FIGURE 6   Interaction grids for two organizations (Pattern 29). The organization above has a healthy distribution of inward-directed inputs; on the facing page, the center is overloaded and turns work requests outward. Above, the core roles work; on the facing page they *make* work.

The rationale is supported by empirical observations from existing projects.

Managers should still make day-to-day decisions for the business process, pursuant to their responsibility to "keep the pests away" (see Pattern 24, Fire Walls).

Pattern 30: Three to Seven Helpers per Role

Problem   The organization has an uneven communication distribution.

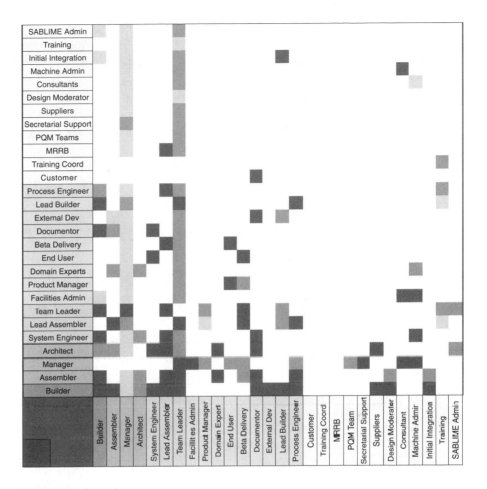

FIGURE 6   *(cont.)*

Context   The organization's basic social network has been built.

Forces   Too much coupling to any given role will overload it; if there's too little coupling, the role can become information starved and underutilized.

Solution   Ensure that each role has between three and seven helpers.

Resulting Context   The result is a more balanced organization with better load sharing and fewer isolated roles.

Rationale   Our empirical results from the organizations studied in the Pasteur project show that any given role can sustain, at most, seven long-term relationships (except in particularly productive organizations, where the number can be as high as nine). Particular needs might suggest that the process designer go outside these bounds, if doing so is supported with a suitable rationale.

Communication between roles in an organization is complete if every role communicates with every other role. An organization's "communication saturation" can be described as the ratio of the number of communication paths within the organization to the total possible number of communication paths. For a given project size, Neil Harrison's studies inside AT&T have found this ratio to be higher in highly productive organizations than in average organizations.

Pattern 31: Named Stable Bases[7]

Problem   How frequently do you integrate?

Context   A schedule framework has been determined.

Forces   With continuous integration, developers must try to follow a moving target. Wait too long between integrations and developers become blocked, unable to progress beyond the limits of the last base.
Stability is a good thing.
Progress should be made, and progress must be perceived.

Solution   Stabilize system interfaces—the architecture—no more than once a week. Other software can be changed (and even integrated) more frequently.

Resulting Context   The project has targets to shoot for. This affects the customer's view of the process, and it has strong ramifications for the architect as well.

Rationale   See the description of the forces. The main point of the pattern is that a project should schedule new changes so that their effects can be anticipated. It is less important to publish the content of a change (it will go unread anyway when there's high change volume) than for the development community to understand that change is taking place. It is important not to violate "the rule of least surprise."

It can be helpful to simultaneously have a number of bases at different levels of stability. For example, one AT&T project had a nightly build (which was

---

[7] This pattern was suggested by Dennis DeBruler at AT&T.

guaranteed only to compile), a weekly integration test build (which was guaranteed to pass systemwide sanity tests), and a (roughly biweekly) service test build (which was considered stable enough for QA's system test).

Pattern 32: Divide and Conquer

Problem   Organizations grow to the point where they cannot easily manage themselves (that is, the organization's decision process breaks down).

Context   The roles have been defined for a process and an organization, and the interactions between them are understood.

Forces   If an organization is too large, it can't be managed. Incohesive organizations are confusing and engender dilution of focus.

Separation of concerns is good. Nevertheless, it is useful to have organization boundaries that are somehow lightweight.

Solution   Find clusters of roles that have strong mutual coupling but are loosely coupled to the rest of the organization. Form a separate organization and process around those roles.

Resulting Context   Each new suborganization is a largely independent entity, to which the remaining patterns in this language can be independently applied.

Rationale   See the description of the forces. Note that each suborganization that arises from this pattern is fodder for most other patterns, since each subsystem is a system in itself. Also, to see an organization that has been reverse-engineered and redivided into new processes, see the picture for Pattern 27, Move Responsibilities.

Pattern 33: Decouple Stages

Problem   How do you decouple stages (architecture, design, coding) in a development process?

Context   A design and implementation process exists for a well-understood domain.

Forces   Stages should be independent to reduce coupling. Independence hampers information flow, but it creates opportunities for parallelism.

Solution   For known and mature domains, serialize the steps. Handoffs between steps should take place via well-defined interfaces. This makes it possible to automate one or more steps or to create a pattern that lets inexpert staff carry out the step.

Resulting Context   The new organization allows for specialization in carrying out parts of the process, rather than emphasizing specialization in solving the customer problem. This approach is "safe" only for well-understood domains, where mapping from needs to implementation is straightforward. Domains that are well understood are also good candidates for mechanization. For less mature domains, the process should build on the creativity of those involved at each stage of the process, and there should be more parallelism and interworking.

    This pattern prepares an organization for Pattern 34, Hub, Spoke, and Rim.

Rationale   See the forces.

Pattern 34: Hub, Spoke, and Rim

Problem   How do you decouple stages (architecture, design, coding) in a serialized development process while maintaining responsiveness?

Context   A design and implementation process exists, for a well-understood domain. Pattern 35, Aesthetic Pattern, has been applied.

Forces   Stages should be independent to reduce coupling.

    Independence hampers information flow, but it creates opportunities for parallelism.

Solution   Link each role to a central role that orchestrates process activities. Parallelism can be reintroduced if the central role pipelines activities.

Resulting Context   The process has more order and is more likely to be repeatable than Pattern 35 alone. The process designer must be wary of the central role becoming a bottleneck. (The designer must address such bottlenecks with other patterns as well, such as Pattern 27, Move Responsibilities.)

Rationale   The pattern is grounded in empirical studies done on a front-end process called CNM for a large AT&T project (unpublished work), and on pipelining theory.

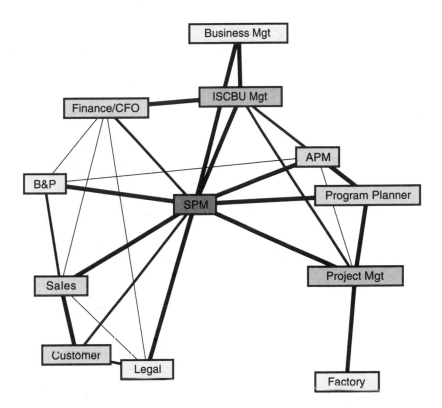

FIGURE 7   A product management organization. A single central role orchestrates this highly responsive front-end process supporting sales and marketing activities (see Pattern 34).

Pattern 35: Aesthetic Pattern

Problem   An organization has an irregular structure.

Context   The organization has been designed up through the preceding patterns. The project is in the early development stage of the first release of its product. The organization must plan how to evolve beyond the product's first release and eventually into the product's maintenance phase.

Forces   Even distribution of responsibility is good, because it distributes the workload. Regular structures (such as hierarchies) can easily be grown, by adding more people, without destroying the spirit of the original structure. A regular hierarchical structure does not distribute responsibility evenly.

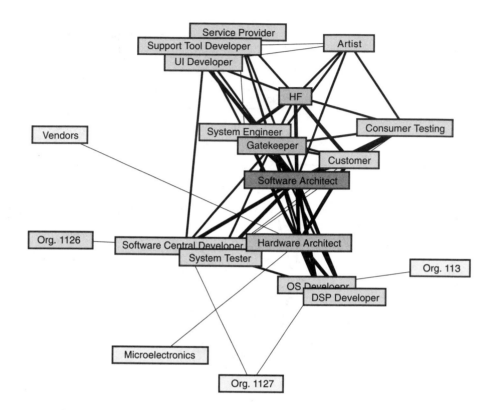

FIGURE 8 Two development organizations. The organization above has no apparent structure, and though it is productive, it is not likely to evolve well. The organization on the facing page has no well-partitioned structures, but one can identify logical partitions within it (customer, developer, management, and so on; see Pattern 35).

Solution   Make sure the organization has identifiable subdomains that can grow into departments of their own as the project thrives and expands to serve a maintained market.

Resulting Context   The organization will have suborganizational foundations on which to grow.

Rationale   This pattern reflects empirical observations of highly productive organizations.

To this point the pattern language has helped ensure a functional, highly productive organization. But work must still be done to allow the organization to grow elegantly. That end can be achieved by identifying the roots of suborganizations within the current organization. If none can be found, the

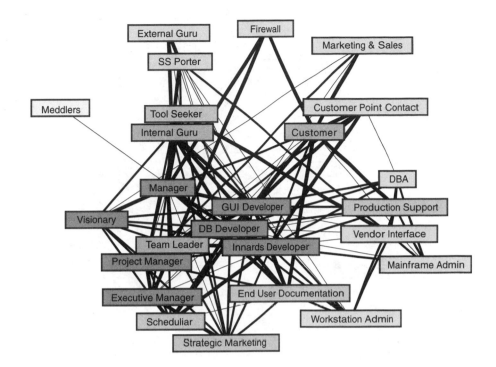

FIGURE 8   (*cont.*)

organization may not be able to grow. (For example, it is difficult to grow a Chief Programmer Team organization.)

Pattern 36: Coupling Decreases Latency

Problem   The process is not responsive enough; development intervals are too long; market windows are not met.

Context   This is for use in a service process and, perhaps in special cases, a small design/implementation process using an iterative or incremental approach.

Forces   Stages should be independent to reduce coupling. Independence improves opportunities for parallelism, but it hampers information flow.

Solution   Open communication paths between roles to increase the overall coupling-to-role ratio. This is particularly important for communication with central process roles. Communication between roles can be shaped using patterns such as Work Flows Inward (Pattern 29) and Move Responsibilities (Pattern 27).

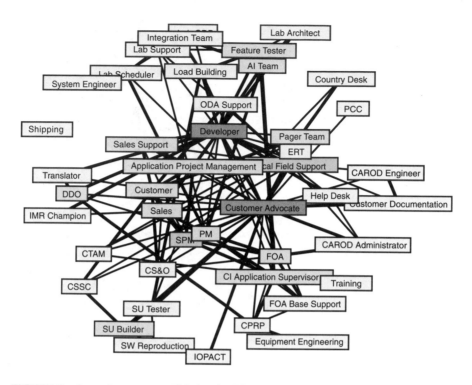

FIGURE 9 A service process. This is a highly responsive process, owing largely to its high degree of internal coupling (see Pattern 36).

Resulting Context Coupling increases dependence between roles, of course, which may not always be a good thing.

This pattern is somehow related to Pattern 40, Interrupts Unjam Blocking.

Handoffs can increase latency. The number of "hops" between roles should be kept small for any given problem.

Rationale This pattern is based on basic software engineering and sociometric principles.

Pattern 37: Prototype

Problem Requirements acquired early in the process are hard to validate without testing.

Context The organization is trying to gather requirements necessary for test planning (as in Pattern 18, Application Design Is Bounded by Test Design) and for the architecture (as for Pattern 15, Architect Also Implements). Alternatively, a high-risk or unfamiliar area surfaces early in development. (This may be used late in development as well, but the earlier it is applied, the better.)

Forces Requirements are always changing. Written requirements are usually too ambiguous. A project needs to get requirement changes early. Designers and implementors must understand requirements directly.

Solution Build a prototype to help you understand the requirements. Prototypes are particularly useful for external interfaces. Throw the prototype away when you're done.

Resulting Context The result is a better assessment of the requirements, to supplement use cases. This pattern nicely complements Pattern 20, Engage Customers; and Pattern 22, Scenarios Define Problem.

Rationale The processes of the visualizations illustrating Developer Controls Process (Pattern 11) and Engage QA (Pattern 19) are based largely on prototyping. Again, software can learn from classic architecture.

   As Frank Lloyd Wright said, "The best friend of the architect is the pencil in the drafting room, and the sledgehammer on the job" (Jacobs 1978).

Pattern 38: Take No Small Slips

Problem How long should the project take?

Context The product is underway and progress must be tracked.

Forces If the project takes too long, developers become complacent and you miss market windows. If it's too quick, developers become burned out and you miss market windows.

   Projects without schedule motivation tend to go on forever or spend too much time polishing details that are either irrelevant or don't serve customer needs.

Solution Paul Chisholm explains the solution: "We found a good way to live by 'Take no small slips' from . . . *The Mythical Man Month.* Every week, measure how close the critical path (at least) of the schedule is doing. If it's three days beyond schedule, track a 'delusion index' of three days. When the delusion index gets too ludicrous, then slip the schedule. This helps avoid churning the schedule. (Chisholm 1994)."

Resulting Context The result is a project with a flexible target date. Dates are always difficult to estimate; DeMarco (1993b) notes that one of the most serious signs of a project in trouble is a schedule set by working backward from a targeted end date.

Rationale   The rationale is based on an MIT project-management simulation, QPW, and *The Mythical Man Month* (Brooks 1982). Most sane projects manage this way.

Pattern 39: Developing in Pairs

Alias   Two Heads Are Better Than One

Problem   People are scared to solve problems alone.

Context   Code ownership has been identified and development is proceeding.

Forces   People sometimes feel they can solve a problem only if they have help. Some problems are bigger than any one individual.
   Too many people sitting in front of a keyboard and screen reduces the effectiveness both of the tool and of the people using it.

Solution   Pair compatible designers to work together; they can produce more together than they can working individually. Furthermore, a pair of people is less likely to be blindsided than is an individual.

Resulting Context   The result is a more effective implementation process.

Rationale   Compare to Pattern 21, Group Validation.

Pattern 40: Interrupts Unjam Blocking

Problem   The events and tasks in a process are too complex to schedule development activities in a linear sequence.

Context   Use this pattern for high-productivity design or implementation processes or low-latency service processes. Scheduling problems are addressed on a small scale (that is, this pattern is not for scheduling entire departments, but the work of cooperating individuals).

Forces   Complete scheduling insight is impossible.

The programmers with the longest development schedules will benefit if more of other programmers' code is complete before they try integrating or testing their own later code, assuming their interval can't otherwise be shortened (see Pattern 17, Code Ownership).

Solution   If a role is about to block on a critical resource, interrupt the role that provides that resource so they stop what they're doing to keep you unblocked.

If the overhead is small enough, it doesn't affect throughput. It will always improve local latency.

Resulting Context   The process should have a higher throughput—again, at the expense of higher coupling. Coupling may have already been facilitated by earlier patterns, such as Pattern 29, Work Flows Inward; Pattern 27, Move Responsibilities; Pattern 28, Buffalo Mountain; and Pattern 36, Coupling Decreases Latency.

Rationale   See the forces. The intent is that this pattern will apply most frequently between cooperating developers working on a single project. This is supported empirically from a high-productivity process at AT&T. There are strong software engineering (operating system) principles at work as well.

It may be useful to prioritize interrupts and service the ones that would optimize the productivity of the organization as a whole. That is, it is better to unblock four people who are currently blocked than to unblock a single squeaky wheel. The decision-making process should be fast; most of the time, it should be distributed. Where arbitration is needed, apply Patron (Pattern 12). The Patron and Manager can help the team audit the project for blocked progress, but they should defer to the Developers (or other directly impacted persons) to resolve the blockage whenever possible.

Maranzano notes a corollary to this pattern is another potential pattern: "Don't put too many critical tasks on one person."

Pattern 41: Don't Interrupt an Interrupt

Problem   The pattern Interrupts Unjam Blocking (Pattern 40) is causing people to thrash.

Context   Pattern 40, Interrupts Unjam Blocking, is being implemented.

Forces   One worker will inevitably be blocked on you—you can't do both things at once.
Expectations for complete, omniscient foresight and scheduling are unreasonable.

Solution   If someone is doing work that was triggered by an interrupt as in Pattern 40, he or she should turn away further interrupts until the current work is complete.

Resulting Context   The resulting context is largely the same as that of Pattern 40, Interrupts Unjam Blocking.

Rationale   This is a simple though somewhat arbitrary rule to keep scheduling from becoming an elaborate ceremony.

Pattern 42: Compensate Success

Problem   How do you best provide appropriate motivation for success?

Context   The organization consists of a group of developers meeting tight schedules in a high-payoff market.

Forces   Schedule motivations tend to be self-fulfilling: a wide range of schedules may be perceived as equally applicable for a given task. Schedules are therefore poor motivators in general.

Altruism and egoless teams are quaint, Victorian notions.

Companies often embark on make-or-break projects; such projects should be managed differently from others.

Disparate individual rewards motivate those who receive them, but they may frustrate their peers.

Solution   Establish lavish rewards for individuals contributing to successful make-or-break projects. The entire team (social unit) should receive comparable rewards, to avoid demoralizing individuals who might assess their value by their salary relative to their peers'.

"Very special" individuals might receive exceptional awards that are tied less strongly to team performance. A celebration is a particularly effective reward (Zuckerman and Hatala 1992).

Resulting Context   The result is an organization that focuses less on schedules and more on customer satisfaction and systemic success (but see Pattern 4, Size the Schedule). Such high rewards may cause individuals to overextend themselves, leading to personal stress and potential risks to the project.

Rationale   The rationale is empirically based. There is a strong correlation between wildly successful software projects and a very lucrative reward structure. Cases include QPW and practice cited at the Risk Derivatives Conference in New York on May 6, 1994; also, see Lawler (1981). The place of reward mechanisms is well established in the literature (see, for example, Kilmann 1984).

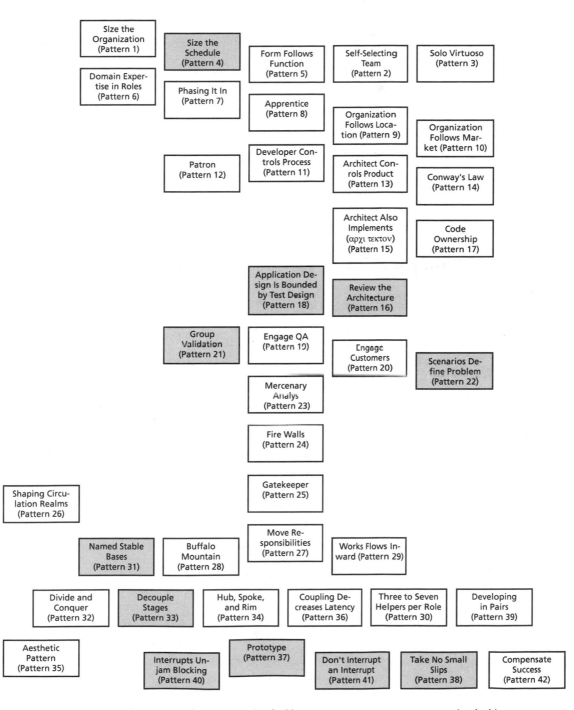

FIGURE 10   A map of the pattern language. Shaded boxes are process patterns; unshaded boxes are organizational patterns.

High rewards to some individuals may still demoralize their peers, but rewarding on a team basis helps remove the "personal" aspect of this problem and helps establish this mechanism as a motivator (in addition to being just a postmortem soother).

Dennis DeBruler noted at the PLoP review of this pattern that most contemporary organizational cultures derive from those of the industrial complex of the 1800s, which was patterned after the only working model available at the time: military management. He notes that most American reward mechanisms are geared more toward weeding out problems than toward encouraging solutions. A good working model is that of groups of doctors and lawyers, where managers are paid less than the employees.

REFERENCES

Alexander, Christopher (1979). *The Timeless Way of Building*. New York: Oxford University Press.

Alexander, Christopher, S. Ishikawa, and M. Silverstein (1977). *A Pattern Language*. New York: Oxford University Press.

Allen, Thomas (1977). *Managing the Flow of Technology*. Boston: MIT Press, pp. 141–182.

Beck, K. (1991). "Think like an object." *UNIX Review* (September 1991).

Berczuk, Steve (1994). Personal communication with the author, August 1994.

Block, R. (1983). *Politics of Projects*. New York: Yourdon Press.

Brooks, F. P. (1982). *The Mythical Man Month*. Reading, MA: Addison-Wesley.

Cain, B. G., and J. O. Coplien (1993). "A role-based empirical process modeling environment." *Proceedings of the Second International Conference on Software Process*. Berlin, February 1993.

Carlin, Jamee (architect) (1994). Personal interview, 1 July 1994.

Chisholm, Paul (1994). Personal discussion with the author, June 1994.

Coplien, J. O. (1994a). "Borland Software craftsmanship: A new look at process, quality, and productivity." *Proceedings of the 5th Annual Borland International Conference*. Orlando, FL, June 1994.

Coplien, J. O. (1994b). "Evaluating the software development process." *Dr. Dobb's Journal* 19, 11 (October).

Curtis, B., et al. (1988). "A field study of the software design process for large systems." *CACM* 31, 11 (November): 1268–1287.

DeMarco, Tom (1993a). Personal discussion with the author, January 1993.

DeMarco, Tom (1993b). CaseWorld Conference, January 1993.

Floyd, Christiane, et al., eds. (1992). *Software Development and Reality Construction*. Berlin: Springer-Verlag.

Gabriel, Richard P. (1994). "Productivity: Is there a silver bullet?" *Journal of Object-Oriented Programming* 7, 1, pp. 89 92.

Hsia, Pei; Jayaranan Samuel; Jerry Gao; and David Kung (1994). "Formal approach to Scenario analysis." *IEEE Software* (11), 2, pp. 33ff.

"An implementation of structured walk-throughs in teaching COBOL programming" (1979). *CACM*, 22, 6, (June).

Jacobs, Herbert. (1978). *Building with Frank Lloyd Wright.* San Fransisco: Chronicle Books.

Jacobson, Ivar, et al. (1992). *Object-Oriented Software Engineering: A Use Case Driven Approach.* Reading, MA: Addison-Wesley.

Johnson, Ralph. Personal communication.

Katz, Daniel, and Robert L. Kahn (1978). *The Social Psychology of Organizations,* 2d ed. New York: John Wiley.

Kerth, Norman (1994). "Caterpillar's Fate." Chapter 16, this volume.

Kilmann, R. H. (1984). *Beyond the Quick Fix.* San Francisco: Jossey-Bass.

Lawler, Edward E. (1981). *Pay and Organization Development.* Reading, MA: Addison-Wesley.

Mackenzie, K. D. (1986). "Organizing high technology operations for success." In J. R. Callahan and G. H. Haines, eds., *Managing High Technology Decisions for Success.*

Maranzano, Joe. Personal discussion with the author.

Meszaros, Gerard (1994). Personal communication at OOPSLA/94 workshop on Teams and Objects, October 24, 1994.

Meyers, G. J. (1978). "A controlled experiment in program testing and code walk-throughs/inspections." *CACM* 21, 9, (September).

Rousseau, Jean Jacques (1972). *Discours sur l'origine de l'inégalité.* Sorbonne: Nouveaux Classiques Larrouse.

Rybczynski, Witold (1989). *The Most Beautiful House in the World.* New York: Penguin.

Sun Tzu (1983). *The Art of War.* Trans. James Clavell. New York: Delacorte Press.

Swieringa, Joop, and André Wierdsma. (1992). *Becoming a Learning Organization.* Reading, MA: Addison-Wesley.

Vitruvius (1960). *The Ten Books of Architecture,* trans. Morris Morgan. New York: Dover.

Whitenack, Bruce (1994). "RAPPeL: A Requirements-Analysis Process Pattern Language for Object-Oriented Development." Chapter 15, this volume.

Zuckerman, M. R., and Lewis J. Hatala (1992). *Incredibly American. Milwaukee: ASQC Quality Press, pp. 81–83.*

James O. Coplien can be reached at AT&T Bell Laboratories, 1000 East Warrenville Road, Naperville, IL 60566; cope@research.att.com.

Lifecycle and Refactoring Patterns That Support Evolution and Reuse

14

Brian Foote and William F. Opdyke

Software development can be characterized as a set of recurring prototype (or initial design) phases, expansion phases, and consolidation phases. During a consolidation phase some relationships, initially modeled using inheritance, may evolve into aggregations. Also during consolidation, abstract classes are sometimes defined to capture behavior common to two or more existing classes. In this paper we define high-level patterns for the prototype, expansion, and consolidation phases of software development. We also define supporting patterns for evolving to aggregations from inheritance hierarchies and for creating abstract classes.

> So the real work of any process of design lies in the task of making up the language, from which you can later generate the one particular design.
>
> And, more subtly, we find also that different patterns in different languages have underlying similarities, which suggest that they can be **reformulated** to make them more general, and usable in a greater variety of cases.
>
> C. Alexander, *The Timeless Way of Building*

Copright © 1995 AT&T and Brian Foote. All Rights Reserved.

1. INTRODUCTION

Most of the work on patterns to date has concentrated on characterizing recurring functional, structural, and behavioral relationships among objects. Less attention has been paid to how classes and frameworks emerge and evolve. However, truly reusable objects are the result of an iterative, evolutionary process. We believe that it is possible, using patterns, to characterize aspects of this process itself. We agree with Kent Beck et al. [10] that an emphasis on the transformations designers make to existing objects to improve them can be as helpful to designers as depictions of the resulting artifacts.

Cunningham et al. [11] claim that many of the objects in a system may be found via a simple examination of the grammatical relationships in the system's specification. Many of the remaining objects, they contend, are uncovered using analysis tools such as CRC cards. Only a few are found late in the lifecycle; however (they concede), these are often of exceptional value, since they embody insights that emerge only from experience and can "make complexity melt away" [11].

We feel it is important to add that while the basic identities of many objects may be discovered early, these objects will change and improve as a system evolves. Truly reusable objects emerge as the result of this evolutionary process. As Dennis DeBruler has noted [9], it is important to allow for downstream changes to avoid design paralysis during the early phases.

We think it may be possible to characterize this process using a four-layered set of patterns. These patterns are far from a full-fledged pattern language for object-oriented software development. They should instead be thought of as a rough, preliminary sketch of where some of the major landmarks in such a language might be located. A full exposition of these potential patterns is beyond the scope of this paper. We have elected instead to focus upon five of them in detail. Nonetheless, we hope that through our discussion of the contexts these patterns complete and the patterns they give rise to, the reader may begin to discern the outlines of this nascent pattern language.

A top-layer pattern, Develop Software That Is Usable Today and Reusable Tomorrow, has forces that are resolved by the second-layer patterns Prototype a First-Pass Design, Expand the Initial Prototype, and Consolidate the Program to Support Evolution and Reuse.

We define each of these second-layer patterns in Sections 3 through 5. Then we define (in Sections 6 and 7) two patterns that apply during the consolidation phase. The consolidation aspects of program evolution have been a focus of our research on object evolution [13], life cycles [14], reuse [16], and refactoring [17, 21, 22]. (While the refactoring examples described herein apply most clearly to C++ programs, we have also researched how these patterns apply to programs written in Smalltalk and CLOS.) Design guidelines for the consolidation phase have also been documented by others [3, 7, 18, 23].

The Evolve Aggregations from Inheritance Hierarchies pattern, also examined in this paper, is one of the third-layer patterns that resolves the forces associated with the consolidation process. Inheritance models the *is-a* relation, while aggregation models the *has-a* relation. However, these relations are less distinct than might at first be thought. Is a pixel a point, or does a pixel have a *location* that is a point [24]? Is a matrix an array with extra behavior, or does a matrix have a *representation* that is an array [12, 21]? Different people give different answers to these questions, and it is common for people's answer to change over time. On the one hand, both points of view can lead to working programs. On the other hand, they differ in how the resulting designs will be reused and the kinds of changes that can easily be made to them. It is important to be able to change software so it reflects the current point of view. Although it is possible to convert aggregation to inheritance, converting inheritance to aggregation (the focus of this paper) seems to be more common, for several reasons [17].

The Create Abstract Superclass pattern is another third-layer pattern defined in this paper. During consolidation, abstractions common to two or more classes can be moved to a common abstract superclass. This pattern describes how that can be done, and what forces must be resolved.

Finally, there is the fourth layer of refactoring (behavior-preserving program transformation) patterns [21] that resolve the forces of this (and similar) patterns.

We have found this layered approach helpful in characterizing the program-consolidation phase, in understanding how refactorings can be interleaved with additions, and in ensuring that refactorings can be safely applied to object-oriented programs [21].

Patterns can exist at all scales.

C. Alexander, *The Timeless Way of Building*

2. BACKGROUND: OBJECT EVOLUTION

The language will evolve, because it can evolve piecemeal, one pattern at a time.

C. Alexander, *The Timeless Way of Building*

There are three distinct phases in the evolution of object-oriented abstract classes, frameworks, and components: a prototype phase, an expansion phase, and a consolidation phase. Associated with each of these phases is a series of high-level patterns that address the forces that must be resolved during that phase. These high-level patterns are realized in turn by applying lower-level patterns that resolve these forces. In the process of software development, we have seen these phases iterated and replicated in and among classes, frameworks, and applications. This pattern of self-similarity at different levels is typical of fractal curves; hence we refer to our characterization as the Fractal Model [14].

The Fractal Model can be thought of as an object-oriented specialization of Boehm's Spiral Model [4]. The Spiral Model is cast broadly, in such a way as to accomodate reuse, iteration, and the independent evolution of subsystems. The Fractal Model emphasizes those characteristics of objects that support change in ways that traditional software cannot. It is also unique in its emphasis on consolidation and refactoring as essential stages in the evolution of truly reusable components.

In the sections that follow, we will describe our patterns in a format similar to Alexander's [2]. The subsections below present the context, problem, solution, and discussion of related patterns.

3. PATTERN: PROTOTYPE A FIRST-PASS DESIGN

3.1 Context

In order to develop software that is usable today and reusable tomorrow, one must first address the problem at hand. Initial user requirements should be determined, even if they are sketchy. There is pressure to produce tangible results relatively quickly.

3.2 Problem

Building systems from the ground up is expensive and time-consuming. Moreover, it is difficult to tell if they really solve the problems they were intended to solve until they are complete.

It is rare to see systems built completely from scratch these days. Modern software systems rely on a variety of domain-independent components and tools. However, reusable domain-specific objects and frameworks are still relatively rare, particularly outside of the realm of graphical user interfaces.

It should come as no surprise that this is so. It is difficult simply to design a system at all. Designing a general, reusable system from first principles is much harder. Designing a system that addresses both the requirements at hand as well as a broad range of potential future problems poses nearly insurmountable challenges.

3.3 Solution

The initial design of a system should focus on the requirements at hand, with broader applicabilty as a secondary concern. It is most important to get *something* running relatively quickly, so that feedback on the design can be obtained. This initial prototype can borrow expediently from existing code.

As Brooks notes [6], software should be grown, not built. Successful large systems begin as successful small systems. A good way to get started is to build a prototype. For object-oriented programs, early prototypes allow designers to get feedback from customers and to understand the architectural issues they need to confront. Often the prototype is a quick, first-pass design, with an emphasis on finding a set of objects that embody the surface structure of the problem at hand.

The prototype phase may involve the application of analysis and design methods [see 5, 8, 26] as well as the development of an initial prototype implementation. During the construction of a prototype, it is common to expediently use existing code in order to get something working quickly. Such a strategy depends not only on the availability of preexisting domain-independent reusable components (like collections), but also on an infra-structure of domain-specific artifacts. Even in those domains where such code does not exist, code from a related domain might be borrowed.

Using existing code to create a new application is sometimes called "program-ming by difference." It is fair to ask where such reusable code (which serves as the foundation for an initial new design) comes from for domains where no code already exists. The next two patterns address this issue.

3.4 Related Patterns

While this phase can realize a reasonable first-pass set of objects, the designs of these objects still need to be refined (and they may later need to be completely redone). The following patterns (not further developed here) are examples of patterns that apply in this phase: Nouns in the Specification Imply Objects, Verbs Imply Operations(P1); Build on Existing Objects Using Inheritance (P2); Get It Running Now, Polish It Later (P3); and Avoid

Premature Generality (P4). This phase also sets the stage for exploration and consolidation, discussed in the following sections.

4. PATTERN: EXPAND THE INITIAL PROTOTYPE

Different neighborhoods, just like different people, will quite often have different versions of the patterns.

C. Alexander, *The Timeless Way of Building*

4.1 Context

Successful systems are seldom static. Instead, success sets the stage for evolution.

4.2 Problem

When software addresses an important need, both users and designers may recognize opportunities to apply the software in new ways. Often, addressing these new applications requires changes to the program—changes that were not envisioned when the software was initially designed. Such software evolution and reuse can undermine a program's structure and, over time, make it more difficult to understand and maintain the software.

During the expansion phase, designers often try to reuse parts of a program for purposes that differ from the program's original purpose, to varying degrees. In traditional languages, such reuse might be undertaken by making copies of the original code or by introducing flags and conditionals into the original code. Such activities tend to compromise a program's structure and make it difficult to understand and change the program later.

4.3 Solution

In object-oriented programs, inheritance is a powerful and useful mechanism for sharing functionality among objects. Placing new code in subclasses can help maintain design integrity, because changes are isolated in these subclasses and the original code in the superclasses remains intact.

Objects can evolve more gracefully than traditional functions or procedures because exploratory changes can be confined to subclasses. Such changes are less potentially disruptive to existing code that depends on a component.

What often results from the expansion phase is a class hierarchy that models a history of changes. The resulting subclasses are not yet truly general. More desirable, from a software maintenance standpoint, would be an inheritance hierarchy that models a type hierarchy [19].

4.4 Related Patterns

During expansion, patterns such as these come into play: Subclass Existing Code Instead of Modifying It (E1); Build on Existing Objects Using Inheritance (E2, like P2); Defer Encapsulation for Shared Resources (E3); Avoid Premature Generality (E4, like P4); and Get It Running Now, Polish It Later (E5, like P3). Note that some of the same patterns that appeared during the prototype phase appear here as well. This reflects genuine underlying similarities between these two phases.

5. PATTERN: CONSOLIDATE THE PROGRAM TO SUPPORT EVOLUTION AND REUSE

But what guarantee is there that this flux, with all its individual acts, will not create chaos?

It hinges on the close relationship between the process of creation and the process of repair.

C. Alexander, *The Timeless Way of Building*

5.1 Context

Initial designs are often loosely structured. As objects evolve, insights emerge on how they might have been better designed.

5.2 Problem

As objects evolve, they are subjected to forces that can undermine their structure if left unchecked. Prototypes are often first-pass designs that are expediently structured. During expansion, the introduction of new, sometimes conflicting requirements can muddle the clarity of parts of the original design. The insight necessary to improve objects is often not available until later in the program's lifecycle. Traditional lifecycle notions do not address the need to exploit this insight.

Truly reusable objects seldom emerge fully formed from an initial analysis of a given problem domain. More commonly they are discovered later or are polished and generalized as a system evolves. As a result, the objects in the system must be changed to embody this structural insight.

Traditional waterfall lifecycle models do not accommodate redesign late in a program's lifecycle. More recent lifecycle models, such as the Spiral Model, embrace iteration but do not address the unique properties of evolving objects.

Objects evolve differently than traditional programs. This is because they can, and do, change within and beyond the applications that spawn them. Some of these changes add breadth or functionality to a system; others improve its structure or reusability. It is easy to understand why the latter types of changes are often deferred indefinitely. This is unfortunate, because it is these changes that can be of the most enduring value.

Prototypes are loosely structured for a variety of reasons. One is that prototypes often are built to allow the designer to gain an initial sense of the layout of the design space. By definition the designer's understanding of the problem is immature at this time. Objects found during this phase may adequately reflect the surface structure of the problem, but they will need to be refined to do so elegantly. Furthermore, they will need to be reused in order to become reusable.

A second reason for the structural informality of prototypes is that they are often constructed in an expedient fashion out of existing, reusable parts. This should not be seen as a bad thing. "Get it running now, polish it later" can be an effective strategy for learning how to employ existing components to address new requirements.

In both cases, the insight necessary to get objects right is not available up front. If the process does not accommodate this insight when it does become available, these rough drafts can become the final objects.

During expansion, objects that have proven useful are redeployed in different contexts. Since the requirements raised by these contexts were not part of the specification for the original objects, they could not, in general, have been anticipated when these objects were designed. In object-oriented systems these new requirements tend to accumulate around the leaves of the inheritance graph; over time the hierarchy can become overgrown with redundant, haphazardly organized code.

5.3 Solution

Exploit opportunities to consolidate the system (by refactoring objects) to embody insights that become evident as the system evolves.

Objects can provide opportunities for reuse that are not available to conventional software. Object-oriented encapsulation encourages more modular initial designs. Inheritance allows changes that are made to accommodate new requirements to be made in subclasses, where they do not undermine the structural integrity of existing objects.

There comes a time when insight gained during the prototype and consolidation phases can be employed to refactor the system. Refactorings typically do not change the way the system works, but rather improve its structure and organization.

Experience accrued during successive reapplications of an object (during the prototype and expansion phases) should be applied during the consolidation phase to increase the object's generality and structural integrity. A program's design should be improved—abstract classes and frameworks should emerge or be made more explicit. During the expansionary phase, the size of a system typically increases. During consolidation, it can shrink.

For example, a designer might notice that two methods added during expansion contain duplicated code or data. The designer might factor this common code into a common superclass. Or a method may have grown larger as the code evolved. A designer might break this code into several methods to increase its level of abstraction and to provide new places to override behavior. As an object evolves, it is common for new objects to emerge. The next section describes a refactoring that addresses this situation. Each refactoring can be seen as addressing and correcting forces that, left unchecked, would undermine the structural integrity of the objects that compose the system. As a system evolves, disorder and entropy can increase; consolidation can be seen as an entropy-reduction phase.

5.4 Related Patterns

Table 1 lists thirteen design rules that are characteristically employed during consolidation. Table 2 lists refactorings that can be employed during consolidation. The next two sections present two of the most common and important refactorings as patterns.

DR1.	Use consistent names.
DR2.	Eliminate case analysis.
DR3.	Reduce the number of arguments.
DR4.	Reduce the size of methods.
DR5.	Class hierarchies should be deep and narrow.
DR6.	The top of the class hierarchy should be abstract.
DR7.	Minimize access to variables.
DR8.	Subclasses should be specializations.
DR9.	Split large classes.
DR10.	Factor implementation differences into subcomponents.
DR11.	Separate methods that do not communicate.
DR12.	Send messages to components instead of to self.
DR13.	Reduce implicit parameter passing.

TABLE 1 Design Rules [16]

6. PATTERN: EVOLVE AGGREGATIONS FROM INHERITANCE HIERARCHIES

6.1 Context

The class hierarchies that emerge during the prototype and expansion phases are often functional but neither elegant nor reusable. During the consolidation phase, designers take time to exploit opportunities to clean up the system, improve its structure and comprehensibility, and increase its reuse potential. The process of deriving aggregations from inheritance hierarchies can play a major role in system consolidation. This pattern can be employed in these superior patterns: Factor Implementation Differences into Subcomponents (DR10), Separate Methods That Do Not Communicate (DR11), and Send Messages to Components Instead of to Self (DR12).

6.2 Problem

Inheritance is sometimes overused during the early phases of an object's evolution. Changing informal, whitebox–based inheritance to blackbox–style aggregate-component relationships can result in better encapsulated, better structured, more resuable, more understandable code.

Category		Refactoring(s)
High-level refactoring	HR1.	Create abstract superclass.
	HR2.	Subclass and simplify conditionals.
	HR3.	Capture aggregations and components.
Supporting refactorings:	SR1.	Create empty class.
Create program entity	SR2.	Create member variable.
	SR3.	Create member function.
Delete program entity	SR4.	Delete unreferenced class.
	SR5.	Delete unreferenced variable.
	SR6.	Delete a set of member functions.
Change program entity	SR7.	Change class name.
	SR8.	Change variable name.
	SR9.	Change member function name.
	SR10.	Change type of a set of variables and functions.
	SR11.	Change access control mode.
	SR12.	Add function argument.
	SR13.	Delete function argument.
	SR14.	Reorder function arguments.
	SR15.	Add function body.
	SR16.	Delete function body.
	SR17.	Convert instance variable to pointer.
	SR18.	Convert variable references to function calls.
	SR19.	Replace statement list with function call.
	SR20.	In-line function call.
	SR21.	Change superclass.
Move member variable	SR22.	Move member variable to superclass.
	SR23.	Move member variable to subclass.
Composite refactoring	SR24.	Abstract access to member variable.
	SR25.	Convert code segment to function.
	SR26.	Move a class.

TABLE 2 Refactoring Patterns [21]

During the prototype and expansion phases of an object's evolution, designers tend to depend heavily on inheritance. Inheritance is often used where aggregation would be better because

- Inheritance is supported at the language level, so using it is easier than constructing aggregates by hand. Since it is a feature of object-oriented languages, programmers are trained to use it when they learn the languages. They do not become familiar with design idioms and patterns like aggregation until they become more experienced.

- It is not obvious that an *is-a* relationship should become a *has-a* relationship until the subclass becomes more mature.

- Inheritance creates a white box relationship that makes sharing resources such as operations and variables easy. It does not become clear how best to untangle intraobject coupling that may exist until the object has been used and reused for a while and the fissures along which new objects may be cleaved become more evident.

There comes a time (that is, the consolidation phase) when designers may notice that certain parts of an object exhibit a degree of cohesion that suggests that a distinct object can be factored from the existing hierarchy. The following benefits might be realized if some inheritance relationships can be changed into aggregations:

1. Cohesion and encapsulation can be improved by changing one large class to two smaller classes.

2. Aggregates can change their components at run time, while inherited subparts are static. That is, components can exploit dynamic polymorphism. A component might become a member of a different aggregate as well.

3. Separate classes can be reused independently, and may independently evolve. Each may spawn subclasses that can be interchangeably used by the other, since they will communicate only via a public interface.

4. An aggregate might have more than one instance of a given component class.

An example of an inheritance-based relationship that could be cast as an aggregate might be a `Matrix` class. The initial design of such a class might be based on the observation that a `Matrix` is a `TwoDimensionalArray` to which a repertoire of arithmetic operations are added. Hence, `Matrix` might be defined as a subclass of `TwoDimensionalArray` that adds operations like `+`, `*`, and `transpose` to the inherited methods for accessing and changing array elements. Changing the relationship from an inheritance-based relationship to an aggregation can take advantage of the fact that the `TwoDimensionalArray` subpart is being used essentially intact as a state repository for the `Matrix` abstraction. Making this part of the `Matrix` a component can permit alternate representations for this repository, such as `SparseArrays` or even stateless identity objects, to be used in place of `TwoDimensionalArrays`.

6.3 Solution

Change inheritance-based relationships into aggregate-component relationships by factoring parts of an existing class into a new, component class. Perform these changes in such a way as to ensure that the program will still work as it did before.

Suppose that A is a subclass of C. A can reuse C's behavior by

- adding an instance of C as a component variable of A
- replacing references to variables and functions inherited from C with references to the component
- removing the inheritance link between A and C

For example, the Matrix class is a subclass of TwoDimensionalArray, with an inherited variable arrayRepr and inherited functions get and put. An instance of class TwoDimensionalArray is added as a component variable of Matrix. References to the inherited members of class TwoDimensional-Array are replaced by references to members of its new component variable. Then the superclass of Matrix is changed (for example, to another class, or to nil if Matrix is now a top-level class).

Ensuring that the program will still work after the changes are performed is easy for steps 1 and 3 but more difficult for step 2, where references to inherited variables and functions must be replaced not only in A (or Matrix) but also in its clients. One way to make step 2 easier is to abstract access to the variables inherited by A (or Matrix) and change the accessing functions to point to the members of the component variable.

6.4 Related Patterns

Changing inheritance-based relationships to aggregate/component relationships can require that a number of supporting refactorings be applied to a program. Creating an instance of the component class and populating it employs the pattern Create Member Variable (SR2). Changing the superclass of the aggregate class employs the pattern Move Class (SR25). Other related patterns include Create Member Variable (SR2), Create Member Function (SR3), Delete Unreferenced Variable (SR5), Delete a Set of Member Functions (SR6), Add Function Body (SR15), Move Member Variable to Superclass (SR22), Move Member Variable to Subclass (SR23), and Move Class (SR25). Changes to argument lists and member names may also be necessary, employing the patterns Change Variable Name (SR8), Change Function Name (SR9), Add Function Argument (SR12), Delete Function Argument

(SR13), and/or Reorder Function Arguments (SR14). Abstracting access to variables employs the pattern Abstract Access to Member Variable (SR23).

7. PATTERN: CREATE ABSTRACT SUPERCLASS

7.1 Context

As previously noted, the class hierarchies that emerge during the prototype and expansion phases are often functional but neither elegant nor reusable. One way to clean up inheritance hierarchies during the consolidation phase is to define abstract classes that capture behavior that is common to one or more existing classes. This pattern can be employed to satisfy the following design rules: *Class hierarchies should be deep and narrow* (DR5), *The top of the class hierarchy should be abstract* (DR6), and *Subclasses should be specializations* (DR8).

7.2 Problem

As programs evolve, abstractions emerge. Abstractions that appear in two or more classes are often implemented differently, and they are often intertwined with code that is specific to a class. Unless abstractions are consolidated in one place, code duplication persists and it is hard to reuse the abstaction.

 Systems grow with age. As they grow, the same abstraction may appear in more than one place in a program. This may happen because

- One common programming practice is to extend a program by copying existing code and modifying it. As this happens, code gets duplicated.
- Different design-team members may implement the same functionality independently in different parts of a program.

During the consolidation phase, these common abstractions are sometimes discovered. If the abstractions are consolidated in one place, several benefits might be realized:

- Defining the abstraction in one place reduces the program's size and possibly its execution time.
- Separating out the abstraction makes it easier to understand and reuse.
- If the abstraction (or its implementation) is flawed, it needs to be fixed in only one place. One problem with the copy-and-modify approach to

software development is that errors in the original code get copied along with the code. If the error is subsequently discovered and fixed in one place, it may still persist somewhere else.

- If abstractions are separated out and made explicit throughout a program, it can make the entire program easier to understand and evolve.

An example of where this pattern might be applied is where two classes, DenseMatrix and SparseMatrix, are defined. Suppose that Dense-Matrix was defined first, and then SparseMatrix was defined later by copying DenseMatrix and modifying it. These two classes contain common behavior and duplicated code. An abstract Matrix superclass could be defined that captures the behavior common to these two classes [22].

7.3 Solution

Factor abstractions common to two or more classes into a common abstract superclass. Perform these changes in such a way as to ensure that the program will still work as it did before.

Suppose that classes C1 and C2 share a common abstraction. An abstract superclass can be defined by

1. Adding a new class A1, which initially contains no locally defined members
2. Making A1 the new superclass of both C1 and C2
3. Determining the common behavior (functions, or parts of functions) in C1 and C2
4. Changing (as needed) function names, argument lists, function bodies, and the attributes of reference variables so that functions that implement common behavior (in C1 and C2) are implemented identically.
5. Moving the common functions to A1 and deleting them from the subclasses.

For example, during the evolution of the Choices file system framework, two classes, BSDInode and SystemVInode, were defined to support two different file formats. This pattern was applied to move common behavior into a common superclass, Inode. While some of the steps in applying this pattern were trivial, changing the function bodies was not. The mapUnit function was defined in both classes; it included much common code but also a few differences. The differing code was split off into new functions, and (in mapUnit) the differing code segments were replaced by calls to these functions, in order to make the function definitions in the two classes conform [22].

7.4 Related Patterns

Creating the abstract superclass may employ the patterns Create Empty Class (SR1), Create Member Variable (SR2), Create Member Function (SR3), Delete Unreferenced Variable (SR5), Delete a Set of Member Functions (SR6), Change Variable Name (SR8), Change Member Function Name (SR9), Change Type of a Set of Variables and Functions (SR10), Change Access Control Mode (SR11), Add Function Argument (SR12), Delete Function Argument (SR13), Reorder Function Arguments (SR14), Replace Statement List with Function Call (SR19), and Move Member Variable to Superclass.

8. DISCUSSION

As people exchange ideas about the environment, and exchange patterns, the overall inventory of patterns in the pattern pool keeps changing.

Of course, this evolution will never end.

C. Alexander, *The Timeless Way of Building*

To reiterate, our emphasis on consolidation does not mean that one should abandon the use "up front" of disciplined design and analysis techniques. On the contrary, one should apply discipline in the up-front stages—while realizing that the design won't remain fixed throughout a program's evolution. Over time, insights are gained and programs are evolved to address new problems that were not understood when the programs were initially designed. The focus on consolidation is not so much to "fix mistakes" as it is to improve a program's structure to accommodate change.

In our aggregation pattern we discuss how inheritance is overused and sometimes incorrectly used. Our pattern addresses how to fix one common misuse of inheritance; but in proposing this pattern, are we (improperly) encouraging an undisciplined use of inheritance, with the idea that one can "fix things later"? We think not. As noted earlier, *is-a* relationships are not always clearly distinct from *has-a* relationships. Points of view change over time, which does not imply that the original view of inheritance was incorrect.

C++ implements subtyping using subclassing. However, inheritance in C++ can also be (and sometimes is) used to implement programming-by-difference—a variant on the copy and modify approach to program development. We agree with Liskov and others that inheritance should primarily be used to represent subtyping relationships; however, inheritance is not always used this way in practice. Our patterns allow one to more clearly reflect typing relationships in programs.

In summary, in this paper we have characterized the evolution of object-oriented programs in terms of three distinct phases: prototype, expansion, and consolidation. We defined a high-level pattern for program consolidation, and we also defined a consolidation pattern for evolving aggregations from inheritance hierarchies.

It has been widely recognized that aggregates are superior to inheritance for expressing some structural relationships [25]. Black box components can better support encapsulation than the white box nature of inheritance. Also, the ability to replace old components with new ones helps in realizing the benefits of polymorphism at run time.

Gamma et al. [15] have compiled a catalog of two dozen structural design patterns. The emergence of aggregate/components relationships together with forwarding methods is a prominent, recurring theme in a sizable number of their patterns. Given the ubiquitous nature of this relationship, we hope to see better linguistic support for aggregation.

9. ACKNOWLEDGMENTS

Ralph Johnson supervised both of our research projects and provided review comments on several drafts. John Brant, Gabrielli Elia, Brian Marick, Don Roberts, and other members of Ralph Johnson's patterns seminar provided insightful review comments on a later draft, as did Ken Auer and the PLoP '94 reviewers. AT&T Bell Laboratories supported William F. Opdyke's refactoring research at the University of Illinois under a full-time doctoral support program.

REFERENCES

[1] C. Alexander. *The Timeless Way of Building*. New York: Oxford University Press, 1979.

[2] C. Alexander, S. Ishikawa, and M. Silverstein. *A Pattern Language*. New York: Oxford University Press, 1977.

[3] Paul L. Bergstein. Object-preserving class transformations. In *Proceedings of OOPSLA '91*. Berlin: Spring-Verlag, 1991.

[4] Barry W. Boehm. A spiral model of software development and enhancement. *IEEE Computer*, 21, 5 (May 1988).

[5] Grady Booch. *Object-Oriented Design*. Redwood City, CA: Benjamin/Cummings, 1990.

[6] Frederick P. Brooks. No silver bullet—essence and accidents of software engineering. *IEEE Computer* (April 1987): 10–19.

[7] Eduardo Casais. *Managing Evolution in Object Oriented Environments: An Algorithmic Approach*. Ph.D. thesis, University of Geneva, 1991.

[8] Peter Coad and Ed Yourdon. *OOA—Object-Oriented Analysis*. Englewood Cliffs, NJ: Prentice-Hall, 1990.

[9] Dennis Debruler. A generative pattern language for distributed processing. Chapter 5, this volume.

[10] Kent Beck et al. Patterns postings related to aggregations. Email exchange on `patterns@cs.uiuc.edu`.

[11] Ward Cunningham et al. When are objects found? email exchange on `patterns@cs.uiuc.edu`.

[12] Brian Foote. *An Object-Oriented Framework for Reflective Meta-Level Architectures*. Ph.D. thesis in preparation, University of Illinois at Urbana-Champaign.

[13] Brian Foote. *Designing to Facilitate Change with Object-Oriented Frameworks*. Master's thesis, University of Illinois at Urbana-Champaign, 1988.

[14] Brian Foote. A fractal model of the life cycle of reusable objects. In *OOPSLA '93 Workshops on Process Standards and Iteration* (J. Coplien, R. Winder, and S. Hutz, organizers). Washington, DC, 1993.

[15] Erich Gamma, Richard Helm, Ralph Johnson, and John Vlissides. *Design Patterns: Elements of Reusable Object-Oriented Software*. Reading, MA: Addison-Wesley, 1995.

[16] Ralph E. Johnson and Brian Foote. Designing reusable classes. *Journal of Object-Oriented Programming* 1,2 (1988): 22–35.

[17] Ralph E. Johnson and William F. Opdyke. Refactoring and aggregation. In *Proceedings of ISOTAS '93: International Symposium on Object Technologies for Advanced Software*. November 1993.

[18] Karl J. Lieberherr and Ian M. Holland. Assuring good style for object-oriented programs. *IEEE Software* (September 1989): 38–48.

[19] Barbara Liskov. Data abstraction and hierarchy. In *Addendum to the Proceedings of OOPSLA '87*. 1987.

[20] Peter W. Madany. *An Object-Oriented Framework for File Systems*. Ph.D. thesis, University of Illinois at Urbana-Champaign, 1992. Also Technical Report No. UIUCDCS-R-92-1751, Department of Computer Science, University of Illinois at Urbana-Champaign.

[21] William F. Opdyke. *Refactoring Object-Oriented Frameworks*. Ph.D. thesis, University of Illinois at Urbana-Champaign, 1992. Also Technical Report No. UIUCDCS-R-92-1759, Department of Computer Science, University of Illinois at Urbana-Champaign.

[22] William F. Opdyke and Ralph E. Johnson. Creating abstract superclasses by refactoring. In *Proceedings of CSC '93: The ACM 1993 Computer Science Conference*. February 1993.

[23] Roxanna Rochat. In search of good Smalltalk programming style. Technical Report CR-86-19, Tektronix, 1986.

[24] J. P. Rosen. What orientation should Ada objects take? *Communications of the ACM* 35, 11 (November 1992): 71–76.

[25] Alan Snyder. Encapsulation and inheritance in object-oriented programming languages. In *Proceedings of OOPSLA '86*, November 1986, pp. 38–45. Printed as SIGPLAN Notices, 21, 11.

[26] Rebecca Wirfs-Brock, Brian Wilkerson, and Lauren Wiener. *Designing Object-Oriented Software*. Englewood Cliffs, NJ: Prentice-Hall, 1990.

Brian Foote can be reached at 209 W. Iowa, Urbana, IL 61801; foote@cs.uiuc.edu. William F. Opdyke can be reached at AT&T Bell Laboratories, Naperville, IL 60566; opdyke@ixserve.att.com.

RAPPeL: A Requirements-Analysis-Process Pattern Language for Object-Oriented Development

15

Bruce Whitenack

ABSTRACT

RAPPeL is a pattern language that provides a direction and rationale for analysts, developers, and project managers engaged in defining requirements for business applications (such as information management systems, decision support systems, work flow management systems, scheduling systems, and so on) to be developed in an object-oriented environment. It weaves through the fabric of a business problem domain, creating threads of techniques for capturing and validating the behavioral and nonbehavioral requirements of a software system. While RAPPeL assumes that the business application is built using object-oriented techniques and implemented in an object-oriented language, some of its patterns are applicable to software requirements analysis in general.

RATIONALE FOR RAPPeL

There currently exists a chronic and severe problem in performing sufficient requirements analysis for successful software development. Customers who

Copyright © 1994 Bruce G. Whitenack and Knowledge Systems Corporation. All Rights Reserved.

come to Knowledge Systems Corporation (KSC) for assistance in developing Smalltalk products typically think their requirements are complete and their problem area well understood. However, upon actually having to design and build a system, they realize that a richer and fuller requirements analysis is required. In KSC's involvement with over one hundred Smalltalk projects, we have found that in a vast majority of cases a project's initial requirements analysis is insufficient to begin a successful design process and to build an object-oriented solution that does not require further analysis and requirement specifications. A large part of the problem is that good requirements analysis for a complex problem domain is challenging and requires hard work and the skillful application of a variety of techniques.

The goals of this pattern language are

1. to guide analysts and product developers to apply a set of techniques and methods appropriately, so as to produce a more thorough analysis and understanding of the problem

2. to provide a framework for defining and capturing requirements before development and then evaluating, designing, building, and testing an appropriate software product

3. to provide a means for tracing a system's design back to the original business and system objectives.

In short, the primary goal of this pattern language is the primary goal of requirements analysis in general—to ensure that systems that "do the right things" are defined and built.

CAVEATS

Please note that items labeled with a boldface, bracketed **D** plus a number (for example, **[D2]**), correspond to the deliverables listed below. These are produced as part of the solution to a pattern. Their descriptions are not included in this paper. Their purpose should be evident from their names and the contexts in which they are built.

This is a work in progress. The reader should assume that there are no other patterns in the language than the ones described in this paper. The pattern numbers indicate that I expect to add new patterns as the language matures and as existing patterns expand. I also expect RAPPeL to be joined with other potential languages (for example, Project Management, Product Design, and so on).

To make the best use of this pattern language, I suggest that you first make a quick pass through the language and read the problem statement for each pattern. Then go back and read each pattern entirely. Few of the patterns stand alone; they need to be read within the context of the language as a whole. I believe those readers involved in developing business applications using object-oriented languages will be rewarded for their efforts in understanding and applying these patterns. I know I have been. It is my hope that software development will eventually become akin to rapidly rappelling down a mountain—from one sure point to another, moving toward a safe destination—rather than to being bloodied as one continually picks one's way around crags and through crevices.

TABLE 1 Pattern References

Pattern	Patterns Referenced	Direct Deliverables Referenced
1. Building the Right Things	5, 14, 9, 17, 20, 34, 99, 97	1–4
5. Customer Expectations	30, 40, 34, 97	4, 14, 29
9. Customer Rapport	97	
14. Sponsor Objectives		3, 5, 6
17. Defining the Requirements	14, 20, 30, 34, 40, 97	31
20. Problem Domain Analysis	22, 24, 25, 26, 28, 30, 36	
22. Information Needs	32, 50, 97	11, 12, 16
24. Finding and Defining the Domain Objects	28, 32	8, 9, 15, 31, 33
25. Classifying, Associating, and Grouping the Domain Objects		13, 14, 34–36
26. Elaboration of the Domain Objects	22, 27, 36	
27. Object Aging (Life Cycles)	30	36
28. Object Stereotypes		34
30. Behavioral Requirements	50, 32	10, 14–27
32. Envisioning	97, 21	15, 25
34. Requirements Specification	20, 30, 99	
36. Business Rules	26	15, 34
40. Pragmatic External Requirements		29
50. User Interface Requirements	97	25–28
97. Prototypes		25, 26
99. Requirements Validation	97	30

Direct Deliverables:

1. Requirements Sources
2. Work Plan
3. Interview Sheets and Group Meeting Results
4. List of Customer Expectations
5. Business Goal Matrix
6. Business Goal Summary Report
7. Model Structure Diagrams
8. Business Process Definitions
9. Business Process Diagrams
10. System Boundary Diagram
11. Information-Source Matrix
12. Information-Flow Diagrams
13. Scenario Script
14. Use-Case Matrix
15. Use-Case Definition
16. Use-Case Models
17. Decision Table
18. Decision Tree
19. Moore State Transition Matrix
20. Harel State Chart
21. Petri Nets
22. Business Rules
23. Information-Views Definitions with Attribute Definitions and Edits
24. Pertinent Object Relationships
25. Low-Fidelity Prototypes
26. High-Fidelity Prototypes
27. CAR Diagrams
28. Window-Flow Diagrams
29. Pragmatic Requirements Template
30. Issues List
31. Glossary of Terms
32. Error Message List

THE PATTERN LANGUAGE

Pattern 1: Building the Right Things

Problem Failure to understand customer needs and difficulties in capturing requirements contribute to software development problems and failures. How do you capture, communicate, and validate software requirements so that successful systems that "do the right things" can be built?

Discussion Capturing and communicating requirements is a difficult task. Customers frequently cannot adequately express their requirements, and developers have difficulty understanding what customers need. Requirements change, or they are incomplete, not well understood by the sponsors, or in conflict with one another. The problem area itself may not be well understood. Systems are often built not for sound business reasons, but because "the powers that be" feel the need to pull the business into the twenty-first century technologically. Often software analysts and developers think they know what is required better than the business experts. This leads to customer dissatisfaction and a product that does not meet their needs. For many projects, all requirements are treated equally—the least important requirement is given the same concern during development as the most important. This can cripple the delivery of the system.

Solution Since requirements originate from sources (people, systems, documents, and so on), identify and categorize requirements sources **[D1]**. These will be your sources of information and will help you decide which requirements are the most important. Devise a work plan **[D2]** for interviewing and examining these sources. This will produce a set of interview results **[D3]** (see Roger Pressman's book [Pressman82] for interview question examples). Because the goal of most business projects is to design and construct a software system that meets customer needs and business goals, the analyst must capture and validate sponsor objectives (see Pattern 14) as well as manage customer expectations (see Pattern 5). The requirements produced by these activities must also be prioritized. If the customer thinks all requirements are of equal importance, watch out—this is a warning sign that you are not dealing with a realistic customer. While accomplishing these and subsequent activities, it is important to establish and keep customer rapport (see Pattern 9). That way you and the customer can work as a team to solve problems, and you can educate each other: the customer can educate you about the business, and you can educate the customer about software development.

Now comes the fun part. When your initial investigation is complete and all the players have been identified, the real requirements analysis game begins. The following paragraph makes the process sound trivial, but in reality it means a lot of varied activities, in which inventiveness and experience play a big part. RAPPeL is meant to provide guidance and experience, to lead you down the right paths.

Use the methods and activities described in Defining the Requirements (Pattern 17) to determine how to best use and bind together the three key activities, or threads, of problem domain analysis (see Pattern 20), requirements specification (see Pattern 34), and requirements validation (see Pattern 99) to produce the specification that will best communicate and model the requirements. It is extremely important to include the use of prototypes (see Pattern 97) as a key part of requirements analysis. The end result of all these activities is a validated requirements specification and one or more product simulations.

Pattern 5: Managing and Meeting Customer Expectations

Problem   How do you meet and manage customer expectations for a product?

Discussion   A product may technically satisfy the requirements specification but still not meet customer expectations. Requirements can always be more completely or precisely defined. It is not possible to ensure that a product will completely meet a customer's expectations through a single massive attempt to completely specify all requirements.

If we listen only to the words a customer uses, we miss a lot of the customer's message. A standard waterfall requirements specification process is estimated to gather roughly two-thirds of a customer's actual requirements [Arthur92].

Solution   The process of discovering expectations is an ongoing one, from the beginning of a project, and is vital to the project's overall success. Consequently, you should produce a list of customer expectations **[D4]** and classify each of them as either a real requirement (a "must-haves") or a customer wish (a "like-to-have"). For example, password security is usually a "must-have," but voice recognition is most likely just a "like-to-have." Each "must-have" should be incorporated as either a behavioral requirement (see Pattern 30) or a pragmatic external requirement (see Pattern 40) in the requirements specification. Again, it is important to eventually prioritize and classify these requirements. This can be done as part of the Use-Case Matrix [D14] and the Pragmatic Requirements Template [D29].

Build one or more prototypes as discussed in Prototypes (Pattern 97), to validate that the defined behaviors of the system will meet customer expectations.

Pattern 9: Customer Rapport

Problem   How do you build and establish a good relationship with a customer?

Discussion   The primary cause of most problems in software development is people not working together. There is often a failure to establish and continue a relationship with the customer during software development. Without a sense of trust and common effort, customers are discouraged and will end conversations prior to really communicating their needs. Meanwhile, when a customer is uncommunicative, the technical people withdraw into the safety of their offices and subsequently write programs with a limited understanding of the customer's needs. Where there is a poor or no relationship between the customer and the analyst or developer, efforts to gather software requirements will probably be unsuccessful [Arthur92].

Solution   It is important to first develop a rapport with the customer and to then move toward specifying the customer's requirements. Seek first to understand, then to be understood. Focus on the user. Talk and work with users at their location. Involve them in the user-interface design. Do not talk down to them, and do not use too much technical jargon.

Build prototypes (see Pattern 97). These are actually a part of the behavioral specification—prototypes provide immediate feedback and validation to the customer. They are a powerful form of requirements gathering and validating. Working together on a prototype connects the analyst or developer to the customer in a way that allows a relationship to develop. This connection facilitates communication at all levels. It provides customers with the most powerful form of feedback the developer can provide—a simulation of the product they want and need [Arthur92]. Every successful Smalltalk project I am aware of used prototypes to model behavior and to build upon.

Pattern 14: Sponsor Objectives

Problem   How do you get the business objectives to line up with what is being built, so the software system can meet real business needs?

Discussion   Systems may be built that are complete according to the requirements but do not really satisfy the customer's business needs. Often there is no clear set of measures for determining what the system is supposed to accomplish or how well it meets those needs. Instead, all requirements are considered to be of equal importance. The most important requirements, however, are those that will meet the business objectives. But what *are* the business objectives? How do you know you have met them?

Solution   Schedule and hold an initial round of interviews. Have group meetings to discuss the objectives, to find and build a consensus on what the most important business objectives are. Record the interview and group meeting results **[D3]**.

The business objectives decided upon in these meetings should essentially reflect the reasons the enterprise is undertaking the development of the system in the first place. A good guideline for determining whether a business objective is appropriate (suggested by American Management Systems, Inc. [AMS92]) is to ask this question: If the system will not substantially meet this objective, is that a sufficient reason to stop the system's development? If the answer is yes, then you have a solid business objective. Try to limit the objectives to no more than eight.

Determine who will support the system and who may oppose it. As a result of these activities, complete a Business Goal Matrix **[D5]**, containing business goals. Each goal will have an accompanying explanation of the metric to be used for measuring performance, as well as a measure of current performance and a target performance value. Also complete a Business Goal Summary Report **[D6]**, which includes consensus answers and significant variances between users.

Use these measurable business goals to negotiate with the customer to deliver requirements that are both valid and reasonable from both the customer's and the developer's perspective.

Pattern 17: Defining Requirements

Problem   How do you produce a requirements specification that is best suited to object-oriented design and to implementation in an object-oriented language? What are the methods and techniques you should use to best determine and define system requirements? When and how should these methods and techniques be applied?

Discussion   If the product is being developed to solve a problem, then the problem must be understood to some degree before a solution can be defined. Problem analysis is required. It is seldom the case, however, that a problem is completely understood before a solution is proposed. For example, in the case of business reengineering, the envisioned business processes must be understood. Even after a careful analysis, it is very common for the customer or the developer to want to add or change features because the prototype implementation revealed misconceptions or it made the user aware of the the system's potential and triggered new ideas on better ways to accomplish tasks. The customer will consequently "require" further changes or behaviors in the system. These will have to be respecified in the next prototype. Meaningful prototyping (see Pattern 97) is essential for good requirements analysis of any software business product.

Also, one organization's design "requirement" may be another organization's design "feature." Company Q may simply state that their salespeople should be able to add a term to a contract. Company B, on the other hand, may state that the Contract window must display a contract in a particular outline form and that a salesperson must be able to select a term and place it in the outline. Natural language is a clumsy way to specify user interface requirements.

Analyzing the problem domain with minimal thought to the functional requirements of the system will lead to well-rounded objects. These are objects that are not slanted toward a particular service, application, or use imposed on them by a particular external user. These objects may be shallow, however, as they have not been called upon to provide a set of services for a number of external users. Consequently there must be activities to focus and define the behaviors of the new system. These activities must answer the following questions:

- Since the system's essential requirements must be defined and prioritized only in accordance with valid business reasons, what are the sponsor objectives (see Pattern 14) to be supported by the system?

- Since the scope of the problem domain must be bounded, what are the boundaries of the system?

- What clients (users) will use the system?

- What external entities will provide services to it?

- Since the system will be built and developed in an environment (both business and technical) that has limitations and standards, what are the pragmatic external requirements (see Pattern 40) affecting the system's development?

- Since users will have special needs and tasks the system must support, what are the information needs of the users?
- What user tasks will the system support?
- How must it support those tasks?
- Since the system will enforce the rules and policies of the domain, which rules of the domain (that is, business rules) are critical? (Which ones *must* be enforced by the system?)

Solution　It is often the case that common business terms (which usually are essential objects in the user's problem domain) have different meanings to different people within the same organization. Terms, policies, rules, processes, and events have to be understood, defined, and agreed upon, or else the behaviors specified to solve the problem will be incomplete and ill defined. This is why it is essential to first create and maintain a glossary of terms **[D31]**.

Requirements analysis may be thought of as a three-stranded process (like a three-stranded rope). The first strand is problem domain analysis, the second is requirements specification, and the third is requirements validation. Each strand overlaps and reinforces the others. The threads are intertwined, not connected end to end as in a waterfall approach. If a product is to solve a problem, then the problem must be understood, by means of analysis, before a solution is defined. The solution is the requirements specification. The validation step is to ascertain that the specified requirements will actually solve the problem analyzed.

Use and study the template discussed in Requirements Specification (Pattern 34). It will serve as a framework for your requirements-analysis efforts. To begin, capture the system's behavioral requirements (see Pattern 30) and do a problem domain analysis (see Pattern 20). As the activities in these patterns are completed and requirements deliverables produced, complete the corresponding sections of the requirements specifications. Validate the deliverables and the sections of the requirements specification with customers. As discrepancies occur, the details of the requirements specification are revisited and reviewed. Finally, the last aspect of the problem is analyzed, all issues are reconciled, and a public version of the specification is completed.

The problem will be better understood as behaviors are specified and modeled. In fact, because most object-oriented development efforts include an object model used to conceptualize the problem domain (and which may be incorporated directly into the system design), there is an increased understanding of the problem domain as development continues. The specification should be validated and understood so the product will conform to the right set of behaviors. As the specification is validated by the customer, the desired behaviors may be refined or changed.

Pattern 20: Problem Domain Analysis

Problem   How do you determine and define the essential nature of the problem domain in which the system is to be built?

Discussion   Problem domain analysis involves the construction of knowledge representations, or models, of the problem domain that give the developer a comprehensive understanding of the problem area. The purpose of problem domain analysis is not to define requirements for a product, it is to provide the developer with the deepest understanding possible of the problem area.

Consider an example in which we are interested in investigating how the human brain works. We would identify its parts, its cells, its regions—and then try to determine what each one does. What are the parts of neurons? What happens when we see, smell, hear, feel, taste? How do these things happen? We could do all kinds of studies to see the effects of different environmental conditions on the brain. We could study memory, language, and thought processes. However, let us say that our sponsors want us to find the best way to treat brain tumors. This narrows our scope, focusing our analysis of the brain on only those aspects that have to be considered in connection to the destruction of brain tumors. After all, this is the reason we are doing the analysis. These two things, analysis and requirements specification, are very much intertwined. The more we specify the requirements, the more it focuses the analysis. Consequently, the identification of required tasks (like the eradication of brain tumors) is considered to some degree during problem analysis. This results in a "Ping-Pong" process of defining behavioral requirements and doing domain analysis at the same time. The questions remains, however, of how this process works.

Solution   In object-oriented analysis the problem domain is seen as a community of interrelated objects. During domain analysis a number of questions are asked and answered. Table 2 lists a series of problem domain analysis questions and the patterns that address them.

What are the essential objects in the problem domain? What is their nature? What are their roles and responsibilities?	The objects' roles depend on how they are viewed by their users. A coffee mug can be viewed as a paperweight, a container for coffee, a container for pencils and other objects, or as a decorative object. It can be a valuable keepsake or a piece of junk. It can even be conceived as a breakable item or a marketing gimmick, depending on the user's point of view. See Finding and Defining the Domain Objects (Pattern 24).
What "important information" is inherent in the objects?	What is important information also depends on the user's point of view. Information associated with a coffee mug could include the logo printed on its side; its color, size, price, material, shape, weight, manufacturer, supplier, and price; or quantity on hand. See Information Needs (Pattern 22).
What are the relationships between objects? What objects are part of other objects?	See Classifying, Associating, and Grouping the Domain Objects (Pattern 25).
What processes are inherent in the community of objects (e.g., as order fulfillment, making a sale, or producing a product)?	See Behavioral Requirements (Pattern 30).
What are significant events (e.g., parts in the warehouse are below threshold, so produce an order and notify purchasing)?	See Behavioral Requirements (Pattern 30).
What rules (or business rules) constrain the objects?	See Elaboration of the Domain Objects (Pattern 26) and Business Rules (Pattern 36).
What is the life cycle of an object? What states can each object be in?	See Elaboration of the Domain Objects (Pattern 26) and Object Aging (Life Cycles) (Pattern 27).

TABLE 2 Problem Domain Analysis Questions and Patterns

The goal of problem domain analysis is to define the world (often called the problem space, product space, or problem domain) in which the product is to be built. The nature of the domain makes some of the questions listed above more important than others. In many business applications, information needs (see Pattern 22) and business rules (see Pattern 36) are the two most important aspects to be defined. The information needs must be identified, and in many cases those needs determine the essential information-holding objects that are part of the business domain (see Pattern 28, Object Stereotypes).

To do a good and meaningful domain analysis, follow the patterns that answer each of the analysis questions in Table 2.

Pattern 22: Information Needs

Problem   How do you capture the information needs of customers and reflect that information as a set of objects?

Discussion   Information needs are paramount to most users of business systems. Users want to display, update, query, analyze, capture, and manipulate information. They want to handle business transactions (such as disbursements, sales, receipts, orders) measure business performance (in sales, shipments, revenues, losses, claims, and so on) and create new products. Many times there is little behavior that is directly associated with this information. This means these objects are not behaviorally complex, but they are terribly important to the success of the product. Projects have been seriously delayed because of inattention to the information requirements of a system. What should be done to ensure that these information needs are met?

Solution   One key way to determine information needs is to identify every possible way users will manipulate information. Through the use-case analysis and low-fidelity prototyping (See Pattern 32, Envisioning; Pattern 50, User Interface Requirements; and Pattern 97, Prototypes), you can envision the views (for example, prototypical windows) users will need and what information those views contain. Based on the use-case and descriptions use-case conversations, identify a set of potential views with all required information items displayed. This helps identify required information elements.

Construct an information-source matrix [D11] that identifies each information object and its source (is it calculated or does it come from an external system?) and includes a description of the object (its semantics). In addition, in order to check for completeness, you might want to indicate what object or class the information may be part of and what prototypical views it is associated with.

To define transformations of information draw information-flow diagrams **[D12]** that show the information flow through the use cases. These data-flow diagrams will show the source of the information and how it gets manipulated in the use cases. To do this successfully requires a fairly complete use-case model **[D16]**. As Norman Kerth points out in Chapter 16, event-partitioned data-flow diagrams provide a number of features that help in translating requirements analysis to design.

Pattern 24: Finding and Defining the Domain Objects

Problem   How do you best determine the objects in the problem domain? How do you define their roles and responsibilities?

Discussion   Every process, every transaction, every piece of information, and every entity in a problem domain can be looked at as an object. That is, every object has an identity and a set of behaviors and is perceived as fulfilling one or more roles (ideally one) and having a corresponding set of responsibilities. Its responsibilities may include conveying states and attributes. (In fact, the primary roles of many objects in informational systems is to hold information and to convey attributes.)

There are complex objects and there are simple objects. There are objects that are known by end users and are visible and essential to the problem domain (commonly called first-class objects). There are also those that support the first-class objects. Most objects in the problem domain can be categorized into one of a number of role types. This type of classification helps in understanding the essential nature of the problem domain (see Pattern 28, Object Stereotypes). Defining the first-class objects in the problem domain is a task that can be done in several ways. An experienced analyst, after careful study of the business processes, should be able to define a large percentage of the domain objects. How does an experienced analyst do it?

Solution   There are several useful approaches to defining domain objects. They all involve class-responsibilities-collaboration (CRC) cards **[D33]**, but they start from different sources, including use-case definitions **[D14],** the glossary of terms **[D31],** current or envisioned business process definitions **[D8],** and business process diagrams **[D9]** (see Pattern 32, Envisioning).

If use cases can be easily defined for the new system, then the first solution is to derive the initial domain model from use cases, using the CRC technique. If the problem area is complex and a system is not easily envisioned, it is difficult to define use cases. If this is the case, it is helpful to start with a written description of the business, in which each business process is well defined. Underline the nouns in the description as possible objects (yes, this really does work). Verbs may reflect responsibilities of the object or use cases. After the business processes and problem domain are better understood, the use cases can be more easily derived.

The optimal size for work groups is three to six persons. Use a small table, with just enough room for all group members to be able to easily read and access the CRC cards. Assign a scribe (with legible handwriting) for writing and editing the cards. Revisit each system use case, identifying any terms that seem common to the business domain being addressed. Use these terms to develop a list of candidate domain objects. Follow these procedures:

- Write each candidate's name on a CRC card.
- Order the cards by their relative importance in the domain.
- Starting with the first card, propose responsibilities for each object, using the use cases and domain experts as a guide.
- Document each responsibility on the CRC card.
- Based on the responsibilities, determine what set of roles the object has. Usually it will have one main role (see Pattern 28, Object Stereotypes for possible roles).

Pattern 25: Classifying, Associating, and Grouping the Domain Objects

Problem   You now need to answer this next set of analysis questions:

- What are the relationships between objects?
- What objects interact with other objects?
- What objects are part of other objects?

Discussion   In many ways, domain analysis is similar to knowledge engineering. A semantic net is built during requirements analysis in order to capture domain objects and their relationships. This semantic net is often called an object model. The domain object model can contain a number of associations between objects, including

- **Containment Hierarchies**. The "has a" or "is part of" relationship. An airplane *has* wheels, for example.
- **Inheritance.** The "is a" relationship. An airplane *is a* flying vehicle, which *is a* vehicle.

- **Collaboration.** The "helper" (client/server) or "uses" relationship. This relationship can have more descriptions, such as "pushes," "writes with," "sees with."
- **Creation.** The "makes a" relationship. A factory *makes a* product. A class *makes an* instance.
- **Dependency.** A subset of collaboration. When one object changes, it triggers a change in a set of dependents.
- **Indirect associations.** When two objects share a resource they have a "shares a" relationship. This association can exist even when each object is not aware of any other object.

This is a very rich set of associations. How does one go about capturing and defining these associations?

Solution   After all the proposed domain objects have had initial responsibilities defined for them, start over with the first object. Follow these steps for each (major) responsibility:

1. Develop a simple scenario in which the object used requires this behavior.
2. Role-play the scenario again. This time, when the behavior is requested from the domain object, determine the collaborators (servers) required and develop a mechanism for fulfilling the defined responsibility.
3. Repeat the role-play until the mechanism works.
4. Consider all the use cases and events that are triggered by external clients.
5. Be sure the use case or triggering event has been captured in the use-case matrix **[D14]**.
6. For each one, develop a simple scenario in which this event or use case is triggered.
7. Role-play the scenario to see if it makes sense.
8. Document the mechanism as a validation scenario in a message-flow diagram **[D35]** or scenario script **[D13]**.

Use the cards and a tool with a notation of choice to group and classify the objects to show the associations. Use model structure diagrams **[D7]** to capture the following relationships among the domain objects within the system:

- Containment
- Inheritance

- Creation
- Dependency
- Indirect associations

Message-flow diagrams **[D35]** are used to show collaboration.

Pattern 26: Elaboration of the Domain Objects

Problem What attributes does each object have? What rules (or business rules) constrain each object? What is the life cycle of each object? What states can each object be in?

Discussion It is thought in some object-oriented design circles that it is detrimental to assign specific attributes to objects during requirements analysis, because at this early point it would cause each object to always possess particular attributes and the designers to think of the object in terms of data and not behavior.

However, during requirements analysis it is important to determine what business rules constrain the objects. It has been our experience that business rules are seldom explicitly specified during product development (regardless of the fact that they are often important constraints on system behavior), even though they may be discussed and identified during the analysis. Most of the time they are explicitly defined only in the database schema, via stored procedures, or at coding, as developers become aware of the constraints on the application behavior. Consequently these rules are spottily defined, are not consistently maintained, and are implemented in an ad hoc manner throughout. Rules, however, are often an effective way to define the behavior of a system. How can the important business rules be identified, captured, and organized?

Solution First of all, instead of assigning attributes to objects, simply state that a responsibility of an object is to convey information (that may be held by an attribute). Whether that information is calculated and whether the object currently possesses it is not essential at this point. Also, whether it is a primitive object like a number or a string or a first-class object is also not relevant. Assume all potential attributes are first-class objects (even though they may have simple values).

To ensure that information is associated with an object, refer to Pattern 22, Information Needs. To capture business rules, refer to Pattern 36, Business Rules. To capture life cycle and states of the domain objects, refer to Pattern 27, Object Aging.

Pattern 27: Object Aging

Problem   What do you do in the case of an object that changes its state during the course of its existence? When and how should you define its life cycle?

Discussion   Certain business objects live a rich life. They go through a regular progression of states, from creation to completion to storage to history. Purchase orders are an example. A typical order gets created, filled out, validated, and finally filled. In most cases the behavior of the object varies as its state changes. How do you capture the states of this object?

Solution   After determining the system's behavioral requirements (see Pattern 30), you should have a good idea of the use cases and business processes that are part of the business domain. In addition, you should have identified the business domain objects. Go through all the domain objects, and for each one evaluate whether there are state changes during any of the business processes or use cases. If there are, name each state and build a state transition diagram **[D36]** for the object, listing the use case event that causes each state to change. If necessary, define what each state means for the business domain.

These state transitions are often reflected in the business rules, and they often determine the work flow. The diagrams are an excellent means of validating and capturing the domain expert's view of what transpires during a use case or business process involving an important business object. For example, a Schedule object may be in one of three states: working, validated, or approved. It must first be validated before it can be approved. If it is approved it will cause other, dependent Schedule objects to have to be updated. If an approved or validated schedule is changed, it becomes a working schedule once again.

In addition, it is not uncommon to discover that objects can also transition to different versions. The same schedule may have several validated versions. This creation of new versions can also be captured in a state-transition diagram **[D36]**.

Pattern 28: Object Stereotypes

Problem   How do you determine the essential nature (that is, the roles) of the objects in the problem domain?

Discussion   While doing problem domain analysis, a number of objects are identified. Each object is really an instance of a class, which is defined by its name, responsibilities, and roles. Because most problem domains involve conveying information, controlling information processing, and interfacing with an external set of clients or servers, there are often objects whose roles involve one of these three areas (that is, information, control, and interfacing). Developers often search long and hard for meaningful behavior and responsibilities to attach to each object. There is often confusion about the roles for each identified object.

Solution   It is beneficial to be able to think of business domain objects in terms of well-understood behavioral stereotypes. These behavioral stereotypes can be used in analysis and design. In the analysis stage, the key question is, Does this object actually perform the role in the problem domain? Rebecca Wirfs-Brock [Wirfs-Brock93a] has come up with a list of behavioral stereotypes for business domain objects that can be considered during analysis. These include the following:

- *Information holders* maintain values that other objects can ask about. These include things like shipping movements, customer accounts, and transactions. Many business objects are simply information holders. They have a set of attributes with primary values that are associated with an instance of a business entity.

- *Structurers* maintain relationships between objects.

- *Controllers* perform a cycle of action. An example of this is a work-flow object (an object that monitors and schedules a set of tasks).

- *Coordinators* pair client requests with objects that can perform a single service. These objects act like brokers or middlemen.

- *Service providers* perform a single business task upon demand. (I like to call these Task Helpers. The problem here is that all objects are essentially service providers.) An example is a helper object for calculating a balance on hand. You give it a raw materials recipe, and it will tell you if the raw materials exist in the warehouse.

- *Interface objects* support communication between the objects within the program and the external systems or users. Interface objects are the windows users work with, like an on-screen schedule, a database broker that stores a persistent object, or an object that helps communicate with a CICS program on a host.

In addition to the above list of stereotypes, there are two specialized role types I find useful during analysis and design:

- *Catalogs* are libraries or repositories for managing the capture, deletion, selection, and modification of business objects. Examples are a parts catalog or a warehouse of items.

- *Display helpers* are objects whose main purpose is to support the display of a business object for a particular window (for example, a spreadsheet). These may also be termed application models (however, I think *application* is an overloaded term). They can be considered to be part of either an Interface object or an information holder. For example, a scheduler may want to examine the weekly shipping movements of products from a warehouse for the same period one year previous to the current week. In addition, he or she wants other related information to be visible, such as current inventory and scheduled use. Special display support models may be needed to view the values in the information holders.

These are role stereotypes. Invent your own, as appropriate, during your analysis. These stereotypes provide a richer set of analysis objects than the usual entity, control, and interface objects used in other analysis methodologies; but they also come close to being design objects themselves, so be careful in their use. However, be sure to assign one or more roles to your objects in the Object Definitions **[D34]**.

Pattern 30: Behavioral Requirements

Problem   What are the system's required behaviors?

Discussion Behavioral requirements are often too amorphous: They include statements like "The system will be able to store versions of objects of all types—text, musical, visual, executable, and so on." Too often requirements are stated in terms of the general abilities of the system. Analysts fail to "grab the bull by the horns" and visualize how the system will actually work for a particular user. The customer often does not know exactly what the system should do.

Solution   Behaviors should first be considered in terms of use cases—how specific clients (actual users, hardware, software, other programs) will use the system. The clients should be identified and defined, as described in the System Boundary Diagram **[D10]**, which shows external clients and servers. The System Boundary Diagram form is used to identify all of the external entities that interface with the system. External entities are divided into two groups—external clients and external servers. External clients are users— they request services from the system. External servers are providers—they provide services to the system.

For each client, list all the use cases in a Use-Case Matrix **[D14]**. The use cases will form the framework of the behavioral specification. Describe each use case in detail in a Use-Case Definition **[D15]**. Complete a set of Use-Case Models **[D16]** to see how the use cases use and extend each other and which use cases have common parts.

A use case describes a specific way of using the envisioned system. It consists of a behaviorally related sequence of exchanges between a user and the system. It can be described textually, as a high-level description of a business scenario; in outline form; or in terms of user-system conversations [Wirfs-Brock93b]. For every complete course of events initiated by a user, identify one use case. Use cases are defined in *Object-Oriented Software Engineering: A Use Case Driven Approach* [Jacobsen+92].

Use cases guide developers in design and implementation, provide test cases for system testers, and communicate the functions of a system to its users and customers. The Use-Case Matrix **[D14]** (which contains all users and their associated use cases) will completely define the functionality of the system. It is best to define the initial set of basic use cases totally independently of any extended functionality.

A user-system conversation is often the best way of defining a use case. This consists of a set of exchanges between users and the system. The system responds to each user action. After each system response, annotate meaningful and useful related items such as user views, steps performed by the system, data validation or business rules that must be enforced, and so on. For this type of requirements definition to be fully effective, a tool is required to organize all the information and its associations.

As Rebecca Wirfs-Brock has pointed out [Wirfs-Brock92b], the identification and organization of use cases can become quite complex. The same tensions that exist in defining objects also exist in defining use cases. Use cases can expand polynomially. They can be generalized into abstract use cases. Wirfs-Brock has noted that, in defining use cases, you need to ask the same types of questions you ask when defining objects. I have attempted below to answer the questions she asks.

What process do you use to build good use cases? Look for the main responsibilities of the external users and identify the tasks they must perform to fulfill those responsibilities. If the business processes are well defined, examine them and select tasks that are potentially automatable as use cases.

How should use cases be captured? Employ the Use-Case Definitions **[D15]** (some of these will contain use-case conversations), use-case matrices **[D14]**, or use-case models **[D16]**, showing extension and uses and prototypical windows. How detailed should they be? They should be as detailed as necessary to specify the requirements where you cannot afford a deviation. When are you done finding and describing them? At least get to a point where you have a complete use-case matrix defined, including all users and all major tasks that each user initiates.

The use-case definitions [D15] will serve as the structure that captures the main external behaviors of the system. When a use case involves information and data-related entities, annotate it with appropriate references to these associated deliverables:

- Business Rules [D22]
- Information-Views Definitions with Attribute Definitions and Edits [D23]
- Pertinent Object Relationships [D24]

If the user interface is an important part of the use case, then, based on the rationale and activities determined with User Interface Requirements (Pattern 50) annotate or reference these deliverables:

- Low-Fidelity Prototypes [D25]
- High-Fidelity Prototypes [D26]
- CAR Diagrams [D27]
- Window Flow Diagrams [D28]

To unambiguously model complex run-time system behavior, augment the use cases with the appropriate formal techniques, using the following guidelines (based on the work of Alan Davis [Davis92]).

If the use case involves a single system behavior that is a function of a set of simultaneously occurring conditions or stimuli, use a decision table [D17]. It is better to use a decision table at first because it helps you make sure you have not omitted any conditions or stimuli. Convert the decision table to a decision tree [D18]. (A decision tree takes up less space and is easier for most people to understand. It also helps capture the order of evaluating conditions, if that is a key criterion.) Use both in the specification.

If the use case involves a series of sequentially occurring stimuli, where system behavior is a function of the previous set of stimuli (a common example is a telephony system for which the user dials a series of numbers after getting a dial tone), then use a model based on a finite state machine. This could be either a Moore state transition matrix [D119] or a Harel state chart [D20]. Use state charts with communication channels, to enable signals to be communicated between specific processes without broadcasting those signals globally.

Harel's state charts provide natural extensions to finite state machines, making them more suitable for dynamic, real-time systems such as automobile cruise control systems and aircraft collision avoidance systems. The extensions support hierarchical decomposition of states and specification of transitions based on global conditions and the active or inactive status of particular states. If the use case involves complex synchronizations, such as process synchronization of time-critical applications, use Petri Nets [D21].

Pattern 32: Envisioning

Problem   How do you go about envisioning a system that will support a business process?

Discussion   Customers frequently want to automate their business processes in order to avoid duplication of effort, increase productivity and sales, prevent errors, downsize their staff, and reduce costs. However, many organizations are beginning to redefine and reengineer the business processes themselves, because automation alone will not yield the desired results. *Envisioning* is a term used to describe both strategies, both imagining a system that will support an existing set of business processes, and conceiving a whole new set of business processes. In reengineering efforts a new set of envisioned business processes are diagrammed alongside the current ones.

It has been our experience at KSC that envisioned business processes for complicated domains are of such a high level and are so lacking in detail that it is difficult to derive use cases from them. This also makes it difficult to envision the new automated system's behavior. How can these problems be remedied?

Solution   You can help ensure that each business process is well defined by writing out the entire process, detailing all its steps. It is often good to first come up with mainstream ideal processes, without considering exceptional conditions. Once these main processes are understood, the exceptions can then be considered systematically. Use-case definitions [D15] can subsequently be derived from the envisioned business processes. Each step of the process should be considered as a potential use case. Potentially, the users will want to interact with the system in a set of coordinated conversations. See Rebecca Wirfs-Brock's work [Wirfs-Brock93a] on use-case conversations.

It is also helpful to use low-fidelity prototypes [D25] as a basis for visualizing how the user will interact with the system. This makes the scenarios described in the use cases more tangible.

Pattern 34: Requirements Specification

Problem   How do you best specify system requirements for the variety of interested parties that need to understand what the system is going to do?

Discussion   Requirements specifications must be clear not only to the customer and developers, but also to the designers, testers, sponsors, and quality assurance personnel. Clear specifications can help compensate for ambiguous, incomplete, and inconsistent requirements. Requirements can be described with

- *Natural language.* Examples include use cases and process descriptions.
- *Formal techniques.* Conceptual models reduce the inherent ambiguity of natural languages by conveying the behavior in a more precise and unambiguous "language," diagram, or notation.
- *Prototypes.* These simulate the external system behavior of the final product.

Given these communication tools, how and when do you use each of them to specify the software product's requirements?

Solution   Use a basic template for a specification, such as the one in Table 3. This organizes the information into sections that mirror the activities and types of deliverables needed for requirements analysis. Initially capture the behavioral requirements (see Pattern 30) and do a problem domain analysis (see Pattern 20). As these activities are completed and requirements deliverables are produced, complete the corresponding sections of the requirements specifications and add the deliverables to the requirements specification. Validate the deliverables and the sections of the requirements specification with customers. See Requirements Validation (Pattern 99). As discrepancies arise or requirements change, the affected areas of the requirements specification are revisited and modified. The requirements specification should be maintained throughout the product development, as it provides a reference point for various issues and for development of future versions of the product.

Pattern 36: Business Rules

Problem   Rules are a very efficient and readable way to specify requirements. What are the best ways to define and capture business rules so they can be verified and used?

Discussion   During requirements analysis it is important to determine what business rules constrain objects (including their associations and values) and what rules constrain the behavior of the system. In addition, it is important to determine what calculations are to be performed to derive the values associated with a business object. It has been our experience that business

1.0 Requirements-Gathering Plan
    1.1 Overview of the proposed system
    1.2 Supporting personnel
    1.3 Business organization
    1.4 Applicable references for requirements
    1.5 Requirements-gathering plan and schedule
    1.6 History of efforts in this area (systems and procedures)
2.0 Business Aspects
    2.1 Business goals and measurements
    2.2 Expectations
    2.3 Summary report with consensus answers and significant variances between users
    2.4 Impact of the system
    2.5 User attitudes*
3.0 System Aspects
    3.1 External clients
    3.2 External servers
    3.3 System Boundary Diagram [D10]
    3.4 System goals with measures
    3.5 Business processes
4.0 Use Cases
    4.1 Use-Case Matrix [D14]
    4.2 Use Case Definitions [D8] (primary)
    4.3 Use-Case Definitions [D8] (secondary and exceptional)
    4.4 Use-Case Models [D16]
5.0 Essential Object Definitions and Models
    5.1 Class specification forms
    5.2 Model structure diagrams
    5.3 Object collaboration diagrams
    5.4 Object life cycles/transitions
6.0 Information Needs
    6.1 Information Source Matrix [D11]
    6.2 Data-flow diagrams
7.0 Interface Design
    7.1 Low-Fidelity Prototypes [D25]
    7.2 High-Fidelity Prototypes [D26]
    7.3 CAR Diagrams [D27]
    7.4 Task analysis and Window-Flow Diagrams [D28]

*This section may be kept internally.

TABLE 3 Specification Template

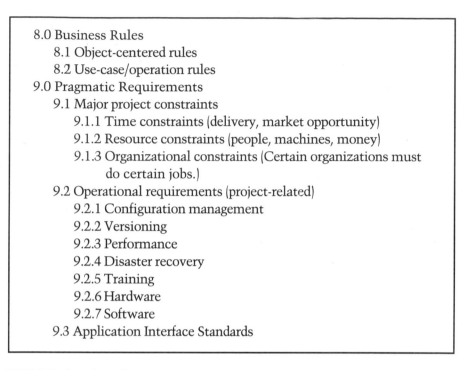

8.0 Business Rules
    8.1 Object-centered rules
    8.2 Use-case/operation rules
9.0 Pragmatic Requirements
    9.1 Major project constraints
        9.1.1 Time constraints (delivery, market opportunity)
        9.1.2 Resource constraints (people, machines, money)
        9.1.3 Organizational constraints (Certain organizations must
            do certain jobs.)
    9.2 Operational requirements (project-related)
        9.2.1 Configuration management
        9.2.2 Versioning
        9.2.3 Performance
        9.2.4 Disaster recovery
        9.2.5 Training
        9.2.6 Hardware
        9.2.7 Software
    9.3 Application Interface Standards

TABLE 3 *(continued)*

rules are seldom explicitly captured during product development (regardless of the fact that they are often important constraints on system behavior), even though they are frequently discussed and identified during the analysis.

Frequently rules are defined only in the database schema—via stored procedures or application code—as developers become more and more aware of the constraints on application behavior. Because there is no well-defined framework in which to plug rules, and because there are a variety of rule types that are not well understood, rules are often ignored until implementation. Consequently, rules are seldom explicitly defined or consistently maintained, and they are implemented in an ad hoc manner throughout the software product. Rules are often the most effective way to define the behavior of a system, however. How should important business rules be identified, captured, and organized?

Solution   It is important to have an understanding of the various types of rules incorporated in a requirement specification. James Odell expounds a simple but comprehensive taxonomy for business rules [Odell94]. This taxonomy proves very useful in understanding rule types and applying them appropriately within a requirements specification. Based on his taxonomy, we can classify business rules into six major rule types, described below. I further divide these into two categories—three that constrain use cases and three that constrain objects and their states.

Rules That Constrain Use Cases

1. ***Stimulus/Response Rules* (also called *Triggering Conditions*)**. These constrain behavior within the context of a use case or an event that may trigger a use case. They specify WHEN and IF conditions that must be true in order for an operation (use case) to be triggered. The examples below are two rules that will trigger the use cases Searching Stores for Copies of a Movie and Placing a Movie Copy on Reserve. (These use cases are part of the larger use case, Requesting a Movie Copy.)

   WHEN a Movie is requested by a Customer
   If a Movie Copy is not available in the store
   Then search other Stores for a Movie Copy
   And
   inform the Customer as to availability.

   WHEN a Movie is requested by a Customer
   If no COPY is available in any STORE
   THEN place next available Copy on reserve.

2. ***Use-Case Precondition Rules***. These specify what conditions must be true before an operation or use case can be guaranteed to perform correctly. For example:

   Schedule production of a Finished Good
   ONLY IF Raw Materials and Plant Resources are allocated successfully.

   The use case Scheduling of a Finished Good cannot proceed unless this condition is true.

3. ***Use-Case Postcondition Rules***. These guarantee the results of a use case or operation.

   A Production Schedule is CORRECTLY COMPLETED (or valid)
   ONLY IF all Raw Materials and Plant Resources for all FINISHED GOODS are allocated successfully.

   Creation of a Validated Production Schedule is the use case guaranteed by this rule.

Rules That Constrain Objects and Their State

1. ***Object-Constraint Rules.*** Most business rules include a constrained object and its associated constraining objects. Rules also make reference to one or more other objects besides the constrained object. The rule Customers Must Have an SSN has *Customer* as the constrained object and *SSN* as the constraining object. To state this rule there must be an association between SSN and Customer. It is the responsibility of each Customer to convey and know its associated SSN. It does not have to possess it as an attribute, although it probably will.

   Object-constraint rules define conditions and policies for objects and their associations that either must not or should not be violated. A "must not be violated" rule should hold under any circumstance and during any use case. For example:

   > IT MUST ALWAYS HOLD THAT
   > A Production Machine's daily batches cannot total greater than 15,000 gallons.

   > IT MUST ALWAYS HOLD THAT
   > If a customer has an SSN, then his DRIVER'S LICENSE NUMBER is his SSN.

   The second example is an object-constraint rule that applies only when an IF condition is true.

   Once they are captured, it is valuable to further categorize the rules as being either inviolable (they can never be broken under any conditions, like the rules above), exceptional (they can be broken under certain conditions), or suggested (they should be followed but do not need to be enforced).

   An example of an exceptional rule is

   > IT MUST ALWAYS HOLD THAT
   > A Production Machine's daily batches cannot total greater than 15,000 gallons UNLESS
   > The Production Manager has Okayed added amounts for the Machine.

   An example of a suggestion is

   > IT SHOULD HOLD THAT
   > A Production Machine's daily batches cannot total greater than 15,000 gallons.

2. ***Inference Rules.*** These state that when certain conditions hold, a new condition can be inferred. They can derive object subtypes, as in this example:

A Product is a Reciped Item IF AND ONLY IF it has an Approved Recipe.

3. ***Computation Rules***. These are rules that derive a result from an equation or algorithm. For example:

Product Quantity IS COMPUTED AS FOLLOWS
Product Need–Current Inventory + Shipping Movement

Now that we know rule classifications, let us consider how to capture business rules:

1. Examine every use case. Determine what stimulus/response rules may trigger the use case or operation and what precondition rules and postcondition rules are true for the use case and for operations within the use case. If there is a business rule evident in the use case and it is not yet captured, add to or modify the rules on the Use-Case Definitions **[D15]**.

2. Examine every essential business object and determine its associated object-constraint rules. For each business object, list and number all the associated business rules (in natural language) in which the business object is the constrained object. Also attach the appropriate inference rules and computation rules with each object definition **[D34]**.

Pattern 40: Pragmatic External Requirements

Problem   How do you determine nonbehavioral and organizationally imposed constraints?

Discussion   During development there can be a number of constraints placed on a system. Some are behavioral and some are not. Examples of this are the concurrent release of a version in multiple national languages, the use of relational databases as the persistent store, and the adoption of a particular user interface standard. All of these constraints have impacts on the design and delivery of the system. It is important that they all be recognized and defined. How can the completeness of these constraints be insured?

Solution   Use a Pragmatic Requirements Template **[D29]** to ensure that most of the nonbehavioral requirements as well as the constraining behavioral requirements are characterized and captured. Review the constraints with all groups that will be involved in delivery, installation, training, and implementation.

Pattern 50: User Interface Requirements

Problem   What is the best way and time to determine the requirements for the user interface?

Discussion   Eighty percent of customer satisfaction comes from the user interface [Arthur92]. Users need information, and they want to be able to perform necessary tasks. When a user sits down at a terminal, he or she must have a clear mental model of the business at hand. The human interface should reflect the user's logical view of the system. One of the fundamental principles of user interface design is that the user's picture of the system should be consistent with the system's actual behavior. In addition, the same metaphors used in the business should be the ones represented on the screen.

User interface requirements need to be determined early on, so as to allow early customer feedback and timely development of user training materials and information documentation. The complexity of the user interface has a big effect on the underlying object models. The more complex it is (for example, using hypertext, speadsheets, graphical networks) the greater the need for supporting display objects, and the longer the development time.

Which user interface design tasks should be accomplished during requirements analysis, and how?

Solution   Use cases provide a mechanism for verbalizing user tasks. They specify the tasks and determine what information is needed for them. Specify as a prototype (see Pattern 97) the views the user has as he or she interacts with the system to perform each use case. These prototypes can be described as low-fidelity windows [D25] and once established can be captured more explicitly in high-fidelity prototypes and CAR and window-flow diagrams [D27 and D28].

Pattern 97: Prototypes

Problem   How do you really capture and determine requirements with prototypes? Aren't you risking a premature design and development of the system with code that will not be maintainable?

Discussion   How does prototyping fit in with the requirements? Requirements cannot all be captured in the initial functional specification. As more prototyping, whiteboarding, and evaluating are done, there will be the need to modify the requirements. The dark side to prototyping is that solutions can be hacked and the software may consequently be weak and poorly designed.

There are several major metaphors for software development, and the particular metaphor used has an effect on the type of requirements specification selected and the rigor with which it is pursued. The manufacturing and construction metaphor likens software development to the construction of a building. At one extreme of this metaphor, requirements are gathered in one shot and a detailed specification is passed off to designers, who then design a working system. The designers, in turn, complete their design and give it to the coders to implement. This metaphor is also known by other names, such as the waterfall approach and the "throw it over the fence" process; it usually culminates in a "big bang" implementation (in which the designer integrates all the pieces at once and then watches the system disintegrate). The more evolutionary, incremental, and iterative your approach, the more likely that there will be a set of prototypes in the requirements analysis. The more that requirements analysis with prototyping occurs early in system development, the more likely the system will work and the more likely the customer will be satisfied.

It takes maturity, discipline, and a very good programming and design environment to reengineer quality back into a product. Without rigorous attention to detail and discipline, a product is in serious risk of failure when features are continually added. As more prototyping and evaluating are done, there will be a need to modify the requirements. Alternating prototyping and use-case modeling occur during requirements analysis. In addition, user expectations have to be kept realistic, since a prototype is not a product. Customers must realize that what they are seeing is a product simulation, not the product itself.

Solution   Work with the customer to build (initially) low-fidelity prototypes **[D25]** using paper widgets, drawings, self-stick notes, and index cards. (These are true throwaway prototypes.) Or, if the necessary skills and tools are available, build high-fidelity prototypes **[D26]**. (You do not want to spend more than 10 percent of your time learning how to use a tool rather than focusing on the actual prototype, however.) Alternate between prototyping and use-case modeling. Prototyping provides user involvement, and use-case modeling provides rigorous analysis. Augment the use-case documentation with references to prototype versions (product simulations).

High-fidelity prototypes developed with a tool that is capable of generating useful code may be used for evolutionary development. Even if it is not a throwaway prototype, however, it should be developed with the understanding that it may radically change as users work with it. It has been my experience with Smalltalk development projects that if developers have a good design in mind and are experienced, the prototype will probably contain code that is usable for a production version. Be sure to plan also for training of beta users and for doing a number of prototypes for prospective users.

Pattern 99: Requirements Validation

Problem   How do you verify that the specified behavioral requirements are correct and compete?

Discussion   You need to have a number of different customers examine and approve the requirements during the requirements analysis process. Requirements vary in their specification needs—some require formal specification, while others can be loosely prototyped.

Requirements validation confirms that a product has and does what is expected or specified. In the case of requirements analysis, the requirements specification is validated by the customer. The appropriate customers must rigorously read, study, and validate the requirements. Use cases are excellent for structuring the specification of behavioral requirements for study and validation. Customers can role-play various use cases, using the domain objects, to get a better feel for whether the system does what is expected.

It is difficult to validate the completeness and consistency of systems that are defined manually. This is an entirely human process, with no automated validation.

According to Gilb [Gilb94], there should ideally be fewer than .5 major defects per page after quality control reviews have been completed and the requirements specification has been edited. A project team can save eight hours of development work for every hour of review. This can possibly lead to the delivery of projects 25 percent ahead of schedule, rather than being late.

Solution   Have all interested parties thoroughly read the requirements specification. Conduct review meetings on sections of the requirements specification. Have a secretary note every issue raised during the reviews in the Issues List **[D30]**. Follow up on all issues raised.

Build prototypes and review them with users. Continue requirements verification through each system development iteration.

If needed, establish an arbitration group to reconcile disagreements on requirements. Distribute prototypes to customers and conduct surveys and usability studies.

BIBLIOGRAPHY

[Adams93] Adams, Sam. *Presentation: KSC Life Cycle Methodology.* Cary, NC: Knowledge Systems Corporation, 1993.

[AMS92] American Management Systems. *Methodology: Management Objectives & Business System Concepts,* American Management Systems, Inc., 1992.

[Arthur92] Arthur, Lowell J. *Rapid Evolutionary Development Requirements, Prototyping & Software Creation.* New York: John Wiley & Sons, 1992.

[Beck94] Beck, Kent. "Smalltalk Idioms: Where Do Objects Come From? Part 2." *Smalltalk Report* (March–April 1994): 15–16.

[Booch94] Booch, Grady. *Object-Oriented Analysis and Design with Applications,* 2nd ed.. Redwood City, CA: Benjamin/Cummings, 1994.

[Davis93] Davis, Alan. M. *Software Requirements Objects, Functions, & States.* Englewood Cliffs, NJ: Prentice-Hall, 1993.

[Gilb94] Gilb, Tom. "IDEA MANAGEMENT: The Results-Driven Quality Planning Method." Paper in progress.

[Jacobsen+92] Jacobsen, Ivar; Christerson, M.; Jonsson, P.; and Overgaard, G. *Object-Oriented Software Engineering: A Use Case Driven Approach.* New York: ACM Press, 1992.

[Kerth94] Kerth, Norman L. "Caterpillar's Fate: A Pattern Language for the Transformation from Analysis to Design." This volume, Chapter 16.

[Love93] Love, Tom. *Object Lessons: Lessons Learned in Object-Oriented Development Projects.* New York: SIGS Books, 1993.

[Odell94] Odell, James. "A Taxonomy for Business Rules." Unpublished paper, 1994.

[Pressman82] Pressman, Roger S. *Software Engineering: A Practitioner's Approach.* New York: McGraw-Hill, 1982.

[Retig94] Retig, Marc. "Practical Programmer." *Communications of the ACM,* April 1994.

[Ross94] Ross, Ronald G. *The Business Rule Book: Classifying, Defining and Modeling Rules.* Boston: Database Research Group, Inc., 1994.

[Schultz92] Schultz, Ron. *A Project Management Handbook for Object-Oriented Software Development.* Gaithersburg, MD: Berard Software Engineering, Inc., 1992.

[Wirfs-Brock93a] Wirfs-Brock, Rebecca. "Characterizing Your Objects." *Smalltalk Report* (February 1993): 7–9.

[Wirfs-Brock93b] Wirfs-Brock, Rebecca. "Designing Scenarios: Making the Case for a Use Case Framework." *Smalltalk Report* (November–December 1993): 9, 10.

Bruce Whitenack can be reached at Knowledge Systems Corporation, 4001 Weston Parkway, Cary, NC 27513; bwhitenack@ksccary.com.

Caterpillar's Fate: A Pattern Language for the Transformation from Analysis to Design

16

Norman L. Kerth

ABSTRACT

Caterpillar's Fate is a pattern language used to support the transformation from fine analysis documents to an initial software design. Just as the concept of metamorphosis is used to explain the magical emergence of butterflies, Caterpillar's Fate explores the magic of constructing a system of objects from an object-free analysis.

1. INTRODUCTION

Caterpillar's Fate is an odd name for a software engineering activity. Nevertheless, the name is a most accurate description of the role this pattern language plays. A caterpillar's fate is metamorphosis—the seemingly magical transformation of an earth-bound creature into an aerial one. The Caterpillar's Fate pattern language is used to guide the transformation of a system from the analysis stage into the design stage—a process that has also been viewed by many as a magical transformation.

Copyright © Norman L. Kerth, Elite Systems. All Rights Reserved.

The structured methodologies of the past suffered during this metamorphosis between analysis and design, I believe in part due to the lack of such a pattern language. I have watched several methodologists try to describe what they do as they transition from analysis to design. To the uninitiated it appears as if they are making it up on the spot. The reality is that the methodologist must use a great deal of acquired wisdom to aid this transformation. A pattern language approach provides an ideal solution to this problem, because a pattern language is built upon acquired wisdom.

Many popular object-oriented methodologies skirt the transformation problem by introducing design issues into the analysis phase (for example, identification of objects, class definitions, and the recording of inheritance). This has put many large projects at risk because of the complexity of making design decisions while one is not sure of what the proposed system should actually do.

To avoid the risk of failure and the cost of rework, a pattern language like Caterpillar's Fate needed to be developed as part of a comprehensive methodology. This methodology consists of an analysis phase and a design phase. The analysis phase is free of any object bias, leaving the questions of where or how to use objects to the design phase. The design phase takes on different design strategies, such as object-oriented, object-based, structured, filter tools–based, algorithmic, or various hybrids, depending on a number of technical and nontechnical factors.

The object-free analysis phase consists of modeling activities intended to answer fundamental questions about *what* the system is to do, without saying *how* it will be implemented (see Table 1). This methodology is discussed further in earlier papers [1, 2].

2. THE CATERPILLAR'S FATE PATTERN LANGUAGE

Caterpillar's Fate captures the wisdom my clients and I have acquired in developing design solutions from fine analysis models. It documents what I do during the transition. It addresses the popular question, "How do I find the objects?"

The format of Caterpillar's Fate is intentionally taken directly from the work of Christopher Alexander [3, 4]. Two deviations have been made: I have included a section on "Suggestions" to the designer, and not every pattern has a "Sketch."

The suggestions seemed too important to ignore just to emulate Alexander. Sketches do exist for each of these patterns, and I believe they are important. They were left out of an earlier version of this paper for reasons of space. I am in the process of adding the sketches; the timing is such that this version of the paper includes only the most necessary sketches. An explanation of the sketch notation can be found in the Appendix.

Analysis Question	Modeling Technique
What information is important in the problem domain?	Information Modeling
How does this information change over time, and what incidents cause it to change?	Entity State Modeling
Who are the users, and what tasks do they turn to the system to get accomplished?	User Task List
What is the data flow for each task?	User-Task Partitioned Data Flow Diagrams
Exactly how does the human interface work?	Four-Dimensional Human Interface Perspective

TABLE 1 Analysis-phase Design Questions and Modeling Techniques

Alexander's sketches are never abstract—they always demonstrate the solution to some real problem. At times I adhere to the same philosophy, but at other times I move into an abstract form. I'm still experimenting, and feedback is welcome.

So, to begin with Caterpillar's Fate, I begin in the same manner as Alexander—at the top, with the first three-design decision to be addressed.

When starting an architectural design from analysis documents, the issues surrounding concurrency seem to be the ones to address first. The patterns addressing these issues are

1. Concurrent Threads of Execution
2. Synchronization of Concurrent Threads
3. Collaborative Work Packets

Pattern 1: Concurrent Threads of Execution

When a system contains processes that run either simultaneously or pseudosimultaneously (a la operating system–supported task switching), then careful planning is necessary.

The requirements documents often discuss functions, but rarely do they discuss exactly what functions will be available from which concurrent process. In fact, such documents shouldn't mention how the functions are deployed, as this is a design decision.

Therefore: Identify threads of execution that have the ability to exist independently from other threads that might exist. In some cases these threads will reside in different machines; in other cases they will represent different users, each with their own agenda, working on the same machine. (In this pattern the word *user* means "an entity, external from the system, requiring service of the system." In some cases a user may be a human; in other cases it may be a device or simply the passing of time.)

Suggestions   Name each thread, and write the purpose of each thread within a system of threads.

When concurrent threads of execution have been identified, you can address the issues of Synchronization of Concurrent Threads (2) and Collaborative Work Packets (3). If your design has only one concurrent thread of execution, then you are ready to address the Shape of Program (9).

Pattern 2: Synchronization of Concurrent Threads

When the Concurrent Threads of Execution have been identified, you are ready to identify the synchronization that needs to occur between concurrent threads.

Often in the execution of a concurrent thread there are situations in which a thread needs to stop processing or remain in a certain form of processing until another, concurrent thread arrives at some well-understood state.

Therefore: Review each concurrent thread of execution throughout its execution life cycle and identify those points where a signal is to be either sent to or received from another concurrent thread. Name the signal for the situation it represents, identifying both the sender and the receiver. In this pattern a signal carries no information; it either has arrived or it has not arrived.

Sketch   Figure 1 illustrates a home heating system with four concurrent threads of execution, three of which involve synchronization.

Suggestions   If your system seems to have a great deal of synchronization, this demonstrates that its various threads have a great deal of interdependency. "A great deal" is determined by noting the amount of concentration needed to

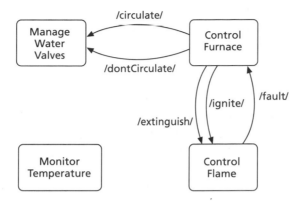

FIGURE 1 A home heating system

understand the purpose and interaction of each signal as a part of the whole system. If the level of concentration begins to exceed some reviewer's patience, then the probability of creating defects increases—as does the cost of enhancement. In such cases, return to Concurrent Threads of Execution (1) and change either the number of threads and/or their purpose in such a way that design decisions from Synchronization of Concurrent Threads (2) become easy to understand.

Now that you have a clear understanding of how concurrent threads synchronize with each other, you are ready to look at Shape of Program (9) and Critical Region Protection (17).

Pattern 3: Collaborative Work Packets

When you have a clear idea of what concurrent threads exist within your system, you are ready to look at the work packets that move between them. Many systems need to split processing work across processors, or they define and schedule work to be accomplished at another time. An example of this is the transaction processing systems found in many business applications.

In this pattern language, the producers and consumers of work packets are the concurrent threads of execution. Over time the producers and consumers may change. The nature of the work to be accomplished may change. As a result, it is important to design a clear separation between the concurrent threads of execution and the work that passes between them.

Therefore: For each pair of concurrent threads, review the life cycle of each thread and identify specific work that is initiated by one thread and continued by the second thread. Name the work packet for the information and work unit it manages or hides. For each work packet, identify the possible producer and consumer concurrent threads.

Suggestions   You should be able to easily state what each work packet is responsible for. Usually the responsibility would read, "All that is known about a _____."

Once you have designed the work packets passed among the concurrent threads of execution, you are ready to design the Work Packet contents (4) and also to start the design of the Shape of Program (9).

Work packets (in some environments, called "transactions") require careful design. This design, like "concurrency," needs to be thought through early on, as it represents a "big-picture" perspective of how concurrent subsystems or concurrent threads of execution collaborate. Work packets contain many details that need to be addressed early in the design process to avoid rework as the system design becomes apparent. The patterns in this section are

4. Work Packet Contents
5. Work Packet Status Report
6. Work Packet Completion Report
7. Work Packet Priority
8. Work Packet Security

Pattern 4: Work Packet Contents

Once a Collaborative Work Packet (3) has been discovered and named, its responsibility recorded, and each of its producing and consuming concurrent threads of execution (see Pattern 1) identified, you are ready to design the internal contents of a work packet.

Work packets contain information and directions for a number of functions. The internal design of a work packet is likely to become a mess if it is not conscientiously constructed.

Therefore: For each work packet, develop a design that contains all the information necessary for the work to be accomplished. Such information includes data, state, statement of need, and history. Data is used for specific processing. The state embodies to the present situation or condition the work packet is in. A statement of need asks the consumer thread to help with some particular goal to be accomplished. The history includes information related to the past experiences of the work packet, often including references to the concurrent threads it has visited in the past (Data Knows Its Roots[21]).

If Work Packet Status Report (5) or Work Packet Completion Report (6) are of value to this design, then the work packet will also need to contain an identifier or name. As Work Packet Priority (7) and Work Packet Security (8) are addressed, they may also have an impact on the contents.

To assure minimal impact on a work packet when either a producer or a consumer changes, the work packet must never contain information related to its future—that is, it must never tell the consumer how to go about processing. A consumer needs to be able to determine the kind of processing by querying about data, state, need, and history. For example, an SQL phrase is a statement of need. The actual processing is left up to the consumer. On the other hand, directions to perform a particular function and then pass the work packet on to yet another consumer are an attempt at controlling the future.

Suggestions   Work packet design follows from the analysis documents. The data within a work packet can be determined by inspecting the information model developed in the analysis phase. State information can be deduced by looking at the entity state model. History is not likely to be found in the analysis documents, as it is dependent on design decisions such as concurrent threads.

If a work packet begins to seem large, study the work packet for variations. If there are a number of kinds of a work packet, consider a design using subtypes of work packets, if that would reduce the amount of data, state, or history that needs to be included.

Where several different kinds of work packets are likely to travel to the same consumer for processing, and where the processing is different depending upon the packet, develop a design where the differences in processing are contained within the work packet. A good test for such a situation is to note if a work packet must answer questions about what type it is—if so, consider a different design. (In this situation, object-oriented designers would consider using polymorphism.)

As work packets become defined, several other design decisions need to be addressed: see Work Packet Status Report (5), Work Packet Completion Report (6), Work Packet Priority (7), Work Packet Security (8), and Data Knows Its Roots (21). With the identification of specific work packets along with their producers and consumers, you are ready to address the Shape of Program (9).

Pattern 5: Work Packet Status Report

When you have made your design decisions around Collaborative Work Packets (3) and Work Packet Contents (4), you have enough knowledge to know if a report on the status of the work packet needs to be generated for the benefit of the producer.

In some designs, a producer's concurrent thread of execution generates work packets, ships them to the consumer thread, and no longer has any interest in that work packet. For such situations this pattern has no value.

In other designs, however, the producer, often at the request of the user, will want to monitor the status of the work packet. For these designs you will need to address the questions of what status information to return to the producer, what stimuli cause the report to be returned, what role the work packet plays, and what role the consumer's concurrent thread of execution plays.

Therefore: Assess the needs identified in your analysis and make these design decisions based on your answers to the following questions:

1. When is the report sent? Here are some possibilities:
    - only upon the producer's request
    - every time the status within the work packet changes
    - when processing within the consumer achieves a particular goal, or
    - with the elapse of some unit of time

2. What information should be in the report? Does the work packet require an identifier? Does the identifier need to be unique? Does a combination of certain pieces of information (such as user name and time sent) make a work packet identifier unique? What status information is part of the report? What data information? What history information? Is the report tailorable?

3. Is the desire for the report known at the time the work packet is passed to the consumer? If so, design the work packet to be responsible for passing the report back to the producer, as it contains the knowledge of its producer.

    If the desire for the report occurs some time after transmission of the work packet, choose a design where the consumer is responsible for producing the report. Such a report is not on one particular work packet, but is a summary of all work packets within its control and knowledge.

4. Determine the needs for security around status reporting. Can a concurrent thread of execution request or automatically receive a status report on work packets generated by some other concurrent thread? Is this request available on a privileged basis? Is it password-protected? Does the status report need to be encrypted?

Decide whether the work packet or the consumer has the primary responsibility for producing and sending the report. Then determine what support is required from the other. Design a mechanism for communicating between concurrent threads of execution to support your answers to these design questions.

Suggestions   Keep the work packet status report design as simple as possible! Do not put any extra "bells and whistles" in this part of your design. Your system needs to produce status reports, but this is not its primary goal; its primary goal is to process work packets. Focus your design creativity there!

Once these design decisions have been made, you will have a clear idea around the design of work packets. Ensure that the specific Shape of Program (9) addresses the receipt of every status report identified.

Pattern 6: Work Packet Completion Report

Once you have made your design decisions concerning collaborative work packets (3), Work Packet Contents (4), and Synchronization of Concurrent Threads (2), you are ready to make the design decisions about what happens when a work packet completes its processing within the consumer's concurrent thread of execution.

Upon completion of the processing of a work packet, there are many different possible design responses. These responses need to be considered now.

Therefore: Assess the needs identified in your analysis and make design decisions based on the following questions:

1.   What gets returned? Is it a success/fail message? Is it an answer to the question contained within the work packet? Is it the work packet itself, in which data, state, and/or history has changed?

2.   If a failure report is returned, how much is communicated about the failure? In some situations, you will want to communicate what the nature of the error was, and suggestions about what should be done differently.

   Note, however, that some systems have a security requirement that will be breached if details of the nature of the failure are shared with the producer thread.

3.   For purposes of security, does the response need to be encrypted? Does it need password protection?

4.   Design a policy to deal with responses if the producer's concurrent thread of execution is not available when the response is ready to

be sent. This may occur in distributed systems because the network goes down, the producing computer goes off-line, or for any number of other reasons. It is possible that the producer, requesting a response, will leave the system forever. How will this situation be handled?

Suggestions   The suggestions offered in Work Packet Status Report (5) apply here too. Keep the completion report simple and concise.

Once these design decisions have been made, you will have a clear idea about the design of work packets. Assure that the specific Shape of Program (9) addresses the receipt of every completion report identified.

Pattern 7: Work Packet Priority

Once you have developed a design for Collaborative Work Packets (3), and while you are transforming the general Shape of Program (9) to a specific one, you need to make decisions about the order in which work packets are consumed.

In some systems work packets are queued for processing at a later time, either because the consumer's processing resource will then be available or cheaper, or because at peak times work packet arrivals exceed the system's processing capacity. Therefore there are design decisions to be made about which work packet to select when there is more than one work packet waiting for processing.

Therefore: Formulate a policy on how waiting work packets are to be selected. (This is something that has been overlooked in most analysis documents.) "First come, first served" might be all that is needed. However, there may be hidden requirements, in the form of general performance statements, that may not be easy to find. Review the documents with the following options for selection in mind:

1.   First come, first served.
2.   Assigned priority. The work packet type may contain a priority, or it might be a privilege priority associated with the producer that created the work packet.
3.   Deadline oriented. Each work packet has a deadline for completion, and work is accepted in such a way that the fewest deadlines are missed.
4.   Cost-penalty analysis. Each work packet has not only a deadline but also an associated cost for missing the deadline. Selection is based on minimizing these costs.

These are basic design issues. It is possible that your system may need a combination of these approaches or may require a different selection policy. What is important is that the policy for selection be consciously made and designed into the consumer's specific Shape of Program (9). Depending on the policy selected, Work Packet Contents (4) may need to be revisited to support the selection policy (you may need to add priorities or deadlines to work packets).

Suggestions Keep the selection system as simple as possible. Be prepared for any kind of change that may be suggested in the future, by adding no "hooks" into the system now and by refusing any assumptions or shortcuts that will prevent future growth. "No hooks" because the future may not play out in the manner you expect. And even if it does, any hooks in the system are not likely to be as well tested as today's working code. This is likely to lead to suspicion, and any maintenance that may have occurred is not likely to have respected the unused hooks.

This "no hooks" suggestion applies not only to this pattern but also throughout the design process. This is the first place where this advice is likely to be important—I will not be repeating it elsewhere, though it is tempting.

Once these design decisions have been made, you will have a clear idea about the design of work packets. Ensure that the consumer's specific Shape of Program (9) addresses selection design decisions and that the producer's Shape of Program (9) and/or Work Packet Contents (4) are refined as needed.

Pattern 8: Work Packet Security

Once Work Packet Contents (4) and Collaborative Work Packets (3) have been addressed, you will be ready to look at work packet security issues.

When work packets containing sensitive information or work directives are constructed on one machine and sent through a network to another machine, there are several security issues that need to be addressed in the design of the work packets as well as the producer and consumer.

Therefore: Consider the following design issues:

- Does the information within the packet need to be encrypted? The answer depends on whether or not someone might benefit from accessing the work packet, rather than whether or not it is possible to access the information (given a particular hardware system configuration). While you may believe you have a secure network, there is no assurance that this will hold true in the future as your configuration changes.

- In systems where some producers of work packets have privileges that others don't (either in information access or functionally permitted), design the prevention of inappropriate function or information access into the producer (for human interface reasons) and design security checks to occur within the consumer. The work packet will need to carry the information necessary for the consumer to perform the security check.

- Some systems perform regular reviews of consumed work packets, looking for anomalies. In other systems an audit trail is used to understand what has happened. If the requirements indicate that either of these security requirements exist, then develop a design for logging the necessary information and activity.

Suggestions   Security is usually left unaddressed or at best vaguely mentioned in most requirements and analysis documents. Most likely you will find a customer's desire for high security to be wishful thinking, based on a limited understanding of the depth of the issues and the costs. If this is the case and security is crucial, stop all design activities, return to analysis, and develop effective security models.

At this point you have addressed a few security-related issues, including encryption, passwords, and logging. As this pattern language matures, there are many more security issues that need to be discussed.

In this section we begin to look at early design issues that occur around one program. This includes the early decisions you need to make in regards to the shape of the program, how stimuli will be acquired and responded to, and how a human interface will be added to the program shape in such a way that it may be replaced without impact to the rest of the system. This section also includes a pattern that revisits concurrency questions to discover critical regions. The patterns in this section are

9. Shape of Program
10. System Citizen's Role
11. Decision Makers' Role
12. Workers' Role
13. Interface's Role
14. Informational Role
15. Small Family Systems
16. Work Accomplished Through Dialogs
17. Critical Region Protection
18. Event Acquisition
19. Event Routing
20. Human Interface Role Is a Special Interface Role

Pattern 9: Shape of Program

Once you have a clear idea of the Concurrent Threads of Execution (1) and the Synchronization of Concurrent Threads (2) across your system and have itemized Collaborative Work Packets (3), you are ready to apply a specific form to the general shape of your program. For systems with only one Concurrent Thread of Execution (1), this will be the first pattern considered.

At the early stages of transforming requirements documents into a software design, there are many issues to consider—usually too many issues to keep in our heads at one time. As a result it is easy to focus on optimizing design issues for the small part of the system that is currently in focus, to the peril of the "big picture."

Therefore: Accept a "typical big-picture design" until it does not serve you (Small Family Systems [15] and Work Accomplished Through Dialogs [16]). This pattern offers a typical program shape. While there are many possible shapes, this one has worked well as a starting point on all the systems I have been involved with.

The shape of this program is best described as tiered. The objects on each tier have the ability to place a call for service to design components on the same or lower tiers, but not on higher tiers.

Sketch The objects in the first tier in Figure 2 are responsible for ensuring that this Concurrent Thread of Execution (1) is a good citizen within a community of concurrent threads, each working toward their own agenda. See System Citizen's Role (10).

The second tier contains objects that are responsible for the decision-making aspects of the system to be built. See Decision Makers' Role (11). The third tier contains objects that perform work needed by the system. See Workers' Role (12). The fourth tier contains objects that are responsible for hiding the interface from some external entity. See Interface's Role (13).

For this tiered system to work, there must be a type of object that moves through the tiered systems, visiting the other objects. This moving object has the responsibility of providing appropriate information as well as tailored functionality. Those familiar with object-oriented thinking will refer to these objects as polymorphic; they are passed as parameters. This object is designated on Figure 2 with the term `anInfoObj`. See Informational Role (14).

The design decisions made using this pattern transform the general shape of the program into a specific one that supports the findings in the analysis documents. To accomplish this transformation, you will find it useful to consider the following patterns, while accepting the tiered shape of programs: System Citizen's Role (10), Decision Makers' Role (11), Workers' Role

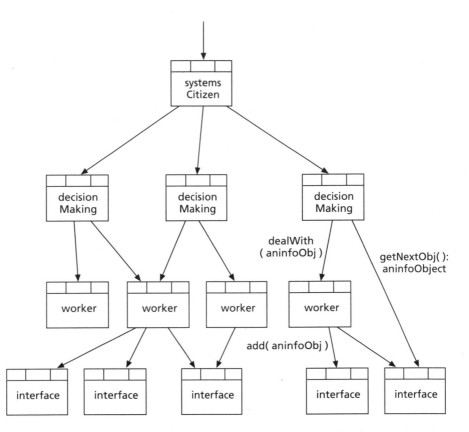

FIGURE 2 The objects in the first tier in Figure 2 are responsible for ensuring that this Concurrent Thread of Execution (1) is a good citizen within a community of concurrent threads, each working toward their own agenda. See System Citizen's Role (10).

(12), Interface's Role (13), and Informational Role (14). When the tiered shape begins to fail, consider Small Family Systems (15) and Work Accomplished Through Dialogs (16). As you begin to consider issues such as how mouse clicks, keystrokes, and the like are handled, you will find Event Acquisition (18) and Event Routing (19) useful.

Suggestions   Services between objects might be called upon within a single tier, but this should be kept to a minimum. The reason for this varies depending on the tier. Generally, as interactions between tier peers grows, the reuse of either without the other decreases. This is particularly true for interface objects and worker objects.

   Since decision-making objects contain knowledge of a particular application, they are not likely to be reused; therefore reuse is not an explanation. Interaction between decision makers requires maintenance engineers to master the operations of both decision makers before either one can be changed. This works within limits, but if taken to an extreme it can cause real problems. When confronted with such situations, revisit the analysis and design decisions that defined the boundaries and responsibilities of these two kinds of objects.

Four tiers may not seem sufficient for large systems. In some cases I have seen a program shape used recursively within one of the object roles described here, most often for decision-maker objects and worker objects. I have also seen the internal working of some of these objects take on the form of a Small Family System (15).

When the general program shape has been transformed into a specific shape for your system, be sure that every signal identified in Synchronization of Concurrent Threads (2) and every work packet identified in Collaborative Work Packets (3) is accounted for.

Once the general tier shape has been transformed into a specific one that reflects the findings of the analysis documents, you are ready to refine the system for various measures of goodness, performance, and other factors that are beyond the scope of this early-architecture pattern language.

Pattern 10: System Citizen's Role

Once there is a clear idea of a Concurrent Thread of Execution (1) and the Shape of Program (9) begins to move from the general to the specific, you are ready to look at creating a single system Citizen object.

Most programs reside on platforms where there are likely to be several applications running at the same time (for example, Mac OS 7.X, OS/2, Windows 3.X, and so on). In these environments the operating environment has expectations for each application running. Each of these environments has its own way of operating. There are likely to be business reasons to design an application that can be moved from platform to platform with ease.

Therefore: Design a single object that is responsible for knowing the protocol that applications must follow to be "good citizens" within a community of applications. As you consider how the particular operating environment handles issues around mouse clicks, keystrokes, and the like, you will find Event Acquisition (18) and Event Routing (19) useful.

Suggestions   Information about the responsibilities of the system's citizen are not found in analysis documents. They are usually found in a programmer's reference manual or the tutorial manual for the operating environment chosen.

Some reviewers have commented that a "single object" with all this knowledge might be quite large. I picture the system Citizen object's internal design as being composed of many objects. The design goal is to localize knowledge of a platform's expectation of application behavior within a single unit.

With this pattern mastered, you are in a good position to apply Decision Makers' Role (11) and Human Interface Role Is a Special Interface Role (20).

Pattern 11: Decision Makers' Role

When the Shape of Program (9) begins to move from the general to the specific and the System Citizen's Role (10) becomes defined, you are ready to design the high-level policy-making aspects of your application.

Most "real life" systems have some interesting design issues around controlling the overall operation of an application. These issues involve the fundamental behavior of the application—the work flow, the control, and the highest level of decision making about the application's behavior. Often it is these decisions that your customers will use to differentiate your application from your competitors'.

If these controlling issues are not respected as being interesting in their own right, then the system's policy/decision-making activities are likely to be distributed across a number of objects. This creates significant maintenance difficulties. Distributed policies and decision making requires a maintenance engineer to master the workings of a large number of objects before any changes to policy or decision-making objects can occur.

Therefore: Create an object or number of objects whose prime role is to be responsible for the decision-making activities of your application. That is, separate policy-making activities from mechanisms that carry out the policy.

Suggestions   Decision-making objects look funny. They often have only one external method—doIt. Nevertheless, they are key to building systems that are maintainable and reusable. Reusability comes from placing all that is not likely to be reused (that is, the policy/decision-making aspects of this application) in one or a number of objects that are not likely to be reused. Decision-making objects are not reused because they are application-specific, unless the application reused involves porting the same application to another environment.

Input for the policy/decision-making object is usually found in the process specification; it is what remains when all the lower-level operations can be allocated to worker objects (see Pattern 12), informational objects (see Pattern 14), and interface objects (see Pattern 13).

At this point you will have a clear idea of how your application will control the work to be accomplished. You are ready to connect the Workers' Role (12) objects, Interface's Role (13) objects, and Human Interface Role Is a

Special Interface Role (20) object. It is quite likely that the decision maker will handle a number of Informational Role objects as they are passed among the worker objects and interface objects.

Pattern 12: Workers' Role

When the Shape of Program (9) begins to move from the general to the specific, you are ready to design the objects that help the application move closer to its goal.

With many programs there are design decisions that can be combined to provide related services that help an application move closer to its goal.

Therefore: Build specific objects with the responsibility to do work that the decision makers would find useful in exercising the policy- and decision-making responsibilities. Collections are a common kind of worker object.

Suggestions   The number one goal of a worker object is to off-load any work from decision makers that is not directly involved with controlling the application. A secondary goal is to build worker objects that are likely to be reused in similar but different applications.

Worker objects are usually easy to find by examining an event-partitioned data-flow diagram. They are often hidden within data stores. The process specifications are used to confirm that they are worker objects and to identify the methods.

Once you have identified the worker objects you will be ready to look at the internal design of these objects; you can be comfortable that the big picture will fit with the small picture, which now becomes of interest to designers.

Pattern 13: Interface's Role

When the Shape of Program (9) begins to move from the general to the specific, you are ready to design the objects that hide the specific behavior of entities that are not part of your system.

Systems are not built in isolation; they interface with something else—it might be hardware devices, or software that is not under the control of the designers. Regardless, since the system is not under the control of the system design, these external entities may change its behavior.

Therefore: To protect your emerging system, hide the external entities' behavior within an object whose responsibility it is to provide high-level abstract services to the rest of your system.

Suggestions   Interface objects can be found on event-partitioned data-flow diagrams; they are usually the external entities. The abstract services can be determined by looking at the process specifications.

Once you have identified the interface objects you will be ready to look at the internal design of these objects; you can be comfortable that the big picture will fit with the small picture, which now becomes of interest to the designers. There is a special kind of interface object that hides the human interface from the decision-maker objects. See Human Interface Role Is a Special Interface Role (20).

Pattern 14: Informational Role

When the Shape of Program (9) begins to move from the general to the specific, you are ready to design the objects that move through the system, visiting interface objects—the worker objects under the direction of the decision-making objects.

We have seen a great deal that is of value from the use of polymorphism. Shape of Program (Pattern 9) structures a number of objects into a rigid tiered system, similar to the old structured-design style of thinking. There are some advantages to such a structure, but polymorphism is not possible. The closest that structured methods could come is to acknowledge the value of passing complex data structures known as "tramp data." This was not considered to be the best of designs, as knowledge of the data structure data was spread across an application. Object-oriented thinking gives us a way to solve this problem, by passing objects.

Therefore: Create objects whose responsibility is to deliver specific information at appropriate places within an application, without letting the structure of the information become known. These are known as informational objects.

Suggestions   Whenever you discover that the design needs to ask an informational object its type in order to resolve a number of IF statements, SWITCH statement, and the like, stop and look for a way to put the type-related work within the informational object.

Informational objects are found by noting how information flows on an event-partitioned data-flow diagram. Solid, meaningful pieces of information that flow to or from Interface Role (13) objects and that have some associated interesting processing (noted in the process specifications) suggest informational objects. This is especially true if you discover that the data dictionary suggests that there are a number of types or variations on this information.

Smalltalk experts recognize the similarities between informational objects and the model component of the Model-View-Controller triad. This is discussed further in Human Interface Role Is a Special Interface Role (20).

Once you have identified the informational objects you will be ready to look at the internal design of these objects; you can be comfortable that the big picture will fit with the small picture, which now becomes of interest to designers.

Pattern 15: Small Family Systems

When the Shape of Program (9) begins to move from the general to the specific, you will encounter times when a tiered system creates awkward designs. In such cases you do not need to discard the program shape, just augment it with another, "mini" shape for the portions of the system you are considering. Often the internal design from Human Interface Role Is a Special Interface Role (20) is benefited by this pattern.

In particular you will find that there are design segments that are well served by building a small number of objects that work well together as a team. The key feature that makes this design segment unique is that, in this "small family" of objects, no one object takes on control responsibilities for the others.

Therefore: Design the small family *as* a family, but make sure it is a *healthy* family. In a healthy family, each object has a distinct responsibility, which is easily differentiated from that of the other family members. For each service provided by this family to the system, there is one object that takes the control responsibility and calls on the other objects for help in accomplishing its goal. The classic Model-View-Controller model is an example of a small family system.

Ensure that the boundaries of responsibilities within a family are never violated. When such a boundary is violated it creates a situation in which it is not clear which object is responsible for accomplishing a given activity. In such cases a maintenance effort is likely to get it wrong, causing some activity to be performed twice or another activity to not be performed at all.

Depending on your language and operating environment, you may not be able to implement a small family system in this manner, from a design perspective; instead you can think of the small family of objects as a single object, when placed within the tiered structure produced by Shape of Program (Pattern 9).

Suggestions Small family systems are composed of only a few kinds of objects—two, three, or, rarely, four kinds is a good benchmark. I have never seen more than four kinds of objects work well as a small family.

Small families are usually not identifiable from the analysis documents; they are usually created to simultaneously support a number of design goals or to simplify an awkward structure that is developing within a tiered structure. They are clever inventions, often adapted from one's previous experience.

I see small family systems as a secondary design strategy—after tiered systems—because of the amount of effort a maintenance engineer must apply in order to master how a family works. Use this measure to guide your own design decisions and documentation plans.

If you have identified a need for a small family system, you may be ready to look at the internal design of these objects; you can be comfortable that the big picture will fit with the small picture, which now becomes of interest to designers.

Pattern 16: Work Accomplished Through Dialogs

As the Shape of Program (9) moves from the general to the specific, you will encounter times when two objects need to invoke methods in each other to get their jobs done. In such cases you do not discard the tier structure developed with Shape of Program (9); rather, you augment it with a design decision that allows some objects to call methods in each other.

There are situations in which the work the system must accomplish involves the blending of two objects' responsibilities. Neither object possesses all the necessary information or processing ability to achieve the requirements. Combining two objects does not seem to be a wise idea, however; each object's responsibilities seem to be well formulated, and there does not seem to be an undiscovered decision-maker object to control the interactions between them.

Therefore: Choose a design that allows the two objects to carry on a dialog with each other. The first object invokes a method in the second object that, in its processing, calls a method in the first. The second object must initiate a dialog with the first object; otherwise you just have a tier connection.

Suggestions   A dialog between two objects is easily understood in moderation. If the method invoked by the dialog (that is, the method invoked when the second object calls the first) is of a questioning nature, it will be easily understood. A method with a questioning nature is a kind of method whose sole purpose is to provide information or answers that help the second object complete its work.

The counter to a questioning nature is a controlling nature. A method with a controlling nature changes the state of the first object; in the worst case it causes the first object to interact with still more objects in a controlling manner. The deep implications of a dialog with a controlling method is hard to comprehend. Reviewers and maintenance engineers are likely to miss subtle implications. Avoid these dialogs!

A dialog that involves more than two objects is called a chain-letter dialog. These are to be avoided at all costs. Picture a design in which an object sends a message to a second object. The second object calls a method in a third object, and eventually the nth object asks the first object for some information. In such a case there is a dependency involving all *(n)* objects. No maintenance change can be made to any one object until all *(n)* objects have been considered. This violates all that we have learned about information hiding and separation of concerns. Never carry on a chain-letter dialog.

With the judicious use of dialogs between questioning-nature methods to refine the design begun with Shape of Program (9), you can return to transforming the program shape from general to specific.

Pattern 17: Critical Region Protection

When Concurrent Threads of Execution (1) have been identified and the Shape of Program (9) for each of those threads has moved from general to specific, you are ready to look for potential critical region problems.

Concurrent systems often use the same resources, usually in the form of interface objects (13), informational objects (14), or worker objects (15). Occasionally they will share decision-making objects (11). If two concurrent threads of execution access the same object at the same point in time, there is a possibility that they will cause harm. This harm might affect the shared object, the work being performed for the other concurrent thread, or, in rare cases, the invoking concurrent thread's own work.

Therefore: For each concurrent thread, review the specific shape of the program and identify the shared objects. For each shared object, determine if protection from simultaneous access is needed. If so, develop a protection mechanism that ensures safe use.

Suggestions   There are several design solutions for this problem; these can be reviewed in any operating systems text. Some solutions include blocking the second thread upon entry to the critical region, requiring each thread to get permission before entering the critical region, aborting a low-priority thread's work when a high-priority thread enters the critical region, and removing the critical region by giving each thread its own data memory space.

Once this pattern has been addressed, you can be sure that you have prevented those potential defects that would be the most difficult to discover.

Pattern 18: Event Acquisition

When the Shape of Program (9) begins to move from the general to the specific and the System Citizen's Role (10) is being considered, this pattern will help resolve some design issues.

Every platform deals with events in its own unique way. By "event," we mean the signal that indicates a mouse click, a keystroke or the like, has occurred. Some operating environments provide a great deal of support, while others lean heavily on the system designer. Nevertheless, the program shape needs to be tailored to assure a consistent design.

Therefore: Review the design's event-acquisition capabilities. Choose those capabilities that make sense for your application and help refine the shape of the program. Key design questions to consider include

- Exactly how is an event acquired? Does the operating environment notice the event, acquire it, and decode it? Or is some or all of that activity left to the designer? Are any events treated as unique or handled in a different manner? Can you override the event acquisition provided by the operating environment? When would you want to do this?

- What operating environment capabilities do you want to accept? How does that impact the Shape of Program (9)? Can these capabilities be contained within the system's citizen object (10)? If not, what consequences does this imply for moving the application to a different platform?

- When do you provide your own event acquisition design? How does that impact the Shape of Program (9)? An example might be when the silhouette of a graphic is dragged across a canvas. When would you not accept the platform's event acquisition mechanism (for example, when the performance or function is not supported).

- Are hardware interrupts supported by the operating environment? Does the operating environment expect a particular design from your "hardware driver"? How does the program shape need to be modified to support these design decisions?

- Does the operating environment support the notion of an "event-consuming object" registering for particular events? If so, how does the program shape change to take advantage of such a powerful capability? When would you not use this registration capability?

Suggestions   If this is the first time you have designed an application for this particular operating environment, sketch a number of variations on the program shape, have them reviewed by a team, and build a number of prototypes. Evaluate each prototype for its advantages and disadvantages. Document your findings for others to follow and for you to review as you work beyond your learning curve.

When you have addressed this pattern, you will have refined the Shape of Program (9) to better meet your design needs. Return to Shape of Program (Pattern 9) and continue to transform the general shape into a specific one. In the future, patterns that address how systems can be tailored during initialization will be referenced from here.

Pattern 19: Event Routing

When the Shape of Program (9) begins to move from the general to the specific and the System's Citizen Role (10) is being considered, this pattern, along with Event Acquisition (18), will help resolve some design issues.

Every platform deals with events in its own unique way. By "event" we mean the signal that a mouse click, a keystroke or the like, has occurred. When these events occur, there are a number of different approaches to ensuring that the event is received and acted upon by all the objects that should respond.

Therefore: Refine the shape of the program to show how events will be consumed. There are several design issues to consider:

- Is each event to be routed to only one object, or are there likely to be a number of objects that want to be informed when the same event occurs?

- How is the routing handled? Is it hard-wired, as you might find in an interrupt handler? Is there a negotiation activity in which event-consuming objects (usually decision makers or human interface objects) will answer if they recognize or are interested in a particular event when it arrives? Is registration the right design for your application? (Registration is a design idea in which objects register for events with a dispatcher. When the event arrives, the dispatcher routes it to the object that registered for it.)

- Under what situations will you consider circumventing the operating environment's way of routing events?

Suggestions   Keep event routing as simple as possible. Dynamic registration of events—that is, registration that occurs continuously throughout the life of a system—yields a system that is impossible to understand by reading the code. A maintenance engineer will have to watch how events are continually registered and removed by using a debugger. In such situations you never know if you have seen all the possible combinations.

Once you have addressed this pattern, you will have refined the Shape of Program (9) to better meet your design needs. Return to Shape of Program (9), and continue to transform the general shape into a specific one. In the future, patterns that address how systems can be tailored during initialization will be referenced from here.

Pattern 20: Human Interface Role Is a Special Interface Role

As you transform the Shape of Program (9) from a general form into a specific design, you will be paying extra attention to how decision-maker objects (11) get their directions from humans.

The human interface is key for providing information and directions to an application. It is found in numerous places throughout an application. Another factor to consider is how difficult it is to port a system from one platform to another if the human interface has been allowed to pervade the system in an unplanned fashion. As a result, the shape of the program needs to be refined to include a human interface component that is isolated from significant portions of the system.

Therefore: Create a special kind of interface object (13) that hides human interface–specific design decisions. Decision maker (11) objects are the most likely to need human input. Refine the program shape to include human interface objects that are accessed by the decision-maker objects. Human interface objects deal with the human interface– and platform-specific issues and leave the more abstract decision making and processing control up to the Decision-Maker objects.

Worker Objects (12) and Interface Objects (13) may also need the same kind of special human interface object to support their lower-level work. This would appear in the form of dialog boxes and the like. Informational objects may also carry around a number of special human interface objects, each providing a unique view on the data in the informational object.

Suggestions   The behavior of human interface objects can be found in the details of the Four-Dimensional Human Interface Perspective model. Deciding what should be the responsibility of the human interface role object and what should be the responsibility of the decision maker can be tricky. Develop several alternative designs and discuss them with a peer. Select the best design by using the guiding principles of simplicity and ease in explaining the design to someone else.

This pattern helps the designer add human interface capabilities to the Shape of Program. You can return to Shape of Program (9) to further refine the general shape into a specific one. You can also look at the internal design of the human interface object. You will discover that Small Family Systems (15) is quite applicable to the internal design. You will also discover that Model-View-Controller is a perfect small-family system and that the Decision Maker object will pass the model, as an Informational object (14), into this human interface object. The actual behavior of the Model, Controller, and View will be hidden within this human interface object. You will be able to follow the design decisions made about Event Acquisitions (18) and Event Routing (19).

> In this section we turn to the design of data. As this pattern language is a work in progress, this section has only one pattern at this moment. This section needs to be expanded, but I did not want to leave this one pattern out, given its importance. The pattern is
>
> 21. Data Knows Its Roots

Pattern 21: Data Knows Its Roots

Once you have identified collaborative work packets, informational role–oriented objects, or any other "entity" that contains information, you are ready to determine if their roots need to be known.

Good systems live for quite some time, and over time they change. Upgrades, added functionality, and new markets are some of the reasons systems change. As new versions are released, it is crucial that work in progress, no matter what state it's in, be accommodated by the new version, thus ensuring a transparent transition from the older version. At the same time, with expanded functionality, work packets, informational objects, and the like must be free to improve as new versions are designed.

Therefore: For any "entity" containing information (work packets, informational objects, etc.) that may persist beyond the life of the program that created it or move between concurrent threads of execution, design the entity so it

- records its type and version
- records the version of the program that created it, the date of its creation, and any information on the environment that it can access (such as

machine type, machine configuration, OS version, file system version, and so on)

- records the date of last access and date of last change
- records, for every concurrent thread of execution visited, the thread's version and the date last visited
- records, for every application that accesses this information, the application's version and the date last visited
- embeds, within this store of information, knowledge about its stored data structure format

Suggestions   For large entities, this additional "roots" information adds little to time and space overhead. For very small entities the overhead may be significant, but in low quantities this information still remains valuable. For small high-volume entities, get creative before you discard this design idea. Consider the design of a transaction log that will record this information and, during slack times, work at condensing the information to save peak processing time.

Upon completion of this pattern you will have ensured that your persistent objects have the information they need for the system to grow; at the same time you will have ensured that work in progress at any stage can be accommodated.

3. USE OF CATERPILLAR'S FATE

A reader might assume that one can traverse through Caterpillar's Fate without any iterations or rework. This is not the case. In some cases the transition from analysis to design points out significant holes or conflicts in the analysis documents. In other cases, as the design begins to emerge it becomes clear that certain design issues have not been considered. Users of Caterpillar's Fate experience iterations of many sorts. This is not necessarily due to a flaw in the methodology, the pattern language, or the project. Building a large system involves learning what the system does. Learning often occurs through iteration. What *does* create a flaw is to ignore the need to iterate, reanalyze, and redesign.

4. STATUS OF CATERPILLAR'S FATE

This document contains about one-third of all the patterns that I have become aware that I currently use. The rest of the patterns have been left out for reasons of space. I say "have become aware" because I discover more common design wisdom every time my clients and I use Caterpillar's Fate. Furthermore, there are occasions when insight through use causes me to rework the patterns I have already documented; thus Caterpillar's Fate is to be seen as a work in progress.

Nevertheless, this work has a high degree of maturity. Caterpillar's Fate has been used by my clients since 1992 to construct several real-life systems: an investment banking system, an interactive voice-response system, a hand-held computer application, and a system for the control of electricity. Teams ranged from three to twenty people. In all cases the pattern language was communicated in a methodology course, followed by personal coaching as necessary. This paper is my first attempt to communicate these concepts solely in a written form.

5. ISSUES

As I developed the text for this pattern language, I was shocked at how rapidly I consider these patterns as I am transforming a system analysis into a first design. This leads to a concern of mine about the amount of effort that another person might have to put into mastering this language before he or she can use the wisdom I have acquired. This is part of the new experiment in exploring pattern languages for developing programs. Can a pattern language be used by someone other than its author, without the aid of a masterful teacher? For us to know if that is possible, written pattern languages need to exist. This is why I have written this paper. It serves as a test-bed to see if pattern languages such as Caterpillar's Fate can be distributed widely.

A second concern I have with Caterpillar's Fate is its dependence on objects as a design paradigm. This is not in keeping with Alexander's view that a pattern language is free of implementation material. Following his lead, I would like to see the transformation from an object-free analysis able to metamorphose into any number of design strategies. Some of the patterns in Caterpillar's Fate, such as Concurrent Threads of Execution (1), are presented without an object bias; others, however, such as Work Accomplished Through Dialogs (16), have a most definite object bias. The bias-free presentation of this acquired wisdom remains a puzzle to me.

Another issue to be resolved, not only for me but for all authors of pattern languages is how to incorporate and honor the work of other authors. There is at least one other pattern language that I'd like to disassemble and partly incorporate into Caterpillar's Fate. Can I do this and still respect the original author's work? I may want to rewrite everything except the idea, or I may not present the author's idea as he or she intended. As a community we need to discuss this and related issues.

A final issue has to do with the fear of public attack. Caterpillar's Fate describes details of how I generally design programs. It is risky to say, "This is what I do." I am certain that Caterpillar's Fate could yield programs I would be embarrassed to show my colleagues. I claim the right to not follow any of its patterns when I believe they will not serve me well. This is how I design today; I claim the right to learn new and different ways to design and, as a result, to create a new version of Caterpillar's Fate.

REFERENCES

[1] Kerth, N. "A Structured Approach to Object-Oriented Design." Addendum to the OOPSLA Proceedings, 1991.

[2] Kerth, N., Rhodes, R.; and Burley, J. "How to Deliver 20,000 Lines of Code with Only Four Defects for under $2.00 Per Line of Code." Invited paper, Pacific Northwest Software Quality Conference, Fall 1990.

[3] Alexander, C. *The Timeless Way of Building*. New York: Oxford University Press, 1979.

[4] Alexander, C., et al. *A Pattern Language*. New York: Oxford University Press, 1977.

Norman L. Kerth can be reached at Elite Systems, P.O. Box 2205, Beaverton, OR 97075; 72073.3222@compuserve.com.

DESIGN PATTERNS AND CATALOGS

PART

5 A design pattern is a recurring architectural theme that provides a solution to a family of common design problems within a particular context. Design patterns help enhance software development by capturing successful expert practice in a systematic yet accessible manner. The term *design patterns* has been established in the lexicon of software design by Gamma, Helm, Johnson, and Vlissides' pioneering book *Design Patterns: Elements of Reusable Object-Oriented Software* (affectionately called the "Gang of Four" book).

The first three chapters in Part 5 present a variety of design pattern catalogs and the fourth chapter describes a library of design patterns. A design pattern catalog provides a battery of solutions to common design problems. In general, we can distinguish pattern languages from design catalogs along the following lines: we think of a pattern language as generating a family of related systems. In contrast, we think of a design catalog as providing a family of individual solution techniques. A pattern library is similar to a class library—it systematically provides selected and readily usable descriptions of specific patterns.

Schemes for classifying patterns are becoming increasingly important as individual pattern catalogs grow, and as the industry matures to the point where designers use multiple pattern catalogs (or pattern languages) together. Contemporary design pattern catalogs typically present a continuum of patterns that range from relatively abstract architectural framework patterns, to design patterns, to relatively concrete idioms. The framework patterns (such as Model-View-Controller and Layered Architecture) are generally domain-independent. In contrast, more concrete idioms (such as James Coplien's "counted body" idiom) are closely tied to specific programming languages (such as C++ or Smalltalk). In general, design patterns are not as systematic at the enterprise level as architectural framework patterns are, nor are they as tied to programming language features as idioms are.

It is likely that catalogs of patterns (at all levels of abstraction) will provide the most payoff for pattern-based software development over the next few years. It turns out that comprehensive pattern languages (as with comprehensive object-oriented application frameworks) are challenging to produce, and require time, effort, and thorough domain analysis to utilize effectively. In contrast, literature on programming idioms is well established. It is in the middle ground of traditional software design where patterns are likely to have their largest impact.

Part 5 introduces a collection of powerful architectural framework patterns and design patterns that developers can put to use immediately. Most patterns presented in the catalogs below are domain-independent. For instance, a given pattern (such as Robert Martin's Three Layer FSM) may be implemented using specific programming language features (such as inheritance and dynamic binding). However, such a pattern may apply equally as well in GUI design as in aerospace flight control software.

Chapter 17, by Frank Buschmann and Regine Meunier, classifies patterns drawn both from existing design literature and from project experience. They propose to classify patterns using three orthogonal dimensions. The first dimension includes the multi-level pattern classification hierarchy described above (i.e., architectural framework patterns, design patterns, and idioms). In addition, Frank and Regine propose two other classifications based on structural principles and functionality. These dimensions are similar to those adopted by Gamma et al., who classify patterns according to creational, structural, and behavioral characteristics.

Walter Zimmer, in Chapter 18, offers another insightful companion to the widely acknowledged Gang of Four patterns by extablishing a new taxonomy to organize them. Walter uses his taxonomy to illustrate how these patterns are related and which patterns offer alternatives for one another; he also map out various dependencies between the patterns. One hazard (or serendipity) of mapping uncharted territory is the discovery of new features. Walter's taxonomy yields a new pattern, Objectifier, that results from a bottom-up generalization of existing design patterns.

Chapter 19, by Robert Martin, is another bottom-up effort, though it starts from a large base of existing C++ framework code rather than from existing design patterns. He "discovers" patterns based on experience he gained while developing GUIs for programs that analyze building architectures. Robert's main premise is that good developers intuitively use patterns to produce successful software designs, whether their method or language supports it or not. Thus, he asserts that existing programs are a good place to look for patterns. Interestingly enough, he finds that the C++ framework his paper is based on embodied all of Gamma et al.'s patterns in some form or another.

In addition, Robert bemoans the fact that his patterns postdate his framework code. He feels that a pattern catalog would have reduced the time spent searching for solutions. The patterns summarized in his chapter may be used to document his application (i.e., reverse engineering). Many are general enough, however, to be reused in subsequent work (forward engineering).

Most of Robert's patterns are at the same level of abstraction and breadth of application as the Buschmann/Meunier patterns or the Gamma et al. patterns. He classifies these patterns in four groups: container patterns, high-level design patterns, low-level design patterns, and C++-related patterns. The latter three groups map directly onto the classification scheme presented by Buschmann and Meunier. In general, there is a significant amount of commonality between form and content of the Buschmann/Meunier patterns, the patterns of Gamma and colleagues, and Martin's patterns. This is particularly striking since each of the pattern catalogs were developed largely independently of each other. This commonality further supports the claim that design patterns capture recurring solutions to common, yet fundamental, problems in software development.

The last chapter in Part 5, by Jiri Soukup, explores a tact orthogonal to most of the other chapters in this section. Soukup believes that existing pattern catalogs (such as the patterns of Gamma and his coauthors) are useful as an abstract guide to software architecture. However, he believes the existing catalogs have two major liabilities: (1) they cannot be directly used by appplication code in their abstract form, but must be customized into an implementation, and (2) except for documentation and comments, patterns do not become an integral part of the code, thus depriving maintenance programmers of critical design information. Soukup suggests a method for creating libraries of directly usable patterns that extend common data structures. Each pattern is encapsulated in a class; it connects to other classes using C++ friends. Soukup posits that this technique removes cyclic relationships among classes, among other benefits.

The chapters in this section illustrate various methods for classifying patterns into catalogs and libraries. Frank Buschmann and Regine Meunier captured their patterns by examining literature and projects in their organization; they built the taxonomy in parallel with their research. Walter Zimmer worked bottom-up from the pattern catalog of Gamma et al. Robert Martin discovered patterns by examining existing C++ frameworks. Jiri Soukup focuses on the reification of patterns in code, rather than on the analysis that created them.

Gamma, Erich, Richard Helm, Ralph Johnson, and John Vlissides (1995). *Design Patterns: Elements of Reusable Object-Oriented Software.* Reading, MA: Addison-Wesley.

17 A System of Patterns

Frank Buschmann and Regine Meunier

ABSTRACT

This paper discusses a system of patterns for constructing the architecture of object-oriented software systems. It comprises patterns at various levels of abstraction, ranging from fundamental paradigms for structuring software systems to concrete implementations of particular design decisions. Each pattern in this system depends on the smaller patterns it contains, the patterns it interacts with, and the larger patterns it is contained within. A template is defined, according to which all the patterns discussed herein are described. To support the selection of a pattern for a given situation, the system includes a classification scheme that organizes patterns according to granularity, functionality, and structural principles. The approach has been successfully applied in several concrete industrial projects from various application domains. This paper summarizes the current status of a project with the goal of developing a pattern-oriented approach to object-oriented software architecture.

Copyright © Siemens AG. All Rights Reserved.

1. INTRODUCTION

Constructing an architecture for a software system, especially for a large-scale or industrial system, is a complex process. Many design decisions must be made: many components must be introduced, the functionality of the software must be attached to these components, the relationships between them must be specified, and the whole architecture must satisfy certain nonfunctional requirements. Various concepts introduced to effectively handle the complexity of building large-scale software systems are based on patterns. Specific examples can be found in the literature [Buschmann92, Coplien92, Gamma+93].

Patterns consist of predefined design structures that can be used as building blocks to compose the architecture of a software system. In our work the object-oriented paradigm is assumed to be the underlying principle for each pattern. However, many of these patterns can be implemented in any programming language that supports abstraction facilities like modules or abstract data types.

Gamma et al. [Gamma+93] describe the fundamental properties of patterns. Each pattern

- Provides a predefined scheme for implementing a particular structural or functional principle for software systems, by describing its different parts as well as their collaboration and responsibilities

- Captures existing, well-proven design experience

- Identifies, names, and specifies abstractions that are above the level of classes and instances

- Provides a common vocabulary and understanding for design principles

- Helps to handle the complexity of software

- Serves as a reusable building block for software development

- May be either domain-independent, like the "Gamma patterns" [Gamma+94], or may address aspects of a specific domain (such as exception handling)

- Addresses both functional and nonfunctional aspects of software design

Patterns cover many aspects that are relevant to software architecture. They explicitly deal with the structure of an application—its components, the relationships between them, and its functional and nonfunctional properties. It has been recognized that these aspects are of great importance to a successful software production [Reenskaug92, Buschmann93, Garlan+93]. They have a great influence on the quality of software systems and the effectiveness and productivity of software development itself. Thus the use of patterns is a very promising approach, fostering the constructive, systematic, and controllable implementation of applications with defined properties.

2. A SYSTEM OF PATTERNS

Patterns exist in a range of scales, beginning with patterns for defining the basic structure of an application and ending with patterns describing how to implement a particular design issue in a concrete programming language. All patterns together form a system of building blocks that can be used to build software architectures.

None of the individual patterns in this system are isolated [Alexander79]. Each pattern depends on the smaller patterns it contains, on the patterns it interacts with, and on the larger patterns it is contained within. With evolving technology, the system of patterns itself may evolve. Existing patterns may be deleted or changed and new ones integrated into the system.

A system of patterns that can be used to build and compose any desired software architecture will consist of many different patterns used for many different purposes. Since the objective of such a system is to support the systematic development of software systems with defined properties, a plain list or brief characterization of all the patterns in the system is not enough to facilitate its effective use or to help designers select and implement the right patterns for a given situation. A usable system of patterns must

- Support the system's evolution. Particular patterns may be changed over the system's life span, new patterns may be added, and existing patterns may "die."

- Describe all the patterns it includes in a uniform way. These descriptions must address all aspects that are relevant to a pattern's characterization, detailed description, implementation, selection, and comparison with other patterns.

- Classify the patterns it contains, to provide a guide when selecting a pattern for a particular design situation. Such a classification scheme must include categories for criteria or design issues that play a significant role in software development.

- Address issues regarding the construction of patterns into more complex and heterogeneous structures. Not every pattern can be effectively combined with any other pattern in the system. In addition, whether a combination of patterns satisfies certain properties such as reusability or changeability often depends on how patterns are combined.

The construction of a system of patterns that satisfies the above criteria is a complex task. Many potential patterns must be investigated, described, and classified, and any constraints on combining them with any other pattern must be specified. However, a comprehensive and well-defined system of patterns forms a uniquely powerful and flexible vehicle for expressing software architectures.

3. HOW TO DESCRIBE PATTERNS

As already mentioned, all patterns within a system of patterns must be described in a uniform way. The following pattern-description template is based on the principles defined by Alexander [Alexander79], who distinguishes three essential parts of a pattern:

- **Context:** A particular recurring situation
- **Problem:** A system of forces that arises in the context
- **Solution:** A spatial configuration that allows the designer to solve the problem

This structure expresses the essence of every pattern and must thus underlie every description form for patterns. However, presenting the idea of a pattern is one aspect, implementing a pattern is another one. Thus it is often helpful to extend this basic scheme with additional aspects. Our description scheme for patterns is closely related to the one Gamma et al. propose [Gamma+93]. Its intention is to support the understanding, comparison, selection, and implementation, of patterns within a given design situation:

1. **Name:** The name of the pattern, conveying its essence [Gamma+93].
2. **Rationale:** The motivation for the pattern (the design issues and problems it addresses).
3. **Applicability:** A rule stating when to use the pattern.
4. **Classification:** Classification of the pattern (according to the scheme developed in the following section).
5. **Description:** Description of the participants and collaborators in the pattern (that is, other patterns), as well as their responsibilities and relationships among each other.
6. **Diagram:** A graphical representation of the pattern's structure.
7. **Dynamic behavior:** A scenario-based illustration of the typical dynamic behavior of a pattern.

8. **Methodology:** The methodological steps for constructing the pattern.

9. **Implementation:** Guidelines for implementing the pattern. When appropriate, the guidelines are illustrated with pseudocode and a concrete C++ code example.

10. **Variants:** Description of possible variants of the pattern.

11. **Examples:** Examples for the use of the pattern.

12. **Discussion:** The constraints of applying the pattern.

13. **See also:** References to related patterns.

All patterns in the system presented in this paper are described according to the above template.

4. CLASSIFICATION OF PATTERNS

As stated above, a system of patterns should include a classification scheme. A meaningful set of categories for classifying patterns will help the user find the pattern needed. Each category must represent a crisp set of criteria or design issues that play a significant and primary role in software development. The following three categories can be identified.

Granularity

Developing a software system requires one to deal with various levels of abstraction, beginning with the basic structure of an application and ending with issues regarding the concrete realization of particular design structures. Thus granularity is an important category for classifying patterns.

Three levels of granularity can be specified:

1. **Architectural Frameworks:** Every software architecture is built according to an overall structuring principle. These principles are described by architectural frameworks:

   An architectural framework expresses a fundamental paradigm for structuring software systems. It provides a set of predefined subsystems, as well as rules and guidelines for organizing the relationships between them.

   Architectural frameworks can be seen as templates for concrete software architectures. They determine an application's basic structure and have an influence on its subsystem architecture. Thus architectural frameworks allow one to handle the structural complexity of software systems. The selection of a particular architectural framework for a software system is a fundamental design decision.

To construct a concrete software architecture based on an architectural framework, the application's functionality must be mapped into its structure. In addition, it must be enhanced and specified in detail. With the help of smaller patterns, its predefined subsystems have to be refined, and the relationships between them have to be fully specified.

Example: The Model-View-Controller framework.

2. **Design Patterns:** A software architecture usually consists of several smaller architectural units. These are described by design patterns.

A design pattern describes a basic scheme for structuring subsystems and components of a software architecture, as well as the relationships between them. It identifies, names, and abstracts a common design principle by describing its different parts and their collaboration and responsibilities [Gamma+93].

Design patterns can be seen as microarchitectures [Gamma+93]. They are software architectures, but because they are used to structure software systems they are microarchitectures. A design pattern is less than a complete software architecture or architectural framework.

A design pattern may also be interlocked with other design patterns and composed out of several smaller patterns.

Example: Mediator-Worker pattern, Forwarder-Receiver pattern (see Section 5).

3. **Idioms:** Idioms deal with the concrete realization and implementation of particular design issues.

An idiom describes how to implement particular components (parts) of a pattern, the components' functionality, or their relationships to other components within a given design. They often are specific for a particular programming language.

Idioms represent the lowest level of a pattern. They are closely related to a particular programming language. Often the same idiom looks different in different languages, and sometimes an idiom that is useful in one programming language does not make sense in others. For example, a C++ idiom may describe how to implement reference counting to correctly handle multiple referenced objects. In Smalltalk such an idiom is not needed because of the garbage collection mechanism integrated in the language.

Since idioms address aspects of both the design and the implementation of a particular structure, they close the gap between the design and implementation phase of software development.

Example: The Counted Body Idiom [Coplien94].

Functionality

The second category for classifying patterns is functionality. Each pattern serves as a template for implementing a particular functionality. However, the various classes of functionality are of a general nature rather than specific for a certain application domain.

The following categories of functionality can be distinguished:

1. **Creation of objects (Creation):** Patterns may specify how to create particular instances of complex recursive or aggregate object structures.

2. **Guiding communication between objects (Communication):** Patterns may describe how to organize communication between a set of collaborating objects that may also be independently developed or remote.

3. **Access to objects (Access):** Patterns may describe how to access the services and state of shared or remote objects in a safe way, without violating their encapsulation of state and behavior.

4. **Organizing the computation of complex tasks:** Patterns may specify how to distribute responsibilities among cooperating objects in order to solve a more complex function or task.

Structural Principles

To realize their functionality, patterns rely on certain architectural principles. These principles form the third and final category.

1. **Abstraction:** A pattern provides an abstract or generalized view of a particular (often complex) entity or task in a software system.

2. **Encapsulation:** A pattern encapsulates details of a particular object, component, or service to remove dependencies on it from its clients or to protect these details from access.

3. **Separation of concerns:** A pattern factors out specific responsibilities into separate objects or components to solve a particular task or provide a certain service.

4.   **Coupling and cohesion:** A pattern removes or relaxes the structural and communicational relationships and dependencies between otherwise strongly coupled objects.

Every pattern within a system of patterns can be classified according to the above categories. The resulting classification scheme forms a guide that designers can use in picking patterns for specific applications. This scheme, together with the designer's experience, will be helpful in determining what patterns best fit the problem and context at hand. (See Figure 1.)

Although the scheme is clearly structured and uses significant characteristics of patterns, neither the classification of patterns nor the search for a suitable pattern is a simple task.

On the one hand, the classification of a pattern around its granularity is sometimes ambiguous. Patterns exist that can be used to structure either a complete software system or just a single component or subsystem. If such a pattern is primarily used to specify the basic architecture of whole applications, it is useful to classify it as an architectural framework rather than a design pattern. Similarly, the boundary between design patterns and idioms is imprecise.

On the other hand, a pattern can have more than one structural or functional characteristic. In this case it is useful to list the pattern in every category of the scheme indicating its properties.

To use a classification scheme in a concrete design situation, take the following steps:

FIGURE 1 A classification scheme for patterns

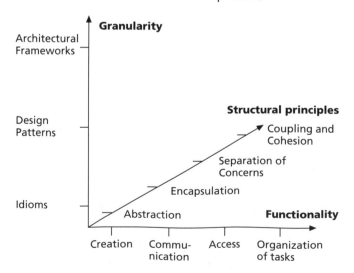

1. Determine the required granularity for the pattern. This is usually easy to decide, since it should be clear if the pattern serves as a basic structure for a whole application, a scheme for structuring a subsystem or component, or a concrete implementation of a specific design requirement.

2. Select the required functionality. This should be clear as well, since usually only one category of functionality is considered for a given design situation. However, it might be necessary to combine several functional aspects within a single structure. In this case, either a pattern that serves all the desired functionalities is selected or several patterns are selected that together provide the required behavior.

3. Determine the desired structural principles. This is the most difficult step. It is certainly a design decision, because often more than one structural solution is possible for a specific functionality requirement. The proposed principles force designers to think about what structural property is the most useful and important for the situation at hand.

The classification scheme is not intended as a means of picking out the one right pattern—the designer must make the decisions. But at least it provides a guide for designers, helping them search for an appropriate pattern for a given situation.

  Note also that the proposed classification scheme reflects only one particular view of design patterns. The focus here is, as mentioned above, on categories that support the choice of a specific pattern in a given design situation. Other classification schemes characterize patterns from a different viewpoint. The most elaborate is described by Gamma et al. [Gamma+93]. The focus of their classification scheme is on major pattern characteristics that can be used to organize patterns into systems. Their scheme makes it easier to talk about patterns and groups of patterns, to learn patterns, and to find new ones.

5. THE PATTERNS

This section lists all the patterns that currently exist in our system and briefly characterizes them by outlining the contexts in which they can be applied. In addition, a summary of their classification is given (without granularity). Some of these patterns are similar to ones described by other authors [Gamma+93, Gamma+94, Coplien92]. Our work on single patterns is still ongoing, and candidates for further design patterns exist. Our work on idioms has just started; no concrete results are currently available.

The Architectural Frameworks

- **Layered architecture:** Can be used to structure applications that can be organized hierarchically, "each layer providing services to the layer above it and serving as a client to the layer below" [Garlan+93].

- **Pipes and Filters architecture:** Can be used to structure applications that can be divided into several completely independent subtasks that are performed in a strongly determined sequential or parallel order.

- **Model-View-Controller architecture:** Can be used to structure software systems that are highly interactive with their users or their environment, systems that have several users with different responsibilities, and systems in which the system abstraction model is controlled and represented in different ways for different versions.

- **Presentation-Abstraction-Controller architecture:** Can be used to structure software systems that are highly interactive with human users, systems that enable multiple controls and presentations of their abstraction model, and systems that can be composed from independent subfunctions.

- **Reflective architecture:** Can be used to structure software systems that need to consider future adaptations to changing environments, technology, and requirements and systems that exist in various configurations and variants or need to be integrated with other software artifacts.

- **Microkernel architecture:** Can be used to structure software systems that have to provide different views on their functionality and that (often) have to be adapted to new system requirements. This architecture is especially useful for the development of operating systems.

Other architectural frameworks exist, but are yet to be described:

- Repository architecture
- Broker architecture
- Abstract Machine
- Client-Server architecture

The Design Patterns

- **Actor-Supplier pattern:** Applicable when a complex task can be divided into several simpler, context-independent subtasks.

  Variants: Actor-Agent-Supplier pattern.

- **Composite-Part pattern:** Can be used to protect components, which are used to compose a complex function from unauthorized access or to treat a number of cooperating components as a single unit within a software system.

  Variant: Wrapper pattern.

- **Mediator-Worker pattern:** Can be used to decouple cooperating components of a software system and to realize them without having direct dependencies among them. This pattern can also be applied when the services offered by existing or individually developed components should be combined to provide a more complex functionality.

  Variants: Adapter pattern, Sensor pattern, Display pattern.

- **Abstract Factory pattern** [Gamma+93]: Can be applied when dependencies and variations on the creation and composition of complex components or subsystems should be removed from a client application or client module.

- **Envelope-Letter pattern:** Can be applied to support multiple implementations of components or to change the implementation or behavior of an object without modifying system clients. The structure of this pattern is related but not identical to a pattern defined by Coplien [Coplien92].

  Variants: Bridge pattern [Gamma+93], Handle-Body pattern [Coplien92].

- **Proxy-Original pattern** [Gamma+93]: Applicable whenever there is a need for a representative for a component in a different address space (remote proxy), a need for a component that should be loaded on demand (virtual proxy), or a need for a protected access to a component (protected proxy) [Gamma+94].

- **Subject-Snapshot pattern** [Gamma+93]: Can be used when it is necessary to "snapshot" the state of a component so as to be able to later restore it to its original state, or to allow other modules to obtain information about the state of a component without obtaining access to its implementation or functionality [Gamma+94].

- **Controller-Command pattern:** Can be used when a request for a service should be decoupled from its execution, when it is desired to provide functionality related to the execution of services, or when the execution of a service may vary.

- **View-Representation pattern:** Can be applied when the general organization of views on a software system should be separated from actions necessary to create and administrate a particular view, or when it is necessary to support different views on the same subject or the same view for various output devices.

- **Collection-Iterator pattern:** Can be used to handle the access to elements of a collection component and to support simultaneous iteration over the same collection. In addition, it can be used to provide multiple traversal strategies for collection components and to support their variation.

- **Master-Slave pattern:** Can be applied whenever it is necessary to handle the computation of replicated services within a software system.

- **Producer-Consumer pattern:** Can be used to organize the access to results of services provided by active suppliers within a structure of cooperating components.

  Variants: Producer-Repository-Consumer pattern, Producer-Sensor-Consumer pattern.

- **Publisher-Subscriber pattern:** Can be used to propagate changes and to maintain consistency among cooperating components of a software system.

- **Forwarder-Receiver pattern:** Can be applied to separate and encapsulate interprocess communication facilities used within distributed software systems with a statically known distribution of services.

Other design patterns exist, but are still to be described:

- **Client-Broker-Server pattern**
- **Client-Trader-Server pattern**
- **Worker-Repository pattern**

Table 1 gives an overview of the further classification of the patterns that currently exist within the system. For reasons of simplicity, the architectural frameworks are not explicitly listed in this scheme. Their main "functionality" is to organize the computation of complex tasks; the major structural principle on which they are based is separation of concerns. Also not shown in this scheme is that a pattern may have more than one functional characteristic. For example, a pattern that organizes the computation of a complex function often has the additional responsibility of guiding communication between its participants. If a pattern is based on several structural principles, its most important principle is highlighted in boldface. Note that for reasons of simplicity and layout the granularity dimension has been flattened (the table does not differentiate patterns of different granularity).

6. HETEROGENEOUS ARCHITECTURES

Patterns are used to build concrete software architectures. Thus no pattern can be seen completely independently of all other patterns. Although each pattern addresses a particular, isolated, complete design issue, in reality it is always part of a larger structure. Any pattern may contain, be contained in,

Creation	Access	Communication	Organizing Complex Tasks
ABSTRACTION			
Abstract Factory	**Controller-Command**	Forwarder-Receiver	Actor-Supplier
	View-Representation	Client-Broker-Server	Actor-Agent-Supplier
		Client-Trader-Server	Composite-Part
			Wrapper
ENCAPSULATION			
	Controller-Command	**Forwarder-Receiver**	**Composite-Part**
	View-Representation	Client-Broker-Server	**Wrapper**
		Client-Trader-Server	
SEPARATION OF CONCERNS			
Abstract Factory	**Proxy-Original**	Forwarder-Receiver	**Actor-Supplier**
	Subject-Snapshot	Client-Broker-Server	**Actor-Agent-Supplier**
	Collection-Iterator	Client-Trader-Server	Composite-Part
			Master-Slave
			Worker-Repository
		Broker Architecture	*All architectural*
		Microkernel	*frameworks*
		Architecture	
COUPLING AND COHESION			
Abstract Factory	**Envelope-Letter**	**Mediator-Worker**	Actor-Supplier
	Bridge	**Adapter**	Actor-Agent-Supplier
	Handle-Body	**Sensor**	
	Proxy-Original	**Display**	
	Subject-Snapshot	**Publisher-Subscriber**	
	Controller-Command	**Client-Broker-Server**	
	View-Representation	**Client-Trader-Server**	
	Producer-Consumer		
	Producer-Repository-		
	Consumer		
	Producer-Sensor-Consumer		

TABLE 1 Classification of Patterns

or be interlocked with other patterns, and will also interact with them. Thus a useful system must consider all possible constraints regarding the combination and composition of the patterns it comprises.

When combined correctly, patterns complement each other. If not they may introduce additional, unnecessary complexity, and the resulting structure may lose the desirable properties each single pattern supports. In such a situation more problems are introduced than solved.

For example, several design patterns can be used to further structure the Model-View-Controller framework. Mediators may be introduced to decouple the subsystems of this architecture, and the Publisher-Subscriber pattern can be used to implement the change propagation mechanism between them. The Composite-Part pattern usually serves as a further structuring mechanism for all three subsystems. Adapters, sensors, and displays are useful for decoupling the application from its environment (that is, its input and output devices or graphical user interfaces). Commands (Controller-Command pattern) and representations (View-Representation pattern) may be used to further structure the controller and to view subsystems of the architecture. Abstract Factories may be used to create complex entities like windows or particular views on the software. The use of snapshots may help avoid violating the model's encapsulation when retrieving information about its state. In this case the correct combination of several patterns leads to a well-structured architecture for a complex system that satisfies both functional and nonfunctional requirements.

On the other hand, the combination of several ActorSupplier or Composite-Part structures with mediators and wrappers is not always appropriate. It may happen that the mediator interface expands and becomes complex and difficult to maintain. Wrappers have to be used very carefully as well. They introduce additional complexity and have a tendency to spread [Hölzle93].

Thus, combining patterns is not a mechanical task; it calls for the skills of an architect to compose the building blocks in an appropriate way. Of course, the experience of a good software architect cannot be completely captured by rules, but it is certainly possible to formulate some guidelines addressing the combination of patterns to heterogeneous structures.

These guidelines must address two aspects:

- For each pattern, directions have to be developed for its integration into larger structures or its composition from smaller ones. It must be specified which other patterns it can be combined with, and how. These directions are part of the description of each pattern.[1]

- Heterogeneous structures themselves introduce forces (and maybe problems) just because of their existence and complexity. These forces are independent of the design issues addressed by each pattern within the

---

[1] The discussion part of the pattern description template introduced in Section 3 covers these aspects. For each pattern in the system, constraints regarding its usage or combination have been specified. The above examples are excerpts from the original pattern descriptions.

structure. Thus, general rules and guidelines must be specified for composing and handling complex, heterogeneous software architectures containing distinct patterns. These guidelines must be specified separately from guidelines for the constituent patterns.

7. EXPERIENCE

The details of this approach have not been fully worked out. However, to determine whether it works in concrete industrial software applications and to get a feel for how *well* it works (and where to improve it), the approach has been tried in several projects (real product development) in various application domains:

- **Automation:** Flexible manufacturing, material-flow control (more informally applied) [Meyer+88]
- **Telecommunications:** Communication component [ATM93]
- **Business:** Car dealer system (still under development)

From these projects we got positive reinforcement of the idea that patterns help develop systems with clearly defined architectures and defined (non-functional) properties (such as changeability and portability). We also received ideas for improvement of some aspects of the system, such as the classification scheme for patterns (see Section 8).

New projects are planned for the near future to further evaluate our approach to patterns in more detail.

8. OPEN ISSUES

Our work on describing and classifying patterns, as well as the application of our approach in real-world projects, has allowed us to identify several issues that need further study.

The first issue is the completeness of a system of patterns. The following questions arise:

- Can a system of patterns be complete?
- Does it have to be complete?

Likewise, it makes sense to think about the consistency and minimal range of a system of patterns.

The second issue concerns the need for a comprehensive method to guide the software architect in the use of a system of patterns throughout an entire design. Such a guide must address classification schemes for identifying appropriate patterns for a given design situation and combining them into heterogeneous structures. Guidelines do exist for combining some patterns, but up to now there has been no systematic approach to this issue. A top-down approach is not possible, since lower-level requirements can affect the structuring of the overall architecture. For example, the use of reference counters to handle multiple referenced objects requires design patterns that allow their implementation, a requirement that may not be foreseeable at a higher level of abstraction.

A third issue addresses pattern classification. There are patterns that cannot be clearly classified according to specific attributes. (For example, the Mediator-Worker pattern can be used either as an architectural framework or as a design pattern, depending on the specific design situation.) Thus the question arises as to whether selected categories and attributes are correct. Feedback from our pilot projects suggests that in general they do work; however, some developers believe that classification schemes restrict them and may keep them from finding the pattern they need. As one developer put it, "A strict classification scheme assigns each pattern to a drawer, and unless you do not open the drawer for a certain pattern you won't find it, even if you can use the pattern for solving your problem." Rather than a classification scheme, some developers suggest using a kind of road map that includes a short description of every pattern and its connections and links to other patterns. It remains to be seen whether a strict classification scheme is the best option or whether it should be replaced by something like a road map or dropped completely.

9. RELATED WORK

Work from several research topics within the wide field of object-oriented software flows together in "Pattern-Oriented Software Architecture." Most work on patterns has focused on software reuse. Other important contributions have come from research in systematic software design.

Our work is most closely related to that of Gamma, Helm, Johnson, and Vlissides [Gamma+93]. They introduce design patterns as reusable microarchitectures, which are regarded as new mechanisms for expressing design experience. The main difference between the work of Gamma et al. and ours is that we try to develop a system for a large number of patterns and a method for finding and combining the right patterns.

Object-oriented frameworks are another approach for reusing software architectures. A framework is an implementation of an architecture for a family of systems. Adaptation and extension are necessary to solve specific problems. Frameworks are closely related to the subgroup of patterns we call architectural frameworks. The main difference is that frameworks are codified in a programming language, whereas architectural frameworks are language-independent. This makes frameworks more concrete but also less flexible and less applicable than architectural frameworks.

The aim of Perry and Wolf is to build a foundation for research in software architecture [Perry+92]. The goal of such research is to formalize the design principles and paradigms that good designers use intuitively (without an underlying theory or system or even a common notation). Garlan and Shaw's work follows the same direction. They define the notion of an architectural style for a software system [Garlan+93]. An architectural style determines a set of components and a set of possible connections between them, and constrains how they can be combined.

The focus of these approaches is on the design of the overall structure of large, complex systems. Thus an architectural style is comparable to an architectural framework, which forms the highest level of abstraction in our system of patterns.

Coplien works on the other end of the spectrum. He focuses on idioms, which are concrete C++ implementations of specific design issues [Coplien92]. In our system of patterns, idioms form the lowest level of abstraction.

Another research direction that has garnered much interest lately, object-oriented analysis and design [see Booch94, Coad+90, Rumbaugh+91], investigates patterns and mechanisms. The reason for this is that current design methods provide only general steps; they do not support the construction of particular architectures with predefined requirements.

Work on patterns has also been done in various OOPSLA workshops, organized by Bruce Anderson, on software architecture and patterns.

Recently the scientific community [see Beck89, Perry+92] has shown interest in "classical" architecture (that is, designing buildings). *The Timeless Way of Building*, by Christopher Alexander [Alexander79] is quoted particularly often. Alexander proposes the use of pattern languages for the architecture of buildings and communities.

10. CONCLUSION AND OUTLOOK

The use of patterns is a promising approach to software development aimed at constructive, systematic, and controllable implementation of applications with defined properties. We believe, however, that patterns alone are not enough. What is needed is a system of patterns that also offers a classification scheme and a method for choosing the right patterns and pattern combinations.

Our goal is to develop such a system. The status of our work is as follows:

- In this paper we propose a scheme for classifying patterns and a template for describing them. We list the patterns we have described using our template.

- The list of patterns is not yet complete. Our work on the description of frameworks and design patterns is almost finished. Some frameworks and design patterns are identified in this paper but are not yet specified, and a few candidates for further design patterns exist. Up to now only the foundations have been laid for our work on idioms.

- No work has been done on methods to guide users of pattern systems. At this time we have only ideas for an outline of this method.

Our work on patterns, systems of patterns, and an overall method for using them (a classification of patterns) will be revised based on feedback from various industrial projects (see above).

We hope that with the help of a pattern-oriented approach to software architecture it is possible to achieve a great step forward toward more productive software development.

REFERENCES

[Alexander79] C. Alexander. *The Timeless Way of Building.* New York: Oxford University Press, 1979.

[ATM93] Siemens AG. Komplexspezifikation ATM-Switch. Internal document, 1993.

[Beck89] K. Beck and W. Cunningham. A Laboratory for Teaching Object-Oriented Thinking, *Proceedings of the Object-Oriented Programming Systems, Languages, and Applications Conference,* New Orleans, LA. October 1989, pp. 1–6.

[Booch94] G. Booch. *Object-Oriented Design with Applications,* 2nd ed. Redwood City, CA: Benjamin/Cummings, 1994.

[Buschmann93] F. Buschmann. Rational Architectures for Object-Oriented Software-Systems. *Journal of Object-Oriented Programming.* (September 1993).

[Buschmann+95] F. Buschmann, R. Meunier, H. Rohnert, P. Sommerlad, and M. Stal. *Pattern-Oriented Software Architecture—A Pattern System.* In preparation.

[Coad+90] P. Coad and E. Yourdon. *OOA—Object-Oriented Analysis.* Englewood Cliffs, NJ: Prentice-Hall, 1990.

[Coplien92] J. Coplien. *Advanced C++ Programming Styles and Idioms.* Reading, MA: Addison-Wesley, 1992.

[Coplien94] J. Coplien. *Description of the Envelope-Letter Idiom.* OOPSLA Pattern Mailing Reflector. 1994.

[Gamma+93] E. Gamma, R. Helm, R. Johnson, and J. Vlissides. Design Patterns: Abstraction and Reuse of Object-Oriented Design, *ECOOP 7 Proceedings.* Berlin: Springer-Verlag, 1993, pp. 406–431.

[Gamma+95] E. Gamma, R. Helm, R. Johnson, and J. Vlissides. *Design Patterns: Elements of Reusable Object-Oriented Software.* Reading, MA: Addison-Wesley, 1995.

[Garlan+93] D. Garlan. and M. Shaw. An Introduction to Software Architecture. *Advances in Software Engineering and Knowledge Engineering,* Vol. I. World Scientific Publishing Company, 1993.

[Hölzle93] Urs Hölzle. Integrating Independently Developed Components in Object-Oriented Languages. *ECOOP 7 Proceedings.* Berlin: Springer-Verlag, 1993, pp. 36–56.

[Meyer+88] Walter Meyer and Siegfried Paul. Objektorientierung in der Automatisierungstechnik. Laboratory report, Siemens AG, ZFE IS SOF 3, 1988.

[Perry+92] D. Perry and A. Wolf. Foundations for the Study of Software Architecture. *ACM SIGSOFT, Software Engineering Notes* 17, 4 (October 1992): 40–52.

[Reenskaug92] Trygve Reenskaug. *Intermediate Smalltalk, Practical Design and Implementation.* Tutorial TOOLS Europe, 1992.

[Rumbaugh+91] J. Rumbaugh, M. Blaha, W. Premerlani, F. Eddy, and W. Lorensen. *Object-Oriented Modeling and Design.* Englewood Cliffs, NJ: Prentice-Hall, 1991.

Frank Buschmann and Regine Meunier can be reached at Siemens AG, Corporate Research and Development, Dept. ZFE BT SE2, Otto-Hahn-Ring, 81730 Munich, Germany; frankbuschmann{reginemeunier}@zfe.siemens.de.

18 Relationships Between Design Patterns

Walter Zimmer

ABSTRACT

The catalog of design patterns presented by Gamma et al. [Gamm95] contains about twenty design patterns and their mutual relationships. In this paper I organize these relationships into different categories and revise both the patterns and their relationships. I am then able to arrange the design patterns in different layers. The results make it easier to understand the overall structure of the catalog, thereby making it easier to classify other design patterns and apply them to software development. During this classification process, a new design pattern resulted from a generalization of several other design patterns.

1. INTRODUCTION

In the last couple of years, object-oriented design has gained much attention in the field of software engineering. However, after some initial experience with object-oriented design, software engineers face fundamental problems

Copyright © 1994 Forschungszentrum Informatik. All Rights Reserved.

designing and reusing applications and libraries—problems that cannot be solved by current methods and tools.

Many people consider design patterns to be a promising approach to overcoming these problems in object-oriented systems [Beck93, Beck94, Gamm93, Gamm95, Coad93a, Copl92, Copl94, Shaw91, John92, Busc93, Pree94]. The main idea behind design patterns is to reuse design information, thus allowing developers to communicate more effectively. New design patterns are being discovered, described, and applied by several research groups. Development tools supporting the design pattern approach are also under way.

In this new field of software engineering, the following important questions are arising:

- Among the many different design patterns being discovered, are any related to each other? What are the characteristics of such relationships?
- Do any two patterns address similar problems?
- Is it possible to combine two design patterns?
- What are the criteria for classifying design patterns into categories?

Few publications [Gamm93, Gamm95][1] have adequately addressed these issues. Similar to Alexander's pattern descriptions [Alex77], each pattern description in Gamma et al. [Gamm95] contains a "See Also" section listing possible relationships between design patterns. Furthermore, their catalog presents a classification of all design patterns according to two criteria: jurisdiction (class, object, compound) and characterization (creational, structural, behavioral).

Gamma et al. describe these relationships informally and in detail, so that each relationship appears to be a little bit different from the other ones. I propose a classification of relationships that will help in understanding the similarities between relationships. Therefore I have modified their catalog slightly and organized the design patterns into several layers.

This paper gives new insights into the relationships between existing design patterns. Its major accomplishments are as follows:

- A classification of the relationships between design patterns
- A new design pattern resulting from a generalization of several other design patterns
- A structuring of design patterns into several layers

---

[1] As this paper refers to a preliminary (unpublished) version of the catalog, some minor points might differ from the current, published version. Gamma et al. [Gamm93] provide a good introductory paper for design patterns and this catalog.

Section 2 presents a graphic view of all the design patterns and relationships in the aforementioned catalog. Section 3 classifies the relationships. This process raises some problems and gives further insight into the relationships between design patterns in general. After modifying the catalog's structure in Section 4, I show in Section 5 how it is possible to arrange the design patterns into layers representing different abstraction levels.

2. OVERALL STRUCTURE OF THE DESIGN PATTERN CATALOG

Figure 1 is a graphic representation of the design patterns and relationships from Gamma et al. [Gamm95]. No further information is added to this figure. The annotations to the arrows are taken almost literally from their catalog. The variables X and Y are placeholders for the source and target of the respective arrows.

Figure 1 gives an impression of the overall structure of the catalog. It serves as a reference point for the rest of this paper, because it contains the most detailed information about the relationships. Figure 1 serves, therefore, as the starting point for the further classification and revision of the relationships.

3. CLASSIFICATION OF RELATIONSHIPS

3.1 Issues to Be Addressed

Starting with Figure 1, we tried to find categories containing similar kinds of design pattern relationships. During this process, the following issues had to be addressed:

Relationships refer to different aspects of design patterns

Figure 1 shows relationships addressing issues ranging from the problem definition ("creating objects," "decoupling of objects") and the solution definition ("Command can use the Composite pattern in its solution") to very specific implementation details ("similar in a level of indirection").

We wanted to improve the comprehensibility of the catalog and its structure. Therefore we focused on the problem and solution aspects. The relationships addressing implementation details played a minor role in this paper. For this reason, they were removed in later figures (Figures 3 and 4).

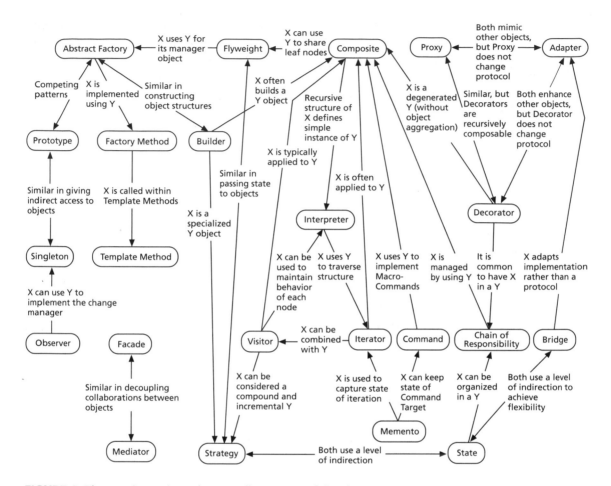

FIGURE 1 The starting point—the overall structure of the design pattern catalog

Relationship direction

The catalog's descriptions do not include the relationships' direction, which may be unidirectional (backward or forward) or bidirectional. Once the category a relationship belongs to is known, the direction can be determined rather quickly. But if one is not sure about the category the direction often remains unclear.

Relationship strength

Is a given relationship quite strong (like that between Abstract Factory and Factory Method), or are the design patterns more loosely coupled (as with Observer and Singleton)? Some design patterns can almost stand alone, while others make sense only in combination with certain other design patterns. Assessing this property is often subjective, based on experience using and combining different design patterns.

3.2 Categories of Relationships

I have classified relationships between the pairs (X, Y) of design patterns into the following categories:

X uses Y in its solution

When building a solution for the problem addressed by X, one subproblem is similar to the problem addressed by Y. Therefore, the design pattern X uses the design pattern Y in its solution. Thus the solution of Y (class structures, for example) represents one part of the solution of X.

Variant of X uses Y in its solution

This kind of relationship differs from the previous one in that the usage of Y by X is optional—some variants of X may use Y; others do not. Y is no essential part of X's solution.[2]

X is similar to Y

X and Y address a similar kind of problem (not a similar kind of solution). In several cases, these similarities are also expressed in the classification in the catalog. For example, the catalog classifies both Prototype and Abstract Factory in the category "Object-Creational."

3.3 Classification

Figure 2 shows how I have classified the relationships depicted in Figure 1 into categories. Instead of justifying all the classifications I have made, in this paper I focus on the most interesting ones. By "interesting" I mean cases where I find it difficult to assign a particular relationship into exactly one category, or I am not sure about the meaning of the relationship at all, or I think some further explanation would be useful.

---

[2] The former name "X can be combined with Y" has been changed, because most pattern combinations contain one central pattern using the other patterns (that is, the combination can be considered a variant of this central pattern).

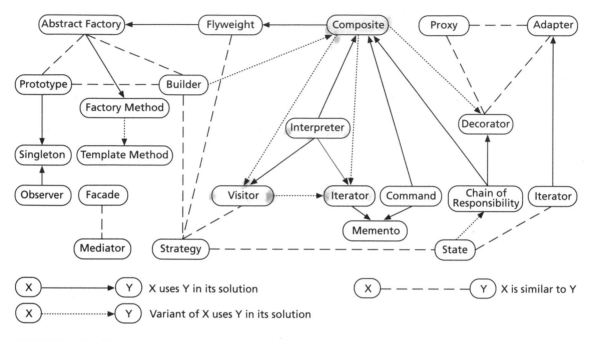

FIGURE 2 Classification of relationships

X uses Y in its solution

In most cases, the assignment of relationships to this category is clear.

Variant of X uses Y in its solution

A Builder often produces Composite objects. A Factory Method is typically called in a Template method.

Composite, Visitor, Iterator: Composite might use Iterator to traverse over composite structures and Visitor to centralize operations on object structures. Depending on the necessary degree of flexibility, one typically combines two or all three design patterns (Interpreter is a typical example).

Composite, Decorator: Composite and Decorator are often used together in applications—for example, for visual objects in ET++, MacApp, and Interviews [Wein88, App89, Lint89]. There are also other kinds of relationships between them: when looking at the solution aspect, Decorator can be seen as a degenerate Composite; when considering the problem aspect, they both support recursively structured objects, whereby Decorator focuses on attaching additional properties to objects. Thus, the design patterns are somehow similar, but it is difficult to state it more precisely. Therefore, we only insert a relationship of the type "Variant of X uses Y," and neglect the other ones.

X is similar to Y

Abstract Factory, Prototype, and Builder are similar in that they all deal with object creation. Builder and Visitor are strategies. Both Facade and Mediator serve to decouple objects. In contrast to Proxy and Decorator, which allow the client to attach additional properties dynamically to an object, Adapter primarily serves to provide a completely different interface to an object.

State (Strategy) is rather loosely coupled with Bridge and Strategy (Flyweight), as this relationship addresses the implementation detail "level of indirection" ("passing of state to objects").

3.4 Using the Classification

This section gives several possibilities for using the presented classification scheme when working with design patterns.

X uses Y in its solution

This relationship makes it clear that Y can be used as a part of the solution of X. The description of X can refer back to that of Y in order to be shorter and easier to understand. Tools supporting the design pattern approach can profit from this information: the relationship can be checked in existing designs, and design patterns like Y can be visualized as blocks, without internal implementation details, in order to raise the abstraction level.

Variant of X uses Y in its solution

When you have already applied a design pattern X in a system, relationships of this kind show how you can adapt X by combining it with other design patterns, resulting in a variant of X. Thus the retrieval of design patterns is supported.

Several design patterns that are so related may also be used as larger building blocks in design, thus raising the abstraction level.

X is similar to Y

Design patterns related in this way address similar problems. When searching for a design pattern to solve a certain kind of problem, you can look at a family of similar design patterns that address similar problems and use the one that best meets your requirements. Thus this relationship supports the retrieval of design patterns.

4. CHANGING RELATIONSHIPS AND DESIGN PATTERNS

This section examines the proposed classification of relationships further. This process results in a new design pattern and some modifications to existing relationships.

4.1 A New Design Pattern: Objectifier

Figure 2 shows that Strategy is similar to the design patterns Builder and Visitor, which can be regarded as special kinds of strategies to objectify certain behaviors. Iterator and Command are also design patterns that objectify certain behaviors; the catalog states that a Command objectifies command-dependent behavior and that an Iterator allows one to vary the traversal of object structures.

I consider the objectification of behavior by means of additional classes to be the central common factor of these and other design patterns. The usage of this design pattern allows one to vary this objectified behavior.

Therefore, I think that the objectification of behavior is a basic design pattern; I call it Objectifier. A detailed description of Objectifier is given in the Appendix. It uses the same description format as Gamma et al. [Gamm93]. The Implementation and Sample Code parts are left out.

4.2 Other Changes

The organization of relationships into different categories is sometimes difficult, because it depends partly upon subjective criteria. The difference between "X uses Y" and "Variant of X uses Y" depends upon a subjective assessment—whether the use of Y is seen as a central part of the solution of X or if it is more a combination of two autonomous design patterns.

Furthermore, two design patterns might be related in different ways; for example, Decorator-Composite and Abstract Factory–Prototype are pairs of design patterns that can be combined and are also similar.

Adapter-Decorator, Adapter-Proxy

Among other things, the catalog says, "Decorator is different from an Adapter, because a Decorator only changes an object's properties and not its interface; an Adapter will give an object a completely new interface." I think this is an important difference, and Adapter is quite different from both Decorator and Proxy. This relationship is therefore removed.

Flyweight–Abstract Factory

As the manager part of Flyweight is not an intrinsic part of the design pattern, this relationship is removed.

Objectifier-Flyweight, Objectifier-State

The relationships between Strategy and other design patterns are transformed in corresponding relationships to Objectifier. As this paper does not examine relationships addressing implementation details, I remove the relationship of Objectifier to Flyweight and State. But as explained in the previous section, State uses Objectifier in its own solution. Therefore a new relationship between State and Objectifier is added.

Adapter-Bridge

Bridge may use Adapter in its own solution. An example of this is the data structure set: Adapter can be used to view lists, arrays, and tables as sets. Thus Adapter standardizes the interfaces of the different ConcreteImplementor classes (lists, arrays, and tables) to the common Implementor interface in the Bridge pattern.

Objectifier–Template Method

As explained in the description of Objectifier (see Appendix), both patterns serve a similar purpose—to vary behavior. Inside a Template Method, methods of Objectifier objects can be invoked.

The integration of all these changes into Figure 2, as well as the addition of the Objectifier pattern, results in Figure 3.

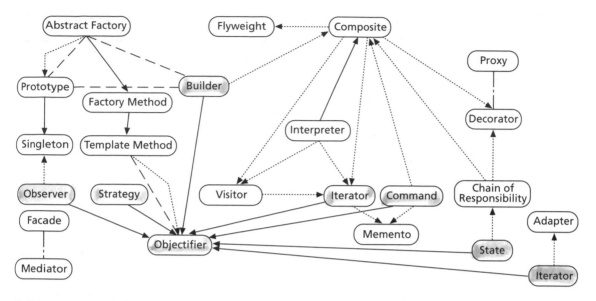

FIGURE 3 Revised classification

5. LAYERS OF DESIGN PATTERNS

5.1 Arrangement in Several Layers

Up to now we have classified relationships between design patterns and modified some of them. As one can see in Figure 3, "Variant of X uses Y" are the most frequent relationships.

I have therefore tried to arrange patterns according to these predominant relationships. The graph defined by these relationships is acyclic. Figure 4 shows that this property allows us to arrange the design patterns in different layers. Thus we can identify three semantically different layers:

- Basic design patterns and techniques
- Design patterns for typical software problems
- Design patterns specific to an application domain

5.2 Basic Design Patterns and Techniques

This layer contains design patterns that are heavily used within the design patterns of higher layers and in object-oriented systems in general. Objectifier seems to be the most important, as it is used by six other design patterns.

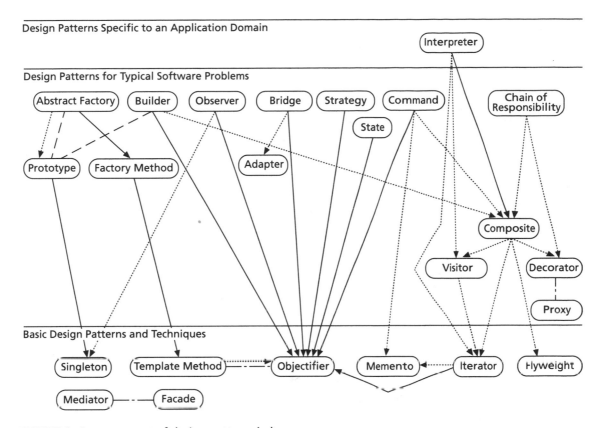

FIGURE 4 Arrangement of design patterns in layers

The problems addressed by these basic design patterns occur again and again in developing object-oriented systems. The design patterns are thus very general. When building a system, one often looks upon them more as basic design techniques than as patterns. The intentions of these design patterns (see Table 1) are very general and applicable to a broad range of problems occurring in the design of object-oriented systems.

5.3 Design Patterns for Typical Software Problems

The middle layer comprises design patterns used for more specific problems in software design. These design patterns are not used in patterns from the basic layer, but in patterns from the application-specific layer and possibly in others from their own layer. The problems addressed by these design patterns are not typical of a certain application domain.

Design Pattern	Purpose of the Design Pattern
Flyweight	Supporting fine-grained objects efficiently through sharing
Facade	Encapsulating a subsystem
Mediator	Managing collaboration between objects
Memento	Encapsulating a snapshot of the internal state of an object
Iterator	Traversing collections of objects or object structures
Objectifier	Objectifying behavior
Singleton	Providing unique access to services or variables
Template Method	Objectifying behavior (primitives will be varied in subclasses)

TABLE 1 Basic Design Patterns, with Their Respective Purposes

Builder, Prototype, Factory Method, and Abstract Factory address problems with the creation of objects, Iterator traverses object structures, Command objectifies an operation, and so on.

I regard the problem addressed by Composite (and Decorator) as a bit more specific than the problems addressed by the basic patterns, and therefore Composite was moved to the next higher layer. But the handling of recursively structured objects is a typical software problem, and Composite is used by several other design patterns. For this reason, it was placed in the lower half of the middle layer.

5.4 Design Patterns Specific to an Application Domain

Design patterns in this layer are the most specific and can often be assigned to one or more application domains.

Although the general problem of parsing some input often occurs, I consider Interpreter to be more specific. Interpreter is used to parse simple languages. The catalog lists some of the known uses of Interpreter, such as parsing constraints and matching regular expressions. Compiler construction is the major application domain.

The current catalog contains almost no application-specific design patterns. Most patterns are generic and applicable to a broad range of problems. The authors support this property by the existence of a "Known Uses" section in the design pattern description, which should include at least two examples from different application domains.

5.5 Other Arrangements

The arrangement of design patterns into layers presented here is only one possible way to separate them. My classification scheme is informal—that is, there is no simple, strict rule to assign a design pattern to a certain layer. This drawback is due to the fact that the classification is based on semantic aspects that are hard to capture formally and precisely. Thus this drawback is intrinsic to classifications such as the classification scheme in Gamma et al. [Gamm95], that is, based on jurisdiction and characterization. Nevertheless, it helps us to understand the overall structure of the catalog and to relate new design patterns to existing ones. It is also an aid for traversing and learning design patterns, as the user can choose between a bottom-up or a top-down traversal.

Another possible method is to group design patterns according to their typical pattern combinations. At this point only some such combinations are known. I believe that in the future they will play a more important role, because such combinations can be used as design building blocks.

The criteria of jurisdiction and characterization used by Gamma et al., result in several clusters of design patterns with a similar intent; this arrangement can help in retrieving an adequate design pattern for a specific problem.

6. RELATED WORK

Alexander introduced the notion of design patterns in traditional architecture [Alex77]. Each of his design patterns is related to other patterns of the same or a higher or lower granularity. These relationships influence the construction process, because one should always look at related patterns when one builds something and one should always apply higher-level patterns first. Alexander provides a classification scheme for his patterns, but not for their mutual relationships.

Gamma et al. [Gamm93, Gamm95] present a large collection of well-described design patterns. The relationships between these patterns are also described; the relationships are not classified, however, although a classification of the design patterns themselves is included. Their classification scheme, based on jurisdiction (class, object, compound) and characterization (creational, structural, behavioral), is orthogonal to the one described in this paper. Patterns within a cluster can be considered as similar to one another; this can help the designer select an appropriate design pattern for a certain problem.

Frameworks [WB90, John91] can be considered high-level design patterns, as they usually consist of many interrelated lower-level design patterns. Beck and Johnson [Beck94] write that "patterns can be used at many levels, and what is derived at one level can be considered a basic pattern at another level." Furthermore, they state that "this is probably typical of most architectures; some patterns will be generic and some will be specific to the application domain," which confirms the organization depicted in Figure 4. Booch [Booc93] also mentions that design patterns range from idioms to frameworks.

Coad [Coad93b] combines several design patterns in an exemplary application, but the relationships are not investigated any further.

7. CONCLUSION

This paper has presented a method for classifying relationships between design patterns, which has led to a new design pattern and to an arrangement of design patterns into different layers. These results partially stem from a former project [Zimm94]; although the design pattern approach and the excellent catalog devised by Gamma et al. [Gamm94] proved effective in this project, the following issues remained:

- The design of important abstractions of the application domain often requires the combination of several, interrelated design patterns.
- Applying design patterns requires a fair knowledge of both single design patterns and their relationships.
- Tool support is needed to apply design patterns to really large applications.

The results reported here address these issues, because they help in

- Understanding the often complex relationships between design patterns
- Organizing existing design patterns, as well as categorizing and describing new design patterns
- Comparing different collections of design patterns
- Building CASE tools that support design patterns.

Thus the results are a step toward the development of a pattern language. I believe this will be very valuable for the development of object-oriented systems.

My colleagues and I are continuing our work with design patterns by formalizing the semantics of the different kinds of relationships and the different layers shown in Figure 4. We are aiming at greater precision and a better semantic definition. This is a prerequisite for defining a generally accepted and usable classification scheme to serve as a basis for further work.

Many new design patterns are currently being discovered and described, especially application-specific design patterns. We will include them and their relationships in our classification scheme. This will enable us to continually evaluate the validity and usefulness of the classification scheme and improve it accordingly.

REFERENCES

[Alex77] C. Alexander, S. Ishikawa, and M. Silverstein. *A Pattern Language.* New York: Oxford University Press, 1977.

[App89] Apple Computer. *Inc. Macintosh Programmers Workshop Pascal 3.0 Reference.* Cupertino, CA, 1989.

[Beck93] K. Beck. Patterns and software development. *Dr. Dobbs Journal* 19, 2 (1993): 18–23.

[Beck94] K. Beck and R. Johnson. Patterns generate architecture. In *Proceedings of ECOOP'94.* 1994.

[Booc93] G. Booch. Patterns. *Object Magazine* 3, 2 (1993)

[Busc93] F. Buschmann. Rational architectures for object-oriented software systems. *Journal of Object Oriented Programming* 6,5 :30–41. (September 1993).

[Casa92] Eduardo Casais, Michael Ranft, Bernhard Schiefer, Dietmar Throbald, and Walter Zimmer. Obst—an overview. Technical report, Forschungszentrum Informatik (FZI). Karlsruhe, Germany, June 1992. FZI.0391.

[Coad93a] P. Coad. Object-oriented patterns. *Communications of the ACM* 35, 9 (September 1993) :153–159.

[Coad93b] P. Coad. Patterns (workshop). In *OOPSLA'92 Addendum to the Proceedings.* Volume 4 of *OOPS Messenger*, pp. 93–96, Vancouver, BC: ACM Press, October 1993.

[Copl92] J. Coplien. *Advanced C++: Programming Styles and Idioms.* Reading, MA: Addison-Wesley, 1991.

[Copl94] J. O. Coplien. Generative pattern languages: An emerging direction of software design. *C++ Report* 6, 6 (July–August 1994)

[Gamm93] E. Gamma, R. Helm, R. Johnson, and J. Vlissides. Design patterns: Abstraction and reuse in object-oriented designs. In O. Nierstrasz (ed.), *Proceedings of ECOOP'93*, pp. 406–431. Berlin: Springer-Verlag, 1993.

[Gamm95] E. Gamma, R. Helm, R. Johnson, and J. Vlissides. *Design Patterns: Elements of Reusable Object-Oriented Software.* Reading, MA: Addison-Wesley, 1995.

[John91] Ralph E. Johnson and Vincent F. Russo. Reusing object-oriented designs. Technical Report UIUCDCS 91–1696, University of Illinois, May 1991.

[John92] R. Johnson. Documenting frameworks using patterns. In *Proceedings of OOPSLA'92*. Vol. 27 of *ACM SIGPLAN Notices*, pp. 63–76. Vancouver, BC: ACM Press, October 1992.

[Lint89] M. Linton, John Vlissides, and P. Calder. Composing user interfaces with Interviews. *IEEE Computer* 22, 2 (February 1989): 8–22.

[Pree94] W. Pree. Meta-patterns: A means for describing the essentials of reusable o-o design. In *Proceedings of ECOOP'94*, 1994.

[Rumb91] J. Rumbaugh, M. Blaha, W. Premerlani, F. Eddy, and W. Lorensen. *Object-Oriented Modeling and Design*. Englewood Cliffs, NJ: Prentice-Hall, 1991.

[Shaw91] M. Shaw. Heterogenous design idioms for software architecture. In *Proceedings of the Sixth International Workshop on Software Specification and Design*, Como, Italy, October 25–26, 1991. IEEE Computer Society, Software Engineering Notes, pp. 158–165.

[WB90] Rebecca J. Wirfs-Brock and Ralph E. Johnson. Surveying current research in object-oriented design. *CACM* 33, 9 (September 1990): 105–123.

[Wein88] André Weinand, Erich Gamma, and Rudolph Marty. ET++—an object-oriented application framework in C++. In *Proceedings OOPSLA '88. ACM SIGPLAN Notices*, Vol. 23, No. 11. pp. 46–57, November 1988.

[Zimm94] Walter Zimmer. Experiences using design patterns to reorganize an object-oriented application. Position paper for the Pattern Workshop at ECOOP'94, July 1994.

APPENDIX: A DESCRIPTION OF OBJECTIFIER

Name   Objectifier

Intent   To objectify similar behavior in additional classes so that clients can vary such behavior independently from other behavior, thus supporting variation-oriented design [see Gamm93]. Instances from those classes represent behavior or properties, but not concrete objects from the real world (similar to reification).

Motivation   Objectifier is a very general design pattern to be applied to a wide range of problems. The idea of objectifying behavior is used in many other design patterns. Thus, knowledge about other design patterns helps a lot in understanding Objectifier (and vice versa). The use of Objectifier is illustrated in the following example, which represents a somewhat simpler variant of the Bridge design pattern.

A frequent problem in design is the separation of an abstraction from its implementation, and the interchange of implementations. For example, the data type Mapping might provide different implementations for different tasks because of efficiency reasons.

A common approach is to have an abstract class for the data type Mapping, with the concrete subclasses MappingList and MappingHash representing

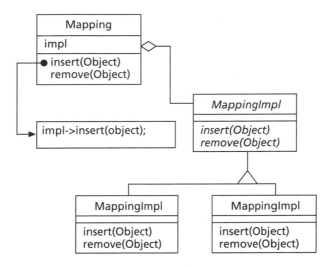

FIGURE 5

different implementations. This allows you to interchange the implementation at compile time, but not at run time.

A more flexible approach is to objectify the varying behavior—that is, to have independent implementation objects that can be interchanged at run time. In the example of Mapping,[3] you have a class, Mapping, representing the abstraction, and an abstract class, MappingImpl, which is the superclass for the concrete implementation classes MappingList and MappingHash. Mapping maintains a reference to MappingImpl, and it delegates the requests to its current implementation object.

This solution allows you to interchange the implementation object at run time.

Applicability   Use the Objectifier pattern when

- Behavior should be decoupled from classes in order to have independent behavior in objects that can be interchanged, saved, modified, shared, or invoked.

- Run-time behavior configuration is required.

- There are several almost identical classes, which differ only in one or a few methods. Objectifying the different behavior in additional classes

---

[3] The OMT Notation [Rumb91] is used in this diagram. Italic letters indicate abstract classes and methods. The method insert from Mapping is represented in pseudocode. The attribute `impl` of Mapping is a reference to MappingImpl.

allows you to unify the former classes in one common class, which can then be configured with a reference to the new, additional classes.

- There is a large amount of conditional code to select behavior.

Participants **The client** has a reference to the Objectifier and can be configured with a concrete Objectifier at run time.

The Objectifier defines the common interface for the different concrete Objectifiers. It may also contain data or references to other objects that are common to all concrete Objectifiers.

Collaborations A client may use Objectifier to delegate parts of its behavior. The Objectifier receives the information needed to fulfill its task during its initialization, or the client passes the information as a parameter when calling the Objectifier. Or a client can be configured with a concrete Objectifier to adapt the behavior to fulfill a certain task.

Class Diagram Figure A-1 depicts the collaborating classes with their inheritance and aggregation relationship.

Consequences **Encapsulation, Modularity:** Behavior is objectified and encapsulated in classes.

Configurability, Customizability: Clients of Objectifier can change the concrete Objectifier at run time.

FIGURE A-1 Class diagram

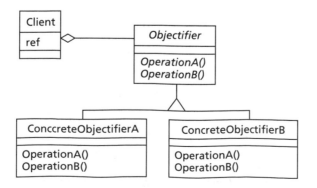

Extensibility, Single Point of Evolution: New behavior can be implemented by adding a new class without affecting existing classes.

Efficiency:

- Loss of time and space by an additional level of indirection.
- The client can dynamically select the class that is most efficient for the current task.
- Stateless Objectifiers (without attributes) can be shared by different objects.

Known Uses   The example of the Mapping data type (see "Motivation" above) is taken from the data structure library of OBST, an object-oriented database system [Casa92]. The type of the current implementation object of a Mapping object depends on the number of elements managed by the Mapping Object; if this number exceeds eight (or falls below four), the list implementation is replaced with a hash implementation (or vice versa). This replacement is triggered by the Mapping object itself, not by the user.

Objectifier is also used in the solution of other design patterns. Therefore one can find real examples of Objectifier by looking at the design patterns referenced in "See Also."

Related Patterns   Although several design patterns contain the common idea of objectifying behavior to solve a problem, their purposes and requirements are more specific than those of Objectifier. Therefore Objectifier is more a generalization of these patterns than a totally new design pattern.

As many other issues have to be addressed when applying these related design patterns, I regard them as independent design patterns, not simply as specialized variants of Objectifier. Referring to Objectifier, the descriptions of these design patterns can often be shortened. Table A-1 contains related design patterns with the corresponding objectified (and potentially varied) behavior.

TABLE A-1 Design Patterns with Their Objectified Behavior

Design Pattern	Objectified Behavior
Bridge	Implementation of some abstraction
Builder	Creation/Representation of objects
Command	Command-dependent behavior
Iterator	Traversal of object structures
Observer	Context-dependent behavior
State	State-dependent behavior
Strategy	(Complex) Algorithm

Strategy Objectifier differs from Strategy in that it objectifies behavior in a broader sense and is not restricted to algorithms in the classic sense of "algorithms and data structures." Thus Objectifier is more general than Strategy.

Template Method This pattern has a similar intent as Objectifier: the variation of some behavior. A Template Method represents the principal structure of an algorithm or behavior, whereby parts of it can be varied in subclasses by (re)defining methods (primitives). In contrast to this, Objectifier puts only the variable parts in additional classes, so that these parts can be varied independently from other behavior. One superclass defines the common interface, and several subclasses implement the concrete behavior in different ways.

Walter Zimmer can be reached at Software Engineering Department, Forschungszentrum Informatik, Haid-und-Neu_Str. 10–14, D-76131 Karlsruhe, Germany; zimmer@fzi.de.

19

Discovering Patterns in Existing Applications

Robert Martin

This chapter discusses a search for object-oriented design patterns in a successfully completed application. The application was designed without patterns in mind and before any of the designers had learned about the concept of patterns. Yet copious, useful patterns were present. From thirty thousand lines of C++ code, we extracted several dozen patterns. Many have already been documented in one form or another in various discussion groups. Those that remain are enumerated here.

INTRODUCTION

My associates and I are engaged in a long-term project involving architectural modeling of buildings. Our project entails the writing of many programs, each attempting to analyze and evaluate an architectural design created by a human using a graphical user interface.

Since this project requires us to write many programs, we have invested a great deal of time in developing a reusable framework that will support them

Copyright © Robert Martin. All Rights Reserved.

all. Over the last year, we have written the first prototype program and put the framework together. We are now producing the rest of the programs.

Even though we had already designed and implemented the first program and much of the framework before we had acquired any knowledge of the concept of patterns, its seemed to us that we had been employing a number of repetitive design elements that might be reused in other designs.

After we had become familiar with the concept of patterns, we decided to reexamine the design and implementation of the first program and framework to see if we could describe any patterns. Not surprisingly, we found quite a few. In fact, in one form or another, every pattern in (Gamma et al.s' *Design Patterns* (1995) was used in our application, yet in very ad hoc and vague ways. Had we known about these patterns to begin with, I believe we would have spent less time searching for solutions and would have created our designs with more discipline and structure.

Over two dozen patterns were found. Most of them build on the *Design Patterns* repertoire, often combining two or three of these patterns into a higher-level, "macro" pattern. Many of the patterns we found are specific to C++, our implementation language. This stems from the fact that polymorphism in C++ is primarily available through inherited interfaces. Thus many of the patterns we found have to do with structuring inheritance relationships to achieve polymorphism, and thereby reducing dependencies.

Pattern Groups

In all, I found four groups of patterns in our designs. Although I am sure that there are more ways to classify these patterns, this is the schema that occurred to me:

1. **Container patterns.** These patterns involve the use of container classes or iterators. Our applications rely heavily on many different template containers. We use Sets, Bags, Ordered Sets, and so on. We also use the method found in the Booch components to differentiate between bounded and unbounded forms of a container.

    Containers form the foundation of our data model. Therefore it is not surprising that several of the patterns we discovered were associated with them. These patterns have to do with creating polymorphic interfaces to the containers, so that container clients do not need to know the specific kind of container being used.

    A container can be created in its bounded or unbounded form, as a Set or Bag container, or in any other form, and then passed to functions that are able to iterate over them and manipulate them in simple ways, without knowing the kind of container they are using.

2. **High-level design patterns.** These are patterns that had a profound effect on the high-level design of our application. All of them were found to repeat, in one form or another, throughout the design. They involve the management of source code dependencies between high-level subsystems, the releasability of each subsystem and of the application as a whole, and the reusability of individual subsystems.

3. **Low-level design patterns.** There were many of these patterns, which appeared over and over again as techniques or tricks in localized portions of the code. They involve localized code reuse, management of dual hierarchies, finite state machines, client/server interfaces, and the query and selection of items in containers.

4. **C++ related patterns.** There were many patterns that dealt with the C++ language. In other languages these patterns would either not exist or would take a very different form. I conclude from this that language-specific patterns may be an important aspect of patterns in general. I know that it took us a long time and a lot of trial and error to find these patterns, which helped us navigate through the special brand of object oriented design required for C++ development. I cannot help but think that their enumeration and explanation will help others.

THE PATTERNS

It is not possible to provide an in-depth analysis of each individual pattern within the confines of this chapter. Therefore I will provide an extremely short description of each pattern in the lexicon below.

Container Patterns

Iterable Container

Containers need to be iterated by clients that don't know the specific kind of container they are using. This pattern arranges all containers into a common inheritance hierarchy that can be linearly iterated. It then applies the Prototype, Strategy, and Factory patterns to create a concrete class, Iterator, that has the ability to iterate over any container in the hierarchy, without knowing what kind of container it is.

Member Container

Many containers have "membership semantics"; that is, they support functions such as `Add`, `Remove`, `IsMember`, and so on. All such containers can be operated upon with the set operations `intersection`, `union`, and `difference`. Clients need to be able to perform these manipulations without a direct knowledge of the kind of container they are using.

For example, a client may wish to take the union of two containers that are passed as function arguments. The caller may decide to pass in a Bounded Set container and an Ordered Unbounded Bag container. The function should be able to deal with this or any other combination of containers.

This pattern uses the Prototype and Envelope Letter patterns to create an inheritance and containment hierarchy for all containers that exhibit membership semantics.

Container Implementation

Although employed by us in our designs, we first saw this pattern used in the Booch components.

Containers can be implemented in a variety of ways. For example, a Stack container can be implemented as a linked list, a static array, or a dynamically growing array. Each implementation has its own particular trade-offs in space, time, and complexity. Users should be able to select the appropriate implementation for their particular needs, and the decision a user makes should not matter to its clients.

For example, I should be able to create an Unbounded Ordered Bag container and then pass it to a client that expects a Bag container. That client should be able to manipulate it as a Bag container without getting confused.

Containers to Arrays

Containers should be copyable into arrays. When asked, a container should be able to create an array of the elements within itself. Thus, I should be able tell a Bounded Ordered Set container to copy itself into an array. Then I can index through the elements of the array as I choose.

Selective Iterator

The concept of iteration is more complex than simply asking for each item in a container in turn. Often a user may wish to iterate over only those items that meet particular criteria. This pattern describes the concept of a Query class, which is used by a Selective Iterator class. Derived Query classes can be implemented by the user and combined through the agencies of AndQuery, OrQuery, and NotQuery into arbitrarily complex queries. Such Queries can be supplied to Selective Iterators so that they will iterate only over those elements that satisfy the query.

Combination Iterator

Iteration sometimes involves combining the elements of a container into pairs. For example, in order to create all the diagonals of a polygon, one must iterate over all the combinations of two points in the polygon. This pattern describes classes, called Combination Iterators, that mix the elements of a container into combinations and permutations. Each combination is the result of a single iteration. Each time the Iterator is asked for the next element, a new combination is formed.

High-Level Design Patterns

Reusable Categories

This is less a pattern of class and object relationships than it is a pattern involving source code dependencies between two groups of classes. Classes are grouped into logical entities called categories. A category can be viewed as the granule of reuse. A reusable category is one that contains mostly abstract classes and has few source code dependencies on other categories.

This pattern defines a reusable category as a category containing high-level policy that can be reused in different detailed contexts. It discusses the qualitative and quantitative attributes of such categories.

Main Sequence Category

This pattern describes those qualities of a class category that bear upon its distance from the "main sequence." The main sequence is a "golden ratio" of dependencies versus dependers and abstraction versus detail. When these factors are in balance the category is said to be "on the main sequence." We can quantify the dependency structure of a category by calculating its distance from the main sequence. See Martin (1995).

Releasable System

A releasable system is composed of categories that can be individually released and whose dependencies are well known. The system is releasable only if the structure of the dependencies forms a directed acyclic graph.

This pattern describes how to build releasable category structures and how to break dependency cycles when they occur.

Abstract Client

Servers often need to send messages to their clients. This is difficult in C++, because the server must use an interface that is part of the client. Static typing makes it necessary for the compiler to be "sure" that the client has the required interface. Thus the server may wind up depending on the client.

This pattern describes how to create abstract client interfaces that carry the required interfaces and are inherited into the client.

Mix-In Client Interface

Sometimes a client must deal with many servers that employ the Abstract Client pattern to create interface classes for the client to inherit from. Multiple inheritance can be used to mix many different client interfaces into a single client.

Application Framework

When there are many similar applications to be written, an application framework can be used to encapsulate the initialization, clean-up, and idle loop, as well as many other common application behaviors.

This pattern describes the concept of an application framework and how to use inheritance to derive new applications.

Transaction Processor Framework

Many applications involve a main loop that gets a transaction from some source and then executes that transaction. This pattern describes such an application in terms of a specialized application framework.

Low-Level Design Patterns

Three-layer FSM

Finite state machines (FSMs) are common in object-oriented applications. They form the translator between incoming events and outgoing behaviors. However, they are often implemented as a mixture of control and behavior. This makes them hard to understand and maintain.

Even when the behavior and control are separated, as in the State pattern (Gamma et al. 1995), it is still difficult to derive new FSMs from old ones. It is also difficult to override old behaviors or add new ones. This is because there is often a cyclic dependency between the behaviors and the control mechanisms of the FSM.

This pattern describes a simple inheritance structure that breaks the dependency cycle. This allows the behaviors to be used with many different FSMs. It also allows new behaviors to be added, or old behaviors overridden, by using inheritance to create new behavior classes.

Finally, the technique lends itself well to FSM compilers (programs that input a textual description of a state table and output C++ code that implements the control structures of the FSM).

Rungs of a Dual Hierarchy

Dual hierarchies have always proven problematic in C++. A dual hierarchy exists when two base classes share a containment relationship that is used by their derived classes.

The two base classes form the root of two very similar inheritance hierarchies. The semantics of the hierarchy are such that each derived container must contain a specific derived object. For example, if our two base classes are Operator and Vehicle, and Operator contains Vehicle, then we might derive Chauffeur, which must contain Limousine; or Pilot, which must contain Airplane.

This pattern describes dual hierarchies and the mechanism of using dy-namic cast to facilitate the communications between derived peers.

RTTI Visitor

This pattern describes a technique for using the Visitor pattern to implement a version of dynamic_cast in C++ compilers that do not currently support RTTI.

Private Mix-In Bridge

This pattern provides an alternate to the Bridge pattern. It builds an imple-mentation/interface bridge by creating classes that publicly inherit their interface from abstract base classes and then privately inherit their imple-mentation from concrete implementation classes.

RTTI Selector

Operating on heterogeneous containers is problematic in C++. Static typing forces you to know the interface of an object. Prior to RTTI, it was difficult to query an object to see if it could respond to a desired interface.

This pattern describes some appropriate uses for dynamic_cast when traversing heterogeneous containers.

Write a Loop Once

Sometimes the same loop will appear over and over again in different parts of the same application. The loop will be similar, but the body of the loop will be different. This is a problem, because if the looping structure changes once, it must be changed everywhere in the application.

This pattern describes a mechanism for writing such a loop once and then using inheritance to provide derivatives of the loop that implement different bodies for it.

SUMMARY

This chapter has shown that existing applications provide fertile ground for discovering new patterns. This is good news; it means there is a huge source of patterns, waiting to be discovered, in object-oriented programs that have already been written. It would be beneficial to all programmers to look over these programs to discover and describe the patterns their designers intuitively used.

REFERENCES

Gamma, Erich, Richard Helm, Ralph Johnson, and John Vlissides (1995). *Design Patterns: Elements of Reusable Object-Oriented Software.* Reading, MA: Addison-Wesley.

Martin, Robert C. (1995). *Designing Object Oriented C++ Applications Using the Booch Method.* Englewood Cliffs, NJ: Prentice-Hall.

APPENDICES

ITERABLE CONTAINER

Containers, C++ Related

Intent   This pattern provides a common interface to containers whose elements can be iterated over one at a time.

Motivation   In C++ it has been common practice to create iterators that are specific for a particular kind of container. Examples include SetIterator for Set containers and QueueIterator for Queue containers. This means, however, that you must know the kind of container you are iterating over before you can create the iterator.

There are many kinds of containers that can be iterated over. The iteration itself has little or no relation to the kind of container. In fact, it is often desirable to iterate over a container without knowing what kind it is. For example, you might create a function that prints every element of a container, regardless of whether it a Bag, Set, Queue, Stack, or other type of container. To do this you need an iteration scheme and interface that is independent of the type of container.

Solution You can use the Factory, Bridge, and Prototype patterns to create a way for users to use the same concrete Iterator object regardless of the container type. All containers are derived from an abstract class named `IterableContainer`. This class provides a pure virtual function named `MakeIteratorMechanism`. Thus `IterableContainer` becomes an abstract Factory pattern for specific kinds of iterator mechanisms. Each derived container is the concrete factory that creates the appropriate derivative of `IterableContainer` (that is, the derivative knows how to iterate that particular container).

`Iterator` is a concrete class with a constructor that takes a reference to an `IterableContainer`. The constructor invokes the `MakeIteratorMechanism` method and then uses the Bridge pattern to delegate the iteration functions to the `IteratorMechanism`. Iterators provide copy semantics by using the contained `IteratorMechanism` as a prototype and asking it to clone itself.

Structure The structure in Figure 1 shows how this pattern can be used with two different containers, Bag and Set. It is trivial to expand its use to other containers.

Implementation Here is one possible implementation of this pattern of C++:

```
template <class T> class Iterator;
template <class T> class IteratorMechanism;


//- - - - - - - - - - - - - - - - - - - - - - - - - - - - - - - - - -
// Name
// IterableContainer
//
// Description
// This class is the abstract base class from which all containers
// that can be linearly iterated derive. It supplies the pure
// virtual MakeIteratorMechanism function.
//
template <class T>
class IterableContainer
{
  public:
    virtual ~IterableContainer() {};
```

```
    private:
      virtual IteratorMechanism<T>* MakeIteratorMechanism() const = 0;
    friend Iterator<T>;
};
// - - - - - - - - -
// Name
// IteratorMechanism
//
// Description
// This is the abstract base class from which all iterator mechanisms
// derive. It supplies the pure interfaces by which all
// iterator mechanisms are controlled.
//
// IsNotAtEnd —  Returns true if the iterator has not yet
//                     reached the
//                     end of the container. Otherwise returns false.
// Next —        Moves the iterator to the next item in the
//                     container. (Undefined if container is at end.)
// Item —        Returns the value of the item in the container
//                     at the position currently referred to by the
//                     iterator.
// Clone —       Creates an exact copy of the Iterator
//                     Mechanism on the heap, and returns its address.
//
template <class T>
class IteratorMechanism
{
    private:
      virtual bool IsNotAtEnd() const = 0;
      virtual void Next() = 0;
      virtual T Item() = 0;
      virtual IteratorMechanism<T>* Clone() const = 0;

      IteratorMechanism& operator= (const IteratorMechanism&);
    friend IterableContainer<T>;
    friend Iterator<T>;
};


//- - - - - - - - -
// Name
// Iterator
//
// Description
// This class is a concrete class that creates and then manipulates
// IteratorMechanisms. It presents the standard Iterator interface:
//
//     operator void*    Used to test the iterator for completion.
//                            This is similar to the error test used in
```

```
//                        iostreams. The void* type is allowed in
//                        conditional expressions. Zero void*
                          values are
//                        taken to be false, and nonzero void* values
//                        are taken to be true. Thus one can test an
//                        iterator for completion as follows:
//                        Iterator i(someIterableContainer);
//                        while (i) // loops till end of container.
//
// operator++             Used to move the iterator to the next item in
//                        the container.
//
// operator*              Used to access the item currently referred to
//                        by the iterator.
//
// With this interface, the following idiom can be used:
//
// for(Iterator<T> i(someIterableContainer); i; i++)
// {
//     T & t = *i;
//     // use the item
// }
//
template <class T>
class Iterator
{
   public:
   Iterator(const IterableContainer<T>& theIterableContainer)
   {itsMechanism = theIterableContainer.MakeIteratorMechanism();}

   virtual ~Iterator() {delete itsMechanism;}

   Iterator(const Iterator<T>& theIterator)

   {itsMechanism = theIterator.itsMechanism->Clone();}

   Iterator& operator= (const Iterator<T>& theIterator)
   {
      delete itsMechanism;
      itsMechanism=theIterator.itsMechanism->Clone();
      return *this;
   }

   virtual operator void*() const
    {return reinterpret_cast<void*>(itsMechanism->IsNotAtEnd());}

   virtual void operator++(int) {itsMechanism->Next();}
   virtual T operator*() {return itsMechanism->Item();}
```

```
      private:
        IteratorMechanism<T> *itsMechanism;
};
```

Applicability   Use the Iterable Container pattern when you have many different kinds of
containers and you need to iterate over them without regard to the type of
container. This applies when

1. You have containers that supply the same containment semantics but
   use different implementations to tweak storage or execution efficiency
   (for example, Set containers that use linked lists, arrays, hash lookups,
   or linear lookups). Clients of these different kinds of containers very
   likely do not want to know the difference.

2. You have clients that need to iterate over many different kinds of
   containers, irrespective of their containment semantics (for example,
   clients that need to iterate over the elements of a container regardless
   of whether it is a Set, Queue, Stack, or Bag container)

FIGURE 1 Implementation

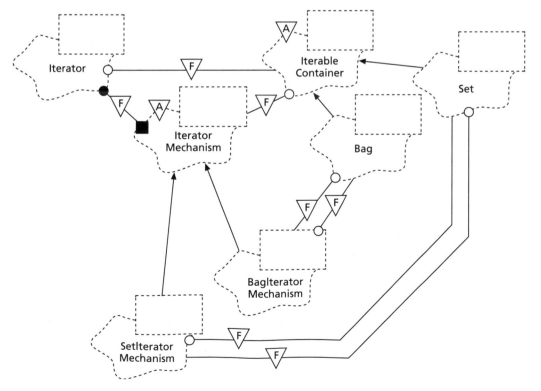

Consequences There are slight inefficiencies related to the use of the Bridge and Factory patterns. The creation of an iterator involves the virtual deployment of the `MakeIterator-Mechanism` function and the allocation of an `IteratorMechanism` on the heap. Special-purpose allocators can mitigate this inefficiency quite a bit.

Also, every use of an Iterator object is delegated through virtual deployment to its iterator mechanism. While virtual deployment in C++ is very fast, it is not as fast as direct function calls. In certain application domains, where efficiency is extremely important, the virtual deployment of functions as common as iterator manipulations may be inappropriate.

Sample Code The following is an example of a function that takes a container, regardless of its type, and then prints every element:

```
void PrintElements(IterableContainer<int>& c)
{
    for (Iterator<int> i(c); i; i++)
        cout << *i <<-endl;
}
```

Related Patterns Bridge, Factory, Prototype

MEMBER CONTAINER

Containers, C++

Intent This pattern provides a common interface for containers whose underlying principle is "membership," so clients can manipulate those containers without having to be aware of their specific type.

Motivation There are many types of containers such as `Bag` or `Set`, that have the concept of "membership." Such containers allow members to be added, removed, and checked for membership.

Usage of these containers is often general, and does not depend upon a specific type of container. For example, a function that scans a container to look for elements meeting particular criteria and then removes them from the container should not care whether it is a `Set`, `Bag`, or `Queue` container.

There are a standard set of membership operators that should apply to such containers. These operators are `intersection`, `union`, and `difference`. These operations can be supplied by overloading the operators `&`, `+`, and `-`, respectively.

Consider the following code:

```
Bag <int> b;
Set<int> s;
Set<int> common = b & s;
```

The intent is clear. We would like to find all the elements that are common to both the Set and Bag containers and place them in another Set container named common. However, what is the return type of the & operation? It appears to be calling b.operator&(s). Since b is a Bag container, the operator is probably returning Bag. How can a Bag container be used to initialize the Set container named common? We could create a constructor for Set that takes a Bag argument, but it would likely result in a geometric explosion of constructors as new types of containers are added. It would also mean that none of the container classes could be closed against new types of containers.

Worse, what if Bag and Set are abstract classes? Then what would b.operator&(s) return?

Solution   All containers that have membership semantics derive from an abstract base class named MemberContainer. MemberContainer uses the Iterable-Container pattern and the Envelope Letter pattern to allow clients to manipulate the membership semantics of a container regardless of its type.

MemberContainer inherits from IterableContainer, so iteration can be achieved irrespective of container type. It adds the simple methods Add, Remove, Clear, IsMember, and Cardinality so that clients can manipulate the membership semantics of any derived containers. MemberContainer also implements the membership operators for union, intersection, and difference.

The Envelope Letter pattern allows MemberContainer to be instantiated as a concrete class that delegates all its operations to a contained derivative. The membership operators for union, intersection, and difference return such an instantiation of MemberContainer by value. The derivative contained by that MemberContainer instance is created by using the Prototype pattern on the left-hand operand.

This allows the membership operators for intersection, union, and difference to be closed against new kinds of containers. Functions that use these operators do not have to know what type of container they are operating on.

Structure   Figure 2 shows that the MemberContainer class is independent of its derivatives. Any derivative of MemberContainer can be used as the delegate of the Envelope Letter pattern.

Implementation   A possible C++ implementation of this pattern is as follows.

```
//- - - - - - - - -
// Name
// MemberContainer
//
// Description
// MemberContainer is a Concrete base class for all containers
// that have membership semantics. The class supplies interfaces
// for all the membership manipulations. The default behavior of
// these interfaces delegates to the contained MemberContainer
// derivative.
//
// MemberContainer is not an abstract class, and so MemberContainer
// objects can be instantiated. However, the only constructor
// available is a copy constructor. Thus MemberContainer objects
// can only be constructed from previously existing derivatives
// of MemberContainers.
//
template <class T>
class MemberContainer : public IterableContainer<T>
{
public:
  MemberContainer(const MemberContainer<T>& t);
   // copy constructor. MUST NOT BE CALLED FROM DERIVED
   // COPY CONSTRUCTORS!!!  Infinite recursion will be the
   // result....

  virtual ~MemberContainer() {delete itsRep;};
  MemberContainer<T>& operator=(const MemberContainer<T>&);
  virtual void Add(const T& t)     {itsRep->Add(t);}
  virtual bool Remove(const T& t) {return itsRep->Remove(t);}
  virtual void Clear()             {itsRep->Clear();}

  virtual bool IsMember(const T& t) const
    {return itsRep->IsMember(t);}

  virtual int  Cardinality() const
    {return itsRep->Cardinality();}

  virtual MemberContainer<T>* Clone()  const
    {return new MemberContainer<T>(*this);}

  MemberContainer<T>& operator+= (const MemberContainer<T>&);
  MemberContainer<T>& operator-= (const MemberContainer<T>&);
  MemberContainer<T>& operator&= (const MemberContainer<T>&);

  MemberContainer<T>  operator+ (const MemberContainer<T>&) const;
  MemberContainer<T>  operator- (const MemberContainer<T>&) const;
  MemberContainer<T>  operator& (const MemberContainer<T>&) const;
```

```cpp
protected:
  // Default constructor is protected and degenerate.
  MemberContainer() : itsRep(0) ;
  void CopyItems(const MemberContainer&);

private:
 virtual IteratorMechanism<T>* MakeIteratorMechanism() const
  {return itsRep->MakeIteratorMechanism();}

  MemberContainer<T>* itsRep;
};

template <class T>
MemberContainer<T>::MemberContainer(const MemberContainer<T>& t)
  : itsRep(0)
{
  if (t.itsRep)
      itsRep = t.itsRep->Clone();
  else
      itsRep = t.Clone();
}

template <class T>
MemberContainer<T>& MemberContainer<T>::operator=(const
MemberContainer<T>& theMemberContainer)
{
    if (this != &theMemberContainer)
    {
        Clear();
        CopyItems(theMemberContainer);
    }
    return *this;
}

template <class T>
void MemberContainer<T>::CopyItems(const MemberContainer<T>&
theMemberContainer)
{
    for (Iterator<T> i(theMemberContainer); i; i++)
        Add(*i);
}

template <class T>
MemberContainer<T>& MemberContainer<T>::
operator+= (const MemberContainer<T>& theMemberContainer)
{
    for (Iterator<T> i(theMemberContainer); i; i++)
        Add(*i);
```

```
        return *this;
    }
    template <class T>
    MemberContainer<T>& MemberContainer<T>::
    operator-= (const MemberContainer<T>& theMemberContainer)
    {
        for (Iterator<T> i(theMemberContainer); i; i++)
            Remove(*i);
        return *this;
    }


    template <class T>
    MemberContainer<T>& MemberContainer<T>::
    operator&= (const MemberContainer<T>& theMemberContainer)
    {
        MemberContainer<T>& difference = *Clone();
        difference -= theMemberContainer;
        operator-=(difference);
        return *this;
    }


    template <class T>
    MemberContainer<T> MemberContainer<T>::
    operator+(const MemberContainer<T>& theMemberContainer) const
    {
        MemberContainer<T> x = *this;
        x += theMemberContainer;
        return x;
    }


    template <class T>
    MemberContainer<T> MemberContainer<T>::
    operator-(const MemberContainer<T>& theMemberContainer) const
    {
        MemberContainer<T> x = *this;
        x -= theMemberContainer;
        return x;
    }


    template <class T>
    MemberContainer<T> MemberContainer<T>::
    operator&(const MemberContainer<T>& theMemberContainer) const
    {
        MemberContainer<T> x = *this;
        x &= theMemberContainer;
        return x;
    }
```

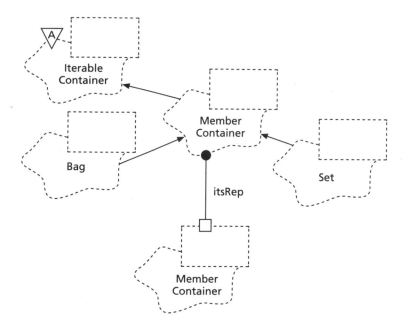

FIGURE 2

Applicability   Use this pattern whenever many different kinds of containers must be operated upon using membership operators such as `intersection`, `union`, or `difference`. The containers may be different because they have differing membership semantics, like `Bag` and `Set`; because they maintain certain orderings of the data they contain, like `Queue` or `Stack`; or because they use different implementations to tweak memory or execution efficiency, like `BoundedSet` and `UnboundedSet`.

Consequences   Virtual deployment of membership primitives such as `Add` and `IsMember` will cause a very slight execution overhead. Deployment through the envelope or letter for those objects returned from the overloaded operators will add yet another layer of virtual deployment and delegation overhead. The letter pointer in the `MemberContainer` base class will add one pointer of storage overhead.

Sample Code   The following code uses sets and membership operators to implement the sieve of Eratosthenes.

```
main()
{
    // Create a set of all the numbers 2..99
    UnboundedSet<int> numbers;
    for (int i=2; i<100; i++)
```

```
        numbers.Add(i);

    // Create the set that has the primes <= sqrt(100)
    UnboundedSet<int> primes;
    primes.Add(2);
    primes.Add(3);
    primes.Add(5);
    primes.Add(7);
    UnboundedSet<int> sieve = numbers;
    for (Iterator<int> p(primes); p; p++)
    {
        UnboundedSet<int> multiples;
        for (int n = *p * 2; n < 100; n += *p)
            multiples.Add(n);
        sieve -= multiples;
    }
    MemberContainer<int> composites = numbers - sieve;
    for (Iterator<int> ci(composites); ci; ci++)
        cout << *ci << ' ';
}
```

Related Patterns   Envelope Letter, Prototype, Iterable Container

THREE-LEVEL FSM

C++, Low Level

Intent   This pattern creates finite-state machines (FSMs) whose behavior is independent of their logic. This allows them to be derivable and extensible.

Motivation   FSMs are often used to describe the logic an application uses to convert incoming events to the resultant behaviors. When the logic and behaviors are intermixed in the same algorithms, they become difficult to change and subject to error.

It is difficult to separate control from logic, because they often form a closed loop. The logic of the FSM invokes a behavior that in turn invokes another event in the FSM. Thus, even when behavior and control are separated into two classes (as in the Objects for States pattern), the two classes share source-code dependencies. Thus it is difficult to use the behavior class with a different control class.

Solution   Describe the FSM in three layers of inheritance. The first layer supplies interfaces and implementations for the behaviors of the FSM. However, the events of the FSM are not known at this level, so this class is independent of control. This means that any of the behaviors that subsequently invoke events will be implemented as pure virtual functions at this level.

The second layer is derived from the first and adds the functions that respond to the events of the FSM. It also employs the Objects for States pattern or the Strategy pattern to implement the control logic of the FSM. It is possible for this level to be automatically generated from a state table or STD, since, except for their names, this layer is independent of the behaviors.

The third layer derives from the second and supplies those behaviors that must invoke subsequent events.

Thus, since the first layer is completely independent of the control mechanisms of the FSM, it can become the base class for derivations that alter or extend the behaviors. It can also be used with different finite state machines by the derivation of additional second and third layers.

Structure   Figure 3 shows the structure of the three levels.

Implementation   The following code shows a typical implementation of the three levels. The second level has been automatically generated by an FSM compiler that employs the Objects for State pattern. The FSM for this example is a model

FIGURE 3

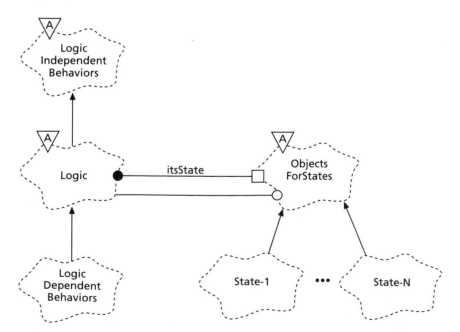

of a subway turnstile. The state table input to the finite state machine compiler is shown below.

State Table

```
Context TurnStyleLevel1 // the name of the context class
FSMName TurnStyleLevel2 // the name of the FSM to create
Initial Locked      // Initial state.
{
  Locked < Lock // Lock upon entry
  {
    Coin      Unlocked    {}
    Pass      *           Alarm
    Failed    Broken      LockError // indicate can't lock.
  }
  Unlocked  <Unlock
  {
    Coin      *           Thankyou
    Pass      Locked      {}
    Failed    Broken      UnlockError // indicate can't unlock
  }
  Broken <OutOfOrder >InOrder
  {
    Fixed     Locked      {}
  }
}
```

This is a simple state machine. It starts out in a locked state. If a coin is detected, the machine changes into an unlocked state. When the turnstile detects a person passing through (Pass), it returns to the locked state. If a person attempts to force his way through while the turnstile is in the locked state, it stays in the locked state and sounds an alarm. If the person deposits a coin while the turnstile is in the unlocked state, it lights up a little "Thank you" light.

Whenever the turnstile enters the locked state, the Lock action is invoked. This action can fail, resulting in a Failed event. Likewise, whenever it enters the unlocked state it calls the Unlock function. This function can also fail, resulting in a Failed event.

Upon failure, the FSM enters a broken state. On entry into this state the OutOfOrder function is invoked, lighting a little light warning people away from the turnstile. When the repair person fixes the turnstile, the Fixed event occurs, and the system returns to the locked state. Upon exiting the broken state, the system calls the InOrder function, which turns off the little out-of-order light.

Level 1—Behaviors Independent of Logic The first level is a class that defines the interfaces for all the behaviors of the turnstile. It also provides implementations for most of those behaviors. Only the Lock and Unlock functions remain unimplemented, because they must invoke the Failed event, which has not been defined at this level.

```
class TurnStyleLevel1
{
  public:
    virtual void Lock() = 0;
    virtual void Unlock() = 0;

    virtual void Alarm();
    virtual void LockError();
    virtual void UnlockError();
    virtual void Thankyou();
    virtual void OutOfOrder();
    virtual void InOrder();
  protected:
    bool LockAndCheck();
    bool UnlockAndCheck();
};
```

The last two member functions provide implementations for the Lock and Unlock functions. However, the bool that these functions return must be translated to an event for the finite state machine. This translation will occur at level 3.

Level 2— The Control Logic This level has been entirely generated by the FSM compiler from the text shown above in the state table.

```
class TurnStyleLevel2;
class TurnStyleLevel2State
{
  public:
    virtual const char* StateName() const = 0;
    virtual void Coin(TurnStyleLevel2&);
    virtual void Pass(TurnStyleLevel2&);
    virtual void Failed(TurnStyleLevel2&);
    virtual void Fixed(TurnStyleLevel2&);
};
class TurnStyleLevel2BrokenState : public TurnStyleLevel2State
{
  public:
    virtual const char* StateName() const
        {return "Broken";}
    virtual void Fixed(TurnStyleLevel2&);
};
```

```cpp
class TurnStyleLevel2UnlockedState : public TurnStyleLevel2State
{
  public:
    virtual const char* StateName() const
        {return "Unlocked";}
    virtual void Coin(TurnStyleLevel2&);
    virtual void Pass(TurnStyleLevel2&);
    virtual void Failed(TurnStyleLevel2&);
};

class TurnStyleLevel2LockedState : public TurnStyleLevel2State
{
  public:
    virtual const char* StateName() const
        {return "Locked";}
    virtual void Coin(TurnStyleLevel2&);
    virtual void Pass(TurnStyleLevel2&);
    virtual void Failed(TurnStyleLevel2&);
};

class TurnStyleLevel2: public TurnStyleLevel1
{
  public:
    // Static State Variables
    static TurnStyleLevel2BrokenState Broken;
    static TurnStyleLevel2UnlockedState Unlocked;
    static TurnStyleLevel2LockedState Locked;
    TurnStyleLevel2(); // Default Constructor
    // Event functions
    void Coin() {itsState->Coin(*this);}
    void Pass() {itsState->Pass(*this);}
    void Failed() {itsState->Failed(*this);}
    void Fixed() {itsState->Fixed(*this);}
    // State Accessor Functions
    void SetState(TurnStyleLevel2State& theState)
      {itsState = &theState;}
    TurnStyleLevel2State& GetState() const {return *itsState;}
  private:
    TurnStyleLevel2State* itsState;
};

TurnStyleLevel2BrokenState TurnStyleLevel2::Broken;
TurnStyleLevel2UnlockedState TurnStyleLevel2::Unlocked;
TurnStyleLevel2LockedState TurnStyleLevel2::Locked;
void TurnStyleLevel2State::Coin(TurnStyleLevel2& s) {}
void TurnStyleLevel2State::Pass(TurnStyleLevel2& s) {}
void TurnStyleLevel2State::Failed(TurnStyleLevel2& s) {}
void TurnStyleLevel2State::Fixed(TurnStyleLevel2& s) {}
void TurnStyleLevel2BrokenState::Fixed(TurnStyleLevel2& s)
```

```
{
    s.SetState(TurnStyleLevel2::Locked);
    s.InOrder();
    s.Lock();
}
void TurnStyleLevel2UnlockedState::Coin(TurnStyleLevel2& s)
{
    s.Thankyou();
}
void TurnStyleLevel2UnlockedState::Pass(TurnStyleLevel2& s)
{
    s.SetState(TurnStyleLevel2::Locked);
    s.Lock();
}
void TurnStyleLevel2UnlockedState::Failed(TurnStyleLevel2& s)
{
    s.UnlockError();
    s.SetState(TurnStyleLevel2::Broken);
    s.OutOfOrder();
}
void TurnStyleLevel2LockedState::Coin(TurnStyleLevel2& s)
{
    s.SetState(TurnStyleLevel2::Unlocked);
    s.Unlock();
}
void TurnStyleLevel2LockedState::Pass(TurnStyleLevel2& s)
{
    s.Alarm();
}
void TurnStyleLevel2LockedState::Failed(TurnStyleLevel2& s)
{
    s.LockError();
    s.SetState(TurnStyleLevel2::Broken);
    s.OutOfOrder();
}
TurnStyleLevel2::TurnStyleLevel2() : itsState(&Locked)
{
    Lock();
}
```

Level 3—Behaviors Dependent upon Control Finally, level 3 derives from
level 2 and implements those behaviors that must invoke events in the FSM.
These functions are Lock and Unlock, which must call the LockAndCheck
and UnlockAndCheck functions, respectively, and then invoke the Failed
event if the functions return false.

```
class TurnStyleLevel3 : public TurnStyleLevel2
{
```

```
public:
  virtual void Lock()
  {
      if (!LockAndCheck()) Failed();
  }
  virtual void Unlock()
  {
      if (!UnlockAndCheck()) Failed();
  }
};
```

Since the first level provides all the substantial behaviors the FSM controls—but in no way depends upon any particular state machine—it can be reused by many state machines. It can also be the target of derivation so that its behaviors can be overridden or extended.

Applicability Use this pattern in any context where behaviors may be controlled by more than one finite state machine or where such behaviors need to be overridden and/or extended through inheritance.

Consequences Virtual deployment of the action functions may add a small amount of execution time overhead. Also, the Objects for States pattern used in level 2 adds lots of classes. Fortunately, since those classes can be generated by a compiler they need not add to the programmer's conceptual burden.

Related Patterns Objects for States, Strategy

ABSTRACT CLIENT

C++, High Level

Intent This pattern provides clients with an interface that servers understand.

Motivation Server classes sometimes need to send messages to their clients. However, in C++ this means that the server must know the interface of the client. This makes it difficult to create servers with many different, unrelated clients. We would like the clients of a server to be unrelated, so new clients can be created without affecting either the server or the other clients.

Solution Servers that need to send messages to their clients provide the client with an abstract base class containing pure virtual functions that represent those messages. The client can then derive from this abstract base, often using multiple inheritance, and implement the pure virtual functions to handle the messages.

For example, consider a `Timer` class whose job it is to send a `Tick` message to a group of clients once every second. Each client sends a message to the `Timer`, registering itself to receive the `Tick` message.

Structure Figure 4 shows the `Timer` example. Notice that the `Timer` class does not depend on the derived client in any way. Thus if that client changes the `Timer` class will be unaffected.

Implementation Here is one way the Timer class could be implemented.

```
class TimerClient
{
  public:
    virtual void Tick() = 0;
};
class Timer
{
  public:
    void Register(TimerCLient& t) {itsCLients.Add(&t);}
  private:
    void SendTick()
    {
        for (Iterator<TimerClient*>i(itsClients); i; i++)
            (*i)->Tick();
    }
    UnboundedSet<TimerClient*> itsClients;
};
```

FIGURE 4

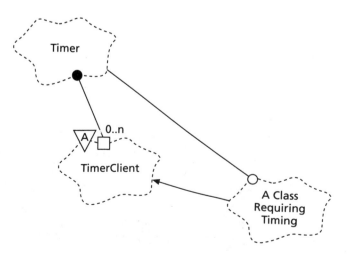

Applicability Use this pattern wherever there are servers that must send messages to their clients and you don't want the server to have source code dependencies upon the client.

Consequences The virtual deployment of the messages through the abstract base class will add a small amount of overhead. Use of this pattern will also promote use of multiple inheritance, since the ability to be called by a server will probably need to be mixed into an already existing hierarchy.

Related Patterns Bridge: The abstract class represents a special case of a bridge from the server to the client.

WRITE A LOOP ONCE

C++, Low Level

Intent This pattern will prevent very common loops from being written over and over again.

Motivation An application will often need to loop through a container in many different parts of the code. Each loop is virtually identical, except for its body. Moreover, the body of each of these loops may contain similar components. But if these loops are all coded separately, when changes occur to the code that affect how these loops are written each loop must be found and corrected.

It ought to be possible to write such loops just once and then plug in different loop bodies where applicable. Thus when changes occur to the structure of the data or the looping mechanism, those changes can be made in one place.

For example, consider an application that models the floor plan of a building in order to determine the quality of the design. Such an application would have an extensive data model describing rooms, walls, doors, corridors, windows, and so on. The application must score the structure of the floor plan against a battery of design rules. Each rule demands that we traverse the data, looking for various components and applying certain scoring algorithms. So each rule must use a variation of the exact same loop, changing only the criteria by which certain elements are selected for processing (thereby changing the processing itself).

Solution   Write an abstract base class with a function that implements the loop and then calls pure virtual functions for selection and processing. Derived classes can then implement their own selection mechanisms and processing algorithms.

Implementation   Consider the following example, which provides a loop that scans for Doors.

```
class DoorScannner
{
  public:
    DoorScanner(IterableContainer<Door*>& c) : itsContainer(c)
      {}
    virtual bool SelectDoor(Door&) = 0;
    virtual void ProcessDoor(Door&) = 0;
    void Scan();
  private:
    IterableContainer<Door*>& itsContainer;
};
void DoorScanner::Scan()
{
    for (Iterator<Door*> di(itsContainer); di; di++)
    {
        Door& d = **di;
        if (SelectDoor(d))
            ProcessDoor(d);
    }
}
class OpenDoorScanner : public DoorScanner
{
  public:
    OpenDoorScanner(IterableContainer<Door*>& c)
        : DoorScanner(c) {}
    bool SelectDoor(Door& d) {return d.IsOpen();}
};
class OpenDoorCounter : public OpenDoorScanner
{
  public:
    OpenDoorCounter(IterableContainer<Door*> c)
        : OpenDoorScanner(c), itsOpenDoors(0) {}

    virtual void ProcessDoor(Door& d) {itsOpenDoors++;}
    int GetOpenDoors() const {return itsOpenDoors;}
  private:
    int itsOpenDoors;
};
void f()
{
    OpenDoorCounter c(DoorList);
```

```
        c.Scan();
        int openDoors = c.GetOpenDoors();
}
```

Applicability Use this pattern whenever you have to write a variation of a loop many times.

Consequences Virtual deployment of the selection criteria and the processing function will add a small execution overhead.

Related Patterns Bridge: The selection function and the processing function are applications of the Bridge pattern in a very specific context.

Robert C. Martin can be reached at 2080 Cranbrook Road, Green Oaks, IL 60048; rmartin@oma.com.

20 Implementing Patterns

Jiri Soukup

1. INTRODUCTION

Until now, activity related to design patterns has focused primarily on collecting new patterns, describing them as precisely as possible, and cataloging and organizing them. Having a good catalog of patterns is important, but is only the first step. The ultimate goal is to use these patterns to design software in a new and better way.

Even though all the ground work has not yet been finished, this paper looks ahead at the problems and possibilities of pattern implementation. There are three basic problems:

1. With the present implementation style, patterns get lost during program coding. This leads to debugging and maintenance problems later. Good documentation certainly helps here, but a safer and cleaner solution would be for the final code to record the patterns.

2. Multiple patterns can lead to large clusters of mutually dependent classes, which is one of the prime reasons why object-oriented systems

Copyright © 1994 Jiri Soukup. All Rights Reserved.

can be difficult to manage. Any method that would break at least some of these dependency cycles would greatly improve the program.

3.   Until now it has been quietly assumed that the programmer will implement patterns in code by designing the classes as prescribed by the pattern. As far as I know, nobody has described a library of concrete reusable patterns.

This paper shows that problems 1 and 2 above can be solved by representing each pattern with a special class called a Pattern class. This class encapsulates all the behavior and logic of the pattern. The classes that form the pattern contain no pattern-related methods, only pointers and the other data required for the pattern. The result is a major decoupling of the application classes, and separation of application classes from patterns. This paper also shows how you can build a reusable library of many common patterns.

The idea of representing each pattern with a special class will first be explained with simple, realistic examples. I will then provide more precise proof. All the examples in this paper have been coded in C++.

2. ABSTRACT AND CONCRETE PATTERNS

One problem with pattern-based design is that there is currently no generally accepted definition of what constitutes a pattern. My definition of a pattern overlaps with Booch's mechanism [3]. A pattern describes a situation in which several classes cooperate on a certain task and form a specific organization and communication pattern. Note that most of the patterns described by Gamma et al. [5] fall into this category. My definition is limited to structural patterns used in software architecture. It includes neither low-level language-related idioms nor general patterns related to the managment of software teams (see chapters throughout this volume).

On the other hand, my definition includes data structures that require the cooperation of several classes, such as graphs, many-to-many associations, and aggregations. Even though there is no accepted definition of what constitues a pattern, there is a general agreement that a pattern description must contain not only the structural information (classes, their relations, and communication), but also the pattern's purpose, the forces it resolves, and conditions necessary for successful implementation. In this paper I am primarily interested in how to design libraries of patterns; for this reason, the structural part of patterns is emphasized. I assume that the remaining information (reasons, forces, conditions, recommended uses) will be recorded in the comment segment associated with each pattern stored in the library.

The software architecture patterns cataloged so far (see Gamma et al. [5]) are mostly abstract, general patterns. However, if we discuss architecture only at this high level, we'll never get a code implemented. At a certain stage of the design process, we have to implement the patterns. This leads to the differentiation between abstract and concrete patterns.

Descriptions of abstract patterns usually include one or more examples of concrete implementations (see Gamma et al. [5] and this volume). Often there are several possible ways to implement a given abstract pattern. For example, a collection can be implemented as a singly linked list, a doubly linked list, or a dynamic array. Elements stored in the collection can be linked directly (as in most custom implementations) or indirectly (as in most class libraries or Smalltalk). Also, once we start the implementation we are no longer language-independent.

When designing software, you may start with abstract patterns and switch to concrete patterns later. Or you can start directly with concrete patterns that imply a certain implementation style and later replace them with other concrete patterns implementing the same abstract pattern. The second method is less abstract, but it may better fit the spiral design model typical of object-oriented software today. In either case you need many more concrete patterns than abstract patterns.

In the remaining part of this paper the word *pattern* refers only to concrete patterns, unless explicitly stated otherwise.

3. LOSING PATTERNS DURING IMPLEMENTATION

In common practice, design patterns are used only during the initial, conceptual design. Once the overall architecture is determined, programmers take over to implement the patterns. Except perhaps for the documentation or comments scattered throughout the code, the patterns are not visible in the final code.

For example, Coad [2] describes a relatively simple design involving eight classes and six patterns. In his diagram (see Figure 1), it is difficult to see which patterns are involved in the final design shown in Figure 1 (see Figure 2). Two different programmers could, perhaps, even arrive at two different sets of patterns.

Programmers tend to lose sight of the original patterns; this is a major source of maintenance problems. Working with the code does not necessarily allow one to see the underlying concepts. Adding or removing patterns is difficult, and the documentation describing the patterns will eventually get lost or become obsolete. Many of these problems would be solved if the final code reflected the existence of the patterns in a simple and straightforward manner.

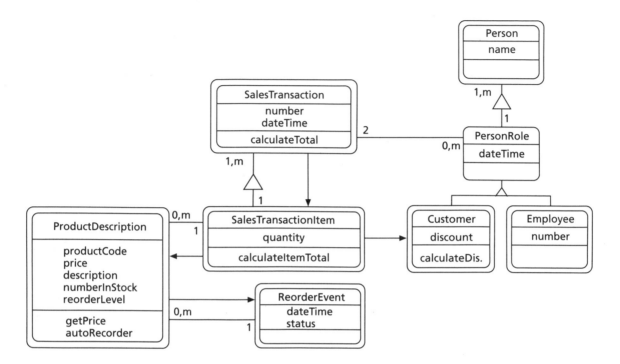

FIGURE 1 A design that includes eight classes and six patterns, as published by Coad [2]. Even if the designer used the pattern approach, the original intent is lost (see Figure 2).

4. CLUSTERS OF INTERDEPENDENT CLASSES

When applying several patterns to the same set of classes (in situations such as those in Figures 1 and 2), pattern behavior is embedded in methods associated with various application classes. By definition, each class in each pattern calls methods of several other classes; as a result of this chain reaction, the class depends directly or indirectly on every other class. The entire design becomes a big knot of interdependent classes and methods.

Note, however, that some relatively less frequent patterns (such as Filters and Pipes in Gamma et al. [5]) do not imply tight communication between the participating classes. Therefore these do not fit the type of class this paper addresses.

Complex interdependency affects both debugging and testing. Code with complex embedded relations is difficult to understand. Classes and patterns cannot be tested individually. Adding, removing, or replacing patterns is a sensitive and error-prone operation.

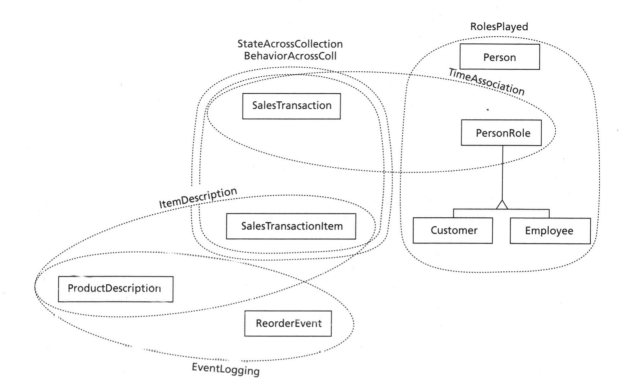

FIGURE 2 Patterns involved in the design shown in Figure 1, according to Coad [2].

The main problem here is that we have to deal with the entire design as one indivisible entity. Imagine maintaining an object-oriented CASE system that has five hundred classes nested up to seven levels deep, interwoven with fifty patterns that each involve two to four additional classes (these numbers are from an actual project).

You may of course say that such a problem is intrinsically complicated. Patterns as such are not the source of the complexity; however, as the next section shows, the implementation of patterns does play a major role.

One of the reviewers of this paper challenged this entire view by stating that, according to his experience, "large systems with lots of patterns are not monolithic jungles of interdependent classes." The difference of opinion may be caused by different personal experiences, different types of application, or use of a particular programming language. For example, class dependencies are a more serious problem for efficient C++ frameworks with many embedded pointers than they are for Smalltalk programs based on indirectly linked container classes. The Introduction and Chapter 9 (Case Studies) in Soukup's book [4] describe some large C++ projects where this became a serious issue.

5. PATTERN CLASSES

Most of the problems described above can be solved by introducing a special type of class to manage each pattern—I will refer to it as a pattern class. This concept is similar to Hogg's Islands and Bridges [6]. In the C++ language the pattern class will be a friend of the classes that form the pattern, and it will encapsulate all the code logic (communication, messages) of the pattern. It will also contain all the external interfaces for the pattern. The classes that form the pattern will contain all the relevant data (pointers, indices, values), but no pattern-related methods. Ideally the pattern class contains no data; its main purpose is the interface.

We will not use the pattern class in situations where the entire interface (all the methods) is assigned to a single class. This class already provides the functionality of the pattern class. Regardless of how many classes are involved, the pattern description will be recorded in the comment part of the pattern class.

Figure 3 shows the Directed Graph pattern implemented in this style. Note that classes Node, Edge, and Root contain only pointers (firstEdge, nextEdge, targetNode, and so on), while the entire pattern interface (addEdge, removeNode, and so on) is associated with the pattern class (DirectedGraph). The iterator class for traversing edges adjacent to a given node is a separate class, again loosely associated with the classes that form the pattern (through friends).

Figure 4 shows the implementation of the example in Figures 1 and 2, using pattern classes. Note how the design splits into two layers of classes, with only friend relations between the two layers. Since the entire implementation of the patterns is separated by the pattern classes, there is very little, if any, interaction between the application classes. Except for the functionality related to the patterns, each application class can be tested independently. The functionality of any given pattern can be tested again, in isolation with only those application classes that form the pattern.

One important feature of the pattern class is that it remains in the final code as a record of what pattern is being used. Adding or removing a pattern is simple: you add or remove a pattern class and modify only a few members in the related application classes (for an example, see the State-Town-Highway program).

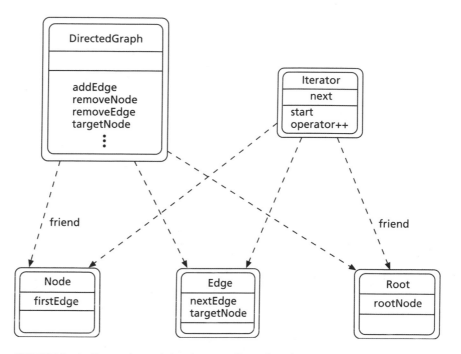

FIGURE 3 A directed graph implemented as a low-level pattern. Directed Graph is the pattern class here; it includes all the methods related to the graph manipulation. Classes Node, Edge, and Root contain pointers that implement the graph, but no graph-related methods.

One of the reviewers, Ralph Johnson, suggested that I present "Pattern as a Class" as a new pattern. (The pattern proposal is included here in Appendix A.) Note, however, that this entire methodology has been developed independently of Alexander, and that the prime focus of this paper is on the implementation of patterns, not on formalizing the method as a new pattern.

6. LIBRARY OF GENERIC PATTERNS

The following coding style has been used for generic data structures in the C/C++ Data Object Library from Code Farms, Inc. (the syntax has been changed slightly for the purpose of this presentation):

Assume that you have classes State, Town, and Highway. State contains Towns (forming the pattern Aggregation), and Highways connect Towns (forming Graph). When coding this problem, your code will have two parts.

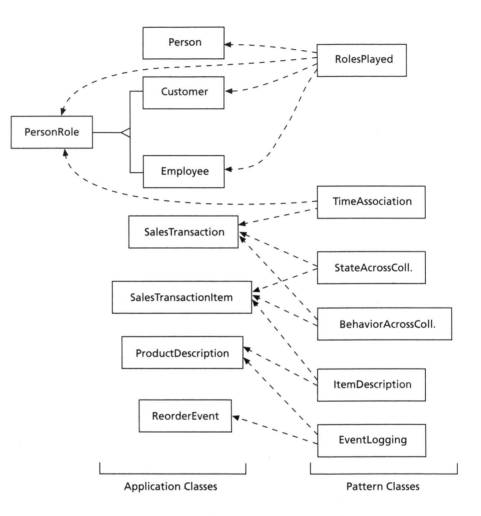

FIGURE 4 Design from Figures 1 and 2 using pattern classes (right column). Even though there are many friend relations (dashed arrows), application classes (left column) are mutually independent.

File `code.hpp` will define classes and patterns, while file `code.cpp` will contain the methods.

This is file `code.hpp`:

```
class State {
   inject_State
   // ... any members or methods you wish
};
class Town {
   inject_Town
```

```
        // ... any members or methods you wish
    };
    class Highway {
        inject_Highway
        // ... any members or methods you wish
    };
        // 'states' identifies the pattern
    pattern_Aggregation(states,State,Town);
        // 'roads' identifies the pattern
    pattern_Graph(roads,Town,Highway);
```

This is file code.cpp:

```
#include "generated.hpp"   // automatically generated classes
#include "code.hpp"
#include "generated.cpp"   // automatically generated methods
    ...
State* s=new State;
Town*   t=new Town;
states.add(s,t); // add town to the state
...
Highway *h;
...
roads.rem(h); // remove the highway
              //   from the road network
```

A special code generator reads file code.hpp and generates files generated.hpp and generated.cpp. The internal implementation of the library is beyond the scope of this paper; however, the two critical steps in this implementation are described below.

First, file generated.hpp defines pointers and other variables needed in all inject_... statements. It also contains definitions of all pattern classes with types and pointers already customized to the particular pattern:

```
#define inject_State \
  friend class pattern_states;\
  Town *child_states;

#define inject_Town \
  friend class pattern_states;\
  friend class pattern_roads;\
  State *parent_states;\
  Town *next_states;\
  Highway *edges_roads;

#define inject_Highway \
  friend class pattern_roads;\
  Town *target_states;\
  Highway *next_roads;
```

```
class pattern_states {
public:
  void add(State *s, Town *t);
  State *parent(Town *t){return(t->parent_states;)}
  Town *next(Town *t){return(t->next_states;)}
  ...
};
class pattern_roads {
public:
  void rem(Highway *h);
  ...
};
#define pattern_Aggregate(id,a,b) pattern##id id
#define pattern_Graph(id,a,b) pattern##id id
#define type1_states State
#define type2_states Town
#define type1_roads Town
#define type2_roads Highway
```

Second, pattern classes are stored in the library in a parametric format, in which both types and variable names depend on a single parameter, $. For example:

```
// generic pattern class pattern_Aggregate(type1,type2) id;
class pattern_$ {
public:
  void add(type1_$ *s, type2_$ *t);
  type1_$ *parent(type2_$ *t){return(t->parent_$;)}
  type2_$ *next(type2_$ *t){return(t->next_$;)}
  ...
};
```

The advantage of this format is that the customized version of the class can be generated simply by replacing $ with the pattern id (in this case the string states). Another advantage is that if you remove $ with a text editor you get a perfectly readable class, which you can debug independently before putting it back into parametric format.

Note that we have only a single parameter, even though several classes form the pattern, and this format cannot be replaced by a template. Not only types, but also some member names (pointers) are parameterized.

This library design permits the implementation of pattern classes, for any pattern, in which the cooperation between classes depends on class members, pointers, and messages being passed between the classes that form the pattern. It does not facilitate patterns that involve the use of inheritance; however, if we move the { symbol from the class definition into the inject_... statement, patterns involving inheritance can be handled in the same style. For example, assume that the pattern Aggregate requires the first class to inherit the second class (this has no practical meaning; we use this assumption simply for demonstration). Then we can have

```
class State inject_State // {
    // ... any members or methods you wish
};
class Town inject_Town // {
   // ... any members or methods you wish
};
...


#define inject_State : public Town { \
    friend class pattern_states;\
    Town *child_states;

#define inject_Town { \
    friend class pattern_states;\
    friend class pattern_roads;\
    State *parent_states;\
    Town *next_states;\
    Highway *edges_roads;
```

The only problem here is that the syntax of the inject_... statement will be different if State also inherits from another class. For example:

```
class territory { ... },
class State : public Territory inject_State // {
   // ... any members or methods you wish
};
#define inject_State , public Town { \
    friend class pattern_states;\
    Town *child_states;
```

This is really not a serious problem, since the existing Code Farms generator already knows the inheritance tree of the application classes.

When storing certain more complex patterns in such a library, the inject_.. statement may also include some private methods. For example, when representing pattern Composite (see Figure 5 and Appendix B) in this style, both inject_Graphic and inject_Picture must include the method detectPicture(). Classes such as Text or Line from Appendix B are not a part of the pattern; they are only derived from class Graphic as a part of the application.

7. PROOF

We have already shown that pattern classes remain in the code as a permanent record of what patterns have been used. This solves the first problem

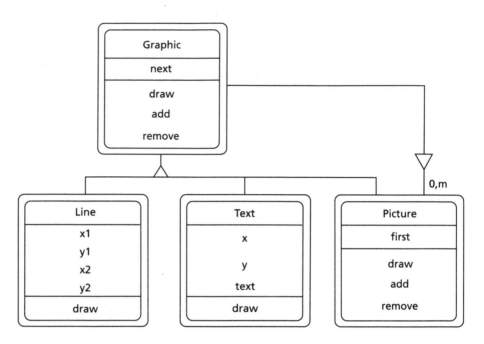

FIGURE 5 An example of the Composite pattern obtained from Erich Gamma. This is the situation before the pattern class is applied.

stated at the beginning of the paper (presently, patterns are lost during coding). For example:

```
pattern_Aggregation(states,State,Town);
pattern_Graph(roads,Town,Highway);
```

Any operations related to the pattern can be easily identified by looking at the pattern id:

```
states.add(s,t);
roads.rem(h);
```

We also showed one possible way of constructing a library of concrete patterns (the third problem stated above). Also, a class library built on this idea has been commercially available for over four years (C++ Data Object Library, from Code Farms, Inc.), and has been successfully used on hundreds of projects (some of them in excess of five hundred classes and 100,000 or more lines of code). However, the present version of the library is limited to patterns that do not involve inheritance, and the modification described above has not been extensively tested. Even though the modified library can store many patterns, it is likely that some patterns will not fit this library format.

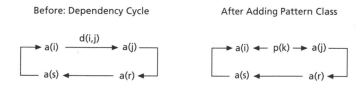

FIGURE 6 One of the edges d(..) must be caused by a dependency other than inheritance. If this is edge d(i,j), then introducing pattern class p(k) will break the dependency cycle.

What remains now is to prove that in the case of multiple, partially overlapping patterns, the use of pattern classes breaks dependency cycles. Let us assume that without pattern classes our design has application classes a(1) to a(n), with mutual dependencies introduced by the patterns (see Figure 6). Class a(j) is dependent on class a(i) if a(j) accesses data from a(i), calls one of its methods, or inherits from it. When a(j) depends on a(i), we add edge d(i,j) between the nodes a(i) and a(j).

If we introduce a pattern class p(k), the original dependency d(i,j) is replaced by friendship dependencies e(k,i) between p(k) and a(i), and e(k,j) between p(k) and a(j). Since all dependencies e(k,..) are directed away from p(k), this automatically breaks any cycle involving d(i,j). After introducing a pattern class and possibly one or several iterators for each pattern (as in Figure 3), all cycles will be removed. In fact, all original edges d(..) will be eliminated, except for those that represent inheritance and those that cannot form cycles.

Every dependency cycle we break makes the application classes more independent and improves the entire architecture.

8. CONCEPTUAL ISSUES

An important question related to the use of pattern classes is whether any pattern can be represented in this form. Perhaps there are patterns that cannot be implemented in this style, but I have not seen one yet. I discussed this with a number of people, and both Erich Gamma and several other programmers suggested that the Composite pattern may be one of those that are difficult to implement. My version of this pattern, using a pattern class, is in Appendix B.

Note that pattern classes permit you to work with two different kinds of instances. For example, when a set of objects is simultaneously involved in two different graphs, each graph corresponds to one instance of the pattern class, but each connected subgraph corresponds to one instance of class Root (see Figure 4).

ACKNOWLEDGMENTS

I would like to thank all reviewers, and in particular Ralph Johnson, for suggestions and comments that much improved this paper.

REFERENCES

[1] Gamma, E., Helm, R., Johnson, R., and Vlissides J. *Design Patterns: Abstraction and Reuse of Object-Oriented Design*, ECOOP'93. Kaiserslautern, Germany, August 1993.

[2] Coad, P. Object-oriented patterns. *Communications of the ACM* 35, 9 (September 1992): 152–159.

[3] Booch, G. *Object-Oriented Design with Applications*. Redwood City, CA: Benjamin/Cummings.

[4] Soukup, J. *Taming C++: Pattern Classes and Persistence for Large Projects*. Reading, MA: Addison-Wesley, 1994.

[5] Gamma, E.; Helm, R.; Johnson, R.; and Vlissides, J. *Design Patterns: Elements of Reusable Object-Oriented Software*. Reading, MA: Addison-Wesley, 1995.

[6] Hogg, J. Islands: Aliasing protection in object-oriented languages. *OOPSLA'91, Conference Proceedings* 9 (ACM), Nov. 1991, pp. 271–285.

APPENDIX A: PATTERN AS A CLASS

Intent   Pattern classes represent entire patterns as objects.

Motivation   Present techniques present three major problems in implementing patterns:

1.   Patterns usually get lost during coding.
2.   Patterns may lead to large clusters of mutually dependent classes.
3.   Patterns are typically hand-coded in each new application.

The first problem is caused by the pattern not being an object. The second problem is caused by the presence of dependency cycles introduced by the patterns. The third problem has its root in the programming language; nobody thought about design patterns when Smalltalk or C++ was invented.

Forces   An architecture with fewer classes is often not the cleanest solution. Adding some classes may improve code clarity and maintenance. The use of friends may appear as a violation of encapsulation; but in the way they are used here, all the walls between application classes remain intact. For the pattern class, accessing the members directly is more efficient.

Applicability This pattern is only applicable to patterns that describe the cooperation of several classes. It can always be used when the pattern does not include inheritance. The implementation of the Composite pattern, generally considered to be very difficult, exists. So far, no pattern has been found for which this method would fail. Do not apply this pattern to patterns where all the methods are already assigned to a single class.

Participants **The pattern class**—represents the pattern and contains all (or almost all) methods.

Several application classes—contain data and pointers, but no pattern-related methods (some virtual functions may be an exception).

Collaborations The pattern class performs all operations on the pattern. Application classes only carry the data.

Structure See Figures 3 and 4.

Consequences This pattern improves and sometimes completely cures the three problems mentioned above. The pattern class breaks dependency cycles, its declaration remains in the code as a record of which pattern has been used, and in a new parametrized style, it can be stored in a reusable library.

The application classes and patterns are, from the user's point of view, orthogonal.

Limitations The technique is limited to patterns that generally coincide with the definition of a mechanism: a group of classes with close cooperation on a certain task. I have added one pattern class and one iterator for a typical pattern.

The pattern class does not contain the entire pattern; it only represents its interface. The overall intent, and some structural details such as inheritance, cannot be expressed by this class alone. Additional structural information must be stored in the library: location of members, pointers, inheritance, and other details.

Implementation In C++, the pattern class is a friend of the application classes. The pattern is typically implemented directly, not with indirect lists or pointers.

Sample Code See Appendix B.

Known Uses   This approach has been used by the Code Farms C/C++ Data Object Library and was successfully applied to hundreds of projects, some of them with over 100,000 lines of code. Patterns with inheritance were subject to only marginal testing.

APPENDIX B: C++ IMPLEMENTATION OF CLASS COMPOSITE

The following code shows an implementation of the Composite pattern using a pattern class (class Composite). The code is based on Figure 5, which was obtained from Erich Gamma. Note that in this case the pattern class represents the pattern (the entire external interface is in class Composite); however, it does not implement the pattern. An important part of the pattern is the inheritance and virtual functions in classes Graphic, Picture, Line, and Text. Note that all pattern-related methods are in class Composite except for one function, pictureDetect().

```cpp
//—-file graphic.h starting here #include <iostream.h>
class Composite;
class Graphic {
friend class Composite;
    Graphic *next;
    virtual int pictureDetect(){return(0);}
public:
    virtual void draw(){}
    Graphic(){next=NULL;}
};
class Line : public Graphic {
    int x1,y1,x2,y2;
public:
    virtual void  draw(void){cout<<"Line:"<<x1<<y1<<x2<<y2<<'\n';}
    Line(int X1,int Y1,int X2,int Y2){x1=X1; y1=Y1; x2=X2; y2=Y2;}
};
class Text : public Graphic {
    int x,y;
    char *text;
public:
    virtual void draw(void){cout<<"Text:"<<x<<y<<text<<'\n';}
    Text(int X,int Y, char *tx){x=X; y=Y; text=tx;}
  };
class Picture : public Graphic {
friend class Composite;
    Graphic *first;
    virtual int pictureDetect(){return(1);}
```

```
public:
    virtual void draw(void){cout<<"Picture:\n";}
    Picture(){first=NULL;}
};
// _____ file graphic.h ending here _____
    class Composite {
public:
    void add(Picture *p, Graphic *g){g->next=p->first;
    p->first=g;}
    void remove(Picture *p, Graphic *g);
    void draw(Graphic *g);
    void dissolve(Graphic *g);
};
void Composite::remove(Picture *p, Graphic *g){
    Graphic *t;
    if(p->first==g){p->first=g->next; g->next=NULL;}
    else {
        for(t=p->first; t; t=t->next) if(t->next==g)break;
        if(t){t->next=g->next; g->next=NULL;}
        else cout<<"error\n";
    }
}


void Composite::draw(Graphic *g){
    static int level-0; // not necessary, just for better
                        // displays
    int i;
    Graphic *t;

    for(i=0;i<level;i++)cout<<"    "; // just to indent the
                                     // print
    g->draw();
    if(g->pictureDetect()){
        level++;
        for(t=((Picture *)g)->first; t; t=t->next) draw(t);
        level-;
    }
}


void Composite::dissolve(Graphic *g){
    Graphic *t,*tn;

    if(g->pictureDetect()){
        for(t=((Picture *)g)->first; t; t=tn){
            tn=t->next;
            t->next=NULL;
        }
        ((Picture *)g)->first=NULL;
```

```
        }
    }

    int main(void){
        Line *n1,*n2,*n3,*n4; Text *t1,*t2,*t3;
        Picture *p1,*p2,*p3;
        n1=new Line(1,1,11,11); n2=new Line(2,2,22,22);
        n3=new Line(3,3,33,33); n4=new Line(4,4,44,44);
        t1=new Text(1,1,"one"); t2=new Text(2,2,"two");
        t3=new Text(3,3,"three");
        p1=new Picture; p2=new Picture; p3=new Picture;
        Composite comp;

        comp.add(p1,n1); comp.add(p1,n2); comp.add(p2,n3);
        comp.add(p2,n4); comp.add(p3,t1); comp.add(p3,t2);
        comp.add(p2,t3); comp.add(p2,p1); comp.add(p3,p2);
        comp.remove(p2,n4); comp.add(p3,n4);

        comp.draw(p3);
        comp.dissolve(p2);
        cout<<'\n'; comp.draw(p3);
        return(0);
    }
```

Jiri Soukup can be reached at Code Farms Inc., 7214 Jock Trail, Richmond, ONT K0A 2A0, Canada; `jiri@debra.dgbt.doc.ca`.

ARCHITECTURE AND COMMUNICATION

PART 6

The chapters in Part 6 identify and evaluate common patterns in communication systems, in which autonomous services collaborate by exchanging information with each other. The patterns are found in many guises in the Internet TCP/IP protocol suite, the ISO Open Systems Integration (OSI) reference model, the UNIX operating system, and distributed object frameworks such as CORBA, OODCE, and OLE/COM.

Communication systems span multiple levels of abstraction and integrate many hardware and software components. To help alleviate complexity, these systems are often composed of layered services that collaborate by exchanging typed messages with adjacent layers. For example, the ISO/OSI reference model uses a "layered services" metaphor to structure its widely known seven-layer protocol stack into services such as the "network service" and the "transport service."

The UNIX operating system provides a similar metaphor with the "pipes and filters" idiom for integrating text-based applications. Single-input, single-output filters are written without any specific knowledge of where the input comes from (keyboard, a network connection, file, or elsewhere) or where the output goes to. Thus, changing filters or modifying filters to accomplish different tasks is relatively straightforward.

Layering is a common design pattern in communication systems since it reduces the complexity of individual services, enhances extensibility, and facilitates vendor independence. In theory, each layer may be specified, designed, and implemented independently and then composed with other layers to form a complete communication system. Moreover, services in each layer may execute autonomously to take advantage of "pipeline parallelism." In practice, however, experience has shown that naively implemented layers may run slowly due to context switching, synchronization, and data movement overhead.

The first two chapters in this section examine the Layered Service Composition pattern. This pattern enhances extensibility by decoupling the service-specific behavior of each layer from core architecture characteristics such as the number of services to be composed; the order in which services are composed; the interprocess communication protocols used to communicate with adjacent services; and the concurrency mechanisms used to execute the services.

The Layered Service Composition pattern is widely used to compose services into layered communication systems.

Stephen Edwards (Chapter 21) describes the formal properties of the Layered Service Composition pattern (which he calls the Streams pattern). He defines a stream algebraically as an ordered sequence of services, all of the same type, that are composed to form a stack, or "stream," of services. Passing messages to adjacent services is the sole communication mechanism between layers.

One mark of a mature pattern is that it informs developers when *not* to apply the pattern. Edwards astutely points out that the Streams pattern is not appropriate for applications with highly dynamic flow of data and control (such as a virtual desktop user interface). However, for applications that interact in a consistent, layered manner, the Streams pattern is directly applicable. Not surprisingly, the pattern is used heavily in frameworks for composing layered communication protocol stacks. Widely available examples of these frameworks include System V UNIX streams, the BSD UNIX TCP/IP network architecture, the x-kernel, the Conduit framework from the Choices OS project, and the ADAPTIVE Service eXecutive (ASX) framework.

In Chapter 22, Regine Meunier focuses on the consequences of various implementations of the Layered Service Composition pattern (which she calls the "pipes and filters architecture"). Key issues that must be addressed when implementing this architecture involve reducing the overhead of context switching, synchronization, and data movement. For example, if data must be copied when moved between two filters through a pipe, then the benefits of parallel execution will be reduced dramatically. For this reason, high-performance implementations of the pipes and filters architecture (such as the BSD UNIX TCP/IP implementation) typically pass messages using shared memory to avoid data copying.

Diane Mularz (Chapter 23) describes several general patterns for integrating application services. In contrast to Edwards and Meunier, who focus on patterns for composing layered communication systems, Mularz addresses architectural patterns for integrating legacy and third-party applications into information systems. Her Broker pattern and Shared Repository pattern may be used to integrate distributed, heterogeneous communication systems (such as financial services applications that buy and sell stocks in real time). Participants in these communication systems interact in a flexible, dynamic manner. Conversely, the layer services (such as protocol stacks) described by Edwards and Meunier interact in a comparatively rigid, hierarchical manner.

Mary Shaw transcends the domain of communication systems by summarizing a suite of common architectural patterns. In Chapter 24, she argues that patterns for packaging components and describing component interactions should be supported directly in a language. To illustrate, she describes features in the Unicon architectural language that support the connection of components: pipes, files, shared memory, procedure local and remote calls, and a stimulus/response scheduler.

Many of the patterns Shaw outlines are covered in depth elsewhere in this book. The "layered pattern" corresponds to Chapter 21, the "pipeline pattern" to Chapter 22; the "repository pattern" to Chapter 23. The "implicit invocation pattern" is similar to the event-handling patterns in Chapters 28 and 29; the "interpreter pattern" resembles the finite state machine patterns in Chapters 19 and 30. The fact that these common patterns were "discovered" and described independently by so many authors reaffirms their fundamental nature.

Streams: A Pattern for "Pull-Driven" Processing

21

Stephen H. Edwards

PATTERN NAME: STREAMS[1]

Problem This pattern allows designers to concentrate on the data flow of a complex piece of software without concern for the techniques individual components will use to distribute the computational burden. Abstractions or "objectified" program fragments obeying this pattern are easy to compose and to reason about, even though they may each use very different control strategies and representations internally.

Context The pattern applies to most imperative languages, including object-oriented and object-based languages. Streams are most effective when the architecture of a software subsystem is best captured by highlighting the data flow within it. Thus, streams work naturally with pipe and filter-style conceptual models of program operation.

Copyright © 1994 Stephen H. Edwards. All Rights Reserved.

[1] This work is supported in part by the National Science Foundation, CCR-9111892 and CCR-9311702; by the Advanced Research Projects Agency under ARPA contract number F30602-93-C-0243, monitored by the USAF Materiel Command, Rome Laboratories, ARPA order number A714; and by the Graduate School of The Ohio State University.

Streams may be more difficult to use in software subsystems that have one or more of the following properties [AAG93, AG92]:

- The data flow within the subsystem is highly dynamic.
- The subsystem is highly interactive, reactive, or event-driven, like a graphical user interface (GUI).
- The processing elements (filters) under consideration are highly parameterized, and these parameters change over time.

Forces   The following key issues must be considered when addressing the problem of how to structure software so that composability is maintained while decisions about computational approaches and strategies are deferred:

- The communications mechanisms that will be used between subsystem components can have a major impact on both maintainability and adaptability. For example, the way the flow of information between software components is represented in the architecture can cause such an effect, as can the way control flow between software components is represented.

- Different components within the subsystem may choose very different processing strategies, such as precomputation, partial precomputation and buffering, demand-driven computation, and so on. If different components choose different strategies, these choices can affect component interfaces, data flow among the components, and control flow among the components. Also, different higher-level communications choices can either enhance or hinder the flexibility needed to make alternate design choices in the course of implementing individual components.

- Achieving composability of independent or semi-independent components is critical for maintainability and adaptability. Furthermore, the designer must be able to reason effectively (and correctly) about any given composition of components, and the architectural choices should support this activity.

Solution   Model each component in the subsystem as a stream of data objects. "Computational elements" (or filters) need not be modeled explicitly, but can be implicitly modeled in the behavior of operations that connect separate streams.

A stream can be informally defined as an ordered sequence of objects, all of the same type, with a distinct point, or cursor, representing the current position within the sequence where activity will occur. More formally, we can mathematically model a stream of objects of type `Item` as an ordered pair, in which each component is a string of `Item`s.[2] If we call these two string components the "past" and "future" of a stream `s`, the entire content of the stream is `s.past * s.future`,[3] and the division between these two substrings represents a cursor pointing to the current position within the stream. This model can be extended to encompass the notion of "open" versus "closed" streams, as shown below, by permitting a stream to have a "bottom" value (also written) that denotes the equivalence class of all "closed" streams.

It is too restrictive, however, to require every class or type obeying the stream pattern to have this abstract state model. All that is really necessary is that a programmer using an object from such a class be able to reason about it as if it had the above structure, without getting into any trouble.

To this end, streams will be described here as a "common interface model" [Edw93] with the following definition:

```
common model Input_Stream_Model

    schema context

    parametric context
        type Item

    interpretation context
        math function
            INITIAL_STREAM : math[concrete[Stream]]

    concept schema
        interface

            type family Stream is modeled by
                bottom union (
                    past   : string of math[Item] ,
                    future : string of math[Item]
                )
                exemplar s
                initialization
```

---

[2] Strings, or "sequences" [GS93], are commonly used primitives in model-based software specification [HLOW94].

[3] Here * is used as shorthand for the concatenation operation on mathematical strings.

```
                          ensures    concrete[s] = INITIAL_STREAM
            operation Read_Item (
                    alters    s : Stream
                    produces x : Item
               )
               requires  s /= bottom  and
                         s.future /= empty_string
               ensures  s /= bottom                    and
                        s.past = #s.past * <x>   and
                        <x> * s.future = #s.future


            operation Test_If_Open (
               preserves s : Stream
               ) : boolean
               ensures    Test_If_Open  iff   s /= bottom


            operation Test_If_EOS (
               preserves s : Stream
               ) : boolean
               requires  s /= bottom
               ensures    Test_If_EOS  iff  s.future = empty_string


      end Input_Stream_Model
```

The `Input_Stream_Model` CIM defines the pattern for input streams. Output streams are the same, with the `Read_Item` operation replaced by the following `Write_Item` operation:

```
operation Write_Item (
      alters    s : Stream
      consumes x : Item
   )
   requires  s /= bottom
   ensures   s /= bottom                    and
             s.past   = #s.past * <x>   and
             s.future = #s.future
```

As one would expect, bidirectional streams simultaneously provide the features of both input and output streams.

Because this interface model is in essence an abstract, model-based specification of a component interface, component implementers using this interface should understand the relationship between the internal, encapsulated state of their stream objects and the abstract, pair-of-strings conceptual model clients will use. "Abstraction functions" [LG86] (which may, in fact, be relations [BHKW94, HLOW94]) are an effective tool for formally defining the correspondence between encapsulated state representations and their high-level conceptual descriptions.

An Example A simple example of where one might use a stream is in tokenizing character data. The code for this process in C++ might be written as follows:

```
class Token  {
    . . . . .
};
class TokenStream {
public:
    TokenStream();
    ~TokenStream();

    // The basic operations for all input streams:
    Token   Read_Item ();
            // Requires: stream is open, and
            // there are more tokens on the
            // stream to read
    Boolean Test_If_Open ();
            // Legal any time
    Boolean Test_If_EOS ();
            // Requires: stream is open

    // Additional operations for this type of stream:
    void Open (CharStream& seed);
            // Consumes the seed, returning an
            // initial value--the seed should NOT be
            // shared
    void Close ();
            // Requires: stream is open
};
```

Given some Token class, a token stream (TokenStream) is an (initially empty) sequence of such tokens. The sequence may be "filled" by calling the Open method, which takes a character stream (CharStream) as input. This character input stream is "consumed," or used up, to create the new value of the token stream. Then Read_Item() and the various tests can be called to retrieve individual tokens, one at a time.

Note that one could actually define this class as an abstract base class and create several alternative implementations. The behavioral descriptions provided with each operation—and particularly with Open—specify to the user a mental model of how to think about streams he or she is manipulating; but they stipulate nothing about the implementation (except the externally observable results).

Thus, in addition to having different internal representations, the alternative implementations of the TokenStream base class might differ in how they actually perform the tokenizing. The work could be distributed among the Open, Read_Item, and Test_If_EOS operations in many possible ways. The implementation strategy used, however, is completely hidden from the user and does not affect the class interface.

The reason this class interface defines a "pull-driven" stream is that, in essence, the Open operation allows the designer to "connect up" a supply stream (in this case, a character stream) to a given TokenStream object. This character stream is visibly "consumed" by the Open operation, which means it is no longer accessible to the outside world. The actual CharStream object might really be held within the internal state of the token stream, however. Whenever the user calls the Read_Item method ("pulling" on the stream of tokens), the TokenStream object can in turn "pull" just enough data off the hidden character stream internally to satisfy the request. This is only one of the many possible implementation alternatives, of course, but it shows the pull-driven nature of interstream communication.

Force Resolution   The pattern balances the various trade-offs involved by promoting the data flow among software parts as the primary architectural feature. This makes the resulting architecture transparent to choices about control flow and computational strategies. It also provides a simple model of composition that supports the informal (and even formal) reasoning efforts of designers and implementers.

Specifically, the forces described above are resolved as follows:

■ Streams become the "channels" through which software components communicate; they are thus the sole communication mechanism. Data flow is explicitly represented in the architecture by showing the "wiring pattern" of the streams involved. Control flow is not represented at the architectural level at all, and is instead an internal feature of each distinct stream abstraction.

■ Because control flow is hidden within stream abstractions, each distinct type of stream can choose an arbitrary processing strategy for any of the method(s) it supports. All such decisions are completely transparent to the architecture and thus have no effect on the interfaces between components or the overall flow of data.

■ Streams allow for a simple model of composition. The Open operation for one stream can take as its parameters one or more "input streams"; subsequent calls to the Open operations of other stream objects will then provide the infrastructure for connecting up networks representing entire software subsystems. If streams are used as the sole communication mechanism, then one can view Open operations as "transformation" steps, which convert streams of input data items into a stream of output data items. As long as the nature of this transformation step is unambiguously described, the process of reasoning about complex pipelines of streams is straightforward.

Design Rationale

The idea of a stream of homogeneous objects has been in use as a practical programming abstraction for a very long time and is well known to LISP and functional programmers. Abelson and Sussman give a textbook description of streams in this context [AS85]. The streams they describe are composite data structures designed to help organize and structure computations on serial collections of data "in a way that corresponds in spirit to an electrical engineer's concept of a signal-processing system" (p. 242). Conceptually, a stream is simply a sequence of data objects. It differs from a regular list in the way it is represented and in the fact that the sequence might be arbitrarily long. This stream concept is used in many functional programming languages for structuring computations that can be thought of in terms of a data flow model, where data objects flow through computational "stages" or filters.

The longevity and versatility of streams as programming objects leads to the questions of whether there is a higher-level abstract pattern here and, if so, what problems it addresses and in what contexts. The problem that streams best address can be uncovered by further examining the "signal-processing" analogy made by Abelson and Sussman [AS85]. Streams allow one to structure computations on (usually long) sequences of data in an intuitive way, using simple data flow ideas, without regard for the details of how the computation will actually be carried out at run time. Conceptually, a stream denotes an entire sequence of data objects, and operations on streams take as input an entire sequence and produce an entire sequence. Because of the operations available on streams, however, one cannot access the sequence arbitrarily—usually only the "head" element in the stream can be accessed. This access restriction means that a stream can simultaneously be viewed, without conflict, as either a channel for transmitting objects one by one or as the entire sequence of objects that will (eventually) be transmitted across that channel.

One of the most interesting ramifications of this duality is that any number of techniques can be used to represent a stream or to implement a stream operation, including any combination of the following:

- directly representing stream elements
- precomputing and buffering groups of stream elements
- computing elements on demand (delayed evaluation)

Regardless of the implementation complexities involved in achieving effective performance, however, streams with any or all of these representational strategies can be intermixed and composed because of the simple conceptual model they all obey. From the outside they can all appear to have pull-driven interfaces, while internally any of the above implementation choices can be made. Stream abstractions derive much of their power from this combination of interoperability and a uniform external treatment of representations that employ radically different control flow paradigms internally.

Examples of streams abound, even in imperative programming environments. The simplest example is a character-oriented device (files, the console, network message connections, and so on) treated as a "stream" of characters. In addition, streams lend themselves naturally to pipeline-style programming, where the main internal components of a program are written as stream filter/transformer operations and then connected up to form a complete end-to-end filter in a manner very similar to UNIX-style command line piping. With this programming style, however, one is not limited to simple character streams; program components can be connected via streams transmitting very sophisticated objects.

Another interesting use of stream-based programming is the construction of stream pipelines in which each stage relies exclusively on delayed evaluation to produce results. This style of programming mixes well with pipeline-style software architectures. It is often called pull-driven computation, since one requests the next output data object from the last stage of the pipeline, which then "pulls" on its supplier, and so on up the line. Each pipeline stage only computes enough to supply its client, which is similar to the "just-in-time" supply policy in logistics. Pull-driven computation contrasts with push-driven computation, in which one "pushes" input into the first stage of the pipeline. The first stage then performs its task and pushes its result to the next stage of the pipeline; this process is repeated until the desired answer is produced by the final stage.

A pull-driven pipeline architecture can be used to describe many transformation-based programs, including a compiler. The process of scanning can be rephrased as the process of transforming a stream of characters into a stream of tokens, producing each new token on demand. Similarly, the process of parsing can be viewed as transforming a stream of tokens into a stream of abstract syntax trees representing the sequence of compilation units, and so on. Many additional examples from the functional programming world are provided by Abelson and Sussman [AS85].

Finally, is a stream really a pattern, or is it merely a hierarchy of related programming abstractions one would expect to find in a class library? Stream class hierarchies can be found in OOP libraries for Smalltalk, C++, and other languages, but these hierarchies really only capture an organized collection of implementations of particular ADTs derived from a particular stream interface. The notion of "behaving" like a stream is not tied to a particular inheritance hierarchy, however, nor to an object's entire interface. As long as some facet of an object, including some subset of its operations and behavior, can be coherently interpreted as "streamlike," there is the potential for using stream-oriented composition techniques when combining it with other objects. For example, iterator objects often behave like streams under controlled circumstances, as do many standard data structures that allow sequential access to their elements (like queues, stacks, or lists). Furthermore, this "pattern" might be discovered at any time, including long after the object definition has been written and its position in a given class library determined. As a result it is useful to describe this recurring commonality as a pattern, rather than simply considering it a "stock" interface in a library of low-level parts.

Related Patterns The above pattern description really talks only about the simplest of stream interfaces' bare bones input, output, and bidirectional streams. A complete pattern language on the subject of streams should be much more comprehensive and should discuss not only these simple starting patterns but also the following:

- push-driven stream interfaces, which are the counterpart to the pull-driven approach
- streams with multiple inputs, which might easily be handled by a more sophisticated argument to an Open operation
- streams with multiple outputs
- stream repositioning operations
- synchronous and asynchronous communications issues
- concurrent versus sequential execution of stream programs (and the resulting problems that can arise)
- the possibility of encapsulating filters or "stream-processing machines" as objects
- the main variations on stream implementation—direct representation of stream data, delayed evaluation, partial computation and buffering, and so on

Most importantly, once the various streaming techniques are presented as patterns, one should address the relative merits of each technique and when each is most suitably applied.

REFERENCES

[AAG93] Gregory Abowd, Robert Allen, and David Garlan. Using style to understand descriptions of software architecture. In *Proceedings of the ACM SIGSOFT'93 Symposium on Foundations of Software Engineering*, December 1993.

[AG92] Robert Allen and David Garlan. Towards formalized software architectures. Technical Report CMU-CS-92-163, School of Computer Science, Carnegie Mellon University, Pittsburgh, PA, July 1992.

[AS85] Harold Abelson and Gerald Jay Sussman. *Structure and Interpretation of Computer Programs*, chapter 3.4: Streams, pages 242–292. MIT Press, Cambridge, MA, 1985.

[BHKW94] Paolo Bucci, Joseph E. Hollingsworth, Joan Krone, and Bruce W. Weide. Implementing components in RESOLVE. *ACM SIGSOFT Software Engineering Notes*, 19(4): 40–52, October 1994.

[Edw93] Stephen H. Edwards. Common interface models for reusable software. *International Journal of Software Engineering and Knowledge Engineering*, 3(2):193–206, 1993.

[GS93] D. Gries and F. B. Schneider. *A Logical Approach to Discrete Math*. Springer-Verlag, New York, 1993.

[HLOW94] Wayne D. Heym, Timothy J. Long, William F. Ogden, and Bruce W. Weide. Mathematical foundations and notation of RESOLVE. Technical Report OSU-CISRC-8/94-TR45, Department of Computer and Information Science, The Ohio State University, August 1994.

[LG86] B. Liskov and J. Guttag. *Abstraction and Specification in Program Development*. MIT Press, Cambridge, MA, 1986.

Stephen H. Edwards can be reached at the Department of Computers and Information Science, The Ohio State University, 2036 Neil Avenue Mall, Columbus, OH 43210-1277; edwards@cis.ohio-state.edu.

22 The Pipes and Filters Architecture

Regine Meunier

ABSTRACT

The pattern presented in this paper, the Pipes and Filters architecture, can be used to structure applications that can be divided into several independent, complete subtasks performed in a strongly determined sequential or parallel order. Each of these subtasks is processed by a filter component of the architecture. A filter reads a stream of data, processes it, and produces a stream of data, which is transferred to another filter by a pipe. The principles behind the Pipes and Filters architecture are organization of complex functions' computation and separation of concerns. The Pipes and Filters architecture is described as a pattern that exists within a comprehensive system of patterns. This description is a result of a project designed to develop a pattern-oriented approach to object-oriented software architecture.

1. INTRODUCTION

The Pipes and Filters architecture has been developed as part of a comprehensive system of patterns for software architecture (see Chapter 17). The aim of this paper is not only to illustrate the Pipes and Filters architecture,

Copyright © Siemens AG. All Rights Reserved.

which has already been done in detail [Perry+92, Garlan+93], but to describe this pattern within a system of patterns. To be able to explain how the Pipes and Filters architecture relates to other patterns, it is necessary to introduce the patterns briefly. Therefore, short descriptions of all referenced patterns are given in the Appendix. They are fully described by Buschmann et al. [Buschmann+95].

Our system of patterns includes patterns of various scales, beginning with ones for defining the basic structure of an application and ending with ones describing how to implement a particular design issue in a concrete programming language. All patterns within this system are described in a uniform way, according to a template consisting of the following slots:

1. **Name:** The pattern's essence is succinctly conveyed.
2. **Rationale:** The motivation for developing the pattern is presented.
3. **Applicability:** A rule is presented stating when to use the pattern.
4. **Classification:** The pattern is classified according to the scheme developed in the following section.
5. **Description:** The participants and collaborators in the pattern are described, as well as their responsibilities and relationships to each other.
6. **Diagram:** A graphical representation of the pattern's structure is given.
7. **Dynamic behavior:** Where appropriate, the dynamic behavior of a pattern is illustrated.
8. **Methodology:** The methodology (steps) for constructing the pattern are listed.
9. **Implementation:** Guidelines for implementing the pattern are presented.
10. **Variants:** Possible variants of the pattern are listed and described.
11. **Examples:** Examples for the pattern's use are presented.
12. **Discussion:** The constraints of applying the pattern are discussed.
13. **See also:** References to related patterns are given.

To guide the selection of a pattern for a given design situation, the system of patterns includes a classification scheme by which all patterns are classified. This classification scheme consists of three categories of criteria or design issues that play a significant role in software development:

1. **Granularity:** Developing a software system requires dealing with various levels of abstraction, beginning with the basic structure of an application and ending with issues regarding the concrete realization of particular design structures. Thus granularity is an important category for classifying patterns.

Three levels of granularity can be specified:

- *Architectural frameworks* represent fundamental paradigms for structuring software systems.

- *Design patterns* describe basic schemes for structuring subsystems and components of software architecture, as well as their relationships.

- *Idioms* describe how to implement particular components (parts) of subsystem and component functionality, or their relationships to other components within a given design.

2. **Functionality:** The second category by which patterns can be classified is functionality. Each pattern serves as a template for implementing a particular functionality. However, the various classes of functionality are of a general nature rather than specific to a certain application domain.

The following functionality categories can be distinguished:

- *Creation of objects:* Patterns may specify how to create particular instances of complex recursive or aggregate object structures.

- *Guiding communication between objects:* Patterns may describe how to organize the communication between a set of collaborating objects that may also be independently developed or remote.

- *Access to objects:* Patterns may describe how to access the services and state of shared or remote objects in a safe way, without violating their encapsulation of state and behavior

- *Organizing the computation of complex functions:* Patterns may specify how to distribute responsibilities among cooperating objects to solve a more complex function or task.

3. **Structural principles:** To realize their functionality, patterns rely on certain structural principles:

- *Abstraction:* A pattern provides an abstract or generalized view of a particular (often complex) entity or task in a software system.

- *Encapsulation:* A pattern encapsulates details of a particular object, component, or service to remove dependency on the pattern from its clients or to protect these details from access.

- *Separation of concerns:* A pattern factors out specific responsibilities into separate objects or components in order to solve a particular task or provide a certain service.

- *Coupling and cohesion:* A pattern removes or relaxes the structural and communicational relationships and dependencies between otherwise strongly coupled objects.

The Pipes and Filters architecture presented in this paper is described and classified according to the overall frame set by the system of patterns.

2. THE PATTERN

Name   The pattern is named the Pipes and Filters architecture.

Rationale   Many data processing systems (compilers, for example) are composed of several independent subtasks. These subtasks are executed in a strongly determined order, and they communicate with each other only by exchanging streams of data. In order to gain high reusability, changeability, and maintainability in such applications and their subsystems, software architectures are needed that reflect the above characteristics in their primary subject matter.

Applicability   The Pipes and Filters architecture is particularly useful for software systems in which different subtasks can be identified and attached to separate components that

- are by themselves complete
- cooperate with each other only by using the output of one component as the input to another
- are to be executed in a sequential or parallel order that can be determined in advance (that is, the order is not changed dynamically)

Examples of such software systems include compilers as well as many distributed applications and signal processing systems [Garlan+93]. The Pipes and Filters architectural framework is not restricted to an object-oriented approach—it is applicable to all programming paradigms supporting abstraction facilities like abstract data types or modules.

The Pipes and Filters architecture is especially suitable for tasks where the data structure consists of a stream of similar data elements and the same processing steps have to be performed on each one. The more a task departs from these conditions, the more the advantages of the architecture are lost. If a task requires a complex data structure and each processing step only changes a small part of this structure, the Pipes and Filters architecture becomes unattractive. Either the whole data structure has to be copied by each filter, which is inefficient, or storage has to be shared, which violates a basic property of the architecture and partly destroys its advantages. This is also why the Pipes and Filters architecture is not suitable for interactive systems. Shared storage is inevitable in those cases.

The Pipes and Filters architectural framework can be used to structure applications that can be divided into several completely independent subtasks performed in a strongly determined sequential or parallel order.

Classification

The Pipes and Filters architecture is an architectural framework. It is mainly used to define the overall structure of a whole software system. The functionality of the Pipes and Filters architecture is to organize the computation of complex functions. The structural principle underpinning it is separation of concerns.

Description

The Pipes and Filters architectural framework consists of components that transform data (filters) and connections between them that transmit data (pipes). A filter component is responsible for a particular, independent, complete subtask of an application's functionality (for example, the lexical analysis within a compiler). Its interface consists of an input and output stream only. A filter reads streams of data from its inputs, processes these data, and produces streams of data to its outputs. Usually the input and output of each filter is restricted to a specific set of values. If there is an ordering correspondence between the input and output data, the filter preserves it. For example, the lexer component of a compiler has to preserve the ordering correspondence between the characters of the program text it analyzes and the tokens it produces [see Perry+92 for a formal description of this order-preserving property]. Usually, transformation of input data is done locally and incrementally, so that output may begin before the input is completely read. This means that a filter may start to work as soon as its predecessor produces its first result.

To preserve the independence of the framework's components, filters may not share a state. The only way to put the results of different filters together is to organize some of them into a sequence such that certain filters perform further transformations on the outputs of others. In addition, a filter should not know the identity of the filters preceding or following it in the computation

TABLE 1 Participants of the Pipes and Filters Architectural Framework

Class	Collaborators
Filter • performs independent subtask or service	Filter(s) Pipes(s)
Pipe • transmits data	Filters

sequence. Two principally different possibilities exist for the realization of pipes: pipes may simply be links between filters (such as message calls) or they may be separate components (such as data repositories or sensors). A pipe's only responsibility is to transmit data between filters, eventually by converting their format from the one produced by their sender to the one required by their receiver.

Thus the Pipes and Filters architectural framework is basically an arrangement of producer-consumer structures. On the one hand, each filter can be seen as a consumer of input, either from the user or from the output of some other filter. On the other hand, it is a (self-activated) producer of output, either for the user or for input to some other filter. In addition, filters provide their service without any request—they are not activated by successors needing results.

Diagram   Figure 1 presents an example of a Pipes and Filters architecture. It uses the notation of the OMT object model [Rumbaugh+91]. The description, using attributes and methods, does not necessarily imply an object-oriented implementation. The described architecture consists of four filters with four pipes connecting them. After processing some user input according to subtask_1, Filter_1 transmits its results using data links (Pipe_1 and Pipe_2) to either Filter_2a or Filter_2b. These filters process the data and add their own results to the repository components, which are used to implement Pipe_3 and Pipe_4, respectively. Filter_3 retrieves results

FIGURE 1   A Pipes and Filters architecture

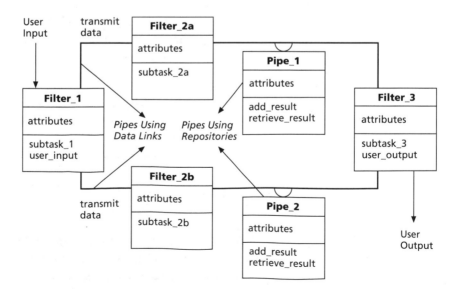

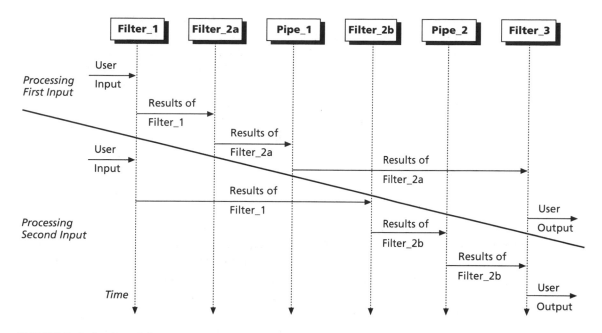

FIGURE 2 Behavior of the Pipes and Filters architecture

from `Pipe_3` and `Pipe_4`, processes them, and provides the output to the user. `Filter_2a` and `Filter_2b` may implement the same or different functions. Note that in Figure 2, `Pipe_1` and `Pipe_2` are simple message links while `Pipe_3` and `Pipe_4` are components.

Dynamic Behavior   A possible scenario for the dynamic behavior of the Pipes and Filters architectural framework modeled in Figure 1 is illustrated in Figure 2. It shows the processing of two items of user input (separated by a diagonal line). Note that `Filter_2a` and `Filter_2b` depend on the results of `Filter_1`, but may start to work before `Filter_1` has consumed all its inputs. The diagram shows the processing of two items of user input. `Filter_2a` starts to work as soon as it gets the first result from `Filter_1`. While the first item of user input is still being processed by `Filter_2a`, the next item of user input is read by `Filter_1`. The result is transferred to `Filter_2b`. Since `Filter_2a` and `Filter_2b` do not depend on each other's results, there is no predefined order for their execution.

Methodology   The first step in structuring a software system around a Pipes and Filters architecture is to identify those subtasks of its primary subject matter that can be independently executed. These subtasks are attached to separate, independent components, each representing a filter in the structure of the application under development. The next step is to determine which input is necessary for each filter and which other filter can deliver it. Based on this information, it can be specified which filters have to be executed sequentially and which can be executed in parallel. The filters must be organized in such a way that each filter gets the input it needs to perform the subtask it is responsible for. According to the needs of its associated subtask, each filter may also be further structured into finer-grained components.

After organizing the filters, the connections between them—the pipes—are considered. A pipe may be either just a way to pass data from one filter to another (such as a message call or data stream) or a separate component (like a repository or a sensor). Repositories may be used if a filter can perform its data transformations incrementally and locally and an ordering correspondence between input and output can be preserved. If such conditions hold for a particular filter, it makes sense for its successor to start work before the result the filter produces is complete. Thus the pipe connecting the filters must allow a continuous transmission of data from the filter producing partial results to the filter consuming them. In such cases the pipe may be implemented as a repository (as a queue, for example).

If a filter should not know the identity of another filter, a control component may be introduced to organize the transmission between the filters, or they may be connected by a repository or a sensorlike pipe.

Implementation   Every filter should be implemented as a separate component so it can be changed and easily reused. A component may be as simple as one class or module or as complex as a subsystem consisting of several parts composed using the Composite-Part design pattern. Handles between two filter components or between a filter component and a pipe component should be implemented as pointers. A filter component must offer functionality to access its results. Since this functionality accesses only prefabricated information, it should not include any means of controlling or influencing the results of the filter. If the filter is to be a self-activated component, it must be able to start the continuous production of its results. If the filter component is to be stimulated from outside the mechanism to produce its results, it must be able to invoke the production of new results.

Different realizations are possible for pipes:

- **Procedure-call with parameter:** A filter calls its successor filter. This requires a handle to its successor within the filter, which should be implemented as a pointer or access to a global variable pointing to it.

- **Control component:** A control component calls all filters and organizes the transmission of data between them.

- **Separate component:** If the pipe's task comprises more than just the transmission of data, it must be modeled as a separate component. This component may be a repository that offers services to add and retrieve data (see Producer-Repository-Consumer pattern in the Appendix). If it is necessary to transform data between two filters, a pipe can act as a sensor that transforms the data one filter produces before it is transmitted to another filter (see Producer-Sensor-Consumer pattern in the Appendix). The sensor's data transformations are restricted to changing the data's format. The sensor may neither process the data nor add or remove data; otherwise it would be a filter, not a pipe.

Data stream structures and parameter formats are important design and implementation issues for the Pipes and Filters architecture. Since no global data structures exist, all data must be transferred from one component to another. In data streams, one data item may be as simple as a single byte (one character) or as complicated as a structure describing a banking transaction. The producer and receiver of the data must agree on special meanings for certain data items ("end of line," for example).

Variants   There are three specializations of the Pipes and Filters architectural framework [Garlan+93]:

- A common specialization is the Pipeline system, which restricts its topology to a linear sequence of filters.

- Another specialization is the Bounded Pipe system, which sets a limit for the amount of data that may reside on a pipe.

- The Typed Pipe system specializes the Pipes and Filters architectural framework by restricting the data transmitted on a pipe to a certain type.

Examples   A compiler is one well-known example of a Pipeline system [Perry+92]. A compiler can be modeled in five phases: lexical analysis, syntactic analysis, semantic analysis, optimization, and code generation. Lexical analysis works on source code characters, transforming them into tokens. These form the input for the syntactic analysis, which produces phrases—either definition or use phrases. Then these definition and use phrases are passed to the semantic analysis, in which they are correlated. The result—correlated phrases—are passed on to code optimization, which annotates them. These annotated phrases form the input for the code generation that produces the object code. Code optimization is preferred but not necessary. The first two phases can be implemented in such a way that they make data transformations locally and incrementally and preserve the ordering between input and output. Therefore, syntactic and semantic analysis can start as soon as the preceding phase produces its first result. This is not true for the last three phases. All phrases have to be correlated before code generation begins. In the classical multiphase compiler, each of the five phases completes its function before the next phase starts. This is necessary because the compiler's name tables and abstract syntax trees have to be complete before they can be used for further transformations of the original program into executable code.

The UNIX shell supports the Pipes and Filters architecture: the Pipe System Call is a run-time mechanism that makes transmission of data between processes possible. The pipe symbol (|) allows connection of UNIX processes in a sequence [Bach86]. Here is an example of using the pipe symbol:

```
cat file1 | sort | grep test > file2
```

The Meta-Information-Protocol (MIP) [Buschmann+92a, Buschmann+92b], a run-time–type information system for C++, includes a toolkit that generates the structure that keeps the type information about a program. This toolkit is based on the Pipes and Filters architectural framework and uses a central component to organize data transmission between the various filters.

Discussion   The Pipes and Filters architecture strongly supports some desirable nonfunctional properties. Because of its simple structure, systems with this architecture are easy to understand and easy to maintain and enhance. The simplicity of their interface makes filters highly reusable. Sequences of completely independent filters support concurrent execution and thus efficiency.

On the other hand, the Pipes and Filters architecture does have some disadvantages [see Garlan93]. Since each filter is a completely independent component, it is often used to transform only whole input data into whole output data; the ability to incrementally change data and preserve the ordering correspondence between input and output data is often not used. This leads to a batched organization of filters, where one filter starts to work only after its predecessor has finished. (Many compilers are implemented this way.) In such cases the architecture's potential parallelism cannot be fully realized. Another drawback occurs if a common data format is necessary for all pipes. The necessity to adjust data to the common format leads to a loss of performance and an increased internal complexity in the filters.

The Pipes and Filters architecture supports parallel execution of components. This does not hold only for filters that appear in parallel lines in the system structure, but also for filters in a sequence where one filter may start to work before its predecessor has consumed all its input. The architecture may thus increase the efficiency of distributed systems, if the benefits of this parallelism outweigh its costs for the particular system.

The Pipes and Filters architectural framework can also be used to structure subsystems of an application. For example, if a software system structured with the Model-View-Controller architecture[1] confronts a task for which a Pipes and Filters organization is suitable, the appropriate part of the software's model subsystem may be implemented as a Pipes and Filters structure.

A correctly structured Pipes and Filters architecture supports the following general objectives for software architecture:

- **Reusability:** The Pipes and Filters architecture supports development with reuse. The existing components already have an interface that allows the use of one component's output as input to another, either directly or with the help of a repository or sensor. The Pipes and Filters architecture strongly supports development for reuse because it leads to components with a simple interface: an input stream with a specification for accepted data and an output stream with a specification for possible results.

- **Changeability/Maintainability:** Since each filter implements a complete functionality by itself and is independent of all other components, the Pipes and Filters architecture supports changeability and maintainability. Filter exchanges and changes within one filter do not have side effects on other components as long as the interface and behavior do not change.

- **Testability:** Testability is supported insofar as the different filters can be tested independently of all other system components. Throughput and deadlock analysis may also be applied.

See Also   The Producer-Consumer pattern can be used to compose a Pipes and Filters architecture. The Composite-Part pattern and the Mediator-Worker pattern can be used to further structure the components of a Pipes and Filters architecture.

3. CONCLUSION

The Pipes and Filters architecture is well known and widely used. The major aim of this paper is not to give yet another description of this architecture, but to present it as a pattern within a system of patterns. This paper, together with the papers "A System of Patterns" (Chapter 17) and "The Master-Slave Pattern" (Chapter 9), describes the current status of a project with the goal of developing a

---

[1] These patterns are briefly introduced in Chapter 17 of this volume and will be fully described in a forthcoming paper [Buschmann+95].

pattern-oriented approach to object-oriented software architecture. "A System of Patterns" describes the system itself and includes a description template, a short description of each pattern investigated to date, and a classification scheme. The other two papers (as well as this one) illustrate how patterns are represented within this system of patterns, by giving two example descriptions of patterns of different granularity: "The Master-Slave Pattern" describes a design pattern, whereas this paper presents an architectural framework.

Work on the description of frameworks and design patterns is almost finished and will be presented in a forthcoming paper [Buschmann+95]. Up to this point only the foundations have been laid for work on idioms. At this point there is only a rough outline of a method of guiding the user of a system of patterns.

Knowledge about sofware design is not easy to capture. We hope that a pattern-oriented approach to software architecture will make design knowledge available and useful for many software engineers and thereby improve the quality and productivity of software development.

REFERENCES

[Bach86] M. Bach. *The Design of the UNIX Operating System,* Prentice-Hall, 1986, pp. 111–119.

[Buschmann+92a] F. Buschmann, K. Kiefer, M. Stal. A Runtime Type Information System for C++, *TOOLS Europe '92 Proceedings,* Prentice Hall, 1992.

[Buschmann+92b] F. Buschmann, K. Kiefer, M. Stal, F. Paulisch. The Meta-Information-Protocol: Run-Time Type Information For C++, *Proceedings of the International Workshop on New Models for Software Architecture '92,* Tokyo, Japan, 1992.

[Buschmann+95] F. Buschmann, R. Meunier, H. Rohnert, P. Sommerland, M. Stal. Pattern-Oriented Software Architecture—A Pattern System. In preparation.

[Garlan+93] D. Garlan, M. Shaw. An Introduction to Software Architecture, *Advances in Software Engineering and Knowledge Engineering,* Vol. I. World Scientific Publishing Company, 1993.

[Perry+92] D. Perry, A. Wolf. Foundations for the Study of Software Architecture, *ACM SIGSOFT, Software Engineering Notes,* 17(4), pp. 40–52, October 1992.

[Rumbaugh+91] J. Rumbaugh, M. Blaha, W. Premerlani, F. Eddy, W. Lorensen. *Object-Oriented Modeling and Design,* Prentice Hall, 1991.

APPENDIX

Mediator-Worker Pattern

The Mediator-Worker design pattern facilitates the decoupling of otherwise strongly coupled, cooperating components of a software system (the workers). It organizes communication between them by introducing a special agent module (the mediator). Direct dependencies are removed between workers and attached to the mediator component. In addition, the Mediator-Worker design pattern supports the composition of complex functionality out of services offered by various individually developed or already existing components. In this case, the mediator acts as glue that connects the various workers to a compound entity.

Adapter Pattern

A Mediator-Worker structure with only two workers is called an Adapter structure. The main task of an adapter is to transform messages and data from the format used by the worker component sending a request to the format required by the worker receiving it. Since only two workers participate in an Adapter structure, no routing of requests is necessary. In other words, the Adapter design pattern performs a bidirectional protocol adaptation between two interfaces. Adapter components serving a similar purpose are often organized in an inheritance hierarchy with an abstract base. The Adapter design pattern is based on the same principles and has the same properties as the Mediator-Worker design pattern.

Sensor Pattern

The Sensor design pattern is a special variant of the Adapter design pattern. It is used to perform a unidirectional protocol adaptation from a specific to a generic interface. Sensor components serving a similar purpose may be organized in an inheritance hierarchy with an abstract base.

Producer-Consumer Pattern

The Producer-Consumer design pattern supports and organizes access to services provided by self-activated suppliers within a structure of cooperating components; this means that these suppliers provide their services without an explicit request. The supplier components are called producers, and the components that use their services are called consumers. The pattern is built around the structural principles of coupling and cohesion. It tries to maintain self-activated suppliers independent of their clients.

Producer-Repository-Consumer Pattern

This is a variant of the Producer-Consumer design pattern, in which the producer deposits its information in a separate, external repository component rather than keeping it in its inner structure and offering access to it. The repository component is responsible for maintaining the information provided by the producer, and allows the consumer to retrieve this information through its interface. The consumer component communicates only with the repository component. The Producer-Repository-Consumer design pattern is based on the same principles and has the same properties as the Producer-Consumer design pattern.

Producer-Sensor-Consumer Pattern

In this variant of the Producer-Consumer design pattern the result provided by the producer has to be transformed before it can be used by the consumer. This task is performed by a special sensor component. It performs a unidirectional data translation, from the format delivered by the producer to the one required by the consumer. The Producer-Sensor-Consumer design pattern is based on the same principles and has the same properties as the Producer-Consumer design pattern, combined with those of the Mediator-Worker design pattern.

Regine Meunier can be reached at Siemens AG, Corporate Research and Development, Dept. ZFE BT SE2, Otto-Hahn-Ring, 81730 Munich, Germany; reginemeunier@zfe.siemens.de.

23 Pattern-Based Integration Architectures

Diane E. Mularz

ABSTRACT

As today's information-systems industry undergoes a paradigm shift from custom development to integration of components, successful new strategies are needed. Although such strategies currently exist, they suffer from three weak characteristics: informality, project-specificity, and product-specificity. As the component space expands, it will preclude explicit product integration as the default method for determining successful integration schemes. This paper explores the use of patterns as an approach to codifying integration schemes. Several examples are used to demonstrate that recurring problems exist in the integration of systems, that these problems can be recognized, and that a solution can be specified for others to use as an "integration pattern."

INTRODUCTION

There is a growing collection of off-the-shelf components and legacy assets that can serve as a basis for integrated systems. To successfully build this

Copyright © 1995 The Mitre Corporation. All Rights Reserved.

kind of system, you need an integration strategy that will resolve the conflicts introduced by the composition of stand-alone components. Although a component's internal structure can lead to integration conflicts, this is not the focus of this paper. Instead the focus is on the integration architecture required given individual components. Two types of structural entities exist in component-based architectures: functional components and integration components. Functional components encapsulate a domain-specific capability (such as word processing, spreadsheets, combat simulations, payroll). Integration components provide the glue for binding functional components together. This glue is highly dependent on the particular components to be integrated, the purpose of the integration (for example, end-to-end processing, data exchange), and the characteristics of each component with respect to the desired integration. These integration components possess a wide range of complexities and structures, depending on the degree of mismatch between component attributes and the desired integration. When functional component attributes are incompatible with the integration, an integration conflict occurs. A viable integration architecture essentially resolves the conflicts between the integration mechanisms made available by a given component, and the desired capabilities for the integrated system.

As an example, consider current military training systems. Many stovepipe simulations were independently developed to model a particular aspect of military conflict (such as logistics planning, combat modeling, deployment). Integration of these individual simulations can provide much more realistic end-to-end training exercises. However, to provide this level of integration requires the resolution of conflicts regarding shared (and often overlapping) states; access to multiplatform, distributed, heterogeneous components; and dynamic entry and exit of components from the exercise. An integration strategy known as the Aggregate Level Simulation Protocol (ALSP) has been successfully developed to provide the desired integration [ALSP93].

Although the previous example casts the integration problem in domain-specific terms, this paper's premise is that recurring patterns are present in the integration strategies used to resolve specific integration conflicts, that these patterns can be cast in an operational form, and that this combination of problem and solution can be defined as a pattern of integration that can be used in similar contexts. The inspiration for this work is drawn from the work of Christopher Alexander [Alexander77; Alexander79] and from the application of his ideas within the object-oriented community [Johnson92]. This work differs from the main thrust of Alexander in that some elements of the architecture (for example, the functional components) are known a priori, which imposes certain constraints on the resultant integration component. It may be more appropriately likened to Alexander's process of repair, in which a partial solution addresses some of the problems, but resolving defects would provide a complete solution.

Note that although patterns have been popularized throughout the object-oriented community, the integration pattern ideas presented in this paper stem largely from experiences in integrating existing components. This is not to say that these patterns are not appropriate for object-oriented systems; in fact I see overlaps with some of the design patterns captured by Gamma et al. [Gamma95].

Integration Patterns

An integration pattern specifies an integration problem and a corresponding integration model that resolves the problem. The model consists of structural entities that can potentially be dispersed throughout an architecture, either as separate integration components or as adjuncts to the functional components. An integration pattern is therefore a well-formed arrangement of entities (that is, their behavior and relative placement is explictly specified as part of the architecture). These structural arrangements depend on two things: the integration attributes of the functional components and the desired integration. For instance, if two components need to exchange information but they do not agree on an exchange format, then a translator must be introduced to convert the information from one form into another. (Note that this could require semantic as well as structural conversion.) In addition, components might have to be modified to import and export the information exchanged (that is, component adjuncts might need to be introduced to facilitate integration). These integration components, and their placement, form the integration model for a given integration problem.

The following template is used to present some sample integration problems and their solutions in the form of integration patterns:

1. **Name:** The pattern is given a descriptive title.

2. **Integration Intent:** The pattern's purpose is summarized in a concise statement.

3. **Integration Context:** A typical context for the pattern's use is presented. The components to be integrated are described, together with the rationale for integration.

4. **Integration Conflict:** The fundamental problem to be resolved is identified. Conflicting forces that must be addressed are indicated. The integration attributes of the functional components are considered (for example, components are distributed across multiple platforms, they are constructed using multiple languages, they have overlapping data

models, or they assume the presence of other components or products).
Such attributes constrain how the conflict can be resolved, potentially
impeding ultimate integration by conflicting with overall goals such as
transparency and seamlessness. (For instance, components that need to
interoperate might not share a common mechanism for information
exchange or communication.)

5. **Solution:** The essential integration components are identified, together
   with their relationships to one another and to the functional
   components required to resolve the conflict.

6. **Applicability:** Appropriate conditions under which to apply the pattern
   are described.

7. **Completing Patterns:** Patterns that complete this pattern are identified.

PLoP'94 Note: It was noted by Mary Shaw during her review of this work
at the conference that performance is an important aspect of an integration
pattern. Trade-offs must be made between functionality and performance;
any possible extensions and variations that will refine the basic pattern's
performance should be captured. The author acknowledges that this is a
necessary refinement of the work; however, such refinements have not yet
been factored into this paper.

INTEGRATION PATTERN EXAMPLES

Pattern 1

Name   (Legacy) Wrapper

Integration Intent   This pattern provides continued access to a legacy application while extending its capability and user base, eventually leading to its replacement.

Integration Context   A legacy application encapsulates an important functionality. While this functionality must continue to exist, a new functionality is required. In addition, users require access to this functionality from distributed, heterogeneous workstations that are separate from the legacy platform. In the short term, multiple users must be able to access the legacy application. In the long term, it will most likely be necesary to replace all or part of the legacy application while maintaining transparent access for the end user. *Note:* Although this pattern is explained in terms of a legacy application, it can be applied to any application with a product-defined API.

Integration Conflict   The key forces at play here are the need for continued access by an expanding user base to existing functionality while allowing for incremental replacement of the implementation in a manner that is transparent to the user.

Solution   Consider the legacy application to be an available service and the user application(s) to be clients of that service (see Figure 1). Define a domain-specific interface, a framework that will serve as the basis for integrating the user application with the legacy system. Encapsulate the legacy application in a wrapper that exposes only the framework interface. To extend the functionality, place the new functionality into additional services that are accessed through the framework. Since this framework interface is not likely to match the existing legacy interface, create a mapping between the framework and the existing API. This mapping may require caching if multiple interfaces must be executed to provide a single response to the user. To achieve run-time implementation independence, provide a locator component (ideally one that is separated from the user application, to allow for independent growth of the user base).

Applicability   Use this pattern whenever an existing application can be considered a server for one or more users and has an established interface that can be masked by a front-end wrapper, and it is not currently desirable or feasible to rebuild the application.

Completing Patterns   To support a heterogeneous, distributed user base, consider the use of a broker. A broker should also be considered if the legacy application's functionality is extended through the introduction of independent new services that may also be distributed (see Figure 2 for an illustration).

Post–PLoP'94 Note: The concept of a wrapper overlaps with the Facade and Adapter patterns described in Gamma et al. [Gamma95]. In fact, an examination of the published design patterns from an integration pattern perspective is probably warranted so that new patterns are not unnecessarily introduced.

Pattern 2

Name   Work Flow Manager

Integration Intent   Provide an integration component that will automatically perform a user-defined task based on a known, repeatable execution sequence performed by stand-alone components.

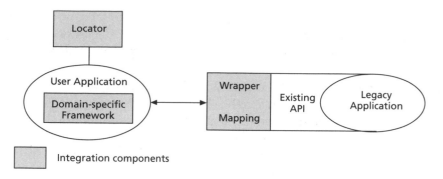

FIGURE 1 Legacy (wrapper) configuration

Integration Context   A collection of stand-alone components provide well-defined functionality (examples include a word processing package, a spreadsheet package, a graphics package, an electronic mail package). A user makes use of the same packages in the same order, transferring the same types of information each time. The only difference between task instances is the actual data.

Integration Conflict   The functional components can be integrated to provide an automatic work flow if the following potential conflicts are resolved: managing required activation, sequencing, and data exchange among actual components; data exchange formats and contents; and interapplication communications.

FIGURE 2 Legacy (wrapper) configuration with additional services

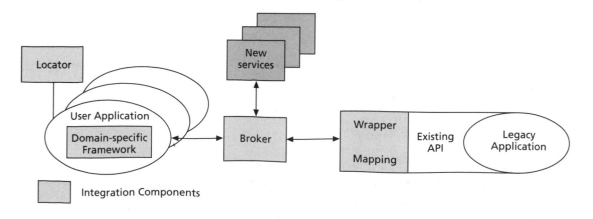

Solution (*Note:* For purposes of this paper, all aspects and generalizations of the solution are not articulated here; only the entities and relationships needed to manage the required relationships between components are presented.) Provide a functional component profile that is separate from the sequencing logic, to ensure generalization and extensibility. The profile should describe the integration attributes of each functional component (for example, its physical location, communication protocol, supported data exchange formats, and so on). Provide a task specifier that defines the type of application and sequencing order. Incorporate a locator for finding files and applications. Provide a task manager to activate and sequence components and invoke data exchanges as needed (see Figure 3).

Applicability Use this integration pattern whenever the integration problem can be modeled as a set of discrete steps in which each functional component in the sequence does not require knowledge of the previous components' state.

Examples A simple example is the use of scripts to activate and control the execution context for an integrated suite of applications. A horizontal template provided by Template Software provides the basic framework for constructing and executing work flows. A commercial product called Synergy by Prodea provides a single-platform application integration capability that extends the

FIGURE 3 Work Flow Manager configuration

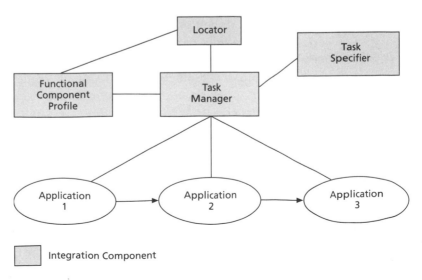

Integration Component

basic integration notions identified here to include run-time flexibility (including selection of actual applications based on execution platform characteristics).

Pattern 3

Name Broker

Integration Intent This pattern provides for communication and location transparency for interoperating applications.

Integration Context Distributed, heterogeneous components are to be integrated. These components have not necessarily been constructed to interoperate with other components. Each component is also required to continue to operate independently. Components can exist on multiple platforms and may be in multiple languages.

Integration Conflict The pattern must support the interoperation of dynamic implementations in a heterogeneous environment, while maintaining the transparency of communication, location, and component attributes (such as the implementation language and platform dependencies).

Solution Consider the functional components to be requesters and providers of one another's services. Employ a broker that will serve as an arbiter and intermediary, accessing services of one component and providing the results to the requestings components. (This is akin to a stockbroker's accessing financial services to buy and sell investments on the client's behalf, and reporting on the results of the transactions.) The broker should include a request handler, a request-to-result correlator, a functional component registration, a locator for finding a service to handle requests, and data encoders/decoders (if needed) to exchange information across language and/or platform boundaries.

Applicability Apply this pattern whenever interoperability is needed in a distributed, heterogeneous environment. (It can also be used in a nondistributed configuration.)

Examples There are several examples of this type of integration component, such as the remote procedure call (RPC), which provides for location transparency, and the Object Request Broker (ORB), as defined by the Object Management

Group [OMG92], for achieving interoperability among distributed applications. In the ALSP example mentioned earlier, a broker-type notion is used, but not explicitly identified as such. An ALSP common module manages the configuration, coordinating entry and exit of functional components and time. An ALSP broadcast emulator provides for distributed communication among the components.

Pattern 4

Name   Shared Repository

Integration Intent   Provide an integration scheme that allows individual components to process information in an internal form while sharing information with other components.

Integration Context   A collection of stand-alone components or tools need to exchange information; the tools process highly overlapping information but maintain separate, internal models of it. Exchange is typically required because multiple groups who have independently developed information using one of the tools must now integrate their models. It is also expected that all tools will potentially require exchange with all others. (See Applicability for details.)

Integration Conflict   The problem is one of minimizing the number of unique interfaces required between components while maximizing the independence of individual components. Note that each integrated component may not be known a priori. Each component is likely to use only a subset of the other components' information, but it is necessary to retain all component information so each component can access all the information provided by any other given component.

Solution   Define a shared-information model that captures all the data that can potentially be exchanged between the components. Build an importer and an exporter for each component to and from the common form (see Figure 4). Such a solution imposes a maximum of two new interfaces for each additional component; otherwise the number of new interfaces is $n - 1$, where n is the number of components to be integrated.

Applicability   Use this approach when all the system components must share their information with all the other components and there is a large set of components, with the likelihood of additions. As an example, consider a

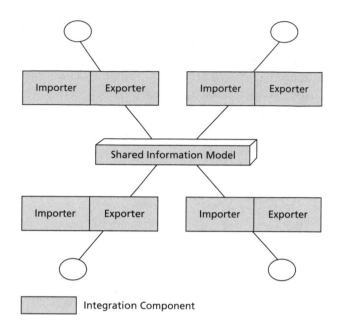

FIGURE 4 Shared Repository configuration

software development project in which each design team uses a different Computer-Aided Software Engineering (CASE) tool but the same software design method. At some point the models must be exchanged and integrated.

PLoP'94 Note: Doug Lea posed an interesting question about this pattern which would lead to variants: What are the general conditions (for example, pattern invariants) that must exist for a translator be fully reversable (that is, to have an import and export capability) as opposed to having strictly a one-way transfer?

CONCLUSIONS

The integration patterns presented here are at a preliminary stage of development and represent integration strategies garnered from a small sample; they are meant to be explanatory rather than exhaustive or fully generalized. The patterns are not connected into an integration language, and the form for capturing them has not been validated. One simple observation I can offer after having captured some of these integration patterns is that the patterns themselves repeatedly indicate the need for recurring internal entities such as locator components. Continued investigations might uncover recurring structural relationships that could be packaged as reusable integration components. (In fact, this is the origin of the ProdeaSynergy product.) Broader integration patterns need to be recognized and captured. Some typing of integration patterns, and the development of a corresponding notation that describes the exact requirements of an integration component in terms of entities and their relationships, would be useful for specifying integration architectures. Finally, if true invariants could be identified in the integration patterns and the patterns were adopted by the community, then validation techniques could be developed to ensure that corresponding implementations conformed to a pattern-based integration architecture. Given all these open questions, it is obvious that the development of an integration pattern is still at an early stage. However, the idea is presented in the hopes that such patterns will be considered useful, and that as others are developed the concept of an integration pattern will be refined.

ACKNOWLEDGMENTS

There is nothing like "taking it out for a spin" for understanding the strengths and weaknesses of one's work. The writer's workshop at PLoP'94 provided an ideal setting for such an experience. I wish to thank the program committee for adopting this approach, and in particular I would like to thank Ken Auer for shepherding my work through the approval process. Feedback from all conference attendees guided the revision of this paper, and the suggestions of Jim Coplien, Doug Lea, Gerard Meszaros, and Mary Shaw were particularly useful. I also wish to acknowledge Daneel Pang Swee Chee, who provided validation of the notion of an integration pattern. In his work on the Singapore Information Infrastructure he has seen evidence of similar patterns. This was very encouraging; we hope to collaborate and to refine our ideas for PLoP'95. Finally, I wish to acknowledge Bill Ruh, Robbie Hutchison, and Clem McGowan of MITRE for their continued encouragement.

REFERENCES

[Alexander77] Christopher Alexander, Sara Isikawa, and Murray Silverstein, with Max Jacobson, Ingrid Fiksdahl-King, and Shlomo Angel. *A Pattern Language.* New York: Oxford University Press, 1977.

[Alexander79] Christopher Alexander. *The Timeless Way of Building.* New York: Oxford University Press, 1979.

[ALSP93] Aggregate Level Simulation Protocol Technical Specification. *MITRE Informal Report.* McLean, VA: Modeling and Simulation Technical Center, June 1993.

[Gamma95] Erich Gamma, Richard Helm, Ralph Johnson, and John Vlissides. *Design Patterns: Elements of Reusable Object-Oriented Software.* Reading, MA: Addison-Wesley, 1995.

[Johnson92] Ralph E. Johnson. "Documenting Frameworks Using Patterns." *OOPSLA'92 Proceedings* (1992): 63–76.

[OMG92] Object Management Architecture Guide, *OMG Technical Report 92.11.1.* Framingham, MA, 1992.

BIBLIOGRAPHY

[Belady91] "Vision of the Software Engineering Industry." Paper presented at the Fourteenth International Conference on Software Engineering, Austin, Texas, 1991.

[Berlin90] Lucy Berlin. "When Objects Collide: Experiences with Reusing Multiple Class Hierarchies." *OOPSLA '90 Proceedings* (October 1990): 181–193.

[Brown92a] Alan W. Brown and Maria H. Penedo. "An Annotated Bibliography on Integration in Software Engineering Environments." *ACM Software Engineering Notes,* 17, 3 (July 1992): 47–55.

[Brown92b] Alan W. Brown. "CASE Tool and Environment Integration." Briefing, July 1992.

[Garlan93] David Garlan and Mary Shaw. "An Introduction to Software Architecture." In *Advances in Software Engineering and Knowledge Engineering,* Volume I. Singapore: World Scientific Publishing Company, 1993.

[Meyers91] Scott Meyers. "Difficulties in Integrating Multiview Development Systems." *IEEE Software* (January 1991): 49–57.

[Perry92] Dewayne E. Perry and Alexander L. Wolf. "Foundations for the Study of Software Architecture." *ACM Software Engineering Notes,* 17, 4 (October 1992): 40–52.

[Taligent93] "Leveraging Object-Oriented Frameworks." Technical Report. Cupertino, CA: Taligent Inc., 1993.

[Wasserman86] Anthony I. Wasserman. "Tool Integration in Software Engineering Environments." *Proceedings of Software Engineering Environments: International Workshop on Environments.* Chinon, France, September 18–20, 1989.

Diane E. Mularz can be reached at The MITRE Corporation, 7525 Colshire Drive, MS Z267, McLean, VA 22102; mularz@mitre.org.

Patterns for Software Architectures

24

Mary Shaw

ABSTRACT

Software designers rely on informal patterns, or idioms, to describe the architectures of their software systems—the configurations of components that make up the systems. My purpose here is to reflect on the role these patterns play in software design. I am particularly interested in how informal patterns shape the configurations. Patterns determine how separate parts are combined, or woven together. The resulting organization is often called the *architecture* of the system. Current programming languages do not support these patterns; indeed, the patterns address problems that lie outside the scope of conventional programming languages. This paper describes the character of these architectural patterns and the status of work on models and tools to support them.

DESIGN PATTERNS FOR SOFTWARE ARCHITECTURES

The conventional view holds that software components interact by importing and exporting access rights to procedures and then calling the procedures (this

Copyright © 1994 Mary Shaw. All Rights Reserved.

is sometimes referred to as invoking the methods). However, software designers describe the interactions among components using a quite rich vocabulary of abstractions. Although the descriptions and the underlying vocabulary are imprecise and informal, designers nevertheless appear to communicate effectively. Even a vocabulary that has been overloaded to the extent that it becomes a collection of buzzwords, when used in context, carries meaning. For example:

- "Camelot is based on the client-server model and uses remote procedure calls both locally and remotely to provide communication among applications and servers" [Spector 87].

- "Abstraction layering and system decomposition provide the appearance of system uniformity to clients, yet allow Helix to accommodate a diversity of autonomous devices. The architecture encourages a client-server model for the structuring of applications" [Fridrich 85].

- "We have chosen a distributed, object-oriented approach to managing information" [Linton 87].

- "The easiest way to make the canonical sequential compiler into a concurrent compiler is to pipeline the execution of the compiler phases over a number of processors. . . . A more effective way [is to] split the source code into many segments, which are concurrently processed through the various phases of compilation [by multiple compiler processes] before a final, merging pass recombines the object code into a single program" [Seshadri 88].

- "The ARC network [follows] the general network architecture specified by the ISO in the Open Systems Interconnection Reference Model. It consists of physical and data layers, a network layer, and transport, session, and presentation layers" [Paulk 85].

The prose is usually accompanied by a box-and-line diagram depicting the intended system architecture. In these diagrams, shapes suggest differences among the components, but there is little discrimination among the lines— that is, among different kinds of interactions. The descriptions are highly specific to the systems they describe, especially in the labeling of components.

  My colleagues and I studied sets of such descriptions and found a number of patterns that recur regularly. Some of these patterns govern the overall style that organizes the components; others identify the character of a component interface or an abstraction for component interaction. A few of the patterns (for example, Objects) have been carefully refined [Booch 86], but others are still used quite informally, even unconsciously. Nevertheless, the idiomatic patterns are widely recognized. System designs often appeal to several of these patterns, combining them in various ways. An inspection of the descriptions of actual systems shows that the motivations for using different patterns are often not carefully separated, and the interactions of the patterns are therefore correspondingly obscure.

Garlan and Shaw [Garlan and Shaw 93] describe several common architectural styles. Ours is not, of course, an exhaustive list; however, it offers rich opportunities both for elaboration and for structure. By abstracting from the details of individual examples, we can identify underlying patterns. These idiomatic patterns differ in four major respects: the pattern's intuitive base (that is, the system model); the kinds of components used to develop a system according to the pattern; the connectors (the kind of interaction among components); and the control structure or execution discipline. By using a uniform descriptive scheme, we improve our ability to identify significant differences between patterns. Once the informal pattern is clear, the details can be formalized [Allen and Garlan 94]. Furthermore, the process of choosing a system's architecture should include matching the architecture's characteristics to the properties of the problem [Lane 90]; uniform descriptions of the available architectures should simplify this task.

Systems are composed from identifiable components of various distinct types. The components interact in distinct, identifiable ways. Components correspond roughly to the compilation units of conventional programming languages and to other user-level objects, such as files. Connectors mediate interactions among components; that is, they establish the rules that govern component interaction and specify any required auxiliary implementation mechanisms. Connectors do not, in general, correspond individually to compilation units; they manifest themselves as table entries, instructions to a linker, dynamic data structures, system calls, initialization parameters, servers that support multiple independent connections, and the like. A pattern is based on selected types of components and connectors, together with a control structure that governs execution. An overall system model captures the intuitive base for determining how these are integrated.

Popular architectural patterns include the following:

Pipeline

System model	Mapping data streams to data streams.
Components	Filters (purely computational, local processing).
Connectors	Data streams (ASCII data streams for UNIX pipelines).
Control structure	Data flow.

Data abstraction (object-oriented)

System model	Localized state maintenance.

Components	Managers (for example, servers, objects, abstract data types).
Connectors	Procedure calls (method invocation is essentially a procedure call with dynamic binding).
Control structure	Decentralized, usually single thread.

Implicit invocation (event-based)

System model	Independent reactive processes.
Components	Processes that signal significant events without knowing signal recipients.
Connectors	Automatic invocations of processes that have a registered interest in events.
Control structure	Decentralized. Individual components are not aware of signal recipients.

Repository (includes databases and blackboard systems)

System model	Centralized data, usually richly structured.
Components	One memory, many purely computational processes.
Connectors	Computational units interact with memory by direct data access or procedure calls.
Control structure	Varies with type of repository; may be external (depends on input data stream, as for databases), predetermined, or internal (depends on state of computation, as for blackboards).

Interpreter

System model	Virtual machine.
Components	One state machine (the execution engine) and three memories (current state of execution engine, program being interpreted, current state of program being interpreted).
Connectors	Data access and procedure calls.
Control structure	Usually state-transition for execution engine and input-driven for selecting what to interpret.

Main program and subroutines

System model	Call and definition hierarchy.
Components	Procedures.
Connectors	Procedure calls.
Control structure	Single thread.

Layered

System model	Hierarchy of opaque layers.
Components	Usually composites; composites are most often collections of procedures.
Connectors	Depends on structure of components; often procedure calls under restricted visibility, might also be client-server.
Control structure	Single thread.

In practice a designer will adopt one or more of these patterns to shape the design. Patterns may be used in combination, either by providing complementary views of the system during the initial design (as both repositories and interpreters [Garlan and Shaw 93]) or by elaborating a component of one pattern using some other pattern (as in a layered system in which some layers are elaborated as pipelines and others as data abstractions). This progressive elaboration can be continued repeatedly until the architectural issues are resolved, at which point conventional programming techniques take over.

Clearly these patterns need to be elaborated and classified. This is the objective of ongoing work. Another important open problem is how to provide guidance on choosing the best architectural pattern for a given problem. Lane [Lane 90] worked through this question in detail for a specific domain—the user interface.

PATTERNS FOR COMPONENT PACKAGING AND INTERACTION

Recognizing, recording, classifying, selecting, and using patterns for architectures is not enough. Different patterns rely on different kinds of components, and those components interact in different ways. Furthermore, most systems are heterogeneous—several patterns are used in combination to define the architecture. A full architectural description language must, therefore, distinguish between different kinds of components and interactions. Yet the tools at the disposal of programmers are the procedure and data references that languages allow them to export from modules. As a result, there is a gap between the concepts and notations used for the architectural descriptions and the concepts and notations used for the resulting programs. My colleagues and I are working on a language and tools to bridge this gap. This section describes the types of components and connectors we support in the current prototype and the way they interact to define legal system configurations.

Conventional views of system composition do not acknowledge the difference between architectural design and program code. Some view systems simply as collections of compilation units that import and export names of procedures and data, using the constructs of the underlying programming language for the interaction. Others choose one organizational pattern and support it exclusively; this often means components are restricted to a particular form and interactions are restricted to one specialized abstraction.

A major shortcoming of both conventional methodology and conventional languages is that people don't generally recognize the distinctions (or the lack thereof) that cause trouble. If a software developer is not sensitive to differences in component packaging, he or she may inadvertently select incompatible components. Consider, for example, the difference between filters and procedures (system calls) in UNIX. Many of the same functions are provided in both forms. Even though a formal specification might indicate that both versions compute the same function (such as `sort`), the two versions are not interchangeable, because they interact with their data in different ways.

The situation is exacerbated because the connectors are invisible—the abstractions used for system style are not evident in the design but are instead hard-coded in procedure calls. Furthermore, component packaging comes in many kinds, and these are not often discriminated. Even the copious literature on reuse ignores the needs of systems that use multiple

TABLE 1 Component Types Supported by UniCon

Component Type	Intuition	Player Types Supported
Module	conventional compilation unit	RoutineDef, RoutineCall, GlobalDataDef, GlobalDataUse, ReadFile, WriteFile
Computation	pure function	RoutineDef, RoutineCall, GlobalDataUse
SharedData	Fortran common with import	GlobalDataDef, GlobalDataUse
SeqFile	UNIX file	ReadNext, WriteNext
Filter	UNIX filter	StreamIn, StreamOut
Process	UNIX process	RPCDef, RPCCall
SchedProcess	real-time process	RPCDef, RPCCall, Segment, Trigger
General	anything goes	all (that is, any player type is allowed)

patterns, because it fails to deal explicitly with different forms of component packaging and different abstractions for component interaction (connection).

The common organization styles listed in the previous section distinguish among different kinds of components and connectors. This establishes a requirement that an architectural language support those distinctions by means of labeling, checking, and analysis. We have argued elsewhere [Shaw94] that interactions should have the same first-class status that components do.

UniCon, our prototype architectural language, takes the first steps [Shaw et al. 95]. *Components* and *connectors* are the primary entities in the language. Each component and connector has a type, a specification, and an implementation. Specifications include the elements of interaction—*players* for components and *roles* for connectors. The types of components currently supported by the language are listed in Table 1, and the types of connectors are listed in Table 2. The specification of a connector, called a protocol, determines how components will interact. It establishes the roles that must be played by various components, and it identifies the player types that can fill these roles. Subsystems are then constructed as nonprimitive components by defining the components and connectors to be used and the manner in which they will be configured.

This is only a first step; as new types must be added manually, no abstraction capabilities are available yet, and enforcement of architectural style patterns is still quite weak.

ALEXANDER'S PATTERNS

Alexander's pattern language [Alexander et al. 77] has helped shape my views on software architecture over the past few years. I first discovered it when I was trying to understand the reuse of design fragments that could not be captured in subroutine or object form. These fragments included

- program skeletons to be fleshed out, often with varying numbers of certain features
- housekeeping activities such as scheduling and synchronization that seem to be impossible to isolate in their own modules
- configuration of modules without reference to the computations in the modules

It was clear that these fragments are reused idiomatically, just as algorithms and data structures are. However, they must be fleshed out with other (unrelated) code in order to be useful, so ordinary library mechanisms are not suitable. Alexander's patterns are of precisely this form.

Connector Type	Intuition	Role Types and the Players They Support
Pipe	UNIX pipe	Source (accepts `StreamOut` of `Filter`, `ReadNext` of `SeqFile`) Sink (accepts `StreamIn` of `Filter`, `WriteNext` of `SeqFile`)
FileIO	UNIX operations between process and file	Reader (accepts `ReadFile` of `Module`) Readee (accepts `ReadNext` of `SeqFile`) Writer (accepts `WriteFile` of `Module`) Writee (accepts `WriteNext` of `SeqFile`)
ProcedureCall	intermodule procedure call	Definer (accepts `RoutineDef` of `Computation` or `Module`) Caller (accepts `RoutineCall` of `Computation` or `Module`)
DataAccess	shared data (between compilation units within a process)	Definer (accepts `GlobalDataDef` of `SharedData` or `Module`) User (accepts `GlobalDataUse` of `SharedData`, `Computation`, or `Module`)
RemoteProcCall	remote procedure call	Definer (accepts `RPCDef` of `Process` or `SchedProcess`) Caller (accepts `RPCCall` of `Process` or `SchedProcess`)
RTScheduler	processes competing for processor cycles	Stimulus (accepts `Trigger` of `SchedProcess`) Action (accepts `Segment` of `SchedProcess`)

TABLE 2 Connector Types Supported by UniCon

Other influences include the use of carefully structured prose rather than formal specifications to express the patterns, discrimination among a variety of patterns and restrictions on which ones can interact with which others, and recognition that it is acceptable for some patterns to operate on a large scale while others operate on a small scale.

A major attraction of Alexander's pattern language is that its forms are modified when they are combined, and the patterns describe how these changes take place. This is in stark contrast to most programming languages, in which the parts are completely, rigidly defined in advance and maintain their identity throughout (except for intermodule optimization, which is invisible to designers).

ACKNOWLEDGMENTS

The technical results reported here were developed jointly with various coauthors, especially David Garlan. A good share of the motivation for this work came from sources outside computer science, most notably Alexander's work on pattern languages and some conversations with Vic Vyssotsky on urban planning. Discussion of the original paper at the August 1994 PLoP workshop showed me a number of ways to improve the content and presentation.

This research was supported by the Carnegie-Mellon University School of Computer Science and Software Engineering Institute (which is sponsored by the U.S. Department of Defense); by a grant from Siemens Corporate Research; by the Wright Laboratory, Aeronautical Systems Center, Air Force Materiel Command, USAF; and by the Advanced Research Projects Agency (ARPA) under grant F33615-93-1-1330. The U.S. government is authorized to reproduce and distribute reprints of this article for government purposes. Views and conclusions contained in this chapter are those of the author and should not be interpreted as representing the official positions of any of the supporters.

REFERENCES

[Allen and Garlan 94] Robert Allen and David Garlan. "Formalizing Architectural Connection." *Proceedings of the 16th International Conference on Software Engineering,* 1994.

[Alexander et al. 77] Christopher Alexander, Sara Ishikawa, Murray Silverstein, et al. *A Pattern Language.* New York: Oxford University Press, 1977.

[Booch 86] Grady Booch. "Object-Oriented Development." *IEEE Transactions on Software Engineering,* SE-12, 2 (February 1986): 211–221.

[Fridrich 85] Marek Fridrich and William Older. "Helix: The Architecture of the XMS Distributed File System." *IEEE Software*, 2, 3 (May 1985): 21–29.

[Garlan and Shaw 93] David Garlan and Mary Shaw. "An Introduction to Software Architecture." V. Ambriola and G. Tortora (eds), In *Advances in Software Engineering and Knowledge Engineering*, Vol. II. World Scientific Publishing Company, 1993.

[Lane 90] Thomas G. Lane. *Studying Software Architecture Through Design Spaces and Rules.* Carnegie-Mellon University Technical Report, September 1990.

[Linton 87] Mark A. Linton. "Distributed Management of a Software Database." *IEEE Software* 4, 6 (November 1987).

[Paulk 85] Mark C. Paulk. "The ARC Network: A Case Study." *IEEE Software*, 2, 3 (May 1985): 62–69.

[Seshadri 88] V. Seshadri et al. "Semantic Analysis in a Concurrent Compiler." *Proceedings of ACM SIGPLAN '88 Conference on Programming Language Design and Implementation.*

[Shaw 94] Mary Shaw. "Procedure Calls Are the Assembly Language of Software Interconnection: Connectors Deserve First-Class Status." *Proceedings of Workshop on Studies of Software Design.* Springer-Verlag, 1994.

[Shaw and Garlan 93] Mary Shaw and David Garlan. "Characteristics of Higher-level Languages for Software Architecture." Unpublished manuscript, 1993.

[Shaw et al. 95] Mary Shaw, Robert DeLine, Daniel V. Klein, Theodore L. Ross, David M. Young, and Gregory Zelesnik. "Abstractions for Software Architecture and Tools to Support Them." *IEEE Transactions on Software Engineering*, forthcoming.

[Spector 87] Alfred Z. Spector et al. *Camelot: A Distributed Transaction Facility for Mach and the Internet—An Interim Report.* Carnegie-Mellon University Computer Science Technical Report CMU-CS-87-129, June 1987.

Mary Shaw can be reached at Computer Science Department, Carnegie Mellon University, Pittsburgh, PA 15213; mary.shaw@cs.cmu.edu.

OBJECT USAGE AND STYLE

PART

7

Patterns are an important contribution to the software community because they address a fundamental challenge in software development: communication of knowledge among developers. The patterns in Part 7 convey principles of good object usage and programming style that are essential to writing high-quality object-oriented software.

Object-oriented programming (OOP) languages are often touted as a significant improvement over alternative programming language paradigms (such as procedural programming or functional programming). Proponents of OOP claim that language features such as classes, inheritance, dynamic binding, and parameterized types enhance software quality factors such as modularity, reuse, and extensibility. The key language design principles that underly these features include the following:

- Separation of interface from implementation — this separation is supported by abstract base classes and enforced by class access control mechanisms;

- Static and dynamic substitution of implementations. Substitution is supported statically by type parameterization and inheritance. It is supported dynamically allowing late binding of methods to objects at run-time.

By combining these principles, developers are encouraged to write programs that invoke operations defined by abstract base classes. This programming model improves modularity and reuse (since programs rely upon behavior rather than representations) and it improves extensibility (since the behavior of an invocation is determined by a parameterized class at link-time or a subclass at run-time).

Experience has shown, however, that OOP language features alone are no panacea for developing high-quality software. Despite the claims of some vendors and pundits, OOP languages are not a silver bullet that will slay all the dragons of software complexity, instantly transform inexperienced programmers into superdesigners, or eliminate the need for creativity, knowledge, and diligence by developers.

A more realistic view is that OOP language features provide a core set of building-block mechanisms. These mechanisms have proved over time to alleviate unnecessary programming complexity when used correctly. To consistently improve software quality, however, these mechanisms must be shaped by an appropriate set of usage and style policies adopted by programmers. The chapters in this section focus on design patterns that help programmers avoid certain pitfalls associated with common OOP language mechanisms such as classes, objects, inheritance, and dynamic binding.

In Chapter 25, Bobby Woolf focuses on the ValueModel framework from VisualWorks, which is a Smalltalk development environment. A ValueModel is a flexible notification mechanism that implements a variant of the Observer pattern described by Gamma et al. The ValueModel framework notifies a set of observing objects that the value of an object under observation has changed. This mechanism leads to style of programming where independently developed software components are connected without tightly coupling their behavior or state. Although this is a very powerful form of object collaboration, learning how to program this model correctly can be challenging. Therefore, Bobby adopts the pattern form to state and answer a wide range of questions regarding the effective use of ValueModels. For example, multiple observers may want to view a shared ValueModel from different perspectives with respect to the value's type. Bobby's recommendation is to use a TypeConverter object to transform the value into the appropriate type expected by its observer. He also presents several style guidelines and conventions for improving the type-safety of Smalltalk programs.

Panu Viljamaa, in Chapter 26, discusses a design pattern that works around the static nature of inheritance in many object-oriented programming languages such as C++, Smalltalk, and Eiffel. These languages don't allow an object to replace the class of any ancestor (base classes). Although this restriction is rarely a showstopper, certain applications and programming styles may be simplified by dynamically changing the behavior of a base class by altering where a given method is inherited from. For example, an object-oriented implementation of a communication protocol (such as TCP or SPX) may be simplified if the object representing each connection could change its class to reflect the current state of the protocol (e.g., idle, connecting, established, disconnecting). Thus, the object's response to the arrival of packets would vary according to the current class of the object. This highly dynamic form of object collaboration is known as "delegation." Panu's pattern describes how to achieve various forms of delegation in languages whose static inheritance mechanisms don't support the feature directly.

In "Reusability Through Self-Encapsulation" (Chapter 27), Ken Auer presents a set of guidelines to ensure that subclasses don't subvert inheritance as a vehicle for reuse. He presents a pattern language that preserves class encapsulation across inheritance boundaries. This is important in programming languages (such as C++ and Smalltalk) that allow subclasses to access the state of their ancestor base classes directly. Taking advantage of this feature causes subclasses and base classes to become tightly coupled, however. Thus, extensibility and reusability will suffer if programmers don't use this feature sparingly. Ken's solution is to define the interaction between subclasses and a base class in terms of their abstract behavior, rather than by directly sharing state. He recommends that subclasses call base class methods, rather than accessing the data directly. Ken describes several benefits from this technique, such as simplifying program design, reducing the number of instance variables, and minimizing the amount of code to maintain. Fortunately, many programming language implementations now agressively optimize method calls from subclasses to superclasses (e.g., by using inlining), so the extra degree of abstraction provided by Ken's pattern doesn't result in significant performance overhead.

Most of the design patterns in this book transcend the programming languages that used to exemplify them. For instance, all three of the design patterns in this section are presented by authors with deep Smalltalk expertise. However, the object usage and style issues are equally applicable to many other languages that provide classes, inheritance, and dynamic binding.

In general, the growing interest in design patterns in the object-oriented community at large signals a healthy shift in focus away from "programming language–centric" views of the object paradigm. This represents a major step forward since it enables experienced developers from different language communities (such as Smalltalk, C++, and Eiffel) to share design expertise of mutual interest. Furthermore, the emphasis on patterns is helping rechannel the prevailing preoccupation with objects. This allows opportunities for the good practices of past programming paradigms to shine through. During the PLoP conference, many participants remarked how refreshing it was to attend an object-oriented event where the lions and lambs of various OOP language communities could collaborate without being distracted by the usual internecine language wars.

Understanding and Using the ValueModel Framework in VisualWorks Smalltalk

25

Bobby Woolf

To answer this question:	Read this section:
How can one object retrieve and change a collaborator object in a uniform way, regardless of what larger object the collaborator may be a part of?	1.1 Use a ValueModel to Generalize an Object's Aspect
How can two objects share a common value in such a way that (1) both can access and change it, and (2) whenever one object changes it, the other will be notified automatically?	1.2 Use a ValueModel to Share a Value
How can an object that is using the value contained in a ValueModel be notified whenever the value changes?	2.1 Use onChangeSend:to: to Register Interests on a Value
What if the update that is performed when a change occurs is so simple that a separate <something>Changed method seems unnecessary?	2.2 Use ValueModel Chains Instead of onChangeSend:to:

Copyright © 1994 Bobby Woolf and Knowledge Systems Corporation. All Rights Reserved.

To answer this question:	Read this section:
When using `ValueModels`, how does the programmer know when to use `value` and `value:`?	2.3 Encapsulate Senders of `value` and `value:`
How can multiple objects that need to share the same value be assured of sharing a single `ValueModel`?	2.4 Ensure That All Objects Sharing a Value Use the Same `ValueModel`
When an object gets a value from a `ValueModel`, how does it know the type of object it will receive?	2.5 Maintain Consistent `ValueModel` Value Types
How can I wrap `ValueModel` behavior around the objects in my instance variables?	3.1 Use a `ValueHolder` to Hold a Stand-Alone Object
How can I wrap `ValueModel` behavior around my retrieval of an aspect of another model?	3.2 Use an `AspectAdaptor` to Hold an Aspect of an Object
My view has a number of values. How can I allow the user to change all of them without changing them in the application model, and then accept or cancel all the changes at one time?	3.3 Use a `BufferedValueHolder` to Delay the Commit of a New Value
How can I easily convert a real-world quantity to a percentage such that whenever the quantity changes, the percentage is automatically recalculated?	3.4 Use a `RangeAdaptor` to Channel a Number's Range
How can I wrap `ValueModel` behavior around a particular element in a collection?	3.5 Use an `IndexedAdaptor` to Hold a Single Index in a Collection
How can I wrap `ValueModel` behavior around a particular instance variable in an object without changing what kind of object an instance variable holds?	3.6 Use a `SlotAdaptor` to Hold a Single Instance Variable
How can I wrap `ValueModel` behavior around an arbitrary portion of an object?	3.7 Use a `PluggableAdaptor` to Hold Some Part of an Object

To answer this question:	Read this section:
Two objects wish to share a value, but one dependent wants it expressed as one type and the other expects another type. How can the value appear as the appropriate type of object for each dependent?	3.8 Use a `TypeConverter` to Convert a Value between Types
What object should I use to keep track of how much a point's position on a grid has changed?	3.9 Use a `ScrollValueHolder` to Hold a Position in n-Dimensional Space
How can I set up a list so that it can tell me which item is currently being used?	3.10 Use a `SelectionInList` to Hold a List and Its Selection

INTRODUCTION

In Objectworks 4.1, ParcPlace introduced the `ValueModel` framework. Back then it only consisted of two concrete classes. The Objectworks code didn't use this framework very much, so neither did most application developers. However, this framework was greatly enhanced to help form the foundation of ParcPlace's next release, VisualWorks 1.0. This version of Smalltalk expanded the framework to contain numerous concrete subclasses and associated classes.

This document will answer these questions:

- What is the `ValueModel` framework?
- Why was this framework developed?
- How should developers use this framework?
- How, specifically, should developers use the framework's concrete classes?

VisualWorks uses this framework to convert users' painted views into application models containing executable code. The framework is used extensively by the generated code in application models and the code developers write to enhance their application models.

However, the framework does more than just enable VisualWorks to automatically generate application model code. It significantly enhances the dependency framework, and it helps developers separate application models and domain models into distinct objects. In fact, although VisualWorks' code generators use `ValueModels` exclusively in `ApplicationModels`, they may be even more useful when employed in domain models.

This paper explains what `ValueModels` are, why they were developed, and how to use them. You, the reader, are expected to be familiar with ParcPlace Smalltalk (either Objectworks 4.x or VisualWorks) as well as basic Smalltalk syntax and object-oriented practices. You should have a basic understanding of the dependency framework whereby an object notifies its dependents of a change by sending itself `changed...`, which causes each dependent to receive `update:....` You should have used the UI Painter facility in VisualWorks to create your own subclass of `ApplicationModel` and design a view for it.

In general, though, intimate knowledge of Smalltalk is not required to understand these guidelines. Although they document the `ValueModel` framework in VisualWorks, the concepts that motivate the framework's use are not VisualWorks-specific or even Smalltalk-specific (although they may be specific to object-oriented programming). Thus, even though these guidelines are designed primarily for VisualWorks programmers, other developers using object-oriented techniques can benefit from them as well.

1. WHAT IS A VALUEMODEL?

"ValueModel" is the name of a framework in VisualWorks. It is implemented by the `ValueModel` hierarchy, but it also has some related classes outside that hierarchy, like `SelectionInList` and `DependencyTransformer`. `ValueModel` itself is an abstract class; you actually use instances of `ValueModel`'s concrete subclasses.

A `ValueModel` has two main characteristics:

- Its aspect is always `value`. This means that its getter message, setter message, and update aspect are `value`, `value:`, and `#value`, respectively.
- It informs its dependents whenever its value changes. It has a standard mechanism for registering interest in the value, and those objects that have done so will be notified in a standard way.

This provides a simple, generic interface between any object (a value) and a value-based object (such as a visual widget that displays a single value). The value and the value-based object do not have to be customized for each other; the `ValueModel` does this by connecting the two and translating the interactions between them as necessary. Thus the value-based object neither knows nor cares where the value comes from or how to access it. The object is able to simply send `value` to its `ValueModel`, which in turn does whatever is necessary to obtain the value, and then returns it.

If the value changes, the model notifies the widget. This is the case even when multiple widgets share the same value; when one widget changes the value, it does not have to perform any notification, because the `ValueModel` does so. In this way, the widget simply uses the value as it sees fit, and it does not have to worry about what the consequences might be to anyone else who might also be using the value.

For additional information about the `ValueModel` framework and how to use it, see ParcPlace's discussion [Par93].

Following are some guidelines that describe what `ValueModels` are and what they do.

1.1 Use a ValueModel to Generalize an Object's Aspect

Problem How can one object retrieve and change a collaborator object in a uniform way, regardless of what larger object the collaborator may be a part of?

Context The object will treat its collaborator as a single value. It will need to be able to retrieve this value and change its setting by storing a new value. Since the value may change, the object will need to be notified when the value changes.

The object will need to send messages to retrieve and set the value. The object's design can be simplified if these messages are always the same. It will also need to listen for notification that the value has changed to a new object. Again, if this notification is always the same, the object's design can be simplified.

The value may be stored in several different ways: it may be a stand-alone object; it may be a part of a larger object; it might not be an object at all, but rather one that can be generated from others whenever it is needed. If these specifics of how the value is stored can be hidden from the object using it, that object's design can be simplified.

Behavior will be needed that allows a value to be accessed using standard messages. More will be needed to access it, depending on how it is stored. This behavior should be implemented in a way that is as reusable as possible. Then the code that handles these issues for one value can be used with all values that have similar circumstances.

Solution Use a `ValueModel` to store the value. `ValueModel` is an abstract class, so you'll actually use an instance of one of `ValueModel`'s concrete subclasses.

Which subclass you'll use will depend on a couple of factors: How is the value stored in the system? How does it need to be retrieved from the system? What conversion needs to be performed on the object during the retrieval process? (See Section 3.)

A ValueModel has the aspect value. This means that to retrieve the value, the getter message is value; to change the value, the setter message is value:; and to listen for updates when the value changes, the update aspect is #value.

Once a ValueModel is established on a value, you don't need to know where the value comes from, what its real name or aspect is, or what other objects might be using it. The ValueModel takes care of these details. You automatically know how to retrieve it and change it using the standard value aspect. In this way you always know how to use the value and you don't need to be concerned about the details.

Examples   **Example 1** Let's say you want to implement a time widget that displays a clock face on a view. (Maybe you want to implement two, analog and digital.) Its state will be based on an instance of Time.

Where might this instance of Time come from? Someone might create one in a workspace and send it displayAsClock. It might be one-half of a DateTime object or an aspect of a LogEvent object. It might sit in a particular place in memory, the result of a primitive that constantly reads the system clock and replaces the Time instance whenever the clock changes. As you can see, you don't know where it might be coming from.

And you shouldn't know where it's coming from. Even if you're implementing the clock view for one particular model, you should generalize your implementation to fit any Time instance that comes along. So you should design it to access its Time object via a ValueModel. That means that it uses value to get the Time from its view's model, value: to set it, and reperforms the get when it receives a #value change notification.

Which concrete subclass of ValueModel you use will depend, case by case, on how the Time is stored in the system. With the appropriate kind of ValueModel, your clock widget will work with any model that contains a Time, including a stand-alone instance of Time itself.

Example 2 Most of the widgets that use ValueModels are visual widgets. For an example of a model widget, see SelectionInList (see also Section 3.10).

Whereas a ValueModel has one aspect, value, SelectionInList has three: list, selectionIndex, and selection. The first two are implemented "physically" through the instance variables listHolder and `selectionIndexHolder`; the third is implemented "logically" in terms of the first two. The two instance variables are (you guessed it) `ValueModels` (actually `ValueHolders`; see Section 3.1).

1.2 Use a ValueModel to Share a Value

Problem   How can two objects share a common value in such a way that (1) both can access and change it, and (2) whenever one object changes it, the other is notified automatically?

Context   The change/update mechanism in VisualWorks enables an object to notify its dependents when its internal state changes. This mechanism does not work when the object is replaced with an entirely new object, however; all of the dependents are still attached to the old object. The dependents and the old object are all unaware that the old object has been replaced with a new one.

The behavior performing the swap could use the message `become:` to change all pointers to the old object so that they point to the new one. However, `become:` is inefficient, makes code difficult to maintain, can cause unwanted side effects, and doesn't notify dependents. It will confuse objects that want to point to the old object even if it is replaced with a new one, and the dependents will not be notified that the replacement has been made.

For a set of objects sharing a value to all automatically share a replacement value, their pointers require a level of indirection. Instead of pointing directly to the shared value, they should point to an object that will not be replaced and which in turn points to the shared value. This intermediary object will be a container that holds the shared value.

Because the objects sharing the value will have to access it through the container, the container will know when the value has been replaced. Thus the container can notify the dependents whenever the value is replaced.

Solution   When two objects need to share a common object, they should place that object in a shared `ValueModel`. They can then register their interests on the value, and the `ValueModel` will notify them when the value changes (see Section 2.1). To manipulate the value they go through the `ValueModel` (see Section 1.1), allowing it to monitor their actions. It will execute overhead behavior as necessary (such as translating the value or notifying dependents of a change).

Example   Let's say two application models need to use the same value in a domain model. Either application model might change the value, in which case the other needs to be informed so that it can update itself accordingly.

A simple way to accomplish this is for the domain model to store the value in a `ValueModel`. Then each application model can latch on to the `ValueModel` and access the value by sending the model `value`. Each one can change the value by sending the model `value:`. Of course, when one object changes the value, the other needs to know about it, so both will register their interest with the `ValueModel` (see Section 2.1). This way, when the value changes, the application models will be notified. In fact, the object changing the value may not be one of the application models. The domain model may decide to change its internal state, and in doing so change the value. Even in this case, all of the value's dependents (who registered themselves as such), including the two application models, will be notified.

2. HOW TO USE VALUEMODELS

A `ValueModel` is a powerful mechanism which will abstract an object's aspect and define its dependents. However, given that `ValueModels` provide this behavior, how should programmers design them into their code to implement useful system functionality?

`ValueModels` also introduce a layer of indirection that can quickly complicate the model's use of its aspects and obscure the interface protocol for the collaborators that use those aspects. When a programmer first starts to use `ValueModels`, he or she can easily become confused about when to send `value` or `value:` to an object. Because of this confusion, he or she will have difficulty getting otherwise simple code to work. Once his or her code does work, it often contains unneeded senders of `value` and `value:`; these can lead to more subtle problems.

This section contains guidelines and tips on how to write code that uses `ValueModels`. A programmer does not have to follow these guidelines to write code successfully, but they will often make the code simpler and better encapsulated. This will be an especially big help to someone trying to learn how to use `ValueModels`.

Here are some guidelines that describe how to use `ValueModel`.

2.1 Use onChangeSend:to: to Register Interests on a Value

Problem   How can an object that is using the value contained in a `ValueModel` be notified whenever the value changes?

Context   When multiple objects share a value, they should share a single `ValueModel` wrapped around that value (see Section 1.2). When the `ValueModel` changes the value, it will notify its dependents.

To be notified, each dependent must register its interest in this value. This will make it a logical dependent of the value (which is implemented as a physical dependent of the `ValueModel`).

Since the only update aspect a `ValueModel` ever sends is #value, this is the only one the dependents must listen for.

It is insufficient for a dependent to simply listen for notification of a change. When it receives such notification, it must perform actions to respond to the change. To encapsulate this series of actions and give it a name, the actions should be collected together into a method (which in turn may use other methods). By collecting this series of actions into a method, the series can be reused whenever it is needed, even if the need is not caused by a change notification. For example, a newly created object might perform these actions to initialize itself, and then reperform them whenever it receives a change notification.

When an object's design dictates that it will be a dependent of a value, the code to implement that assumption should be encapsulated inside the object.

When an object is no longer being used, it should release its dependencies so that it will no longer receive notification of changes.

Solution   To register your interest in a `ValueModel`'s value, send the `ValueModel`

```
aValueModel onChangeSend: aSelector to: aDependent
```

in which `aSelector` is the name of the method you want run when the value changes, and `aDependent` is the object that contains the method (usually yourself).

The `onChangeSend:to:` message should be sent by the `initialize` method of the dependent object; this means that the `to:` parameter will be `self`. By establishing the dependency during initialization, this ensures that it will be established only once and that it will be established before the object is used.

The dependent object should also implement `release` to release its dependencies by sending

```
aValueModel retractInterestsFor: aDependent
```

to the `ValueModel`. In this way, for each sender of `onChangeSend:to:` in `initialize`, there will be a corresponding sender of `retractInter-estsFor:` in `release`.

Note: In practice, sending `retractInterestsFor:` when the dependent is released is not always necessary. When the `ValueModel`'s container is released and garbage collected at the same time as the dependent, it is irrelevant whether or not their dependency is disconnected. However, in many cases the dependent is released while the ValueModel's container remains in use. In such cases, to keep the obsolete dependent from receiving updates from the ValueModel, the dependent should release its dependency as part of its releasing itself. Thus it's safest to always release the dependency, even though this sometimes is not necessary.

Examples   **Example 1** An application model needs to know when the value in the domain model changes. Luckily the domain model stores the value in a ValueModel so that the application model can easily register its interest in the value and receive notification when the value changes. The application model has a method, domainValueChanged, that it wants to run whenever the value in the domain model changes. Here's the code in the application model to do this:

```
initialize
    . . .
    self domainModel sharedAspectHolder
        onChangeSend: #domainValueChanged
        to: self.
    . . .


domainValueChanged
    "The domain model changed; update the app model"
    self sharedAspect: self domainModel sharedAspect

release
    . . .
    self domainModel sharedAspectHolder
        retractInterestsFor: self.
    . . .
```

Note: In the above examples, domainModel is a method that returns the application model's domain model, sharedAspectHolder returns the ValueModel holding the value of interest (see Section 2.3), and domainValueChanged performs the steps in the application model that are necessary when the value changes. In real code, these methods would have more descriptive names.

Example 2 A list of Things is being displayed in my view, and I want selectedThingChanged run whenever the selection in the list changes. Here's the code (see also Section 3.10):

- **initialize:** self thingsSelectionInList selectionIndex-Holder onChangeSend: #selectedThingChanged to: self

- **selectedThingChanged:** `self selectedThing: self thingsSelectionInList selection`
- **release:** `self thingsSelectionInList selectionIndexHolder retractInterestsFor: self`

2.2 Use ValueModel Chains Instead of onChangeSend:to:

Problem   What if the update performed when a change occurs is so simple that a separate `<something>Changed` method seems unnecessary?

Context   If an object is to understand a particular message, it must implement or inherit the corresponding method. Each such method adds to the object's bulk and the amount of code a developer must learn to maintain the object. Thus an object should not contain methods it does not need.

Each time a dependent registers its interest on a value using `onChangeSend:to:` (see Section 2.1), it must specify a `<something>Changed` message in itself to be sent. Thus the dependent must implement or inherit a method for this message.

Complex methods are necessary; they are how objects implement their behavior. But simple `<something>Changed` methods that do nothing more than re-fetch the changed value do not significantly enhance the overall behavior provided by the object.

An object designed to automatically re-fetch a value whenever it changes would encapsulate this functionality. It would automatically initialize its value in the dependent object, then update it when the value in the parent changes. This behavior would be easy to reuse, and its role would be easily recognizable, simplifying maintenance.

Solution   Rather than implementing an extremely simple `<something>Changed` method in the dependent to be sent by `onChangeSend:to:`, eliminate that extra step by using a `ValueModel` instead. This will connect the parent and dependent models, using two `ValueModels`. The parent object will contain the first `ValueModel`; that `ValueModel` will be the subject of the second, which will in turn be contained by the dependent object. Whenever the value in the parent changes, the first notifies its dependents, which causes the second to update its value in the dependent.

Examples   **Example 1** A domain model has an aspect `address`. The application model needs to hold this address so that it can display it in its view. The domain model should store its address in a value holder (see Section 3.1) so that the application model can register its interest on the value by sending the `ValueHolder onChangeSend: #addressChanged to: self` (see Section 1.2). The `addressChanged` method would simply read the new value from the `ValueHolder` and store it into the application model `self address: self domainModel address`.

However, the `addressChanged` method is so simple it's not even necessary. Instead, make a variable in the application model that stores the value in an `AspectAdaptor` (see Section 3.2). The `AspectAdaptor`'s subject channel is the address `ValueModel` in the domain model, and its aspect is `value`. This way, whenever the address value in the domain model changes, its `ValueHolder` will issue an update. This will trigger the `AspectAdaptor` to issue an update, which will cause its dependents (such as the field subview that displays the address) to update. All of this is done as a chain of events, without you needing to write any further code (such as `addressChanged`).

Note: You could almost have the instance variable in the domain model and the one in the application model contain the same `ValueHolder`. Unfortunately this typically doesn't work, because VisualWorks feels compelled to insert a `TypeConverter` (see Section 3.8) between the domain model's `Value-Holder` and the application model. It does this because the `ValueHolder` can hold any object, but the application model requires a specific type, such as a string or a number. Thus the `TypeConverter` is needed to guard against the `ValueHolder` containing `nil`, which will be converted to the empty string or zero. Having both models share the same `ValueModel` might seem to be the simplest solution, since it uses only one `ValueModel` instead of two. However, VisualWorks will insert one anyway, so you get two `ValueModels` even if you only specify one. Since an `AspectAdaptor` is a little more efficient than a `TypeConverter`, you might as well specify which type of `ValueModel` to use.

Example 2   The application model contains a list and a field that should display the current selection in the list. You could use a `SelectionInList`, and send its `selectionIndexHolder onChangeSend: #selectionChanged to: self`, where `selectionChanged` reads the selection and stores that in the field's `ValueModel` (typically a `ValueHolder`).

There is, however, a simpler way that avoids implementing the `selectionChanged` method. Make the field's `ValueModel` a `PluggableAdaptor`, like this:

```
field :=
    (PluggableAdaptor on: listSelectionInList)
        getBlock: [ :m | m selection]
        putBlock: [ :m :v | m selection: v]
        updateBlock: [ :m :a :p | a ==
                    #selectionIndex].
```

This way, whenever the selection changes, the `PluggableAdaptor` will catch the update and update the field with the new value (see Section 3.7).

Note: The field should really just use an `AspectAdaptor` whose aspect is `selection` (see Section 3.2). However, when a `SelectionInList`'s selection changes, it issues the update aspect `#selectionIndex`, not `#selection`. Since an `AspectAdaptor`'s update aspect must be the same as its get selector, you have to use a `PluggableAdaptor`, because it allows you to specify them separately. This would no longer be necessary if `SelectionInList` were fixed to issue both `#selection` and `#selectionIndex` update aspects whenever the selection or the selection index changes.

Example 3 Use `AspectAdaptors` (see Section 3.2) on a "selection channel" to allow the selection of an object and to display its aspects. In this technique, a `ValueModel` is set up to hold the current selection. If this selection is made via a `SelectionInList`, use the technique described above to attach the `ValueModel` to the `SelectionInList`. This `ValueModel` that holds the selection is called a *selection channel*. With the selection channel established, attach `AspectAdaptors` (or other `ValueModels`) to it to display the object's aspects (or other values).

With this arrangement, whenever the selection changes, the selection channel's value changes, which triggers the `AspectAdaptors`. They in turn reread their values and update their dependents, which redisplay or otherwise update themselves.

This selection channel technique is well documented by ParcPlace [Par93].

2.3 Encapsulate Senders of value and value:

Problem When using `ValueModels`, how does the programmer know when to use `value` and `value:`?

Context To use a variable's value, a programmer must know what type of object the value is. This way he or she knows what protocols the value supports and thus what messages it will understand. (For more information about enforcing an object's type in Smalltalk, see [Woo01].)

When a message returns a value (besides `self`), the message name should describe or suggest the value returned.

When using `ValueModels`, the programmer must know which messages return the `ValueModels` and which return the values themselves. Usually the sender will be interested in a value, not the `ValueModel` that contains it.

An object's accessing protocol should simply provide its aspects while hiding how those aspects are implemented. This will better encapsulate the object and make it simpler to maintain. (For more information about interface design, see [Aue95].)

Solution   Implement separate messages for accessing an object's aspects (values) versus accessing the ValueModels that contain those aspects.

If a model has an aspect called aspect that is being stored in a ValueModel that will be held in an instance variable, name the instance variable aspectHolder. Initialize the instance variable in the initialize method to be the necessary kind of ValueModel. Create a getter for it that is named after the instance variable (aspectHolder), but do not implement a setter for it (see Section 2.4). Also implement a pair of getter/setter methods for the values — aspect and aspect: — that use the aspectHolder method.

Use the message aspectHolder when you need the ValueModel (to send onChangeSend:to: to it, for example; see Section 2.1). Otherwise, use aspect and aspect: to get and set the value; they encapsulate the object that implements them, simplify its accessing protocol, and hide exactly how the value is stored.

Examples   **Example 1** A model has the aspect address, which the model stores in an instance variable. You need to be able to update other values when the address changes, so you'll store the address in a ValueModel and the other values will register their interests on it using onChangeSend:to:. You want to avoid using senders of value and value: in your code.

Name the instance variable addressHolder and initialize it in initialize to be an appropriate kind of ValueModel. Implement addressHolder to return the instance variable's value, but don't implement addressHolder:. Implement address as ^ self addressHolder value and address: as self addressHolder value: newAddress.

Now, to get and set the address, use the messages address and address:. To be notified when the address changes, send onChangeSend:to: to the result of the message addressHolder.

Example 2 The model in Example 1 is an ApplicationModel; the aspect address is being set via the Properties Tool or Multi Tool.

Specify the aspect as addressHolder (to get VisualWorks to give the instance variable the name you want). When you install and define the model, it will create the instance variable addressHolder and implement the method addressHolder for you (it will not implement addressHolder:, which is fine). Now implement address and address: as directed above.

Example 3 If the instance variable is to hold a `SelectionInList` (not a `ValueModel`), don't call it `<list>Holder`, because that's misleading. A variable named `<aspect>Holder` should understand the `value` aspect, but a `SelectionInList` will not. Instead, name the variable `<aspect>SelectionInList` or `<aspect>SIL`, which indicates that it understands the aspects `list` and `selection`.

2.4 Ensure That All Objects Sharing a Value Use the Same ValueModel

Problem   How can multiple objects that need to share the same value be assured of sharing a single `ValueModel`?

Context   When two objects need to share the same object, they should share a single `ValueModel` wrapped around that object (see Section 1.2).

   The shared `ValueModel` will have to be stored in a commonly accessible place; usually one of the objects will store the `ValueModel` and make it accessible to the others.

   If the ValueModel stored in this common place is shared by a couple of objects and then changed to contain a different ValueModel instance, not all of the objects will be sharing the same ValueModel. To make sure they are all sharing the same ValueModel instance, the ValueModel should be set once and then never changed.

Solution   When an instance variable holds a `ValueModel`, create a getter method for it, but not a setter method, and initialize it in the `initialize` method. This way it gets set once and will never get reset.

   This technique will be sufficient for typical uses. There are some fairly advanced uses of `ValueModel`s, however, for which a method to set the `ValueModel` externally is necessary.

Examples   See the examples in Section 2.3.

2.5 Maintain Consistent ValueModel Value Types

Problem   When an object gets a value from a `ValueModel`, how does it know the type of object it will receive?

Context   ValueModel is a container object. The object it contains, its value, can be any type of Object. ValueModel is implemented to work with any type of Object as its value.

Collaborators using an object interact with it through one or more behavior protocols. Thus the object must be able to perform the protocols. In implementation terms this means that the object must understand the messages being sent to it, which are the messages in those protocols.

An object's type is defined by the protocols it is able to perform. The more specialized an object's behavior, the more specialized some of its protocols. Collaborators will interact with specialized objects using specialized protocols that most objects don't perform.

Although a ValueModel can hold any type of object as its value, the collaborators using that value may use a protocol that not all objects perform. Thus the value in a ValueModel cannot be just any type of object, it must be of a type that supports the protocol its collaborators will use. If its collaborators use several protocols, the value must be of a type that supports all of them.

Solution   When defining a variable's type as ValueModel, also specify the ValueModel's value's type. Declare and initialize the ValueModel with a valid value. When changing the ValueModel's value, ensure that the new value is of the specified type. (See [Woo01].)

When implementing code, you must make sure that the object used as an argument to value: is of the specified type. This way, when other objects retrieve the value, they can assume its type is correct and that it will support the protocols they will use.

Example   Let's say a Person domain object contains an age aspect which must be a nonnegative integer. The age aspect is stored in a ValueHolder to simplify its use.

These code segments represent valid uses of age that will keep its type, Integer, consistent:

- **definition comment in Person:** <ValueModel on: Integer>
- **Person>>initialize:** ageHolder := ValueHolder on: 0 (0 is an integer)
- **Person>>age::** newAge>= 0 ifTrue: [self ageHolder value: newAge] (enforces that age is positive)
- self age: 21 (21 is an Integer)
- self age + 1 (Integers understand +)
- self age: self age // 2 (// returns an Integer)

These code segments show invalid uses of age because they do not preserve the Integer type specification:

- **definition comment in Person:** <ValueModel on: Integer> (same as above, this is OK)

- **Person>>initialize:** ageHolder := ValueHolder on: 0.0 (0.0 is not an Integer)

- **Person>>age::** self ageHolder value: newAge (this is OK, but assumes that newAge is valid)

- self age: 5.5 (5.5 is not an Integer)

- self age tooYoung ifTrue: [...] (Integers do not understand tooYoung)

- self age: self age //2 (// does always return an Integer)

Be careful to write code like the first set, not the second, in order to keep a variable's type consistent.

3. TYPES OF VALUEMODELS

Typically, discussions about the ValueModel framework center around the class ValueModel, because it is the abstract class that defines the basic behavior and interface of all ValueModels. It is, however, an abstract class; there are no instances of ValueModel to use. A programmer must actually use instances of ValueModel's subclasses.

In VisualWorks 1.0, the ValueModel hierarchy contains a number of concrete subclasses. Their front end is always the same: a single aspect named value that remembers the interests registered on that value. What distinguishes them is their back ends: how they attach to other models, how they hold and retrieve their values, and how they convert and/or translate their values. By knowing what each one does, a programmer can choose which one to use for the job at hand.

Here are some guidelines that describe how to use the different types of ValueModels and their associated classes.

3.1 Use a ValueHolder to Hold a Stand-Alone Object

Problem   How can I wrap ValueModel behavior around the objects in my instance variables?

Context   `ValueModel` behavior is often desirable (see Section 1).

The `ValueModel` must store the object it is holding, because there are no other objects available to do so. The `ValueModel` does not need to perform any sort of conversion or translation on the value; it should just return the value as is.

Solution   Use a `ValueHolder`, the simplest and most commonly used type of `ValueModel`. It will wrap the object within itself, thus giving the object `ValueModel` behavior. Store the `ValueHolder` in the instance variable.

Example   A domain model has multiple aspects; the value of each of these is stored in an instance variable. Multiple `ApplicationModels` may need to share each of these values.

Make each instance variable a `ValueHolder` to store the aspect's value. This will facilitate abstracting the value's aspect and make it easy to register interest on the value, without introducing any unnecessary overhead. A simple way to wrap a `ValueHolder` around a value is to send the value `asValue` (although the message `asValueModel` would probably be more intuitive). So, to set up a domain model with a number of aspects in `ValueHolders` (see Section 2), your `initialize` method will look like this:

```
initialize
    . . .
    aspect1Holder :=
        self aspect1DefaultValue asValue.
    aspect2Holder :=
        self aspect2DefaultValue asValue.
    <etc.>
    . . .
```

Then it will need getters for the aspect holders and getters and setters for the aspect values.

3.2 Use an AspectAdaptor to Hold an Aspect of an Object

Problem   How can I wrap `ValueModel` behavior around my retrieval of an aspect of another model?

Context   `ValueModel` behavior is often desirable (see Section 1).

The `ValueModel` does not need to actually store the value, because it is already being stored by another model. When the value of that model's aspect changes (and the model notifies its dependents), the `ValueModel` should update its value. If the model does not notify its dependents when

Aspect Name	Getter name	Setter Name	Update Aspect
name	name	name:	#name
address	getAddress	setAddress:	#getAddress

TABLE 1   Specifics for Two Example Aspects

its aspect's value changes, its dependents (including your `ValueModel`) won't get updated.

The `ValueModel` does not need to perform any sort of conversion or translation on the value; it should just return the value as is.

Solution   Use an `AspectAdaptor`. These are popular because models with simple aspects are popular. Unlike a `ValueHolder` (see Section 3.1), the object itself won't be wrapped with `ValueModel` behavior. But the process of retrieving and storing the object as an aspect of its container model will be wrapped as a `ValueModel`. This is how this kind of `ValueModel` is able to monitor the container model for changes in the aspect.

Example   A domain model has multiple aspects; the value of each of these is stored in an instance variable. The developer who implemented the domain model used simple aspects to store and retrieve the values, but he didn't use `ValueModels` to make registering dependencies easy. Your `Application-Model` needs to use some of these aspects.

Your `ApplicationModel` will need an `AspectAdaptor` for each aspect it wishes to share with the domain model. Let's say the specifics in Table 1 are for two of the aspects (from an article by ParcPlace [Par93]):

Note: The update aspect must always be the same as the getter name. If the aspect you're adapting does not follow this convention, use a `PluggableAdaptor` (see Section 3.7).

The `initialize` code to set up these two adaptors would be

```
initialize
    nameHolder :=
            (AspectAdaptor
              subject: domainModel sendsUpdates: true)
                forAspect: #name.
    addressHolder :=
            (AspectAdaptor
                   subject: domainModel sendsUpdates: true)
            accessWith: #getAddress
            assignWith: #setAddress.
```

Then it will need getters for the aspect holders and getters and setters for the aspect values.

3.3 Use a BufferedValueHolder to Delay the Commit of a New Value

Problem   My view has a number of values. How can I allow the user to change all of them without changing them in the `ApplicationModel`, and then accept or cancel all of the changes at one time?

Context   This mechanism should be a `ValueModel` so that it will have the generic aspect `value`. That way it can be used to store any aspect necessary (see Section 1.1). It should get its value from another `ValueModel`, so that it can retrieve its value generically.

This mechanism will need a trigger with three positions: commit, neutral, and flush. Nothing happens to the values in the `ApplicationModel` until the trigger flips out of neutral. If multiple fields are to trigger simultaneously, their `ValueModels` will need to share a single trigger.

Solution   Use a `BufferedValueHolder` as a layer of separation between the model and the `ValueModel` for a field. A regular `ValueModel` will immediately store a new value in the model (and notify dependents accordingly). However, `ValueModel` stored inside a `BufferedValueHolder` will suspend the new value until you tell it to commit it to the model.

Example   Let's say an `ApplicationModel` has three fields and a pair of *accept/cancel* buttons. You want to allow the user to edit the fields but not commit the edits to the model until the user presses *accept*. If he or she presses *cancel*, the edits should be discarded and the fields should display the original values from the model.

To implement this behavior, use two layers of `ValueModels` instead of just one. The top layer will consist of unbuffered `ValueModels` — like `ValueHolder`, `AspectAdaptor`, `PluggableAdaptor`, and so on — depending on how they must retrieve and translate their values. The bottom layer, between the `ValueModels` and the `ApplicationModel`, consists of `BufferedValueHolders`, one for each `ValueModel` in the top layer.

Connect the `BufferedValueHolders` together with a single trigger, a `ValueModel` whose value is `Boolean` or `nil`. As long as the trigger is `nil`, nothing happens. If the trigger changes its state to `true`, the `BufferedValueHolders` commit their values; if it changes to `false`, they discard their values and reset to the original values from the `ValueModels`. Thus the *accept* button should set the trigger to `true`, and *cancel* should set it to `false`.

It is conceivable that one view could contain multiple groups of `BufferedValueHolders`, each group sharing its own trigger. This would allow each group to be committed individually.

3.4 Use a RangeAdaptor to Channel a Number's Range

Problem   How can I easily convert a real-world quantity to a percentage such that whenever the quantity changes, the percentage is automatically recalculated?

Context   A quantity is often more easily understood by expressing it as a percentage (a number between 0 and 100 percent). A percentage quantity can be easily displayed in intuitive ways: a dial, a needle on a gauge, and the like. A group of percentage quantities can be displayed together as a bar graph, a pie chart, and so on. When a quantity is confined to a range, it can be easily converted into a percentage quantity.

The object holding a percentage quantity should be a `ValueModel` so that it can be used to store any aspect necessary and so the quantity can be easily shared (see Section 1).

The getter and setter `value` and `value:` should return a percentage. If the sender wants the original number within a range, it'll access the value directly.

Solution   Use a `RangeAdaptor`, a `ValueModel` that converts a number in a specified range into a percentage quantity. It sits between the `ValueModel` holding the value within the range and the model wanting a percentage quantity. The percentage quantity will be expressed as a number between 0 and 1.

Example   Slider visual widgets use a `RangeAdaptor` to convert a number in a specified range into a set range, 0 to 1. The `RangeAdaptor` must know the minimum and maximum values in the range, and it must know the step size to use when converting the percentage back into a number in the range. Because a `RangeAdaptor` is a `ValueModel`, when the number in the range changes, the `RangeAdaptor` recalculates the percentage and notifies its dependents automatically.

3.5 Use an IndexedAdaptor to Hold a Single Index in a Collection

Problem   How can I wrap `ValueModel` behavior around a particular element in a collection?

Context   `ValueModel` behavior is often desirable (see Section 1).

The `ValueModel` does not need to actually store the value, because it is already being stored by the collection. To hide the fact that this object is stored in a collection, use a `ValueModel`, so that it will have the generic aspect `value`.

The `ValueModel` does not need to perform any sort of conversion or translation on the value; it should just return the value as is.

Solution   Use an `IndexedAdaptor` to give a `Collection` element the aspect `value`. Since an `IndexedAdaptor` interfaces with the `Collection` via the element's index, the `Collection` must understand `at:` and `at:put:` (thus it must be an `Array` or `OrderedCollection`). The `IndexedAdaptor` will also allow the element to be shared by multiple dependents. If an `IndexedAdaptor` changes an element to another, the new element will appear in the old element's position in the `Collection`.

Example   Let's say you have a list[1] of `Person` elements and a view that displays the fields for `Person`. The fields should all be `AspectAdaptor`s on a selection channel. Since the list is a `SequenceableCollection`, the user can walk through the list by incrementing an index pointer into the list. Thus the selection channel should be an `IndexedAdaptor` that is a `ValueModel` on an element in the list.

Here's how to initialize the `IndexedAdaptor`:

```
selectionChannel :=
    (IndexedAdaptor subject: personList) forIndex: 1.
```

The view will initially display the information for the first `Person` in the list. To display `Person` n, set the `IndexedAdaptor`'s index to n. To walk through the list, increment or decrement the index.

---

[1] This list is presumably a `Collection` and does not have `ValueModel` behavior. If it were a `Collection` wrapped in a `SelectionInList`, the list would have `ValueModel` behavior, including a selection channel, so implementing a separate selection channel using an `IndexedAdaptor` would be unnecessary.

3.6 Use a SlotAdaptor to Hold a Single Instance Variable

Problem   How can I wrap `ValueModel` behavior around a particular instance variable in an object without changing what kind of object an instance variable holds?

Context   `ValueModel` behavior is often desirable (see Section 1).

If the nature of the instance variable can be changed from a variable that holds the value to a variable that holds a `ValueModel` that holds the value, use a `ValueHolder` (see Section 3.1). This will require changing some of the object's methods, such as the getter and setter for the instance variable, as well as any other methods that access the variable directly, such as `initialize`.

If the instance variable is an aspect of the object, with getter and setter methods to access the instance variable, use an `AspectAdaptor` (see Section 3.2).

If there are other means available in the object's public interface to get and set the value of this instance variable, use a `PluggableAdaptor` (see Section 3.7). The `ValueModel` does not need to actually store the value, because it is already being stored by another object.

To hide the fact that this object is an instance variable with no accessor methods, use a `ValueModel` so that it will have the generic aspect `value`. The `ValueModel` does not need to perform any sort of conversion or translation on the value; it should just return the value as is.

Solution   Use a `SlotAdaptor` to give an object's instance variable the aspect `value`. The `SlotAdaptor` will also allow the element to be shared by multiple dependents. If the `SlotAdaptor` is used to change the value, the object's instance variable will now have the new value.

Note: Changing an instance variable out from under an object in this manner is a bad idea. You should use a setter method in the object's public interface to make such changes. Changing an instance variable directly is a private procedure that could make the object's state (or those of its dependents) inconsistent. Whenever possible, use an `AspectAdaptor` or a `PluggableAdaptor`, not a `SlotAdaptor`.

Example   Let's say `aThing` contains the instance variable `amount`, but `aThing` does not provide sufficient behavior for getting and setting `amount`. You can attach a `SlotAdaptor` directly to the instance variable with this code:

```
amountHolder := SlotAdaptor subject: aThing.
amountHolder forIndex:
        (amountHolder subject class
            allInstVarNames indexOf: 'amount').
```

The instance variable `amountHolder` is now a `ValueModel` whose value is the exact same object as the one in the instance variable `amount`. If the `SlotAdaptor` puts a different object in that instance variable, `aThing` will never know. The next time `aThing` uses that instance variable, the variable will contain a different value than it did the last time `aThing` used it.

3.7 Use a PluggableAdaptor to Hold Some Part of an Object

Problem   How can I wrap `ValueModel` behavior around an arbitrary portion of an object?

Context   `ValueModel` behavior is often desirable (see Section 1).

The `ValueModel` does not need to actually store the value, because it is already being stored by another object. If the value is stored in the model as an aspect, use an `AspectAdaptor` (see Section 3.2). If the value is an element in a `Collection`, use an `IndexedAdaptor` (see Section 3.5). If the value is stored in an instance variable that cannot be accessed adequately through the model's behavior, use a `SlotAdaptor` (see Section 3.6).

Obtaining the value from the model may be tricky. The value may need to be derived from explicit values in the model; to store it back, the `ValueModel` may need to dissect the value to get its components, and then store them in the model. The `ValueModel` may need to make a series of decisions to decide if its value should be updated. In fact, the `ValueModel` may not appear to hold a value at all, but rather it may appear to be a detection system for an event that may occur.

Solution   Use a `PluggableAdaptor` to hold an arbitrary portion of an object when no other kind of `ValueModel` will work. `PluggableAdaptor` is a very brute-force style of `ValueModel`; in many cases using it is overkill. However, when the value one model wants is very different from the value the other model has, a `PluggableAdaptor` is often able to bridge the difference when no other kind of `ValueModel` can.

Examples   **Example 1** Let's say the domain model holds the aspects `firstName` and `lastName`. The `ApplicationModel` wants an instance of the `FullName` that contains the information in the domain model. To store a new name, the `FullName` will have to be broken apart into the domain model's aspects. When either of these aspects of the domain model changes, the `FullName` in the `ApplicationModel` will have to be updated accordingly.

```
(PluggableAdaptor on: self domianModel)
    getBlock:
        [ :model |
        FullName
                firstName: model firstName
                lastName: model lastName]
    putBlock:
        [ :model :value "aFullName" |
        model
                firstName: value firstName;
                lastName: value lastName]
    updateBlock:
        [ :model :aspect :parameter |
                aspect == #firstName |
                aspect == #lastName].
```

Example 2   ParcPlace has already implemented some specialized messages;
browse `PluggableAdaptor` to review them:

- `collectionIndex:` — Makes the `PluggableAdaptor` work like an `IndexedAdaptor`.

- `getSelector:putSelector:` — Makes it work like an `AspectAdaptor`.

- `performAction:` Used to make a `Button` act like an `ActionButton`.

- `selectValue:` — Acts like a `Boolean` whose value reflects whether or
  not the value being held is equal to `aValue`.

3.8 Use a TypeConverter to Convert a Value Between Types

Problem   Two objects wish to share a value, but one dependent wants it expressed as
one type and the other expects another type. How can the value appear as
the appropriate type of object for each dependent?

Context   When two dependents want two types of objects for the same value, this
assumes that the value can be converted from one type of object to the other
and back again. If not, they cannot share the same value instance.

The value to be converted should be accessed via the generic aspect `value`.
The converted value should be accessed via the generic aspect `value`.

Solution   Use a `TypeConverter` to convert the type of object being held as a value in
one `ValueModel` into the type expected by the model. When storing a new
value, the `TypeConverter` will perform the inverse conversion.

Note: The `updateBlock` for a `TypeConverter` is always true. `TypeConverter` redefines `value:` so it does not send out updates. This way, the objects at either end of the converter handle send out updates, and the converter just conveys them transparently.

Examples   **Example 1** Let's say a couple of objects want to share a value as a `Number`, and a couple of other objects want to share the same value as a `String`. Here's how:

```
valueAsNumberHolder := ValueHolder on: theNumber.
converter :=
        (TypeConverter on: valueAsNumberHolder) numberToText.
valueAsStringHolder :=
        (AspectAdaptor subject: converter
                sendsUpdates: true)
        forAspect: #value.
```

With this setup, objects that want to share the value as a `Number` register their interests on `valueAsNumberHolder`; those that want the value as a `String` register with `valueAsStringHolder`.

Example 2 Many of the most common conversions have already been defined for you, like `numberToText`. Browse `TypeConverter` to see others, like `dateToText`, `stringOrSymbolToText`, and `stringToNumber`.

3.9 Use a ScrollValueHolder to Hold a Position in *n*-Dimensional Space

Problem   What object should I use to keep track of how much a point's position on a grid has changed?

Context   A single `Number` will be insufficient. It can keep track of the point's distance from the grid's origin, but that will not be enough information to calculate the point's unique position on the grid. There will need to be one `Number` for each dimension of the grid.

Just knowing the position on the grid (the point) is insufficient. If the point must move across the grid in quantum steps, the size of the minimum step must be available. When the point tries to move, its movements must be constrained to those which are a multiple of the grid step size.

Solution   Use a `ScrollValueHolder` to hold the scroll position of a point (which may or may not be an instance of `Point`, which is two-dimensional). Set the grid to be the minimum size of each step the point must take when it moves.

Example   ScrollWrappers are the heart of how the scroll bars on a view work; they connect the scroll bars to the view. The ScrollWrapper must remember what its position is; the position is stored in a ScrollValueHolder. The view's scroll position cannot change without a valid scroll position being stored in the ScrollValueHolder.

Before storing a new scroll position, the ScrollValueHolder will round it off to the nearest grid position. This position is incremented or decremented by one grid size when a scroll bar button is pushed. The position will be adjusted, if necessary, to make it stay within the wrapper's bounds.

The value of the ScrollValueHolder can be adjusted programatically. To auto-scroll the view for the user, store a new scroll position in the ScrollValueHolder. The new value will be validated and stored, and the wrapper will be informed of the new value, at which time the wrapper will scroll the view.

3.10 Use SelectionInList to Hold a List and Its Selection

Problem   How can I set up a list so that it can tell me which item is currently being used?

Context   A Collection knows which items it contains, and can allow you to reference one item at a time, but it cannot tell you which one is currently being referenced.

An item cannot tell you which Collection it is a part of. In fact, it may not be part of any Collection, or it may be part of several. Thus another object will need to contain the list and keep track of which item is currently being used. It should work with any list and selection, regardless of what their aspects are.

You may need to know when the currently referenced item changes. You may also need to know when the items in the list change.

Solution   Use a SelectionInList to track a list and its current selection. If you register your interest in one of its aspects (list or selectionIndex), it will notify you of changes.

Editorial comment: SelectionInList's interface isn't actually as clean as it ought to be. It implements two aspects, list and selectionIndex, using two ValueModels, listHolder and selectionIndexHolder. It then implements a third aspect, selection, but it does not implement it using a ValueModel. So there is no selectionHolder to register interest with, nor to send out selection changed aspects (see also Section 2.2).

Example Here's how to create a `SelectionInList` of `Person` objects:

```
personSelectionInList :=
     (SelectionInList with: self peopleList)
          selectionIndex: 1.
```

This will contain the list of `Persons`; the first one is selected. To be notified when the list is replaced with another, register your interest with `listHolder`. Register interest with `selectionIndexHolder` and you'll be notified when the selection (actually the selection index) changes. To change its list, selection index, or selection programatically, use `list:`, `selectionIndex:`, and `selection:`.

REFERENCES

[Aue95] Auer, Ken. Reusability through self-encapsulation. Chapter 27, this volume.

[Par93] ParcPlace Systems, Sunnyvale, CA. The discrete charm of the ValueModel. *ParcNotices, 4,2 (Summer 1993): 1, 8–9.*

[Woo01] Woolf, Bobby. Variable typing in Smalltalk. Unpublished.

Bobby Woolf can be reached at Knowledge Systems Corporation, 4001 Weston Parkway, Cary, NC 27513-2303; `bwoolf@ksccary.com`.

26 Client-Specified Self

Panu Viljamaa

ABSTRACT

A design pattern is presented for replacing messages to self with messages to an argument. Using the sender itself as the argument allows it to "inherit" or "borrow" methods from others besides its superclasses. A trade-off between adaptability and applicability is discussed. An example is presented in which a problem is solved using Smalltalk's super. An application that implements state-dependent behavior is described, and the pattern is compared to dynamic classes, instance-specific methods, and delegation. Key words used in the paper include *dynamic inheritance, implementation reuse, self, super,* and *delegation.* The style of presentation is adapted from Gamma et al. [1].

1. INTENT

Replacing messages to the pseudovariable self in Smalltalk (this in C++) with messages to an argument allows the sender to effectively change the

Copyright © 1994 Panu Viljamaa. All Rights Reserved.

value of the recipient's `self` at run time. Using the sender as the value of this argument allows the sender to "borrow" the method from the recipient; therefore it can "inherit" from others besides its superclasses.

2. MOTIVATION

An object, like a person, may sometimes assume a new role or behavior. (For instance, a policeman may sometimes behave as a bank robber.) How does one implement objects whose behavior may vary according to the role they are currently acting? A solution is to use special "role objects" that carry the behavior needed in a given role. But how can the methods of those role objects be executed in the context of the "real" object "acting" the role? This can be accomplished if we can make the `self` in the role object's methods refer to the role actor. Unfortunately, `self` is a pseudovariable; its contents cannot be set. Therefore, instead of `self`, define and use an extra method argument, `SELF`, whose contents *can* be set by the caller. I refer to this method argument as a "Client-Specified Self."

3. APPLICABILITY

The Client-Specified Self pattern is a form of delegation. Few object-oriented languages support true delegation, but Client-Specified Self can be used to implement it. Listed below are reasons for using Client-Specified Self when delegation is not supported, and cases in which it may be more preferable than built-in delegation, even when that is available. (Delegation is described in detail in Section 11.)

Use Client-Specified Self (or delegation)

- When implementing methods of general utility that need access to the state of an object.
- When you are using useful but longish methods that have an arbitrary connection to their class.
- To implement classes with dynamic, varying behavior (see Section 10).
- When you want to reuse an implementation across branches of the class hierarchy.
- When you want to redefine a method that sends to `super` and the supercode does things that are hard to undo (like sounding a bell; see Section 9).

- When a method sends many messages to `self` that are defined in a superclass with lots of descendants. If Client-Specified Self is used, the method becomes valuable because it can be reused by all those descendants (see Implementation Issues to Consider in Section 8).

Use Client-Specified Self instead of delegation

- When the delegation relation is very dynamic or it is used only once.
- When you want to broadcast and delegate the message to a set of objects.
- When you want to create flexible, dynamic inheritance schemes such as these:

  Inherit the method versions from all superclasses and collect their results.

  Apply the subclass method to the superclass method's result recursively.

  Inherit from successively higher superclasses until a specific result is returned.

- When you want to redistribute the methods among the classes later. In such cases you want the interface of a method to its owner to be visible, to show what it requires from classes it could be transferred to.

4. STRUCTURE

The relationships between the collaborators in Client-Specified Self (in the typical case of "borrowing") are depicted in Figure 1. The dynamics of the situation are illustrated in Figure 2.

The participants in Figure 1 are as follows:

- The Borrower: an object that wants to use another object's method as its own.
- The Lender: an object whose method takes a SELF argument, thereby offering it for lending.
- SELF: A special argument that may contain a borrower. By default its value is the message recipient.

5. DYNAMICS

1. The sender may set the SELF argument to be the same as the message target. In such cases it is really requesting the services of the target, not borrowing methods from it.

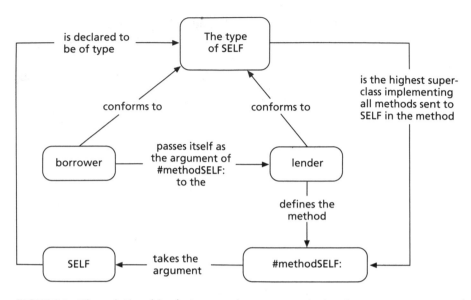

FIGURE 1   The relationships between a borrower and a lender

2. The sender may set the argument to itself (meaning that the sender will perform the methods previously executed by the target, in the sender's own context, as if they were its own).

6. CONSEQUENCES

1. Objects can dynamically "inherit" methods from different branches of the class hierarchy.

2. The class hierarchy's role is clarified: it supports the definition of subtypes by requiring conformity in interfaces to the subclasses. (Implementations of individual methods need not follow the constraints of the hierarchy, however.)

3. The self is generalized to a parameter of the situation, like any other argument.

4. Classes can be used to define context-free groups of related methods. Methods become first-class citizens. They can be subclassed and stored in variables, like objects.

5. The requirements a method has of its owner become explicit because the type of SELF is declared. This increases the understandability of the code.

6. The length of individual methods increases (this may be offset by increased reuse, however).

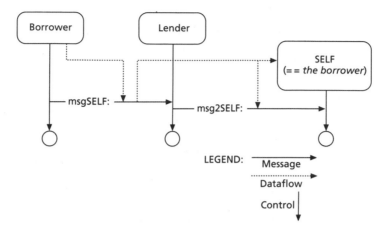

FIGURE 2   The borrower and lender acting in concert

7. IMPLEMENTATION

In Smalltalk, a method intended for public typically has this form:

publicMethod
```
    self privateMethod
```

The method is transformed to accommodate Client-Specified Self by modifying it this way:

publicMethodSELF: SELF
```
    SELF privateMethod
```

Note the intentional use of capitalized SELF in the method name, to indicate the special nature of the argument. When such a method is encountered, the client programmer knows that the protocol required from the argument is a subset of the recipient's protocol.

In C++, Client-Specified Self member functions look like this:[1]

```
#define  SETSELF      if (!SELF) SELF = this;

virtual  ResultType
    AClass::publicMethodSELF(AClassOrItsBase* SELF = 0)
    {SETSELF;
     SELF->privateMethod(...);

     ....
    }
```

---

[1] We can't simply declare AClass::publicMethodSELF(AClassOrItsBase* SELF = this), because few (if any) C++ compilers allow this in a declaration.

In C++, SELF can be defined as an optional argument whose default value is the recipient. The clients need not be aware of the added functionality, so in most cases it makes sense to define the SELF argument: it adds to the value of the service offered, without requiring anything from clients that don't need it.

Implementation Issues to Consider

1. A borrowed method can directly access only the lender's instance variables. It is better to access instance variables with messages.[2] Then "all" of the method can be borrowed, even by classes with different internal structure.

2. Messages to SELF may take a SELF argument of their own (see Figure 2). The value of SELF is best passed on unchanged (meaning no second round of borrowing takes place). If SELF contains a borrower, the lender only knows its interface. It would be foolish to borrow an unknown implementation from it.

3. Some messages may be better sent to self after all. A heuristic technique is to strive for the highest possible declared type of SELF, because the method can then be borrowed by all its subclasses. If a method is defined in the current class only, it may be better to send it to self — the type of SELF can then be set to a superclass, widening the group of borrowers. This leads us to the next implementation issue . . .

4. There is a trade-off in Client-Specified Self between adaptability and applicability.

    - A method that sends only to its arguments can be borrowed individually. The granule of reuse then becomes the individual method, which means the number of their combinations is maximized. If a method sends to self, other methods always come along. But that can make it possible to use a higher superclass as the type of SELF, increasing the number of potential borrowers. There is a trade-off between maximizing the number of methods that can be individually replaced and the number of their potential borrowers.

    - If a method can be borrowed individually, it can adapt to situations in which other methods it calls need to be different. But an adaptable

---

[2] This is a well-known "pattern," whose usefulness gains further support here.

method that never sends to self requires a more specialized SELF, meaning that the method is applicable in fewer situations. The more adaptable we make a method, the less applicable it seems to become.

- This problem occurs because we have to decide at coding time which messages go to SELF and which go to self, limiting either the number of borrowers or the granularity of reuse. One way out of the dilemma could be to always use SELF and to redirect the messages it can't handle back to the lender (the self).[3]

8. SAMPLE CODE

In Smalltalk, sending to the the pseudovariable super means the message goes to self but the definition of the called method in the next higher superclass defining it is used. This makes additive inheritance possible where subclasses execute their own methods in addition to the inherited ones.

A problem emerges if you want to redefine a method that refers to super while holding on to the behavior super offers. The super in the redefined method refers to the method you want to modify; it no longer refers to the useful version above it. The problem is acute when the redefining method does things that can't be undone in the redefined method, like sounding a bell or drawing something on screen.

In the listing below SpecialRadioButton redefines #button1Down: to add the sound of a bell to the inherited behavior. This class has other great functionalities, which we want to reuse in further subclasses like VerySpecial-RadioButton. But we want the new subclasses to be silent. To get rid of the sound, we would have to stop calling upon super. It seems that "additive" and "redefinitive" styles of inheritance are hard to combine:

```
SpecialRadioButton>>button1Down: aPoint
"
Act like the superclass RadioButton but also sound a bell.
"
MacSoundManager bell.
^super button1Down: aPoint
```

---

[3] This becomes a pattern of its own, probably implemented with Smalltalk's #doesNotUnderstand: mechanism.

```
VerySpecialRadioButton>>button1Down: aPoint
    "
    Act like the superclass SpecialRadioButton but
    (try to) comment away the sound of a bell.
    But the bell still tolls !
    "
    "-MacSoundManager bell.-"    "Can't be commented away !"
    ^super button1Down: aPoint
```

The solution with Client-Specified Self is shown below. The SELF argument allows the bottom subclass VerySpecialRadioButton to skip the #button1Down: of its superclass and inherit directly from super's super:

```
VerySpecialRadioButton>>button1Down: aPoint
    "
    Act like the superclass but DO NOT sound a bell.
    Skip-inherit the method from super's super.
    "

    "--MacSoundManager bell. --"        "Commented away ok"

    ^(self class superclass               "Skip over to super's super"
                superclass  new)
        button1Down: aPoint SELF: self  "using Client-Specified Self"
```

```
RadioButton>>button1Down: aPoint SELF: s
    "
     Acts like the original #button1Down: but can
    be explicitly inherited to any descendant.
    (The difference is that all references to
    'self' have been replaced by the argument 's').
    "
    s value
       ifFalse:
           [s contents: true.
            s triggerEvent: #clicked: with: s label.
            s value ifTrue: [s triggerEvent: #turnedOn]
           ]
```

9. USES

An object can dynamically alter whatever it borrows from, typically depending on its state. Beck and Johnson [2] call this the Objects for States pattern.[4]

---

[4] The mechanism is the same in Objects for States, but Client-Specified Self covers a wider set of problems, emphasizing preparing for future "borrowing" by systematic use of the SELF argument.

Instead of deciding on which actions to take by testing your properties, borrow the currently relevant procedures from lender objects in your instance variables. Depending on the state, the lenders will be different and will produce different behavior.

The total state can be decomposed into several State objects. States can be defined as subclasses of a "root" state that defines behavior common to most substates. Substates need only define how the object's behavior differs in them. The mechanisms of inheritance and aggregation can thus be applied to modeling and implementation of time-dependent behavior.

10. RELATED PATTERNS

Client-Specified Self resembles the patterns of dynamic classes, instance-specific methods, and delegation. First, it is conceivable that the class of an object will be changed at run time, allowing it to dynamically change the set of methods offered. Second, instance-specific methods (See Beck [3]) allow us to change the methods of an instance dynamically. Third, true delegation can be supported, as in the language SELF [4]. In SELF, a message can be "delegated" to another object that is stored in an instance variable of the delegator. When the delegated method gets executed, self is bound to the sender-delegator.

Thomas Wu [5] describes the pattern Protocol Objects (in the context of the language Actor 4.0) as a way to separate the inheritance of implementation and behavior. The idea is to singly inherit variables and private methods while using multiple protocol objects as the public interface. The emphasis is on "external" static modeling of individuals with multiple roles. In contrast, Section 10 above describes similar objects for implementing internal state-dependent behavior. Client-Specified Self is in general more of an implementation technique, which allows individual methods to be borrowed regardless of the type of their owner.

Delegation and the other patterns discussed above differ from Client-Specified Self in that they remain rather static. The change affects all callers in a given time interval, and the delegation must be explicitly canceled at the end. In Client-Specified Self, the lender and the borrower are determined individually for each usage. The pattern is also simple to implement in conventional object-oriented languages.

Client-Specified Self builds upon the programmer's rule of avoiding the hard-wiring of decisions into source code. Instead of doing tests to decide on the appropriate actions, use a single message but vary the target. Instead of fixing the recipient as `self`, use a variable that potentially contains `self` but can contain something else as well. This will make your code more adaptable, more applicable, and more reusable.

REFERENCES

[1] E. Gamma, R. Helm, R. Johnson, and J. Vlissides. *Design Patterns: Elements of Reusable Object-Oriented Software.* Reading, MA: Addison-Wesley, 1995.

[2] K. Beck and R. Johnson. "Patterns Generate Architectures." *Proceedings of the Object-Oriented Programming 8th European Conference, ECOOP'94.* Berlin: Springer-Verlag, 1994.

[3] K. Beck. "Instance-Specific Behavior: How and Why." *Smalltalk Report* 2, 6(1992).

[4] C. Chambers, D. Ungar, and E. Lee. "An Efficient Implementation of SELF, a Dynamically-Typed Object-Oriented Language Based on Prototypes." *Proceedings of OOPSLA'89.* New Orleans: ACM, 1989.

[5] C. Thomas Wu. "Improving Reusability with Actor 4.0's Protocol Mechanism." *Journal of Object-Oriented Programming* (March/April 1992).

Panu Viljamaa can be reached at Telcom Finland Ltd., P.O. Box 140, FIN-00511 Helsinki, Finland; `panu@ajk.tele.fi`.

27

Reusability Through Self-Encapsulation

Ken Auer

INTRODUCTION

Reusability has long been a promise of object-oriented technology, and the use of inheritance has been promoted as a significant means to that end. In practice, however, extending existing classes through inheritance can be difficult. Once inheritance is successfully exploited, changing the definition or implementation of a class can often wreak havoc on its subclasses. Many of these difficulties are due to the fact that the benefits of encapsulation are easily ignored when exercising inheritance.

Adherence to the pattern language presented here will lead to classes and class hierarchies that overcome many of these difficulties. The language exploits the notion of encapsulation to isolate implementation decisions to a small number of methods. I call this technique *self-encapsulation*.

This pattern language has been successfully applied in Smalltalk. It may also be appropriate, in whole or in part, in other programming languages. It is best used when implementing new classes from scratch. However, it can also be used to refactor existing classes to improve their reusability. See the context for each pattern to determine when it is appropriate to apply.

Copyright © 1994 Knowledge Systems Corporation and Ken Auer. All Rights Reserved.

THE PATTERN LANGUAGE

Pattern 1: Define Classes by Behavior, Not State

Context You are creating a new class, and you would like to avoid inserting implementation characteristics that would be detrimental to its reliability or to that of its subclasses as they evolve.

Problem Inheritance of behavior is what we typically want to exploit. How do we define classes in such a way that behavior is reliable?

Constraints The essence of an object that is part of a collaborating system of objects is its responsibilities. Other objects rely on it to fulfill these responsibilities. The manner in which it fulfills them is relatively unimportant. Even less important in an object-oriented system is the data structure of an object (that is, the number of slots, the slots' names, and the type of object that is expected to live in those slots).

But an object's responsibilities cannot be fulfilled without message passing. Defining method details is typically much more time-consuming than defining message names (protocols). (*Note:* I refer here to the time necessary to define these names for the rest of the system. This should not be confused with the time needed to determine high-quality message names, which should always be done with care). Additionally, the data structure of an object is often important in making received messages actually respond in a meaningful way.

The data structure of objects is important, as there is very little that can be done without eventually manipulating some sort of data. Trade-offs between space and speed are often closely tied to the data structure used to implement an object. However, subclasses automatically inherit the data structure of their superclass. Any decisions about data structure are virtually irreversible by subclasses without overriding every method that refers to the data structure. Each time detail is added to the data structure, some implementation options are lost and others are imposed on the class and its subclasses.

Solution When creating a new class, define its public protocol and specify its behavior without regard to data structure (such as instance variables, class variables, and so on).

For example:

Class:	Rectangle
Protocol:	area
	corners

```
intersects:
contains:
perimeter
width
height
insetBy:
translateBy:
center
```

and so on.

Pattern 2: Implement Behavior with Abstract State

Context The public behavior of a class is identified (see Pattern 1, Define Classes by Behavior, Not State) but the actual implementation of this behavior is undefined.

Problem How do we approach implementation without prematurely and unnecessarily forcing data structure design decisions on subclasses?

Constraints Identifying names and intents of protocols does not provide functionality. Methods associated with these protocols must be implemented. In order to implement certain methods, access to the implied state of the object is necessary. For example, in order to calculate the area of a Circle, its radius is required.

If portions of the data structure (such as an instance variable) are defined as soon as the need for particular state is identified, there may be an abundance of state variables that may not be necessary, as they can be derived from other state variables (for example, a Circle's diameter can be derived from its radius). Additionally, each detail introduced into the data structure reduces the flexibility of subclass implementations.

Solution If implied state information is needed in order to complete the implementation details of behavior, identify the state by defining a message that returns that state instead of defining a variable.

For example, use

```
Circle>>area
    ^self radius squared * self pi
```

not

```
Circle>>area
    ^radius squared * pi.
```

This implies that methods for `radius` and `pi` must be implemented, but it does not yet determine any particular data structure. Both the details for how the radius is retrieved (or derived) and the details of retrieval and precision for which pi is used are determined in one place and changed in one place. Changes in any of these details will proliferate throughout the rest of the class with no further intervention.

This technique can also be used for "indexed" state by identifying abstract state messages such as `atIndex:` or `atIndex:put:`.

Note that the author acknowledges that there may already be a global variable for pi that would alleviate the need to encapsulate this constant in a method. This example is used to make the reader think twice before determining whether what is thought of as a constant may need to be modifiable due to potential constraints imposed upon the system (for example, precision, performance, special cases, and so on).

Pattern 3: Identify Message Layers

Context   This pattern is applicable to either of these contexts:

1. Basic public behavior has been defined and implemented, and many abstract state messages have been identified but not yet defined (see Pattern 2, Implement Behavior with Abstract State).

2. A class has been fully defined, and specialization through subclassing is now desired (with as few undesirable side effects as possible).

Problem   How can methods be factored to make the class both efficient and simple to subclass?

Constraints   Larger data structures impose less flexibility and a less efficient use of space on a class and its subclasses. It is desirable to keep the data structure to a minimum unless a conscious decision (such as trading off space for speed) necessitates the initiation of additional details. This implies that we should avoid implementing abstract state methods as concrete state methods whenever possible. It also implies that we should examine implementations of other methods for efficient execution so as to avoid prematurely initiating additional data structures for the sake of efficiency.

Many abstract state methods can be identified in terms of others in order to minimize the amount of concrete states necessary. Additionally, protocols that are not bound to state references can often be defined in terms of other protocols. However, this can also lead to circular dependencies like this:

```
Circle>>radius
    ^self diameter / 2
Circle>>diameter
    ^self radius * 2
```

It can also lead to gross inefficiencies or convoluted code, as shown here:

```
Rectangle>>center
    ^self topLeft + (self bottomRight - self topLeft / 2).
Rectangle>>topLeft
    ^self bottomLeft x @ self topRight y
Rectangle>>bottomLeft
    ^self leftCenter x @ self bottomCenter y
Rectangle>>leftCenter
    ^self left @ self center y
```

and so on.

Solution   Identify a small subset of abstract state and behavior methods which all other methods can rely on as kernel methods. Alter other methods so they use these kernel methods wherever possible without duplicating the logic of other nonkernel methods (for example, do not use `self radius * 2` if you can use `self diameter`). Often logic that is duplicated in several methods can be extracted into additional private methods. These new methods can be included with existing "self-reusable" nonkernel methods to form an additional layer of self-encapsulated methods that remaining nonkernel "leaf" methods should be altered to use. (*Note:* This may take several iterations.) Concrete classes then only need to implement (or override) the kernel methods appropriately to reliably provide all the implied functionality. Changing the functionality of "leaf" methods will not produce undesirable side effects. Each layer will have a known sphere of influence.

For example, identify `Circle`'s kernel methods as `radius`, `radius:`, `center`, `center:`, and `pi`. Other methods would use these kernel methods. Methods like `diameter` would become second-layer methods:

```
Circle>>radius
    ^???
Circle>>radius:
    ???
Circle>>pi
    ^???
Circle>>center
    ^???
Circle>>center:
    ???
Circle>>diameter
    ^self radius * 2
```

```
Circle>>area
    ^self radius squared * self pi
Circle>>topCenter
    ^self center - (0 @ self radius)
Circle>>circumference
    ^self diameter * self pi
Circle>>moveBy: aPoint
    ^self center: self center + aPoint
Circle>>scaleBy: aNumber
    ^self radius: self radius * aNumber
```

Pattern 4: Defer Identification of State Variables

Context   This pattern is applicable to either of these contexts:

1. The kernel methods of the class have been identified (see Pattern 3, Identify Message Layers).
2. A class has been fully defined, and specialization through subclassing is now desired (with as few undesirable side effects as possible).

Problem   Once a data structure is defined and methods refer to it, subclasses inherit these assumptions whether or not they are desirable. Can this be avoided?

Constraints   It is very tempting to add state variables (such as instance or class variables) to the class we've been defining. However, as soon as we do we've imposed implementation decisions on our subclasses, requiring them to allocate at least as much space as the base class. If we later need a more space-efficient version of the class, we'll have to rearrange things.

For example, suppose we added the instance variables left, right, top, and bottom to Rectangle. Later, a highly specialized subclass of Rectangle called SmallConstrainedSquare is added. Instances of this new class must take up as little memory as possible. The width and height of the square must be a positive integer less than or equal to 16, and the center of the square must always be an integer between 0 and 1023 in both the X and Y directions. We can hold all the info necessary (for example, centerX, centerY, width) packed into a single SmallInteger. Unfortunately, we've already got four slots allocated per object.

Usually the space issue mentioned in the above example is just not very relevant in today's systems. There are times when space issues are very relevant, especially when space is multiplied in large sets of objects. The techniques described earlier (in Patterns 1–3, Define Classes by Behavior, Not State; Implement Behavior with Abstract State; Identify Message Layers) usually render a fairly minimal set of state variable requirements. However, there is the possibility that even these relatively few variables will become a point of confusion if they are reused or rendered useless by later subclasses.

Lastly, as soon as the base class is turned into a concrete class there is the temptation to add more data structure details. Each time more detail is added (such as an additional instance variable), more behavior often follows. Subclasses will be big and bulky before they ever add their first ounce of behavior.

Solution   Defer identification of state variables for as long as possible. It is often a good idea to make the base class stateless and let the subclasses add state. Future developers of subclasses can then choose either to inherit the state from one of the concrete (or more concrete) subclasses or to start with a clean slate using the abstract class as its base.

For example, create a class `AbstractTwoDimensionalPoint` with the kernel methods `radius`, `theta`, `x`, and `y`, with no instance variables. A concrete subclass, `Point`, is created, which defines two instance variables, `x` and `y`. Later, another concrete subclass, `PolarCoordinate`, is added. Although there are several ways `PolarCoordinate` may be able to subclass `Point` successfully, it would be much more elegant (not to mention efficient) to subclass `AbstractTwoDimensionalPoint`.

Pattern 5: Encapsulate Concrete State

Context   The data structure of a class has been identified and its behavior has been defined.

Problem   How do we minimize the negative effect data structure decisions have on the flexibility of the class hierarchy and reduce the implications of change as the class hierarchy evolves?

Constraints   Adding a state variable and defining what it holds is a single implementation decision. Every method that refers to the state variable will be impacted by that decision. If the decision is altered in any way in the base class or a subclass, it is possible that a new implementation will be required for every method that references the state variable (including those defined in its superclasses).

It is typically extremely efficient to reference a variable directly. Although methods that have only a single line of code that returns or sets a variable are also very efficient due to language implementation shortcuts (as per Dave

Liebs of ParcPlace Systems), they are not as efficient as directly referenced variables. However, in either case the overhead is not usually significant enough to introduce any sort of perceived performance problems.

Additionally, it is often necessary during maintenance, or even at run time, for classes (or subclasses) to determine exactly when an attribute is retrieved or set.

Solution   When adding state variables, only refer to them directly in "getter" or "setter" methods. (See "Variables Limit Reusability," Wilkerson, Wirfs-Brock, *Journal of Object-Oriented Programming*, 1989.) These methods will often exist already (although undefined; see Pattern 2, Implement Behavior with Abstract State, and Pattern 3, Identify Message Layers) and may already be defined as public or private protocols. The fact that such a method provides access to a variable is irrelevant to every object except the one in which it is implemented. As additional behavior is added, continue to access state variables only through these getter and setter methods, to allow for simple modifications in the future. Modify any other methods which refer to state variables directly (if earlier patterns were not followed) so that they instead refer to them indirectly, via these getter and setter methods.

For example, if we followed these rules and later changed our implementation of `Circle` to hold an instance variable of `diameter` instead of `radius`, we would only have to change the methods `radius`, `radius:`, `diameter`, and `diameter:` in the class where the change was made. Any subclasses (such as `Sphere`) should not be affected in any way, other than a possible change in performance on a method-by-method basis.

As an additional benefit, any modifications or side effects (like change notification, rounding, and so on) to the manner in which these variables are treated can be easily confined to a single location.

Pattern 6: Use Lazy Initialization

Context   The data structure of a class has been identified, its behavior has been defined, and the data structure has been encapsulated via accessing methods (see Pattern 5, Encapsulate Concrete State). The programmer would like to initialize certain elements of the data structure to specific values.

Problem   When state variables have an initial or default value, how can we set them in a way that best retains their flexibility?

Constraints   There are several ways to set initial, default values of state variables. The most common are explicit initialization and lazy initialization.

Lazy initialization is done in a getter method if the state variable is `nil`. This offers several benefits:

1. It provides an obvious place to set the value uncluttered by other variables and initialization routines.

2. The overhead of initialization does not take place if the variable is never accessed.

3. Value can easily be reset to its default independently of other variables.

Explicit initialization adds an `initialize` method to a class and has the metaclass send the message to any newly created object. This can provide slightly more efficient objects than lazy initialization, due to the lack of having to check for `nil` on each access of the variable. But it can have several undesirable side effects:

1. Variables may be set to nontrivial values (that is, variables that take some calculation to derive) and never used.

2. A subclass can override its superclass version, in one of two ways:
   - calling `super initialize` and adding behavior, which can sometimes result in setting the same variable multiple times
   - rewriting it completely, which makes the subclass vulnerable to missing future changes in the superclass

3. It adds another place where variables are accessed directly, exposing them to problems when implementation decisions are later altered. If setter methods are used in place of direct reference in order to avoid this problem, it forces default settings and explicit settings to be treated the same, which may not be desirable if setter methods have side effects.

Although some would argue that there are aesthetic or maintainability benefits to using explicit initialization, this is mostly a cultural issue or one of personal taste. The most significant argument for explicit initialization is execution efficiency.

Solution   Use lazy intialization to set initial, default values of a state variable whenever default values are desired. Set the variable to the value returned by a default message (see Pattern 7, Define Default Values via Explicit Protocol).

If a variable needs to be reset to its default value for future use, reset it by sending the setter message with `nil` as the argument. This avoids the overhead of initialization of the value if it is not needed again.

For example, if we followed these rules we could have the following methods in `Circle`:

```
Circle>>radius
    radius == nil
        ifTrue: [radius := self defaultRadius].
    ^radius
Circle>>defaultRadius
    ^10
```

Note the use of `== nil` instead of `isNil`. This is much more efficient due to the language implementation (for most dialects of Smalltalk), as it avoids the overhead of a message send, making the potential performance benefit of the alternative explicit initialization much less significant.

This technique is especially valuable for the initialization of variables that exist as a cache for a calculated value. For example, a `SquareMatrix` may need to refer to its determinant for many algebraic operations. Since the calculation of a determinant is fairly complex and lengthy, it may be valuable to cache this value in a variable called `determinant`. Whenever a new entry is placed anywhere in the matrix, the determinant can be flushed (`self determinant: nil`). If the determinant is never needed again, it will never be recalculated. If it is used, it will be recalculated once and used each time the determinant is needed, until one or more new entries are made to the matrix.

Pattern 7: Define Default Values via Explicit Protocol

Context Initial, default values for class-specific variables are desired, either to encapsulate the need for this state (see Pattern 5, Encapsulate Concrete State) from creators of instances of a class, or to simplify the number of parameters needed at creation time for typical cases.

Problem Where should these default values be defined for maximum flexibility?

Constraints For maintainability, reliability, and understandability, default values should be identified in one place. This allows changes to any default value to be made only once in the base class or its subclasses. For each such case, there are many potential methods in which this single value could be defined.

If explicit initialization is used (in spite of the dangers described in Pattern 6, Use Lazy Initialization) the `initialize` method could house the default value(s). For example:

```
Circle>>initialize
    super initialize.
```

```
    radius := 10.
    center := 0@0.
```

or

```
Circle>>initialize
    super initialize.
    self radius: 10.
    self center: 0@0.
```

In addition to the problems associated with explicit initialization that were mentioned above (an additional method referring to a variable, and side effects at initialization time), this would force a subclass to override the method, even if it only desired a change of one default value (such as `center`). The result would be one of the following:

- A rewrite that does not include `super initialize`. This would break the inheritance link to the base class for future modifications of this method.

- A new version of the method that retained the inheritance link via `super initialize`. This would end up setting the value of the variable multiple times — once for each time the subclass desires a different default value than its parent.

If lazy initialization is used, the getter method could be used to house the default value. For example:

```
Circle>>center
    center == nil
        ifTrue: [center := 0@0].
    ^center
```

This forces subclasses to override the getter method if they want to change the default value, rewriting all three lines of code (most of which is redundant) and breaking the inheritance link to the base class for future modifications if any other side effects of the getter method are desired. (*Note:* Employing getter method side effects is not often recommended in run-time code, although it can prove useful during development.)

  No matter which sort of initialization is defined, a significant amount of code (greater than one line) will be overriden, and there will be no way to test at either development or run time whether a default value is being used, other than to express the default value in a second method.

Solution   Define initial, default values in an explicit method with a selector that has `default` as its prefix and the capitalized variable name as its root. Have other methods which need the value for initialization, testing, and so on send the message to `self` to retrieve the value. For example, an explicit default method for a `Circle`'s center would look like this:

```
Circle>>defaultCenter
   ^0@0
```

This allows subclasses to easily override the default value without repeating other code or breaking inheritance links. It also allows for simple testing to determine whether a particular value is the default value or not (for example, `aCircle center = aCircle defaultCenter`). Following this pattern consistently will allow maintenance programmers to reliably find and change default values without having to determine or care about the type of initialization used or where the default value may be defined.

CONCLUSION

If you use these patterns to produce classes, the classes will invite reuse through inheritance. Self-encapsulation discourages preoccupation with data structures and produces cleaner, behavior-driven designs. These classes will be easier to understand and document due to their internal consistency. A developer is more likely to subclass that which he can understand. Through this technique, much of the promised benefits of inheritance can be realized.

Ken Auer can be reached at Knowledge Systems Corporation, 4001 Weston Parkway, Cary, NC 27513; kauer@ksccary.com.

EVENTS AND EVENT HANDLERS

PART

8 Design and programming techniques that support event-driven processing are becoming increasingly popular. Event-driven processing structures the control flow in interactive and asynchronous applications that interact with their environment. Communication protocol stacks, network management agents, real-time process control systems, user interface toolkits, and telecommunication switches are applications built around event-driven software.

Three characteristics distinguish event-driven applications from programs with self-directed control flow. First, they are "reactive," which means that their behavior is triggered asynchronously by external events. Each event brings information from the outside world into the application. Sources of this information include device drivers, I/O ports, sensors, keyboards or mice, signals, timers, or other asynchronous software. Second, since the application generally has no control over the order that events arrive, finite-state machines are often used to detect illegal transitions. Third, to prevent processor starvation, improve response time, and to keep hardware devices with real-time constraints from failing, event-driven applications handle most events promptly.

There are three basic components in an event-driven application: (1) Event sensors detect and retrieve events from various sources (such as keyboards or network adapters); (2) event demultiplexers dispatch events to the appropriate event handlers; and (3) event handlers process incoming events received by sensors in an application-specific way. Traditional event-driven software employs an explicit event loop. This loop waits continuously for events from one or more sensors. When an event arrives, demultiplexing code in the loop maps the event to its associated event handler, which services the event. One drawback with this approach is that it tightly couples the low-level details (event demultiplexing and dispatching) with high-level behavior (application-specific semantics). Although explicitly coding the event loops may increase performance, it also may cause developers to expend more effort porting, repairing, and extending their applications.

The contemporary patterns of event-driven system design share a common theme of separating application policies from event mechanisms. For example, frameworks for defining user-interfaces (such as Motif or Interviews) and distributed objects (such as CORBA) use features such as callbacks, inheritance, and dynamic binding to decouple application-specific processing policies from application-independent event demultiplexing and event handler dispatching mechanisms. Placing these reusable mechanisms in the framework allows programmers to concentrate on application-specific functionality. Thus, rather than explicitly coding the event loop, programmers define objects for application-specific event processing. These objects are registered with a central event dispatcher. When particular events occur, the dispatcher calls back to the appropriate object method(s).

Decoupling of high-level application processing policies from low-level event processing is a central theme underlying the patterns in this section. These patterns employ object-oriented language features (such as abstract base classes, inheritance, and dynamic binding) to enhance the extensibility of event-driven software. In Chapter 28, Steve Berczuk describes how a fundamental event-handling pattern is used to aid scientific experiments conducted on data arriving from space satellites. This "reassembly/processing pattern" describes how to decouple the reassembly of an event composed of multiple fields and/or fragments from the processing activities performed once a complete event is reassembled.

Steve's project used the reassembly/processing pattern to partition responsibilities between teams of developers. By using the pattern, one team could work on handling complete units of work (represented as events), without interfering with another team that was parsing raw satellite data into fully assembled work units. Each event object produced by the reassembly code is consumed by the corresponding processing code. This reassembly/processing pattern is also used heavily in many other contexts (such as in communication protocol stacks).

Steve's focuses primarily on the division of responsibilities between reassembling and processing events, without regard for how events from multiple sources are detected, demultiplexed, and dispatched concurrently. These latter topics are the focus of Doug Schmidt's chapter on the Reactor pattern (Chapter 29). This pattern is another fundamental event handling pattern that is used in practically all event-driven object-oriented frameworks (such as Interviews, CORBA, ACE, Choices, and OODCE).

Doug has applied the Reactor pattern in a wide range of commercial telecommunication applications. Reactor combines the simplicity of single-threaded event loops with the extensibility offered by object-oriented programming. It provides applications with coarse-grained concurrency control; it serializes event handling within a process or thread but orchestrates dispatching when events are demultiplexed. This often eliminates the need for more complicated threading, synchronization, or locking within an application. Like Steve Berczuk's reassembly/processing pattern, the Reactor pattern improves the modularity, reusability, and configurability of event-driven application software. In particular, it decouples the concurrent event demultiplexing mechanisms (which are application-independent and thus reusable) from event handler processing policies (which are application-specific).

Steve and Doug each provide in depth coverage of an individual pattern. Alexander Ran, in contrast, provides broader coverage of four patterns that have been used to process events in a distributed real-time control and information system. His Event-Centered Architecture pattern (Chapter 30) offers a design paradigm that facilitates the reuse and evolution of event processing mechanisms. His Classes of Event Objects pattern addresses the need for modeling power in representing events. His Fine-grain Classification of Events pattern creates a specific context for event subscription and processing, which helps improve clarity and performance of the system. Finally, his OO State Machine pattern models abstract states and state-dependent behavior in object-oriented programs. It is instructive to compare the OO State Machine pattern to the one presented by Robert Martin in Chapter 19. While the patterns have similar names, their intents and structure are quite different.

The patterns in Part 8 complement each other by addressing events and event handling from different perspectives and different levels of abstraction. Both Doug Schmidt and Steve Berczuk describe patterns for structuring the basic building blocks of event-driven applications. Their patterns emphasize the architectural interplay between policy and mechanism to handle multiple events from different sources concurrently and to decouple the reassembly of events from subsequent event processing, respectively. In contrast, Alexander Ran's patterns focus more on mechanisms for processing the events themselves, rather than on the architecture of event-driven applications. He describes the use of inheritance to structure events, as well as state machines that guide the application-specific processing of events.

28 A Pattern for Separating Assembly and Processing

Stephen P. Berczuk

CONTEXT

After a system involving a number of geographically distributed development teams is designed, functions are assigned to different teams. It is necessary to decouple the work performed by development teams working on different system components in order to prevent development bottlenecks. To facilitate this decoupling, upstream components need not be directly concerned with downstream processing.

Using a pattern such as Builder [Gamma et al. 1995], which constructs objects from a generic data stream based on the stream's contents, will decouple the interfaces between different development groups by insulating the operations team (which, under this pattern, knows neither the definition of units of work nor the details regarding which packets belong in which collections). It is still necessary to decouple the upstream and downstream components, however.

Problem In an environment where components developed by separate teams with different focuses must interoperate, it is necessary to partition responsibilities

Copyright © Stephen P. Berczuk (MIT Center for Space Research). All Rights Reserved.

in such a way that dependencies can be reduced while interoperability is maintained. In particular, the well-defined portions of the system should be isolated from the pieces to be specified. This may be particularly important if the teams are geographically distributed.

A telemetry application is used here as an example. Telemetry processing systems are examples of applications in which one subsystem creates objects from external inputs (in a well-defined manner) and another subsystem processes these collected data (in a less clearly defined manner). This context can, however, be generalized to include any system in which the interfaces between producers and consumers need to be cleanly divided.

SATELLITE DATA PROCESSING

A science satellite is composed of instruments developed by different institutions.[1] Typically the system is divided into at least two subsystems:

- One team is responsible for converting a byte stream into telemetry packets and assembling these packets into units that represent the information in its original form.[2]
- Other teams are responsible for processing the data from the telemetry.

In a science satellite's telemetry processing application, the requirements for different software components evolve at different rates. This is partially due to the fact that these applications are developed by different teams. Often these teams have different operational and scientific requirements. Telemetry handling is divided into two phases (see Figure 1):

- *Assembly*, which processes objects from an input stream, classifies them, and assembles larger units, as necessary. Some of the units are composed of a number of packets; an example of this is a partition. Some of the units are simply individual packets; an example is a packet containing status information about the spacecraft or the instrument. These software requirements are typically well defined; and being key to any downstream processing, it is preferable that such software be built and tested as soon as possible.

---

[1] An instrument is any component of the spacecraft, including items such as telescopes, detectors, or an on-board data processing system.

[2] Telemetry is a transportation medium. The satellite collects data into a buffer and then divides the buffer into smaller pieces for transport. The ground systems must then reassemble the packets into a representation of the buffer, so it can be interpreted.

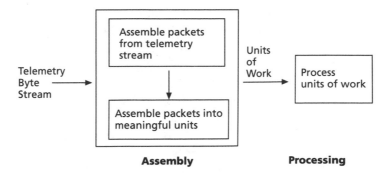

FIGURE 1   A typical telemetry processing system

- *Processing,* which analyzes or reports on the data. This is typically more
  loosely defined, since there are often many ways to process data (consider
  scientific data analysis applications). Because of the variety of ways in
  which data can be processed, we wish to maintain a flexible system. The
  processing requirements may also take longer to come to closure, since
  they are subject to the influence of more players.

The operational requirements for the transmission and assembly of telemetry packets are well defined, since they are based on established standards
and on the specifications of the satellite hardware and the controlling
software. Telemetry assembly is also rather similar from mission to mission,
and thus requirements can be more easily defined.

Processing the assembled units of data is a less well-defined task, since
the operational requirements vary from mission to mission. Furthermore,
these requirements may depend on the preliminary analysis performed
by scientists who designed the experiments on the satellite.[3] Additionally, there may be a desire to have a variety of processing operations
performed in different clients, which would require the services of the
assembly system.

We need a way to isolate the assembly system from the processing
system so the assembly system can be developed and tested without
waiting for the processing system's requirements to firm up (thus liberating
one part of the system from development delays caused by ill-defined
requirements for the downstream part of the system). Each component is

---

[3] As an example, the hardware for the *X-Ray Timing Explorer* was designed to transmit quite a bit of
status information for verification, with the idea that some of it would be useful downstream; it is still
being decided how the ground operation team will use all the information.

developed by a distinct team of developers, so a great deal of uncertainty is created in the schedule when the teams turn to building a tightly integrated system.

The systems are traditionally designed with end-to-end processing in mind. If the end-to-end processing is not well defined, then the entire system can be held back while the details of downstream processing are resolved.

We wish to isolate the assembler from the processor, so we need a way for the assembler to hand off the completed unit to the processor when the unit is available. We want a processing function to be added to the system dynamically, without changing the assembly software.

To summarize the forces at work:

- Requirements for one system component are available before downstream processing is defined.

- There is a need to test the assembly code independent of the processing software.

- Assembly and downstream processing may be developed by separate, often noncollocated groups.

- The assembly system should be developed without assuming anything about downstream processing.

We can resolve the problem of decoupling the development of two systems while maintaining their operational coupling by providing a facility to set handlers to be invoked when a complete unit is available for processing. Thus we are able to isolate the assembly software from the processing software. Virtual functions help make the details of the assembly operation transparent.

This is similar to a callback pattern, in which a handler is specified for an object, to be called when an event occurs, but the motivation is different. The emphasis in this pattern is on providing a way to allow teams of developers to decouple their work.

The classes representing the units of work that the assembly software processes have a method to set a handler that will be called when the unit is complete. The units of work can be individual data objects or objects created by assembling objects from a data stream. The interface to the assembly mechanism can be hidden using a Factory pattern or an Exemplar idiom [Coplien 1992]. In doing this we would provide that each data object received by the assembly stream is classified as an instance of a subclass of a processable unit, the packet, and that a virtual `apply()` method is invoked. In the context of each `apply()` call, an object is inserted into the appropriate collection, and if the collection is complete, the handler is called.

Examples of collections include partitions (which represent buffers of data) and status message packets.

The client creates a handler object (it can also be a pointer to a function) and sets the handler for objects of the same collection class. Only units that interest the client will be sent to it. The handler can perform a variety of operations, such as interpreting the data stream and performing analysis or simply reporting the information to scientists or operations staff.

The participants in this pattern are

- the *collection* classes, which have methods to set handlers to be invoked when the collection is complete
- the *handler*, which will process an instance of collection
- the *client*, which associates a handler with a collection

The solution is illustrated in Figure 2.

EXAMPLE SYNTAX (C++)

The following example shows a use of this pattern. Though the example implies that collection and handling processing occur in the same address space, it is simple to extend the pattern to work with components on different processors

The collection class (in this case, Partition) has a method to set a classwide handler to be called when a complete unit is available, and a dispose() method to invoke the handler on the unit of work. The collection can also have an isComplete() method.

FIGURE 2   Processing flow in the Handler pattern

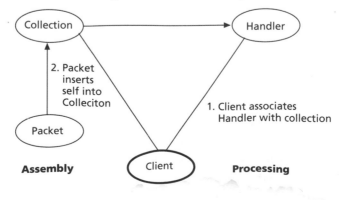

3. Collection goes to Handler when complete

The processing client sets the handlers to be called when a unit of work is available using the setHandler() method on the collection class. The unit-of-work handler is set for each class of collections. The client then gets the next packet from the data stream, using a technique based on a Factory pattern which classifies the bytes that represent a packet into the appropriate subclass. The virtual process() method is then invoked on the packet. The process method assembles the packet into a larger collection, if necessary. If the packet completes the unit of work (recall that a single packet can represent a unit of work) the handler is invoked.

```
PartitionHandler aCHandler;
// Handler to be called for a full partition collection

StatusMsgHandler aSOMsgHandler;
// Handler to be called for a single packet unit

class Collection
// a collection that is assembled from a number of related packets
{
public:
  // constructors and the like

  setHandler(/*function taking a pointer to a Partition*/);
  // set the handler to be called for all complete partitions

  void dispose();
  // apply the handler to the object
};

ingest_client(){
  StandAloneObject::setHandler(aSOMsgHandler);
  Collection::setHandler(aCHandler);
  Packet* pkt = getNextPacket();
  // create a subclass of packet based on info in data stream.

  pkt->process();
  // virtual function puts the packet into the right collection if
  // appropriate) and the collection checks to see if it is full.
  // if pkt is standalone, the handler is called.
}

Packet::process()
{
  // takes the packet and inserts it into the collection, perhaps
  // doing some processing to determine
  // which of a number of collections is appropriate
  // theCollection->insert(this);
```

```
  if(theCollection->isComplete())
    theCollection->dispose();
  // dispatch the collection to the appropriate handler
}
```

This pattern results in a situation in which the assembly software needs know only the following about the downstream processing:

- What the units of work that will be dispatched are. The details of this, which depend on the individual instruments, can be hidden from the assembly client through uses of the Factory pattern and virtual functions.
- The methods used to set the handlers

Additionally, the downstream processing client needs to know only:

- The type of units of work to expect
- The handling that each unit of work should be afforded

Applications of this pattern include telemetry processing, where packets from a telemetry stream must be classified and assembled into partitions (except certain packets representing status messages, which are not assembled into partitions). This pattern can be also be applied in any system where there is a need for one system to perform an operation and then hand the results over to another system for further processing. It can be extended by allowing a list of handlers to be called whenever a unit of work is available, in a manner similar to the way the standard C library provides the atexit() function.[4]

Related Patterns   The use of a generic constructor to classify and build objects from a data stream is a variant of the Factory pattern [Gamma et al. 1995]. The particular variation of Factory used in the implementation this pattern is based on is from the Exemplar idiom [Coplien 1992]. The use of virtual functions on objects to hide assembly details from the assembly application can be expanded into a separate pattern.

---

[4] The need to register multiple handlers can be avoided by defining a handler object that performs some arbitrary list of functions on the complete unit of work. The UNIX atexit() function is used to register a handler that is to be called as the process exits. By calling atexit() with a pointer to a function, a user adds an *additional* handler that is to be called when the process exits.

ACKNOWLEDGMENTS

The PLoP'94 workshop attendees, especially Doug Schmidt, made many useful comments on the early drafts of this paper. Discussions with Lena Davis helped me clarify my thinking about patterns and pattern languages in general.

This work was supported in part by NASA/GSFC contract number NAS5-30612.

REFERENCES

Coplien, James O. (1992). *Advanced C++ Programming Styles and Idioms.* Reading, MA: Addison-Wesley.

Gamma, Erich, Richard Helm, Ralph Johnson, and John Vlissides (1995). *Design Patterns: Elements of Reusable Object-Oriented Software.* Reading, MA: Addison-Wesley.

Stephen P. Berczuk can be reached at the Massachusetts Institute of Technology, Center for Space Research, Room 37-561, 77 Massachusetts Avenue, Cambridge, MA 02139; berczuk@mit.edu.

Reactor: An Object Behavioral Pattern for Concurrent Event Demultiplexing and Event Handler Dispatching

Douglas C. Schmidt

1. INTENT

This pattern supports the demultiplexing and dispatching of multiple event handlers, which are triggered concurrently by multiple events. The Reactor pattern simplifies event-driven applications by integrating the demultiplexing of events and the dispatching of the corresponding event handlers.

2. MOTIVATION

To illustrate the Reactor pattern, consider an event-driven server for a distributed logging service (see Figure 1). Client applications use this service to log information (such as error notifications, debugging traces, and status updates) in a distributed environment. In this service, logging records are sent to a central logging server. The logging server outputs the logging records to various destinations, such as a console, a printer, a file, a network management database, and so on.

Copyright © Douglas C. Schmidt. All Rights Reserved.

In the architecture of a distributed logging service, the logging server in Figure 1 handles logging records and connection requests sent by clients. These records and requests may arrive concurrently on multiple I/O handles. An I/O handle identifies a resource-control block managed by the operating system.[1]

The logging server listens on one I/O handle for connection requests to arrive from new clients. In addition, a separate I/O handle is associated with each connected client. Input from multiple clients may arrive concurrently. Therefore, a single-threaded server must not indefinitely block reading from any individual I/O handle. A blocking `read()` on one handle may significantly delay the response time for clients associated with other handles.

One way to develop a logging server is to use multithreading [Birrell:89]. In this approach, the server spawns a separate thread for every connected client. Each thread blocks on a `read()` system call. A thread unblocks when it receives a logging message from its associated client. At this point, the logging record is processed within the thread. The thread then reblocks, awaiting subsequent input from `read()`. The key participants in the thread-based logging server are illustrated in Figure 2.

Using multithreading to implement event handling in the logging server has several drawbacks:

- It may require complex concurrency control schemes.
- It may lead to poor performance on uniprocessors [Schmidt:94a].
- It may not be available on an operating system platform.

Often a more convenient and portable way to develop a logging server is to use the Reactor pattern. The Reactor pattern is useful for managing a single-threaded event loop that performs concurrent event demultiplexing and event handler dispatching in response to events.

The Reactor pattern provides several major benefits for event-driven applications. It facilitates the development of flexible applications using reusable components. In particular, it helps decouple application-independent mechanisms from application-specific functionality. Application-independent mechanisms are reusable components that demultiplex events and dispatch preregistered event handlers. Application-specific functionality is performed by user-defined methods in the event handlers.

In addition, the Reactor pattern facilitates application extensibility. For example, application-specific event handlers may evolve independently of

---

[1] Different operating systems use different terms for I/O handles. For example, UNIX programmers typically refer to these as file descriptors, whereas Windows programmers typically refer to them as I/O Handles. In both cases, the underlying concepts are basically the same.

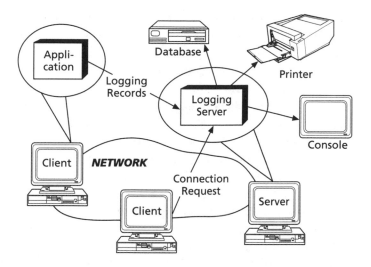

FIGURE 1   A distributed logging service

the event demultiplexing mechanisms provided by the underlying OS platform. By using the Reactor pattern, developers are able to concentrate on
application-specific functionality. In turn, the lower-level event demultiplexing and handler dispatching mechanisms are performed automatically
by the Reactor pattern.

FIGURE 2   Multithread-based logging server

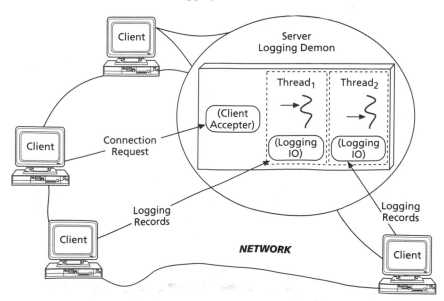

Figure 3 uses OMT notation [Rumbaugh:91] to illustrate the structure of a logging server designed according to the Reactor pattern.

The Event Handler base class provides a standard interface for dispatching event handlers. The Reactor pattern uses this interface to dispatch application-specific methods automatically when certain types of events occur. There are two subclasses of Event_Handler in the logging server: Logging_IO and Client_Accepter. Objects of these subclasses handle events arriving on client I/O handles. The Logging_IO event handler is responsible for receiving and processing logging records. The Client_Accepter event handler is a factory object. It accepts a new connection request from a client, dynamically allocates a new Logging_IO object to process logging records from this client, and registers the new Logging_IO event handler with the Reactor object.

Figure 4 illustrates a run-time view of the key participants in a Reactor pattern–based logging server. Note that the Client_Accepter and Logging_IO event handlers shown in the figure all execute within a single thread of control. The Reactor manages the event loop within this thread.

3. APPLICABILITY

Use the Reactor pattern when

- One or more events may arrive concurrently from different sources, and blocking or continuously polling for incoming events on any individual source of events is inefficient.

FIGURE 3   A logging server structure in the Reactor pattern

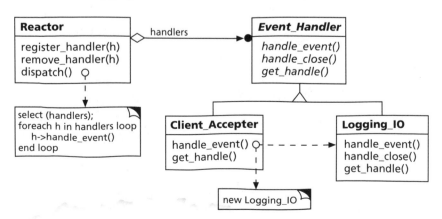

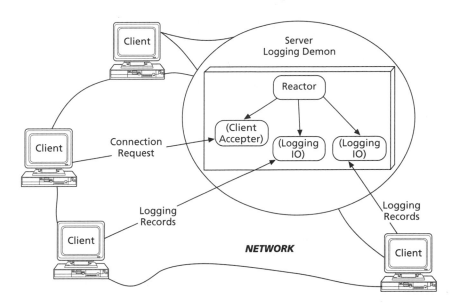

FIGURE 4   Reactor-based logging server

- An event handler exchanges fixed-size or bounded-size messages with its peers without requiring blocking I/O and processes each message it receives relatively quickly.

- Multithreading to implement event demultiplexing is

  infeasible due to lack of multithreading support on an OS platform.

  undesirable due to poor performance on uniprocessors or a need for overly complex concurrency control schemes.

  redundant due to the use of multithreading at a higher level within an application's architecture.[2]

- The functionality of application-specific event handlers will benefit by being decoupled from the application-independent mechanisms that perform event demultiplexing and event handler dispatching.

4. STRUCTURE

The structure of the Reactor pattern is illustrated in Figure 5.

---

[2] For example, the `handle_event()` method of an event handler may spawn a separate thread and then handle one or more incoming events within this thread.

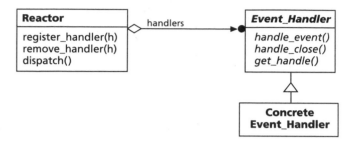

FIGURE 5   Structure of the Reactor pattern

5. PARTICIPANTS

The key participants in the Reactor pattern include the following:

- **Reactor** (`Reactor`): Defines an interface for registering, removing, and dispatching event handler objects. Implementing this interface produces a set of application-independent mechanisms. These mechanisms demultiplex events and dispatch application-specific event handlers in response to events.

- **Event Handler** (`Event_Handler`): Specifies the interface used by the `Reactor` to dispatch callback methods defined by objects that are preregistered to handle certain events.

- **Concrete Event Handler** (`Client_Accepter`, `Logging_IO`): Implement the callback methods that process events in an application-specific manner.

6. COLLABORATIONS

The `Reactor` triggers event handler methods in response to events. These events are associated with handles bound to event sources (such as I/O ports, synchronization objects, or signals). To bind the `Reactor` together with these handles, a subclass of `Event_Handler` must override its `get_handle()` method. When the `Reactor` registers an `Event_Handler` subclass object, it obtains the object's handle by invoking the `Event_Handler::get_handle()` method. The `Reactor` then combines this handle with other registered event handlers and waits for events to occur on them.

When events occur, the `Reactor` uses the handles activated by the events as keys to locate and dispatch the appropriate event handler methods. This collaboration is structured using method callbacks (see Figure 6). The `handle_event()` method is called by the `Reactor` to perform application-specific functionality in response to an event. Likewise, the `Reactor` invokes the `handle_close()` method to perform application-specific cleanup operations before it removes an `Event_Handler` subclass object.

7. CONSEQUENCES

Consequences of implementing the Reactor pattern include the following:

1. The Reactor pattern decouples application-independent mechanisms from application-specific functionality. The application-independent mechanisms become reusable components. They know how to demultiplex events and dispatch the appropriate callback methods defined by event handlers. In contrast, the application-specific functionality knows how to perform a particular type of service.

2. The Reactor pattern helps improve the modularity, reusability, and configurability of event-driven application software. For example, it decouples the functionality in the logging server into two separate classes: one for establishing connections and another for receiving and processing logging records. This decoupling enables reuse of the connection-establishment class for different types of connection-oriented services (such as file transfer, remote login, and video-on-demand). Therefore, to modify or extend the functionality of the logging server, only the implementation of the logging class must change.

3. The Reactor pattern improves application portability. Its interface may be reused independently of the underlying OS system calls that perform event demultiplexing. These system calls detect and report events that may occur simultaneously on multiple event sources (including I/O ports, timers, synchronization objects, signals, and so on). On UNIX platforms, the event demultiplexing system calls are called `select()` and `poll()` [Stevens:90]. In the Windows NT WIN32 API, the `WaitForMultipleObjects()` system call performs event demultiplexing [Custer:93].

4. The Reactor pattern provides applications with a coarse-grained form of concurrency control. It serializes the invocation of event handlers at the level of event demultiplexing and dispatching within a process or thread. Often this eliminates the need for more complicated synchronization or locking within an application process.

One consequence of the Reactor pattern's coarse-grained concurrency control is that event handlers are not preempted while they are executing. Therefore, event handlers generally should not perform blocking I/O. Neither should they perform long-duration operations (such as bulk data transfers of multimegabyte files) on individual I/O handles; if they do, the responsiveness of services offered on other I/O handles will decrease significantly.

To perform long-duration services, it may be necessary to spawn a separate process or thread. This separate process or thread will complete its tasks in parallel with the Reactor's main event loop.

5. On certain OS platforms, it may be necessary to allocate more than one Reactor object. For example, both UNIX and Windows NT restrict the number of I/O handles and events that may be waited for by a single system call (such as select() or WaitForMultipleObjects()). This limitation may be overcome by allocating separate processes or separate threads, each running its own Reactor event loop.

6. The control flow of the Reactor pattern is complicated by the fact that it performs method callbacks on application-specific event handlers. This increases the difficulty of "single stepping" through the run-time behavior of a Reactor (and its registered event handlers) from within a debugger.

8. IMPLEMENTATION

The Reactor pattern may be implemented in many ways. This section discusses several topics related to implementing the Reactor pattern.

Event demultiplexing. A Reactor maintains a table of objects derived from the Event_Handler base class. Public methods in the Reactor's interface register and remove these objects from this table at run time. The Reactor also provides a means to dispatch the handle_event() method on an Event_Handler object in response to events.

The Reactor's dispatching mechanism is typically used as the main event loop of an event-driven application. Its dispatch() method may be implemented using an OS event demultiplexing system call (such as select(), poll(), or WaitForMultipleObjects()).

The Reactor's dispatch() method blocks on the OS event demultiplexing system call until one or more events occur. When events occur, the Reactor returns from the event demultiplexing system call. It then dispatches the handle_event() method on any Event_Handler object that is registered to handle these events. This callback method executes user-defined code and returns control to the Reactor when it completes.

Synchronization.   The `Reactor` may be used in a multithreaded application. In this case, critical sections within the `Reactor` must be serialized to prevent race conditions when modifying or accessing shared data (such as the table holding the `Event_Handler` subclass objects). A common technique for preventing race conditions involves mutual exclusion mechanisms such as semaphores or mutex variables [Birrell:89].

To prevent deadlock, it may be necessary to implement the mutual exclusion mechanisms using recursive locks [Schmidt:94b]. A recursive lock may be reacquired by the thread that owns the lock, without blocking the thread. This property is important since the `Reactor`'s `dispatch()` method performs callbacks on application-specific `Event_Handler` objects. Application callback code may subsequently reenter the `Reactor` object using its `register_handler()` and `remove_handler()` methods. Recursive locks are an efficient mechanism for preventing deadlock on locks that are held by the same thread across `Event_Handler` method callbacks within the `Reactor`.

I/O semantics.   The I/O semantics of the underlying OS significantly affect the implementation of the Reactor pattern. The standard I/O mechanisms on UNIX systems provide "reactive" semantics [Stevens:90]. For example, the `select()` and `poll()` system calls indicate the subset of I/O handles that may be read from or written to synchronously without blocking.

Implementing the Reactor pattern using reactive I/O is straightforward. In UNIX, `select()` or `poll()` is used to indicate which handles have become ready for I/O. The `Reactor` object then "reacts" by invoking the `Event_Handler::handle_event()` callback method, which performs the I/O operation and the associated application-specific processing.

In contrast, Windows NT provides "proactive" I/O semantics [Custer:93]. Proactive I/O operations proceed asynchronously and do not cause the caller to block. An application may subsequently use the WIN32 `WaitForMultipleObjects()` system call to determine when its outstanding asynchronous I/O operations have completed.

Variations in the I/O semantics of different operating systems may cause the class interfaces and class implementations of the Reactor pattern to vary across platforms. For instance, Schmidt and Stephenson [Schmidt:94d] describe the interfaces and implementations of several versions of the Reactor pattern. These different versions were ported from BSD and System V UNIX platforms to a Windows NT platform.

Based on the porting experience Schmidt and Stephenson describe, it appears that implementing the Reactor pattern using proactive I/O is more complicated than using reactive I/O. Unlike the reactive I/O scenario described above, proactive I/O operations must be invoked immediately by the `Reactor`, rather than waiting until it becomes possible to perform an operation. Therefore, additional information (such as a data buffer or an I/O handle) must be supplied to the `Reactor` by the event handler before an I/O system call is invoked. This reduces the `Reactor`'s flexibility and efficiency somewhat, since the size of the data buffer must be specified in advance.

Event handler flexibility and extensibility.   It is possible to develop highly extensible event handlers that may be configured into a `Reactor` at installation time or run time. This enables applications to be updated and extended without modifying, recompiling, relinking, or restarting the applications at run time [Schmidt:94c]. Achieving this degree of flexibility and extensibility requires the use of object-oriented language features (such as templates, inheritance, and dynamic binding [Stroustrup:91]), object-oriented design techniques (such as the Factory Method or Abstract Factory design patterns [Gamma:95]), and advanced operating system mechanisms (such as explicit dynamic linking and multithreading [Schmidt:94a]).

Regardless of the underlying OS I/O semantics, the Reactor pattern is applicable for event-driven applications that must process multiple event handlers triggered concurrently by various types of synchronous or asynchronous events. Although differences between the I/O semantics of OS platforms may preclude the direct reuse of implementations or interfaces, the Reactor pattern may still be reused. In general, the ability to reuse an abstract architecture independent of its concrete realization is an important contribution of the design pattern paradigm.

9. SAMPLE CODE

The following code illustrates an example of the Reactor pattern's object behavior. The example implements portions of the logging server described in Section 2. It also illustrates the use of an object-creation pattern called Accepter [Schmidt:94d]. The Accepter pattern decouples the act of establishing a connection from the service(s) provided once a connection is established. This pattern enables the application-specific portion of a service to be modified independently of the mechanism used to establish the connection. The Accepter pattern is useful for simplifying the development of connection-oriented network services (such as file transfers, remote login, distributed logging, and video-on-demand applications).

The structure of the Accepter pattern is illustrated in Figure 6. In the example below, the general `Client_Handler` class in the OMT class diagram in Figure 6 is represented by the `Logging_IO` class.

The C++ code illustrated in this section implements the `Client_Accepter` and `Logging_IO` classes as well as the main driver function for the logging server. This implementation of the `Reactor` runs on UNIX platforms. A functionally equivalent version of this code that illustrates the Windows NT `Reactor` interface appears in Schmidt and Stephenson [Schmidt:94d].

9.1 The `Client_Accepter` Class

The `Client_Accepter` class establishes connections with client applications. In addition, it provides a factory for creating `Logging_IO` objects, which receive and process logging records from clients. The `Logging_IO` class is described in Section 9.2.

The `Client_Accepter` class inherits from the `Event_Handler` base class. This enables a `Client_Accepter` to be registered with a `Reactor` object. When a client connection request arrives, the Reactor dispatches the `Client_Accep-ter` object's `handle_event()` method. This method invokes the `accept()` method of the `SOCK_Listener` object, which retrieves the new connection.

The `SOCK_Listener` object is a concrete factory object that enables the Client Accepter object to listen and accept connection requests on a communication port. When a connection arrives from a client, the `SOCK_Lis-tener` object accepts the connection and produces a `SOCK_Stream` object.

FIGURE 6   Interaction Diagram for the Reactor Pattern

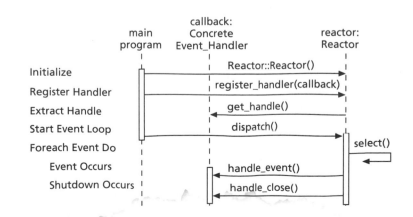

Henceforth, the SOCK_Stream object is used to transfer data reliably between the client and the logging server.

```
// Global per-process Reactor object.
extern Reactor reactor;

// Handles connection requests from clients.

class Client_Accepter : public Event_Handler
{
public:

    // Initialize the accepter endpoint.
    Client_Accepter (const INET_Addr &addr)
      : listener_ (addr) {}

    // Callback method that accepts a new
    // SOCK_Stream connection, creates a
    // Logging_IO object to handle logging
    // records sent using the connection, and
    // registers the object with the Reactor.

    virtual void handle_event (void)
    {
      SOCK_Stream new_connection;

      this->listener_.accept (new_connection);

      Logging_IO *cli_handler =
        new Logging_IO (new_connection);
      reactor.register_handler (cli_handler);
    }

    // Retrieve the underlying I/O handle
    // (called by the Reactor when a
    // Client_Accepter object is registered).

    virtual HANDLE get_handle (void) const
    {
      return this->listener_.get_handle ();
    }

    // Close down the I/O handle when the
    // Client_Accepter is shut down.
    virtual void handle_close (void)
    {
      this->listener_.close ();
    }
```

```
private:
    // Factory that accepts client connections.
    SOCK_Listener listener_;
};
```

The SOCK_Listener and SOCK_Stream classes used to implement the logging
server are part of the SOCK_SAP C++ wrapper library for BSD and Windows
sockets [Schmidt:92]. SOCK_SAP encapsulates the SOCK_STREAM semantics of
the socket interface within a portable and type-secure object-oriented interface.
In the Internet domain, SOCK_STREAM sockets are implemented using the TCP
transport protocol [Stevens:90]. TCP provides a reliable, bidirectional byte
stream–oriented transport service between two user processes.

9.2 The Logging_IO Class

The logging server uses the Logging_IO class, shown below, to receive logging
records sent from client applications. In the code, the Logging_IO class inherits
from the Event_Handler class. This enables a Logging IO object to be
registered with the Reactor. When a logging record arrives, the Reactor
automatically dispatches the handle_event() method of the associated
Logging_IO object. This object then receives and processes the logging record.

```
// Receive and process logging records
// sent by a client application.

class Logging_IO : public Event_Handler
{
public:

    // Initialize the clientStream.
    Logging_IO (SOCK_Stream &cs)
      : client_stream_ (cs) {}

    // Callback method that handles the
    // reception of logging records
    // from client applications.

    virtual void handle_event (void)
    {
      Log_Record log_record;

      this->client_stream_.recv (log_record);
      // Print logging record to output.
      log_record.print ();
    }
```

```
    // Retrieve the underlying I/O handle
    // (called by the Reactor when a Logging_IO
    // object is first registered).

    virtual HANDLE get_handle (void) const
    {
      return this->client_stream_.get_handle ();
    }

    // Close down the I/O handle and delete
    // the object when a client closes down the
    // connection.

    virtual void handle_close (void)
    {
      this->client_stream_.close ();
    }

private:
    // Receives logging records from a client.
    SOCK_Stream client_stream_;
};
```

The `Client_Accepter` and `Logging_IO` code shown above "hard-code" the interprocess communication (IPC) classes (that is, `SOCK_Listener` and `SOCK_Stream`, respectively) used to communicate between clients and the logging server. To remove the reliance on this particular class of IPC mechanisms, this example could be generalized to use the Abstract Factory or Factory Method patterns described in Gamma et al. [Gamma:95].

9.3 The Logging Server Main Function

The following code illustrates the main entry point into the logging server. This code creates a global `Reactor` object and a local `Client_Accepter` object. The `Client_Accepter` object is initialized with the network address and port number of the logging server. The program then registers the `Client_Accepter` object with the `Reactor` and enters the `Reactor`'s main event-loop. There, the `Reactor` uses the `select()` or `poll()` OS event demultiplexing system call to block awaiting connection requests and logging records arriving from clients.

```
// Global per-process Reactor object.
Reactor reactor;

// Server port number.
```

```
const unsigned int PORT = 10000;

int
main (void)
{
    // Logging server address and port number.
    INET_Addr addr (PORT);

    // Initialize logging server endpoint.
    Client_Accepter ca (addr);

    // Register logging server object with
    // Reactor to set up the callback scheme.
    reactor.register_handler (&ca, READMASK);

    // Main event loop that handles client
    // logging records and connection requests.
    reactor.dispatch ();

    /* NOTREACHED */
    return 0;
}
```

The interaction diagram in Figure 7 illustrates the collaboration between the objects participating in the logging server example. Once the Reactor object is initialized, it becomes the primary focus of the control flow within the logging server. All subsequent activity is triggered by callback methods on the Client_Accepter and Logging_IO objects that are registered with, and controlled by, the Reactor.

10. KNOWN USES

The Reactor pattern has been used in a number of object-oriented frameworks. It is provided by the InterViews window system distribution as the Dispatcher class category [Linton:87]. The Dispatcher class is used to define an application's main event loop and to manage connections to one or more physical GUI displays. The ADAPTIVE Service eXecutive (ASX) framework [Schmidt:94a] uses the Reactor pattern as the central event demultiplexer/dispatcher in an object-oriented toolkit for experimenting with high-performance parallel communication protocol stacks. A freely available subset of the ASX framework described in this paper may be obtained via anonymous ftp from ics.uci.edu in the files gnu/C++_wrappers.tar.Z and gnu/C++_wrappers_doc.tar.Z.

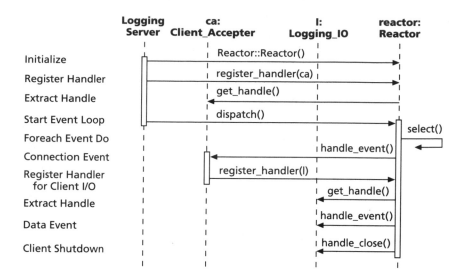

FIGURE 7   Interaction diagram for the logging server

The Reactor pattern has also been used in a number of commercial products. These products include Bellcore's Q.port ATM signaling software, the Ericsson EOS family of telecommunications switch monitoring applications, and the network management portion of the Motorola Iridium global personal communications system.

11. RELATED PATTERNS

The Reactor provides a Facade [Gamma:95] for event demultiplexing. A Facade is an interface that shields applications from complex object relationships within a subsystem.

The virtual methods provided by the Event_Handler base class are Template Methods [Gamma:95]. These Template Methods are used by the Reactor to trigger callbacks to the appropriate application-specific processing functions in response to events.

An event handler (such as the Logging_IO class described in Section 9) may be created using a Factory Method [Gamma:95]. This allows an application to decide which type of Event_Handler subclass to create.

The Reactor may be implemented as a Singleton object [Gamma:95]. This is useful for centralizing event demultiplexing and dispatching into a single location within an application.

A `Reactor` may be used as the basis for demultiplexing messages and events that flow through a "pipes and filters" architecture (see Chapter 22).

ACKNOWLEDGMENTS

This work was supported in part by grants from the University of California MICRO program, Hughes Aircraft, Nippon Steel Information and Communication Systems Inc. (ENICOM), Hitachi Ltd., Hitachi America, Tokyo Electric Power Company, and Hewlett Packard (HP).

BIBLIOGRAPHY

[Birrell:89] A. D. Birrell. "An Introduction to Programming with Threads." Tech. Rep. SRC-035, Digital Equipment Corporation, January 1989.

[Custer:93] H. Custer. *Inside Windows NT*. Redmond, WA: Microsoft Press, 1993.

[Gamma:95] E. Gamma, R. Helm, R. Johnson, and J. Vlissides. *Design Patterns: Elements of Reusable Object-Oriented Software*. Reading, MA: Addison-Wesley, 1995.

[Linton:87] M. A. Linton and P. R. Calder. "The Design and Implementation of InterViews." *Proceedings of the USENIX C++ Workshop*, November 1987.

[Rumbaugh:91] J. Rumbaugh, M. Blaha, W. Premerlani, F. Eddy, and W. Lorensen. *Object-Oriented Modeling and Design*. Englewood Cliffs, NJ: Prentice-Hall, 1991.

[Schmidt:92] D. C. Schmidt. "IPC_SAP: An Object-Oriented Interface to Interprocess Communication Services." *C++ Report*, 4 (November/December 1992).

[Schmidt:94a] D. C. Schmidt. "ASX: An Object-Oriented Framework for Developing Distributed Applications." *Proceedings of the 6th USENIX C++ Technical Conference*. Cambridge, MA: USENIX Association, April 1994.

[Schmidt:94b] D. C. Schmidt. "Transparently Parameterizing Synchronization Mechanisms into a Concurrent Distributed Application." *C++ Report*, 6 (July/August 1994).

[Schmidt:94c] D. C. Schmidt and T. Suda. "An Object-Oriented Framework for Dynamically Configuring Extensible Distributed Communication Systems." *IEE Distributed Systems Engineering Journal* (Special Issue on Configurable Distributed Systems), December 1994.

[Schmidt:94d] D. C. Schmidt and P. Stephenson. "Achieving Reuse Through Design Patterns." *Proceedings of the 3rd C++ World Conference*. Austin, TX: SIGS, November 1994.

[Stevens:90] W. R. Stevens. *UNIX Network Programming*. Englewood Cliffs, NJ: Prentice-Hall, 1990.

[Stroustrup:91] Bjarne Stroustrup. *The C++ Programming Language*, 2nd ed. Reading, MA: Addison-Wesley, 1991.

Douglas C. Schmidt can be reached at Department of Computer Science, Washington University, One Brookings Drive, St. Louis, MO 63130; schmidt@cs.wustl.edu.

30 Patterns of Events

Alexander S. Ran

We must begin by understanding that every place is given its character by certain patterns of events that keep on happening there.

Christopher Alexander

1. EVENT-CENTERED ARCHITECTURE

Context   In many domains products are organized into families, in which each member-product is a slightly different version of the same prototype. These product families are the result either of the evolution of one product or of the parallel development of related products designed to satisfy different requirements of the same problem.

Product families are extremely important, because they help minimize the costs of concurrent evolution of similar products. This is only possible, of course, if the products are related not only by their function, but also by their

Copyright © 1994 Alexander Ran. All Rights Reserved.

internal structure. As a product family evolves, developers should preserve the distinction between what the family members share and what is specific to each member. This goal is hard to attain in the context of evolving families of software products.

Objectives   In most circumstances software designers should strive to optimize the development and maintenance of the entire software family rather than just individual programs. Usually we wish all the members of the family to be constructed from the same set of reusable components. Ideally, members of a family are identical architecturally and differ only in subsets of their components.

The architecture of a family should represent the essential core shared by all members that is unlikely to change but may be incrementally extended or specialized for a particular application. In such an architecture the components should not be bound to each other directly, but only through their interaction with the core. Furthermore, the core should not depend on the presence or functionality of particular components.

Approach   Architecture of a program family is often understood as a common structure made by the major parts of the member-programs. In this approach the structure depends on the components. Changes in the components affect the structure.

In *The Timeless Way of Building,* Christopher Alexander [1979] wrote, "We must begin by understanding that every place is given its character by certain patterns of events that keep on happening there. . . . And indeed, the world does have a structure, just because these patterns of events which repeat themselves are always anchored in the space."

A family of programs defines a specific application domain. Each application domain is given its character by certain patterns of events that keep on happening there. And indeed, the structure of an application is just a consequence of some components of the application causing and some responding to these events. Thus, we may achieve a greater stability of program family architecture if it is based on the major events that occur in the domain. The advantage to event-centered architecture is that, by starting from important events and then decomposing a system into components bound not to each other but to events, it helps to create a stable architecture for an evolving program family.

Notes   The term *event* is often used to mean a special type of communication mechanism (interrupt, signal, operating system message) that is different from the function call mechanism. These should not be confused with the events discussed here, which are conceptual entities unrelated to implementation details.

Events represent and communicate important changes in the state of a system. However, event-centered architecture does not assume that this state is explicitly represented anywhere.

2. CLASSES OF EVENT OBJECTS

Context   In event-centered architecture events become rather complex entities—significant modeling power is required to properly capture their different aspects.

Objectives   Some information may be associated with each event. Different event-generating components may use different kinds of information to generate the same type of events. Events must eventually transfer control to reactive components. Reactive components may require different views of the same event.

Complex relationships may exist between events: events may cause or imply other events, they may shadow or disable other events, and so on. Generation of an event must be independent of the response to the event. This is required in order to avoid binding between components and to allow more freedom in scheduling of the response.

Approach   When an object-oriented programming language is used for software construction, it is appropriate to use classes to model events as system-level concepts. Event classes allow the programmer to treat events as a group. Event-generating components instantiate event objects. Different components may use different instantiation methods to generate events, based on different types of information.

Event objects allow the programmer to separate event generation from event handling. Notification of reactive components about event occurrence is the responsibility of the event objects. Event objects encapsulate information associated with the event and may provide different views of this information to different reactive components.

Registration of the reactive components may be handled by subscription services provided by the event classes. Event classes may establish requirements to subscribers. A minimal requirement may be the capability to handle events of this class. Subscription protocol may also ensure that additional conditions are fulfilled by a prospective subscriber.

Notes The behavior of components that dynamically subscribe and unsubscribe event classes—possibly as a result of receiving events—is difficult to understand. A program that relies on such capability resists static analysis and is often impossible to understand by reading. It is usually better to regard the relationship between a component and the event classes as static. The lost flexibility of dynamic changes in the coordination behavior may be regained by other means. Component invocation procedures associated with different event classes may depend on some system-level condition. State-dependent event response of reactive components is addressed by the object-oriented state machine pattern.

3. FINE-GRAINED CLASSIFICATION OF EVENTS

Context A reactive component is usually interested in only a small subset of all possible events. Invocation of components for irrelevant events may significantly increase the computational cost of invocation. This approach also requires components to be ready to receive events of different types, making component behavior more complicated and even sacrificing type safety.

When it is invoked by an arbitrary event, a component must decide if the event is a member of its set of interest. Different components may be interested in the same or different sets of events; furthermore, these sets may be disjoint or intersecting, or one set of events may be a subset of another. If several components are interested in the same set of events, it is wasteful when invoking the components to repeatedly perform the computation of the membership for the same event in the same set.

An event's membership in different sets of interest may be determined more efficiently if the relationships between the sets are known in advance. When sets of interest are static, it is possible to compute and efficiently encode membership information for every possible event prior to the deployment of the system.

Objectives Event classes provide the context in which reactive components operate. This context must be specific enough to make the definition and operation of reactive components more effective. How specific this context is depends on how specific the classification of the events in the program is. Merging event classification into the functionality of reactive components complicates their behavior, as it hides and replicates important information. This increases the cognitive effort required to understand the program, and also results in computationally inefficient systems. Fine-grained classification of events explicitly represents important information that is otherwise hidden in the computations performed by the reactive components.

Approach Design a hierarchy of event classes that models the generalization/specialization relationship between events generated and expected by different components in the system. It is possible using multiple inheritance to express an arbitrary partition of the set of all possible events so that each set of interest is represented by a class of events.

A component may register its interest in one or several classes of events. A component that is registered for a class of events is considered to be registered for all the subclasses of this class as well. Thus queues of registered components are inherited in the event hierarchy. An event object invokes only the components registered in the event class of which it is an instance. This approach essentially substitutes run-time computation of event membership in the sets of interest of different components with compile-time typing of the events. Since the inheritance relationship between event classes is known prior to the creation of events, the invocation of reactive components may be optimized.

Notes The hierarchy of event classes establishes a natural ordering for invocation of subscribed components. A reactive component with more specific interests or responsibilities with respect to an event should be notified of the event before a reactive component with more generic interests or responsibilities.

Each class of events may specify its own invocation procedure used to invoke the components registered for it. Invocation methods should be combined in order of descending specificity in relation to the class of the event object. Since method combination is essential in the process of object initialization, even languages that do not support method combination in general will combine the initialization methods. This may be used to construct the invocation plan that is executed by the event object after it is constructed.

4. OBJECT-ORIENTED STATE MACHINE

Context Reactive components integrated into systems with event-centered architectures are essentially independent and are often distributed and concurrent. Each reactive component is attached to some event classes. A reactive component should provide the necessary interface for invocation by event objects. The actual response of the reactive components may be rather complex and often depends on the state of the component at the time of invocation.

Objectives The states of a reactive component are essential for understanding its functionality and must be explicitly represented. A state is a condition that implies more specific component behavior than may be generally assumed. Event response of reactive components may be specified in correspondence with their state. This helps to specify the dynamic component behavior that is otherwise too complex. The specification of behavior is divided into several cases; each corresponds to a different state. Jointly, all states specify the component behavior.

Much the same way that subclasses are used to refine the behavior specified by their superclasses, states may be further partitioned by substates. When objects in a state exhibit complicated behavior that depends on additional conditions, substates may be identified that guarantee simpler behavior of the objects. This process of incremental specialization of conditions and the corresponding behavior may be continued until each state is characterized by sufficiently simple behavior.

It is important that the selection of the event-response method is done in correspondence to the state of the reactive component and does not need to be explicitly programmed.

Approach   The representation and behavior of a component are specified jointly by a cluster of classes. The root of the cluster specifies the public interface of the component and the state-independent part of its representation and behavior. Each state is represented as a class that directly or indirectly inherits the root of the state cluster. State classes specify the state-dependent aspects of representation and behavior of the component. State classes may include in their definition a predicate that specifies the condition of the state. States with complicated dynamic behavior may be specified using substates, represented by further subclasses. A dispatcher class with standard behavior that inherits from all the states of the cluster may be automatically generated. Objects that represent reactive components are instances of the corresponding dispatcher classes. Dispatchers use a standard state classification procedure to control event-response method selection for the reactive component in accordance with its state.

5. SEE ALSO

Event-based integration, also called implicit invocation, is discussed in detail and compared to other architectures in [SullivanNotkin] and in [GarlanShaw]. Design space for implementation of implicit invocation in different programming languages is explored in [NotGarGrisSul]. In the object-oriented systems, implicit invocation is commonly associated with automatic change propagation.

Active values [StefikBobrowKahn] of LOOPS allow association of arbitrary actions with access to a variable. Model-View-Controller [KrasnerPope] of Smalltalk-80 is probably the best known framework for change notification specialized for user interfaces. A pattern for event objects was discussed in [Beck]. Several related design patterns—like Subject-Observer, Chain of Responsibility, Mediator, State, and so on—are presented in [GamHelJohnVlis]. Modeling states as classes is discussed in [Ran].

REFERENCES

[Alexander] Christopher Alexander. *The Timeless Way of Building.* New York: Oxford University Press, 1979.

[Beck] Kent Beck. "Using Patterns: Design." *The Smalltalk Report* 3, 9 (July–August 1994).

[GamHelJohnVlis] Erich Gamma, Richard Helm, Ralph Johnson, and John Vlissides. *Design Patterns: Elements of Reusable Object-Oriented Software.* Reading, MA: Addison-Wesley, 1995.

[GarlanShaw] David Garlan and Mary Shaw. "An Introduction to Software Architecture." In V. Ambriola and G. Tortora, eds., *Advances in Software Engineering and Knowledge Engineering,* Vol. 1. World Scientific Publishing Company, 1993.

[KrasnerPope] Glen E. Krasner and Stephen T. Pope. "A Cookbook for Using the Model-View-Controller User Interface Paradigm in Smalltalk-80." *Journal of Object-Oriented Programming* 1, 3 (1988): 26–49.

[NotGarGrisSul] David Notkin, David Garlan, William G. Griswold, and Kevin Sullivan. "Adding Implicit Invocation to Languages: Three Approaches." In Shojiro Nishio and Akinori Yonezawa, eds., *Object Technology for Advanced Software.* New York: Springer-Verlag, 1993, pp. 489–510.

[Ran] A. Ran. "Modelling States as Classes." In Raimund Ege, Madhu Singh, and Bertrand Meyer, eds., *Proceedings of the TOOLS USA 94.* Englewood Cliffs, NJ: Prentice-Hall, 1994.

[StefikBobrowKahn] M. J. Stefik, D. G. Bobrow, and K. M. Kahn. "Integrating Access-Oriented Programming into a Multiparadigm Environment." *IEEE Software,* January 1986.

[SullivanNotkin] Kevin J. Sullivan and David Notkin. "Reconciling Environment Integration and Software Evolution." *ACM Transactions on Software Engineering and Methodology* 1, 3 (July 1992): 229–268.

Alexander S. Ran can be reached at Nokia Research Center, P.O. Box 45, 00211 Helsinki, Finland; ran@research.nokia.com.

Appendix:
Request Screen Modification

Dwayne Towell

Editors' Note: *At PLoP, each day ended with home group meetings. Home groups provided an opportunity for unstructured reflection and discussion about the day's events in a small-group setting. The conference published a daily newsletter, "The Home Group News," that summarized home group activities.*

The pattern presented here, Request Screen Modification, is a product of one of the home group sessions. It first appeared in the "Home Group News" at PLoP. It was written by Dwayne Towell as part of a larger pattern language for graphical interfaces, whose other patterns are yet uncaptured. It is the only work in this volume that first took form at PLoP.

Context   A common multimedia problem consists of on-screen presentation of multiple "actors." A multimedia application will typically include simple pictures (such as a background and static foreground objects), animations (a series of frames, locations, and time triples), user interface objects (buttons, menus, and so on), and possibly other visible components. To give the impression of depth, the objects are ordered; this allows an object to be partially covered by a "closer" object, which promotes the illusion.

Problem   How does each object update its appearance as time and events dictate?

Copyright © Dwayne Towell. All Rights Reserved.

Forces   One possible solution requires the object to "take a snapshot" of the screen contents before modifying it. When the object wishes to change its appearance, it returns the screen to its original appearance and then redraws itself. However, this only works if the object has no other objects in front of it and its background does not change. If an object is obscured in part (or in whole), restoring the "snapshot" corrupts the appearance of the foreground object. Some mechanism is needed to allow an object to query the extent of the objects overlapping it, and only update those areas that are not covered. Also, if the background changed since the object took the snapshot, restoring it would change the expected appearance of the background object.

Solution   Objects request a third party to modify an area of the screen. The third party then requests that each object (from back to front) redraw the appropriate section (if any) of itself. This allows an object to change its appearance and/or location without knowing what is behind or in front of it or even if it is visible.

Example   An animation object is moving the image of a train along a track on the background picture. A tunnel can be added to the picture as a static picture of a mountain in front of the train. When the animation object prepares to show the next frame, it updates its internal state and then "invalidates" the area covered by the old and new locations. The invalidation service eventually iterates the list of objects requesting each to redraw itself in the "invalid" region. First the background is drawn, then the animation, and finally the mountain. The train image has been successfully "moved'" from the old location to the new location, and it will now be able to "enter" the tunnel.

Applicability   Use the Request Screen Modification pattern when visible screen components have no specific knowledge of other objects, may intersect other objects, and are required to change appearance or location.

Consequences   If drawing operations occur directly to the screen, "flicker" occurs; Double Buffer the Screen can be used to correct this. Request Screen Modification (especially when used in combination with Double Buffer the Screen) can add significant overhead to a system; Consolidate Redraws can improve efficiency.

Dwayne Towell can be reached at Image Builder Software, Inc., 7300 S.W. Hunziker Road, Tigard, OR 97223; dwayne@image.com.

Index